Digital
Marketing
Fundamentals

Digital Marketing Fundamentals

OMCP's Official Guide to OMCA™ Certification

Greg Jarboe, Matt Bailey, Michael Stebbins
with Brad Geddes, Kim Krause Berg, and Cindy Krum
Foreword by Avinash Kaushik

WILEY

For general information on our other products and services or for technical support, please contact our Customer Care Department within the United States at (800) 762-2974, outside the United States at (317) 572-3993 or fax (317) 572-4002.

If you believe you've found a mistake in this book, please bring it to our attention by emailing our reader support team at wileysupport@wiley.com with the subject line "Possible Book Errata Submission."

Wiley also publishes its books in a variety of electronic formats. Some content that appears in print may not be available in electronic formats. For more information about Wiley products, visit our web site at **www.wiley.com**.

Library of Congress Cataloging-in-Publication Data

Names: Jarboe, Greg, 1949-author. | Bailey, Matt, 1969-author. |
  Stebbins, Michael, 1971-author.
Title: Digital marketing fundamentals: omcp's official guide to omcatm
  certification / Greg Jarboe, Matt Bailey, Michael Stebbins.
Description: First Edition. | Hoboken, NJ: Wiley, [2023] | Includes index.
Identifiers: LCCN 2022053833 (print) | LCCN 2022053834 (ebook) | ISBN
  9781119894575 (paperback) | ISBN 9781119894612 (adobe pdf) | ISBN
  9781119894605 (epub)
Subjects: LCSH: Internet marketing. | Marketing–Data processing.
Classification: LCC HF5415.1265.J3697 2023 (print) | LCC HF5415.1265
  (ebook) | DDC 658.8/72—dc23/eng/20221104
LC record available at https://lccn.loc.gov/2022053833
LC ebook record available at https://lccn.loc.gov/2022053834

Cover Design: Wiley
Cover Image: © davooda/Shutterstock
SKY10040881_010523

Contents

Foreword

Almost 20 years ago I postulated the 10/90 Rule for Digital Marketing: If you have $100 to spend on being successful, spend $10 on tools and $90 on people!

Since then, this rule has only become truer, as free tools for every digital task have proliferated and others have become cheaper. What remains expensive are the smart people that you need to successfully imagine competitive strategies, convert them into effective marketing tactics, and measure what matters.

I'm super-excited about OMCP, since it is a program that offers a high-quality signal reflecting knowledge and experience. You know…it helps answer whether this human is the right investment for your $90.

Hence, I'm thrilled that Greg, Matt, and Michael decided to write the biblical guide to OMCA certification. Their knowledge spans strategy, brand and performance marketing, comprehensive guidance on digital analytics, crucial areas like SEO, digital advertising, content marketing, social media marketing, as well as conversion optimization, email marketing, and mobile marketing! Each chapter has the detail you need to learn core concepts and pointers on how you can use this book as a jumping-off point into the deep end of any of the topics.

Greg, Matt, and Michael also persuaded Brad, Kim, and Cindy to contribute their wisdom and industry insights, making the book that much more valuable.

Like me, you will read the book to be among those who have the rare honor of earning OMCA certification, but I believe you'll keep it as a handy reference guide at work to look up the guidance you'll need to deliver an outsized impact.

All the best!

Avinash Kaushik

Author: *Web Analytics: An Hour a Day, Web Analytics 2.0*

Digital Marketing Evangelist: Google

Introduction

Who Should Read This Book?

This book is intended for those who will drive digital marketing initiatives, manage digital marketing teams, or communicate digital marketing concepts. It is perfect for those who are transitioning into a career in digital marketing or for students who wish to learn generally accepted practices of digital marketing.

It can also be used as a study guide or to supplement a digital marketer's preparation for OMCA certification. The OMCA certification verifies knowledge across multiple digital marketing disciplines. It is often used as a minimum requirement for marketing team members at advertising agencies or other businesses that perform in-house marketing. Groups who train or hire to OMCA standards lead the industry in digital marketing performance.

Why Get a Digital Marketing Certification?

It's no longer enough to simply claim expertise as a digital marketer. Employers and clients know that they are best served by marketers whose knowledge and skills are current and verified.

According to the 2019 OMCP Role Study, which asked more than 4,000 professionals about their digital marketing priorities, companies and agencies are no longer looking for one-trick ponies. Hiring managers unanimously require employees to have conceptual knowledge and skills across five of the top eight disciplines—search engine optimization, content marketing, social media marketing, digital advertising (including price-per-click), mobile marketing, email marketing, conversion rate optimization, and digital analytics. In addition, subject matter experts must master two or more disciplines as well as digital marketing strategy to be considered for a senior position.

So, whether you are one of the 52,000 individuals preparing for the OMCA exam, 100,000 students trained at more than 900 universities and training institutes that teach to OMCA standards worldwide, or 316,800 advertising, promotions, and marketing managers in the United States, this official guide can help you get a Digital Marketing Certification from OMCP, an industry association that maintains the competency and exam standards for online marketing in coordination with industry leaders from Google, Dell, Microsoft (Bing), Procter & Gamble, Home Depot, and many others.

What Are the Benefits of OMCA Certification?

Individuals who earn the OMCA certification

- stand out to employers and clients as having verified digital marketing skills, education, and experience;
- earn between 16 percent and 26 percent more than noncertified digital marketers; and
- operate more effectively as a marketing professional, sharing common language and generally accepted practices across multiple disciplines.

This book is written by respected authors and members of OMCP's standards committees, past and present. The co-authors and contributors are Greg Jarboe, Matt Bailey, Michael Stebbins, Brad Geddes, Cindy Krum, and Kim Krause Berg.

CHAPTER 1

Digital Marketing Strategy

By Greg Jarboe

It's no longer enough to simply claim expertise as a digital marketer. Employers and clients know that they are best served by marketers whose knowledge and skills are current and certified.

According to the 2019 OMCP Role Study, which asked more than 4,000 hiring managers about their digital marketing priorities, companies and agencies are no longer looking for one-trick ponies. Today, they require employees to have conceptual knowledge and skills across eight disciplines:

- Digital analytics
- Digital advertising (including price-per-click)
- Search engine optimization (SEO)
- Content marketing
- Social media marketing
- Conversion optimization (UX)
- Mobile marketing
- Email marketing

This book includes a chapter on each of these disciplines. So, whether you are one of the professionals preparing for the OMCA exam, or one of the students at more than 900 universities and training institutes that teach to OMCA standards worldwide, this official guide can help you get OMCA certification from OMCP, an industry association that maintains the competency and exam standards for digital marketing in coordination with industry leaders.

Is digital marketing certification worth it? Well, individuals who earn the OMCA certification

- stand out to employers and clients as having verified digital marketing skills, education, and experience,
- earn between 16 percent and 26 percent more than noncertified digital marketers, and
- operate more effectively as a marketing professional, sharing common language and generally accepted practices across multiple disciplines.

The 2019 OMCP Role Study also found that the industry's marketing leaders wanted the addition of digital marketing strategy as its own discipline. Although there are no OMCP competencies for digital marketing strategy yet, that's the challenge this chapter will tackle.

By the end of this chapter, you will have accomplished the following:

- Learned some of the lessons that other fast-moving consumer goods and consumer packaged goods brands have learned from the struggles of Kraft Heinz
- Discovered what other retail brands in the U.K. have observed just by watching the annual Christmas adverts created by John Lewis & Partners and Adam & Eve/DDB
- Will understand how to use the modern marketing model (M3) as a framework to develop an effective digital marketing strategy for your organization

You will also learn why creating an effective digital marketing strategy is a challenge. There are three key reasons:

- There is no "one-size-fits-all" way to build an audience.
- Strategy without tactics is the slowest route to victory.
- Tactics without strategy is the noise before defeat.

I'll tackle each one of these challenges in this chapter so that you can overcome them successfully.

There Is No "One-Size-Fits-All" Way to Build an Audience

Here's the first key reason why teaching digital marketing strategy is a challenge: In the 19th century, John Stuart Mill said, "There is no 'one-size-fits-all' way to build an audience." In the 21st century, digital marketers have discovered that there is no "one-size-fits-all" way to

- create brand awareness,
- build credibility/trust,
- educate audience(s),
- build loyalty with existing clients/customers,
- generate demand/leads,
- nurture subscribers/audience/leads,
- drive attendance to one or more in-person or virtual events,
- generate sales/revenue,
- support the launch of a new product, or
- build a subscribed audience.

These are all goals that B2B (business-to-business) and B2C (business-to-consumer) marketers have successfully achieved by using content marketing in the last 12 months, according to the "12th Annual Content Marketing Benchmarks, Budgets, and Trends: Insights for 2022" report produced by Content Marketing Institute and Marketing Profs. And content marketing is just one of the top eight disciplines of digital marketing.

So what is the best digital marketing strategy for successfully achieving these goals?

There isn't a simple answer to this frequently asked question. Why? Because your company is unique, your customers are unique, and your competitors are unique, too. So one size does not fit all.

Using AnswerThePublic to "listen into" autocomplete data from Google and other search engines, I recently discovered that people in Great Britain are asking about a "digital marketing strategy" for . . . a brand, a hotel, a product, a restaurant, a startup, airlines, app, automotive industry, B2B, B2C, banks, beauty salon, beginners, brand awareness, business, business growth, cafe, cement industry, charities, clothing brand, coaching institutes, coffee shop, colleges, construction company, consumer goods, cosmetics, dairy products, dentists, detergent, doctors, ecommerce, ecommerce website, edtech, educational institutes, event management, events, example crossword, example crossword clue, Facebook, fashion, fashion brands, financial services, FMCG, food products, furniture company, grocery, gym, healthcare, higher education, hospitals, hotels, HR, ice cream, Instagram, insurance companies, interior design, IT companies, jewelry brand, law firms, lead generation, local business, logistics companies, luxury brands, manufacturers, manufacturing industry, mobile app, movies, new brand, new business, new product launch, newspapers, NGO, nonprofit, online business, online store, organization, pharmaceutical, pharmaceutical companies, pharmacy, photographers, political campaigns, preschool, product launch, professionals, radio stations, real estate, recruitment agency, resort, restaurants, SaaS, schools, service industry, small business, social media, software companies, startups, technology companies, tourism, travel agency, university, video, website, and wedding planners.

In other words, people are asking about more digital marketing strategies than there are unique pizza toppings!

Until OMCP can develop the digital marketing strategy standards for training providers and standardized testing, most of the co-authors and contributors to this book have been using illustrative case studies to provide marketing professionals and students with an up-close, in-depth, and detailed examination of a specific digital marketing strategy as well as its related contextual conditions.

Professors at Harvard Business School (HBS) have been using "the case method" since 1921. Central to the case method is the idea that students aren't provided the "answer" to the problem. Instead, the student is forced to analyze a situation and find solutions without full knowledge of all the facts. The case method has been the most widely applied and successful teaching instrument to come out of HBS, and it is used in hundreds of other top business schools around the world.

For example, a couple of years ago, I was a member of a team of subject matter experts who taught a bespoke (custom) digital marketing training program for marketers at a Fortune 500 company in the fast-moving consumer goods (FMCG) and consumer-packaged goods (CPG) industries.

We selected case studies that offered relevant sets of circumstances. Why is this important? Because the typical case study may offer interesting information, but it often doesn't teach useful lessons to marketers in different fields.

Since the marketing team that we were training wanted to see case studies from other companies in their field, I shared a case study that analyzed the failure of a company in the FMCG and CPG industries.

With permission from *Search Engine Journal*, the next section contains a lightly edited version of what I wrote back on July 12, 2019, and shared during the bespoke digital marketing training program.

Kraft Heinz: Isn't Anyone Going to Help That Poor Brand?

According to Mark Ritson of *Marketing Week*, "Kraft Heinz is in 57 varieties of trouble," which is a real pity. The American food company formed in 2015 by the merger of Kraft Foods and H. J. Heinz is the fifth-largest food and beverage company in the world with 2018 net sales of approximately $26 billion.

Ritson, an award-winning marketing columnist, professor, and consultant in the United Kingdom, thinks Kraft Heinz is suffering from a number of self-inflicted wounds, from underinvestment in its brands to a failure to adapt its portfolio to modern tastes.

However, no company aims to inflict wounds on itself, so that explanation is too clever by half.

It reminds me of the scene in *Blazing Saddles* when Sheriff Bart takes himself hostage by pressing his gun against his own head, prompting Harriet Johnson to cry out, "Isn't anyone going to help that poor man?"

YouTube and Kraft Heinz: A Strategic Threat and Opportunity
Even though it may be too late, I'm going to help that poor brand. Again.

Yes, I've tried to help before.

Back in March 2015, I took a look at the combined Kraft Heinz Company's YouTube channels for Tubular Insights and was surprised to see "an archipelago of small, isolated islands. Considering the high percentage of Millennials who eat up YouTube food videos, this represented both a strategic threat AND a strategic opportunity for the food giant."

So, did they heed my advice? Judge for yourself.

Back in Q1 2015, YouTube videos uploaded by Kraft Heinz Company brands got a total of 8.4 million views, according to data from Tubular Labs.

But that was a minuscule percentage of the 2.7 billion views amassed by all of the brands in the food and beverage during industry that quarter.

In Q1 2019, the Kraft Heinz Company's brands got a total of 57.2 million views on YouTube. At first glance, that appears to be significant progress.

But all of the brands in the food and beverage industry got 10.2 billion combined views during this quarter, so any gains seem like a rounding error.

So, four years later, YouTube remains both a strategic threat and a strategic opportunity for Kraft Heinz.

Recently, I've been a subject matter expert for a bespoke, online digital marketing training program for a Fortune 500 company in the FMCG and CPG industries. I can say without violating my nondisclosure agreement that big companies in these sectors on both sides of the pond have struggled to make a smooth transition from the old world of television advertising in the 20th century to the new world of digital marketing in the 21st century.

What Went Wrong?
So, why did Kraft Heinz and other FMCG and CPG companies continue to struggle longer and later than many other companies in most other industries?

Well, they were probably using the wrong metrics as key performance indicators (KPIs). In other words, they were measuring the wrong things.

When you measure the wrong things, you mistakenly think you're reaching your business goals and marketing objectives. But, more often than not, you're getting into 57 varieties of trouble.

Let me share my scientific, wild guess on exactly which metric got Kraft Heinz and far too many other FMCG and CPG companies into 57 varieties of trouble. They have continued to measure success using a metric that was created in the 1950s during the TV era: gross rating points (GRPs).

GRPs measure the size of an advertising campaign by potential impressions using a problematic formula that multiplies estimated reach by frequency.

For example, if you run a commercial five times on a TV show that reaches 7 percent of your target audience, then you get 35 GRPs.

That appears to be a metric that matters because it's been used for decades. But in real life, most of the people in this small segment of your target audience probably ignored your TV spot the fourth and fifth time that it appeared.

Some may have even been annoyed that the same commercial kept popping up so many times during the same bloody show. And this assumes that seeing your advertising the first three times increased your sales to some degree.

Maybe it did.

But maybe it didn't.

As David Ogilvy (1985) wrote in his classic book, *Ogilvy on Advertising*, "The wrong advertising can actually reduce the sales of a product" (p. 9).

He then cited two studies to support his provocative conclusion. In the first, Ford marketing research found that "people who had not been exposed to (their) advertising had bought more Fords than those who had." In the second, consumption of an unnamed brand of beer "was lower among people who remembered its advertising than those who did not. The brewer had spent millions of dollars on advertising which un-sold his beer" (Ogilvy 1985).

So, GRPs measure how many impressions you've purchased, not how your target audience responds to your advertising.

In other words, GRPs measure inputs, not outcomes.

That's why, despite the fact that they've been used since the 1950s as metrics for TV advertising, GRPs shouldn't be used today as KPIs for digital marketing.

Which Metrics Should Kraft Heinz Use as KPIs? This begs the question: Which metrics should Kraft Heinz use as KPIs?

The vast majority of most FMCGs and CPGs will continue to be sold through brick-and-mortar stores for the foreseeable future.

This kind of explains why it took longer for Kraft Heinz and other companies that still rely on retail channels of distribution to embrace digital marketing. But it only sort of explains why they didn't question some of the assumptions that their college professors, marketing predecessors, and advertising agencies had made in an analog era when it came time for them to decide which metrics to use as KPIs in the digital age.

Brand Lift   For example, more marketers at FMCG and CPG companies should have noticed a speech in February 2013 by Susan Wojcicki, who was the senior vice president of advertising at Google back then.

In her speech, she announced that Google was launching *brand lift* surveys. These enabled marketers to measure the impact of their YouTube ads on metrics such as the following:

- Ad recall
- Brand awareness
- Favorability
- Consideration
- Purchase intent

This is possible by using surveys of a randomized control group that was not shown your ad and an exposed group that did see your ad.

You'd think that some of the marketers at Kraft Foods would have spotted the Mondelēz International case study published in Think with Google in October 2014. Why? Because the snack brands of Mondelēz were once part of Kraft Foods until they were spun off in October 2012.

The case study explained how Mondelēz used Google's brand lift solution to measure the marketing effectiveness of the launches of its belVita and Trident Unlimited brands in Brazil.

Here's the story behind the success story: Brand lift revealed valuable insights into the campaigns' viewer retention rates, target audiences, and frequency caps. Based on these findings, the marketers at Mondelēz quickly adjusted the company's targeting and its creatives within days and saw its YouTube campaigns lift brand awareness of its apple-and-cinnamon breakfast biscuit by 26 percent and its gum brand by 36 percent.

Now, brand lift is an infinitely better KPI than some random number of GRPs. If you have any doubt about this assertion, then ask your college professor, marketing predecessor, or ad agency, "How many GRPs do we need to lift our brand awareness by 26 percent or 36 percent?"

As you've already figured out, this is a trick question—because there are no known correlations between GRPs and lifts in brand awareness.

Sales Lift   But wait, there's more!

In January 2019, YouTube and Nielsen Catalina Solutions announced a new way to measure sales lift. So marketers at Kraft Heinz can now measure, in aggregate, how effective their YouTube campaigns are at moving products off of store shelves in the United States.

That's both a strategic opportunity AND a strategic threat.

With more than 2 billion logged-in users visiting YouTube each month, the strategic opportunity is obvious. But the strategic threat is obvious too.

Marketers at other FMCG and CPG companies are already using the combination of brand lift and sales lift studies to measure their digital advertising campaigns.

They're also using tools like YouTube Director Mix to create customized video ads and serve them to suit the interests and intent of different audience segments. This means marketers can customize a base video asset with relevant creative elements, including the following:

- Headlines
- Images
- Prices
- Translations

Then, the video and these elements are stitched together, produced quickly and at scale, reducing the need for endless edits. This results in hundreds of video variations in relatively little time with relatively little effort.

FIGURE 1.1 YouTube Presents: Kellogg's Rice Krispies Treats Case Study (**https://youtu.be/zzdujh5LG80**)

For example, Kellogg's used YouTube Director Mix, Google Correlate, and six-second bumper ads to reintroduce Rice Krispies Treats to parents across the country during the busy and emotional back-to-school season.

They used Director Mix to bring their new packaging to life online with more than 100 customized videos. In the end, the campaign drove best in class brand lift and sales lift, despite fewer retail displays (Figure 1.1).

Selecting the Right KPIs Is the Key Being able to measure brand lift and sales lift doesn't mean that marketers at Kraft Heinz or other FMCG and CPG brands will be able to create the perfect digital advertising campaign their first time out.

However, if they've selected the right metrics as KPIs and are finally measuring the right things, they will learn what they need to do to improve their results in days, not years.

Or as Avinash Kaushik, who is an author, a blogger, and the digital marketing evangelist for Google, wrote on LinkedIn in May 2018, "Companies set inspiring goals. They tend to want to constantly exceed the (often less-than-optimally informed) expectations of Wall Street analysts. They tend to invite motivational speakers to get the employees to think differently, push through to new frontiers, CHANGE THE WORLD!!!!"

He added, "I completely understand this pattern. Who does not want to shoot for the moon or massively exceed their mom's expectations? [But,] I've come to learn that this desire to overachieve also comes at a very heavy cost—it drives sub-optimal behavior. Instead, I recommend this as the #1 goal for your company: Suck less, every day. Whatever you do today, consciously suck less at it."

Although I gasped when I first read his article, I later wished that I had written it myself. It's the perfect advice for a poor brand that's in 57 varieties of trouble. And it's great advice for other FMCG and CPG brands too.

Apply What You Just Learned

To assess whether the marketers at the Fortune 500 company that we were training could apply what they had just learned, our team of subject matter experts assigned a capstone project. We broke them into teams and gave them a couple of weeks to develop a new digital marketing strategy.

Because the marketing teams were located in multiple countries around the globe and worked on a variety of goods and products, we told them they could create a digital marketing strategy for their own market or brand. This ensured that the online training course wasn't a distraction from their day jobs.

The quality of their capstone projects indicated that the marketing teams could apply what they had just learned. And a series of recent interviews with senior leadership verifies that our bespoke digital marketing training program had also helped the company to pivot after the coronavirus pandemic dramatically affected consumers and brands around the world.

From 2020 to 2021, the Fortune 500 company improved its return on marketing investment by more than 70 percent. But it didn't improve overnight.

They achieved this remarkable success over 2 years by rethinking measurement, exploring actionable solutions to help their company gain deeper insights, creating growth opportunities, redefining budgets, being more agile, and building resilience for the future.

The key to their success was selecting the right metrics as KPIs so they were finally measuring the right things. Then they were able to learn what they need to do to improve their results. And that enabled them to suck less, every day.

I know this still sounds like it took a lot of time and effort. Because it did. This is just one reason why creating an effective digital marketing strategy is a challenge.

Strategy Without Tactics Is the Slowest Route to Victory

This brings us to the second key reason why an effective digital marketing strategy is a challenge: far too many CMOs are under tremendous pressure to create a brilliant marketing strategy that will deliver spectacular results in the short term.

You need at least a concept-level understanding of digital analytics, digital advertising, SEO, content marketing, social media marketing, conversion optimization, mobile marketing, and email marketing before you are ready to develop a digital marketing strategy for your organization.

Or as Sun Tzu, a Chinese general, military strategist, writer, and philosopher who lived in ancient China, observed about 2,500 years ago, "Strategy without tactics is the slowest route to victory."

Let me illustrate this by sharing a second case study that analyzes the 2021 Christmas advert from John Lewis & Partners, a brand of high-end department stores operating throughout Great Britain, with concessions also located in the Republic of Ireland and Australia.

The brand sells general merchandise as part of the employee-owned mutual organization known as the John Lewis Partnership, the largest co-operative in the United Kingdom.

The first John Lewis store was opened in 1864 in Oxford Street, London. Since 1925, the chain has promised that it is "never knowingly undersold"—it will always at least match a lower price offered by a national high street competitor.

With permission from *Search Engine Journal,* the following section contains a lightly edited version of the column that I wrote on December 8, 2021.

Nostalgia Marketing and What We Can Learn From John Lewis Ads

You've probably noticed an influx of seasonal television advertising campaigns by retail brands in the build-up to Christmas. These spots tend to attract widespread media coverage and acclaim upon their release. Just look at department store brand John Lewis & Partners, which launched their first Christmas advert back in 2007.

Their nostalgic ads have become something of an annual tradition in the United Kingdom, and one of the signals that the countdown to Christmas has begun. In 2011, John Lewis uploaded their Christmas advert to YouTube for the first time.

Since then, the British department store chain and its London-based agency, Adam & Eve/DDB, have followed suit each and every year. Judging by the quality of ads other brands in the United Kingdom have been releasing this past decade, they may have learned some important lessons from those John Lewis spots.

Let's take a look at how these brands are effectively harnessing the power of nostalgia marketing and what you can learn from them to make it a part of your own marketing strategy.

What Is Nostalgia Marketing? Nostalgia marketing is the strategy of evoking a sentimental longing or wistful affection for the past, in order to build brands for the future. It's the tactic of associating your company with a period or place that triggers happy personal associations for your ideal customer, for the purpose of marketing goods and products in the present.

Why Nostalgia Marketing Works So Well Nostalgia marketing typically works well because the psychological response triggered by watching a deeply nostalgic video tends to be intense, since it is influenced by the viewer's own positive emotions and memories. Nostalgic content also makes advertising campaigns appear more down-to-earth and authentic to the audience.

However, John Lewis may (or may not) have learned what works (and what doesn't).

TABLE 1.1	Tubular Labs Data on YouTube Views and Engagements of John Lewis Christmas Ads		
Title of Video		**Views**	**Engagements**
John Lewis Christmas Advert 2011—The Long Wait		8.3M	43K
John Lewis Christmas Advert 2012—The Journey		7.0M	35K
John Lewis Christmas Advert 2013—The Bear & The Hare		17.7M	124K
John Lewis Christmas Advert 2014—#MontyThePenguin		27.8M	130K
John Lewis Christmas Advert 2015—#ManOnTheMoon		30.4M	163K
John Lewis Christmas Advert 2016—#BusterTheBoxer		28.3M	123K
John Lewis Christmas Ad 2017—#MozTheMonster		10.6M	77K
John Lewis & Partners Christmas Ad 2018—#EltonJohnLewis		14.7M	142K
Christmas 2019 Ad	John Lewis & Partners and Waitrose & Partners		11.1M	99K
Christmas 2020 Ad	Give A Little Love	Waitrose & John Lewis		4.7M	34K

As the data in Table 1.1 from Tubular Labs shows, the John Lewis Christmas ads uploaded to YouTube got more views and engagements several years ago than they've received more recently. That was a troublesome trend even before the pandemic turned last Christmas into a season that most high street shops would rather forget!

Google Trends Data for the Christmas Advert   You can use Google Trends to learn some surprising lessons about interest in the Christmas advert.

For starters, web search interest in the United Kingdom for the search term "Christmas advert" peaked back in November 2016 and was thereafter likely to be just 38 percent of that level.

But if you narrow the time frame on Google Trends to just the last 30 days, you can scroll down and see that the top-related queries for the search term include the following (Figure 1.2):

- John Lewis Christmas advert (100)
- Aldi Christmas advert (42)
- M&S Christmas advert (20)

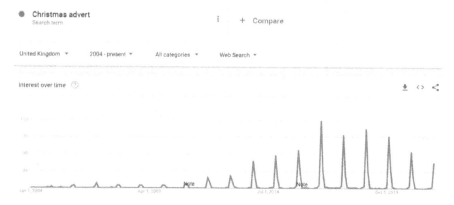

FIGURE 1.2   Google Trends U.K. for Christmas Advert

So people on the other side of the pond are so interested in seeing a brand's Christmas ad that they actually search for it.

Which Christmas Ads Harness Nostalgia Marketing Effectively In 2021?   Let's examine some of these Christmas adverts to determine if any of them effectively harnessed nostalgia marketing in 2021.

John Lewis Ad's Content Doesn't Live Up to Viewers' High Expectations   We'll start with "Unexpected Guest | John Lewis & Partners | Christmas Ad 2021."

The description of this YouTube video asks, "What happens when an unexpected guest lands in your forest? You show them how Christmas is done, of course!"

John Lewis has created a ton of related content. Maybe they have been learning some important lessons over the years. For example, there's an extended version of "Unexpected Guest." And there's a related page on their website that provides the backstory of the "Unexpected Guest." There's also a behind-the-scenes article and video on the making of "Unexpected Guest."

It seems like John Lewis has learned a lesson about merchandising. Why? Because the brand's website includes content about the special Christmas jumper, customized with a star and twinkly lights, that Nathan gives Skye. Plus, John Lewis is donating 10 percent of the sales from their Christmas advert jumper to support families in need.

There's also content about decorating the tree—with links to "Shop in the Gemstone Forest" and "Shop all Christmas decorations." There's additional content about setting the table too, with links to "Shop the advert table look" and "Shop all Christmas tableware."

There's even a new interactive game, "Unexpected Guest: The Experience," which My John Lewis members get exclusive access to play.

FIGURE 1.3   Unexpected Guest | John Lewis & Partners | Christmas Ad 2021 (**https://youtu.be/ZTttgc0DPA4**)

So, everything is queued up to "market goods and products in the present" —as long as the video's content associates John Lewis "with a period or place with happy personal associations." (See Figure 1.3.)

How did the brand do? Well, according to data from Tubular Labs, "Unexpected Guest" got 2.5 million views and 17,500 engagements in its first 30 days. That's a worse start than any of the brand's other Christmas adverts from the previous decade.

If you read some of the 1,200+ comments on "Unexpected Guest," you have to wonder if John Lewis has lost its touch for evoking a sentimental longing or wistful affection for the past:

- Nature bunny said, "Ah. . . there's nothing more festive than a crash-landed UFO in the local woods."
- Wayne Prezzler said, "Let's be honest. John Lewis will never ever beat the lad waiting to give gifts rather than receiving them. It captured an essence lost and that Christmas is more about the giving of gifts than receiving. I believe it was their first and it was definitely their best ad."
- Ethan Clarke said, "The 2012 snowman advert is still the best for me."
- Strong Coffee said, "Monty the Penguin still makes me sob like an idiot. Love the song choice on this though!"
- Edward Osmond said, "Nothing will ever beat the rabbit and the bear."

John Lewis replied to this last comment. Someone representing the brand said, "Those two certainly pulled on the heart strings! But glad you like Nathan and Skye's story too."

Key Insights

- It appears that nostalgia marketing still works. Tying your company to a period or place with happy personal associations to market goods and products doesn't work if your video's content fails to trigger that deeply nostalgic psychological response, though.
- Plan supplemental content to get more mileage out of your video ads and enable the experience to go on.

Now, let's evaluate Christmas adverts from some other brands.

Aldi Video Ad Combines Humor with Deeper Emotional Sentiment According to Kantar's latest research using facial coding to determine the power of the ad to provoke an emotional reaction, the most effective of 24 festive adverts was "Aldi Christmas Launch Advert 2021." (See Figure 1.4.)

It's worth noting that the version of this TV ad that was uploaded to YouTube got 2.9 million views and 7,400 engagements.

Featuring Kevin the Carrot for the sixth year in a row, this year's Christmas advert has been Aldi's most successful so far. In fact, it scored in the top 6 percent of all U.K. ads in terms of being both "distinctive" and "enjoyable," and was also the campaign that sparked the most conversation.

The description of Aldi's Christmas advert asks, "Will Ebanana Scrooge discover his Christmas spirit?" Um, who is Ebanana Scrooge? The brand uploaded a teaser for this year's Christmas advert to provide the backstory for this new character.

According to Kantar, Aldi focused on traditional Christmas themes such as kindness and togetherness. Data from their research found that 35 percent of people feel this Christmas is more important than last year, with a particular emphasis on friends and family and less focus on extravagant spending.

FIGURE 1.4 Aldi Christmas Launch Advert 2021 (**https://youtu.be/MIL8Kl-r0bo**)

Lynne Deason, head of creative excellence at Kantar, said, "Aldi's new take on a Christmas classic is a great example of how a brand can convey serious messages about purpose and social impact while still being great fun.

Aldi uses humor effectively, something especially important in a year when we all need an extra laugh, but it also has a deeper sentiment.

The clever inclusion of "Marcus Radishford" highlights a worthy cause—the campaign to provide meals to those in need—without coming across as too somber to viewers.

And by borrowing from one of the most well-known and loved Christmas stories of all time, it sets out a complicated narrative without ever being confusing."

Key Insights

- The most successful Christmas ads in 2021 captured a positive mood while making the ads highly relevant to their brands and products.
- Those that struggled to get resonance have been the ones with sad or complex storylines, where the intended happy ending doesn't stand out or the audience is left feeling confused.

Marks & Spencer Uses Character and Storyline to Elicit Emotion   Another standout campaign was "Percy Pig comes to life for the first time EVER! | 2021 Christmas Advert | M&S FOOD." (See Figure 1.5.)

In addition, Percy Pig along with his fairy friend discover the delicious delights of the Marks & Spencer festive foodhall, from triple chocolate panettone to collection smoked salmon. This video has 1.8 million views and 7,200 engagements.

FIGURE 1.5   Percy Pig Comes to Life for the First Time EVER! | 2021 Christmas Advert | M&S FOOD (**https://youtu.be/Dlem-MOMZOs**)

Much like Aldi, Marks & Spencer relied on the help of "recognizable" characters, a tactic that proved effective in linking messages and storylines with brand names.

In this case, Marks & Spencer leaned on its well-loved and highly recognizable Percy Pig voiced by English actor Tom Holland, and the "fairy that fell off the top of the Christmas tree" voiced by British actress Dawn French.

Key Insights

- According to Kantar, the characters created a greater emotional reaction among audiences than previous years' ads from the brand, contributing to its increased effectiveness.
- Familiarity—in characters, voiceovers, and other storyline elements—supports nostalgia marketing.

Coca-Cola Has Brand Loyalty and Connection on Its Side   I asked Deason, "Which brand was the most effective at harnessing the power of nostalgia?"

She said, "Coca-Cola's ad is by far the most nostalgic Christmas ad, achieving iconic status in the minds of many." (See Figure 1.6.)

The version of this TV ad that was uploaded to YouTube, "Coca-Cola Christmas Commercial 2021," is unlisted, which explains why it only got 2,573 views and 22 engagements.

FIGURE 1.6   Coca-Cola Christmas Commercial 2021 (**https://youtu.be/vpHxmt8JZeo**)

She added, "Coke's festive truck sings out Christmas to most viewers, but it is also intrinsically associated with the Coca-Cola brand. It is in the top 2 percent of all ads in the U.K. in terms of brand connection, so the success of the festive campaign will translate to long-term brand loyalty."

Final Thoughts I asked Deason via email, "What happened to John Lewis? Why didn't an 'Unexpected Guest' named Skye do better than Kevin the Carrot?"

She said, "It's great to see John Lewis back with an ad that people have really enjoyed. Although not quite as emotionally evocative as some of its previous hits, it still lands in the top 16 percent of all U.K. ads and was the second most enjoyed Christmas campaign of 2021."

"Music continues to be a key driver of emotional engagement for John Lewis, its track was the second most enjoyed this year. The ad is distinctive (top 16 percent) and is one of the top ones which people would share with others," Deason added.

While the role of the John Lewis brand is weaker than in previous years, she said, it always benefits from the anticipation and conversation around the ad each Christmas. The absence of an obvious must-have mascot might also impact its ability to drive traffic to the brand.

This could explain why it may not grab potential shoppers in the way it has before. Even so, Deason pointed out that it is still keeping viewers entertained, as it has done consistently over the past decade.

If the John Lewis team wants some inspiration, then I would encourage them to get their SEO, content marketing, social media, and paid search teams together and watch "John Lewis Christmas Advert 2015—#ManOnTheMoon," It has 30.4 million views and 163,000 engagements.

That demonstrates the potential power of nostalgia marketing during the Christmas season. Unfortunately, it is no longer available.

In fact, none of the John Lewis Christmas adverts listed in the chart at the beginning of this section are available, even though they would have all ranked in the top 20 videos created by a brand in the United Kingdom with Christmas in the title with the most engagements of all time. That's a great pity.

Why should they still be available? Three explanations come to mind.

- First, when people continue to watch old Christmas adverts that evoke a sentimental longing or wistful affection for the past, it can continue to build brands for the future.

- Second, your social media and paid search teams can add up to five cards to each old Christmas advert to make them more interactive. These cards enable you to link your old Christmas adverts to you newest one. If you're in the YouTube Partner Program, you can add a card that allows you to link to your external website to share the latest merchandising opportunities with your audience.

- And third, John Lewis should review their old Christmas adverts to discover how the emotions elicited by video content is related to engagement. As Winston Churchill said in 1948, "Those who fail to learn from history are condemned to repeat it."

Apply What You Just Learned

Based on this case study, it appears that the marketing strategists at John Lewis and Adam & Eve/DDB underestimate the role that YouTube can play in the build-up to Christmas. That would explain why their advertising strategy, which doesn't leverage a concept-level understanding of YouTube and video marketing tactics, looks like it's the slowest route to victory.

They don't seem to realize that the potential audience marketers can reach in the United Kingdom using adverts on YouTube is 53.0 million, according to Digital 2021: The United Kingdom from Hootsuite and We Are Social. That's 84 percent of the U.K.'s total population aged 18+.

By comparison,

- ITV reaches 35.9 million viewers a week.
- Channel 4's audience peaks at 6 million viewers for *The Great British Bake Off*.
- The BBC domestic television channels do not broadcast advertisements.

The marketing strategists at John Lewis and Adam & Eve/DDB might also be surprised to discover the outsized role that digital video marketing can play throughout the customer journey—from discovery to consideration to conversion.

An article entitled, "A new way to think about online video's role in the purchase funnel," which was written by Debbie Weinstein, vice president of YouTube/Video Global Solutions, and published in Think with Google in January 2019, reported:

- More than 90 percent of people say they discover new brands or products on YouTube.
- More than half of shoppers say online video has helped them decide which specific brand or product to buy.
- More than 40 percent of global shoppers say they have purchased products they discovered on YouTube.

Now, video marketing isn't one of the top eight disciplines. At least, not today. But you will probably want at least a concept-level understanding of

YouTube and other social video tactics before you develop a digital marketing strategy for your organization in 2023 and beyond.

Tactics Without Strategy Is the Noise Before Defeat

This brings us to the third and final reason that creating an effective digital marketing strategy is a challenge.

The ongoing development of OMCP standards and practices has been a cooperative effort by the industry's leading marketers, authors, employers, and educators. But there are no generally accepted standards and practices for developing a digital marketing strategy that will generate magnificent success.

But the industry's marketing leaders wanted digital marketing strategy to be its own discipline in 2019. And the vast majority of CMOs can't afford to wait until standards and practices eventually get adopted by a critical mass of organizations a couple of years from now.

Why all the urgency?

Well, according to the latest CMO Tenure Study by Spencer Stuart, which is based on the analysis of the tenures of CMOs from 100 of the most-advertised U.S. brands, the average CMO tenure in 2020 dropped to 40 months, which is the lowest it has been since 2009. Median tenure fell to 25.5 months, which is the lowest on record.

Most certainly, the pandemic fueled some of the decline in CMO tenure as executive teams across industries faced unprecedented change in the market. But developing a digital marketing strategy that will generate magnificent success is the key to increasing CMO tenure.

Or as Sun Tzu also said, "Tactics without strategy is the noise before defeat."

If you need to develop a digital marketing strategy today, I recommend using the Modern Marketing Model (M3), which Ashley Friedlein, the founder of Econsultancy, unveiled in October 2017. It fuses digital and classic marketing into one future-facing framework.

Friedlein provided this rationale for his model: "The increase in new channels and technologies has dramatically changed the environment in which marketers operate. But the way in which marketing is taught, understood and operates has not really changed. This is not sustainable. We need a new unifying framework as a reference for what marketing has become."

He added, "Alongside this need for a new framework, there are new requirements for marketing competencies and capabilities around domains of expertise like data and analytics, customer experience, content, multichannel, and personalization, which are neither properly understood nor being met.

This is acknowledged in the marketing industry, but not reflected in any definitive model."

So, let's use the M3 flywheel, a self-sustaining model, as a starting point and take a closer look at the 10 key questions that Friedlein said a digital marketing strategy should answer.

How Is Marketing Going to Help Deliver on Your Business Strategy?

The first stage of M3 is marketing strategy. And the first question that you need to answer is: "How is marketing going to help deliver on your business strategy?" The marketing competencies and capabilities required to execute the marketing strategy element are as follows:

- Articulating the marketing approach and plan you'll use to deliver against your business objectives
- Outlining your approach and key decisions around each element and the resources (including budget) required to execute the marketing strategy

At a basic level, "suck less, every day" articulates the marketing approach you need to use to deliver against your business objectives. But I suspect that telling your CEO and CFO that your plan is to "consciously suck less" at whatever you're doing today may not help you get the resources (including budget) that you need to execute your marketing strategy.

At an intermediate level, Avinash Kaushik outlined the evolutionary approach that works in a post entitled, "Digital Marketing and Analytics: Two Ladders for Magnificent Success," which was published on Occam's Razor on December 9, 2013.

Google's digital marketing evangelist shared this strategic insight: "More often than not, magnificent success results from executing a business plan that is rooted in a strong understanding of the landscape of possibilities, and a deep self-awareness of business capabilities. These business plans will contain a structured approach...."

Then, he shared a digital marketing ladder of awesomeness (Figure 1.7.).

The ladder articulates the marketing approach and plan we'll use to deliver against our business objectives. This should help us convince the CEO to give us the time that we'll need to pivot our teams, which were built for traditional mass marketing, and train them to OMCA digital marketing standards.

Then he introduced a Digital Analytics Ladder of Awesomeness, which outlines our approach and KPIs for each element. That should convince the chief finance officer (CFO) to give us the resources (including budget) required to execute our marketing strategy.

FIGURE 1.7   Digital Marketing Ladder of Success

These two ladders of awesomeness might look a little different, because this is 2023, not 2013. And both digital marketing and digital analytics have evolved. But the process that he outlined will help us make the hard choices that are most relevant for the company and the evolutionary position it finds itself in.

And if you have a graphic artist on your team, then you can update the illustrations for these two ladders and create something that looks like a double helix, because the marketing strategy requires you to change more than the skills, education, and experience of some of your teams. In other words, magnificent success results from using digital marketing to change the DNA of your entire organization.

Why? Because at an advanced level, your marketing strategy is not just to tackle the challenge of digital transformation, but to embrace it.

And "digital transformation" isn't a nebulous buzzword. It's a process, not a project. By taking incremental steps toward transformation, you can ready your business to drive results today and build resilience for tomorrow (Figure 1.8).

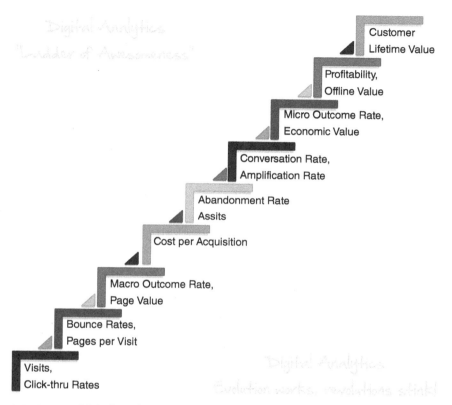

FIGURE 1.8   Digital Analytics Ladder of Success

Every company is at a different point in its digital transformation. But the marketers at Kraft Heinz and John Lewis will really, really want to read, "Results, resilience, and the Route to Ready for 3 brands." Written by Bethany Poole, Google's senior director of ads marketing, this perspective on getting started with digital transformation was published in Think with Google in October 2021.

She said, "We're in a new era, in which COVID-19 has accelerated digital consumption habits so much that analysts talk about seeing a decade's worth of change happening in a few short months. Marketers must create messaging that's agile and responsive enough to capture short-term opportunities, while also building long-term business resilience. But how? The standard answer has been 'digital transformation,' but, too often, the term is used as a buzz-word. And if we aren't clear about what we mean by 'digital transformation,' then it's easy to imagine a long, complicated journey."

She shared examples of how successful brands got started on their journeys.

One was Mondelēz International. (Them again!) Their journey began with a single insight: meeting each consumer where they are means evolving from a mass-marketing strategy to one that delivers a more personalized, helpful set of experiences. This helped galvanize the entire company.

With customer-centricity as their guiding principle, teams from across Mondelēz International—from marketing and information business systems to finance and customer service—broke down their organizational silos to align on shared goals and adopt an agile approach to a companywide initiative called "empathy at scale."

For example, the company launched the "Don't go far for hunger" campaign in India for its Cadbury brand, which used the latest advances in machine learning and programmatic buying to drive consideration among specific audiences. Optimized ad creative combined eight consumer passion points, like cricket or *Game of Thrones,* with six other contextual elements, including time, day of the week, and location. This process generated 92,000 unique, personalized assets that drove a 50 percent increase in ad recall and a click-through rate 2.6 times higher than the CPG benchmark.

Deploying its digital strategy across multiple markets has helped Mondelēz International outpace the rest of its sector and deliver double-digit growth. It has also given the company a template for reorganizing its entire long-term business strategy to focus on building deeper, longer-lasting relationships with consumers.

She also shared the story of how the pandemic accelerated the digital transformation underway at Crate & Barrel, an international home decor brand with more than 100 stores in the United States and Canada. Its online sales have jumped more than 40 percent since the pandemic started, and online sales now comprise more than 65 percent of its overall business.

But the retailer's transformation hasn't been about abandoning its physical stores for an exclusively digital storefront. It has focused instead on making shopping experiences more inventive and inspirational, both online and offline.

Crate & Barrel knew it needed a better way to understand and measure the full customer journey and to respond to those insights in near real time. So the company's transformation journey has centered on building a more unified view of its customers, through a strategy that prioritizes organizational agility and outcomes.

Crate & Barrel began by leaning into the power of cloud computing to gather diverse data from various touchpoints—like traffic information in-store, mobile shopping patterns, and other online purchasing behaviors. Then they created a single data source to represent a holistic picture of the customer.

The company relies heavily on Google Cloud's BigQuery data warehousing and analysis tool, which allows it to draw on 10 times more information sources compared to a few years ago. Data are then analyzed and transformed into actionable insights that can influence a customer's next interaction and, in turn, drive revenue.

So how should you articulate this marketing approach? Well, you could say it's "suck less, every day," "climbing two digital ladders of amazing success," or "tackling the challenge of digital transformation."

But, no matter what you call it, your evolutionary approach is more likely to work than a revolutionary one. Why? Because it will help you infuse agility into your plan, create marketing-driven growth for your company's bottom line, and future-proof your business so you're ready for whatever comes next.

Are You Adequately Aligned and Capable of Succeeding in this Market?

This brings us to the Analysis stage in the M3 model. The second question that you need to answer is: "Are you adequately aligned and capable of succeeding in this market?" The marketing competencies and capabilities required to execute the market/customer orientation element are as follows:

- Avoiding product and sales orientation, how to achieve market orientation and customer focus
- Including market/competitor insight and analysis

Despite the traditional pressures to be product-centric or sales-oriented, most CMOs understand the importance of being customer-centric and market-oriented. So they are adequately aligned to succeed even when market dynamics change rapidly or competitive threats appear unexpectedly.

Why? Because most have read one of the more than 80 books written by Philip Kotler, the S. C. Johnson & Son Distinguished Professor of International Marketing at the Kellogg School of Management at Northwestern University. He's regarded as "The Father of Modern Marketing" by many scholars.

But many of these same CMOs have difficulty making the business case for getting an adequate budget to be capable of succeeding.

Why? Because they haven't read _Return on Marketing Investment_ by Guy R. Powell, which was published in February 2003.

Powell explained that the traditional return on investment' (ROI) metric measures money that is "tied up" in plants and inventories for years, which is a capital expenditure or CAPEX. But spending on marketing is typically "invested" in the current quarter, which makes it an operational expenditure or OPEX.

So he proposed a new metric for measuring the return on marketing investment (ROMI): [Incremental Revenue Attributable to Marketing ($) * Contribution Margin (%) – Marketing Spending ($)] / Marketing Spending ($).

For example, if a company spends $100,000 on digital marketing and it generates $500,000 in incremental revenue, then the ROMI factor is 5.0. If the incremental contribution margin for that $500,000 in revenue is 60 percent, then the margin ROMI (the incremental margin for $100,000 of marketing spent) is $300,000 (= $500,000 × 60%). Of which, the $100,000 spent on digital marketing will be subtracted and the difference will be divided by the same $100,000. So, every dollar expended on digital marketing translates to an additional $2 on the company's bottom line.

Once you learn how to calculate ROMI, you're in a much stronger position to make the business case for getting an adequate budget to be capable of succeeding in your market. If your CEO wants you to generate more revenue, then you can make the business case for a bigger marketing budget. And if your CFO wants you to spend less, then you can reduce the incremental revenue that you need to generate to be successful.

Who Are Your Customers and What Are Their Needs and Expectations?

The third question that you need to answer is: "Who are your customers and what are their needs and expectations?' The marketing competencies and capabilities required to execute the customer insight element are as follows:

- Using qualitative, quantitative, traditional, and digital techniques to gather customer insights
- Designing customer surveys, conducting market research, and analyzing the data to identify or validate who your customers are as well as what they need and expect

Customer insight is always important, but you often don't have the budget to use expensive surveys or the time to conduct market research to gather them. Fortunately, a new audience intelligence tool was launched in April 2020 that solves this problem.

The tool was created by SparkToro, a software company co-founded by Casey Henry and Rand Fishkin. Their tool, which is also named SparkToro, quickly crawls tens of millions of social and web profiles to find what (and who) your audience reads, listens to, watches, follows, shares, and talks about online (Figure 1.9).

For example, SparkToro's database quickly found 117,949 people who talk about "digital marketing." And the following top words appear in their bios/profiles/about fields on Twitter, Instagram, Facebook, LinkedIn, and other social platforms:

- Agency (11 percent)
- Marketing agency (8.6 percent)
- Consultant (6.2 percent)

- Web (5.4 percent)
- Marketing consultant (4.9 percent)

SparkToro's database has found 117,949 people that talk about digital marketing

Get more search ideas related to this audience

Here are the behaviors and demographics of this audience

FIGURE 1.9   SparkToro Digital Marketing

This tells me I should probably find a place somewhere in this book to mention that agencies like GTB, formerly known as Team Detroit, and Media-Com, a leading agency based in the United Kingdom, have trained their teams to OMCP digital marketing standards and lead the industry in marketing performance.

SparkToro also tells me that "marketing strategy" is the most frequently used phrase used by this niche audience over the past 3–4 months on Twitter, Instagram, Facebook, etc.

If one of your clients agrees to provide the resources (including budget) required to execute your marketing strategy, then you should use tools like Google Surveys, a market research tool that allows you to easily create online surveys in order to make more informed business decisions. Unfortunately, far too many account executives at agencies assume that the client knows who their customers are as well as what their customers need and expect.

But, it rarely hurts—and it often helps—to double-check these assumptions.

For example, let me share a story that I told on September 19, 2019, at "Telling Y/Our Story," Intrado's second annual digital media client summit in New York City, and again on October 8, 2019, at Pubcon Pro Las Vegas. This story is part of a longer case study.

In January 2019, my award-winning digital marketing agency helped the Rutgers School of Management and Labor Relations (SMLR) to launch an Online Professional Master's in Human Resource Management (MHRM) program. Our objective was to generate 30 applications by August 1, 2019. Graduate students could complete the 12-course online MHRM program in as few as 18 months and as long as 5 years. And tuition is $3,174 per 3-credit course, or $38,016 for 12 courses.

I used Google Surveys to double-check some of the assumptions that my client had made about graduate students as well as their needs and expectations. Google Surveys enabled me to ask up to 10 questions, including a screening question, which let me target questions to a specific audience by filtering respondents.

I ran my survey on Google's network of publishers. It went live on Friday, January 11, 2019. The results were available on Monday, January 14, 2019, giving me time to analyze them before presenting my findings at a meeting later that afternoon in Piscataway, New Jersey.

Rutgers SMLR had planned to target human resource (HR) professionals, managers, and supervisors with four or more years of experience who wanted to advance their careers to senior HR or management positions. But Google Surveys found that you should also target professionals in personnel, staffing and recruiting, and talent acquisition.

This insight more than doubled the total size of the target audiences.

Respondents also said the following factors were important when selecting a university that offers an online master's degree in human resources management:

- No GRE/GMAT required
- Top-ranked university
- Fully 100 percent online program

So we emphasized these key factors in our digital marketing campaign, which included Google Ads, LinkedIn advertising, SEO, and an optimize press release.

We also used Digital Analytics to evaluate the source/medium of the 8,337 new users and 694 leads generated by our campaign:

- Our press release generated 1 percent of the new users, but 8 percent of the leads.
- SEO generated 3 percent of the new users, but 19 percent of the leads.
- Google Ads generated 11 percent of the new users, but 18 percent of the leads.
- LinkedIn advertising generated 81 percent of the new users, but 37 percent of the leads.

More importantly, the campaign had generated 38 completed applications, worth up to $1,444,608 in tuition over the next 18 months to 5 years.

That's the benefit of using Google Surveys to double-check some of the assumptions that my client had made about graduate students as well as their needs and expectations. The surveys cost less than $2,000, and the insights produced award-winning results.

I shared this story a third time in July 2021, when I taught a two-part course on "Creating a Digital Marketing Strategy" in the first Impact Digital Creator Program at the New Media Academy in the United Arab Emirates (UAE).

One of the 22 influential and creative individuals taking my course, Abdullah AlMheiri, a self-identified coffee connoisseur, asked if he could show how he had used Google Forms to easily create surveys and questionnaires to gather information about his target audience for free.

Google Forms let him select from multiple question types, embed forms on his website, or share them via Instagram, Facebook, or Twitter. And he could watch responses appear in real time as well as access the raw data and analyze it with Google Sheets or other software.

It's worth noting that coffee is a huge part of Arabic culture, and specialty coffee has been on the rise in the UAE. New Media Academy created a show with Abdulla AlMheiri, who is the co-founder of Coarse Coffee, a member of the Specialty Coffee Association, and the 2019 Aeropress champion, to educate and entertain coffee enthusiasts in the region. The show, *Cooooffeeeee with Abdulla,* initially launched on YouTube.

It was then recognized by Snapchat and featured as Cooooffeeeee with Abdulla on their platform. His Snapchat show is specifically designed for coffee lovers and enthusiasts in the region from one of the best coffee specialists in the UAE. It has more than 10 million views and over 20,000 subscribers.

This teaches us all another important lesson: it rarely hurts—and it often helps—when a "student" double-checks what an "instructor" knows about using Google Forms to create online surveys.

Why Should Anyone Care or Take Notice? What Unique Value Are You Providing?

This brings us to the Planning stage in the M3 model. The fourth set of questions that you need to answer are: "Why should anyone care or take notice? What unique value are you providing?"

The marketing competencies and capabilities required to execute the brand and value element are as follows:

- Brand purpose, promise
- The value proposition of the brand, including (but not exclusively) price

In other words, you need a brand purpose and value proposition that can change the hearts, minds, and actions of people. And the best book on this topic is *Enchantment: The Art of Changing Hearts, Minds, and Actions* by Guy Kawasaki, which was published in January 2011.

We've known each other since 1989, when he was a columnist for *Mac-User* and I was the director of marketing at *PC/Computing*, a sister magazine that was also published by Ziff-Davis. But I was still surprised when he reached out in late 2010 and asked me to contribute about four pages to his 10th book, *Enchantment*. He wanted me to help him explain how to use You-Tube to enchant people.

I immediately said, "Yes." And then I asked him, "What do you mean by enchantment? Is this just a synonym for engagement?" Actually, he had something very different in mind.

As defined by my old friend and former colleague, "Enchantment is not about manipulating people. It transforms situations and relationships. It converts hostility into civility and civility into affinity. It changes skeptics and cynics into believers and the undecided into the loyal."

He added, "Enchantment can happen during a retail transaction, a high-level corporate negotiation, or a Facebook update. And when done right, it's more powerful than traditional persuasion, influence, or marketing techniques."

And he concluded, "In business and personal interactions, your goal is not merely to get what you want but to bring about a voluntary, enduring, and delightful change in other people. By enlisting their own goals and desires, by being likable and trustworthy, and by framing a cause that others can embrace, you can change hearts, minds, and actions."

Now, that's a big idea. So instead of sending him some examples from the first edition of my book, *YouTube and Video Marketing: An Hour a Day* (2009), I spent some time thinking about what this bestselling business guru was really asking me to deliver.

When I got back to him, I shared this strategic insight, "Video content that can enchant people must provide intrinsic value to your viewers." This value comes in four forms:

- **Inspiration:** Tell stories of courage, bravery, or personal triumph.
- **Entertainment:** Make people laugh out loud with a hilarious video.
- **Enlightenment:** Leave viewers in-the-know with a documentary film.
- **Education:** Show your target audience how to do something useful.

In the book, he says, "One way to remember these four categories is that they form the acronym 'IEEE,' which is funny in a nerd humor way. If you don't get it, don't worry."

He adds, "One important point: The goal of companies is often to create a 'viral video.' You know, the kind that millions of people watch in a few days—for example, the Old Spice guy videos. This is the kind of video every other company wishes it or its expensive agency created."

And he concludes, "Don't make this your goal. Luck makes a video go viral, and 'get lucky' is not a good strategy. The right goal is to provide a steady supply of video that is inspiring, entertaining, enlightening, or educational and that, over time, enchants people."

Perhaps a case study can illustrate this point.

Procter & Gamble Case Study

The Procter & Gamble Company (P&G) was founded in 1837. Throughout their 185-year history, their business has grown and changed while their purpose, values, and principles have endured—and will continue to be passed down to generations of P&G people to come.

Their website clearly states P&G's purpose: "We will provide branded products and services of superior quality and value that improve the lives of the world's consumers, now and for generations to come. As a result, consumers will reward us with leadership sales, profit and value creation, allowing our people, our shareholders and the communities in which we live and work to prosper."

One of their values is integrity: "We always try to do the right thing."

And one of their principles is to show respect for all individuals: "We believe that all individuals can and want to contribute to their fullest potential."

Taken together, P&G's purpose, values, and principles are the foundation for their unique culture. So the leading CPG company, which is headquartered in downtown Cincinnati, Ohio, didn't need any lessons on how to create a brand purpose or value proposition before earning the OMCP Talent leadership Award for Digital Marketing Certification Pass Rates in 2018.

Nevertheless, with strong support from senior leaders, Katy Moeggenberg and Carrie Rathod unified brand, IT, marketing technology, and other groups to achieve a company-wide 94 percent certification rate—the highest rate that OMCP has seen.

And you can begin to see the impact that combining a clear brand purpose and value proposition with a training and certification program based on industry standards set by OMCP has had on P&G just by looking at their 350 brand and 22 corporate properties on YouTube, Facebook, and other platforms in more than 50 countries in over 30 languages.

As I mentioned earlier in this chapter, video marketing isn't one of the top eight disciplines. So it wasn't explicitly covered on the exams that 94 percent of P&G's brand, IT, marketing technology, and other groups passed.

But content marketing and social media marketing were both part of the programs that two providers had designed for the OMCA curriculum: Simplilearn's OMCA preparatory course, and LinkedIn's OMCA Course. So you could say that P&G has applied what they have learned in a related discipline.

Over the last 3 years, P&G has uploaded 35,400 videos to YouTube, Facebook, and other platforms. Collectively, they've gotten 14.6 billion (with a "b") views and 35.7 million (with an "m") engagements.

And the video with the most engagements is _We Believe: The Best Men Can Be_ (Gillette). Uploaded on January 13, 2019, this enlightening and inspiring video has 35.7 million views and 1.2 million engagements, according to data from Tubular Labs (Figure 1.10).

FIGURE 1.10   We Believe: The Best Men Can Be | Gillette (Short Film) (**https://youtu.be/koPmuEyP3a0**)

The Twitter version of this video has 31.2 million views and 768,000 engagements, Facebook's version has 11.3 million views and 494,000 engagements, and Instagram's version has 443,000 views and 85,100 engagements.

The YouTube video's description says, "Bullying. Harassment. Is this the best a man can get? It's only by challenging ourselves to do more, that we can get closer to our best. To say the right thing, to act the right way. We are taking action . . . Join us."

The initial release of _The Best Men Can Be_ was the subject of controversy. But Ace Metrix found the creative for _The Best Men Can Be_ actually developed the strongest positive purchase intent among recent "social stand" ads, including Nike's _Dream Crazy_ featuring Colin Kaepernick. In fact, 65 percent of the viewers of Gillette's corporate social responsibility (CSR) ad indicated the short film made them more/much more likely to purchase from the brand, and two-thirds rated the message the single best thing about the ad.

You can also begin to see the impact that having a clear brand purpose and value proposition has had on P&G's global rankings by video views of brand properties in the CPG industry. As the chart in Figure 1.11 shows,

P&G's global rankings bounced around from 2016 to 2018. In January 2019, P&G ranked #34. But, within 3 months, the brand property had shot up to #2—where it remained fairly consistently for the next 32 months until P&G passed Unilever to rank #1 in December 2021.

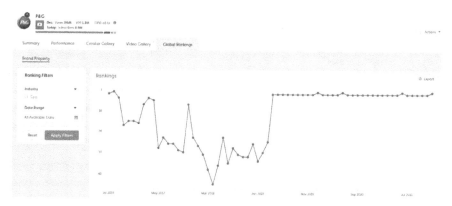

FIGURE 1.11   P&G's Global Rankings by Video Views of Brand Properties

More importantly, P&G has reported a notable improvement in the effectiveness of its marketing after increasing its investment in digital media.

How Does Your Market Break Down into Groups, and Which Will You Go After?

The fifth question that you need to answer is: "How does your market break down into groups, and which will you go after? And the marketing competencies and capabilities required to execute the segmentation and targeting element are as follows:

- Use classic (geo/demographic, behavioral, and psychographic) and digital (in-market and affinity) segmentation to map our market.
- Select target segments based on relevance and attractiveness.
- Decide how wide/narrow to target (e.g., is mass marketing still a valid approach?).

To break down their market into groups, many marketers create fictional characters called "personas." This is a fundamental and powerful concept—when done right.

David Meerman Scott, a friend and the author of 12 books, wrote an article entitled, "Back to the Basics: The Importance of Buyer Personas," which was published on his blog and in *The New Rules of Marketing,* his weekly newsletter on LinkedIn, on December 13, 2021.

He observed, "Organizations filled with people who take the time to understand the needs of buyers they wish to reach, and then develop information to educate and inform those buyers, are more successful than organizations that just make stuff up."

He added, "Buyer personas, the distinct demographic groupings of your potential customers, are critically important for successful marketing that leads to sales success."

And he concluded, "Creating marketing and sales initiatives that target specific buyer personas is a strategy that easily outperforms the results you get from sitting on your butt in your comfortable office making stuff up about your products."

But if you rely solely on demographics to create your personas, you can miss significant segments of potential consumers.

Why? Because demographics rarely tell the whole story. Customer intent—what customers are looking for—is a smarter way to segment our market and target the groups we'll go after.

I've written a column on this topic entitled, "<u>Customer Personas Can Transform SEO, PPC and Content Marketing</u>," which was published in *Search Engine Journal* on March 12, 2021. It's more than 2,600 words long, so I won't republish all of it here.

But with permission from *Search Engine Journal*, let me share a lightly edited excerpt on the research and insights of Justin De Graaf, who is (appropriately) head of ads research and insights at Google.

De Graff says, "Acting on consumer intent is one of the keys to unlocking growth."

He adds, "The things they search, sites they visit, and videos they watch are not only expressing intent, they're reshaping the traditional marketing funnel. And with the help of marketing technology, marketers can sift through all the signals left behind and gain insight that can help them predict intent."

I agree. Too many marketers rely too heavily on demographics when they create customer personas.

Why? Because that's the only data that TV networks could provide about their audiences back in the 20th century. But demographics rarely tell SEO professionals, PPC advertisers, or content marketers what you need to know in the 21st century about search intent.

Keyword research, on the other hand, gives you a better way of unlocking search intent—although you don't have access to a fraction of the marketing technology that Google does. That's why I was amazed that De Graff shared some strategic insights from research that Google partnered with Kantar to conduct. They wanted to get a better understanding of the underlying motivations driving search behaviors. You might assume (as I did) that Google doesn't need any help with this. It turns out that Google knows "what" people search for, but it's often puzzled about "why."

So they leveraged Kantar's NeedScope, which is an approach to segmentation that can help you to uncover the functional, social, and emotional drivers of consumer behavior within a target market.

In other words, NeedScope provides a framework for understanding why people make the decisions that they do, which, in turn, can reveal significant opportunities for companies and brands to create personas that represent those underlying needs more effectively.

De Graff admits that he wasn't initially sure if NeedScope's approach to segmentation could be applied to search, let alone to creating customer personas.

Well, it could. It was. And the result was revolutionary.

According to NeedScope, there are six "canonical" consumer needs and each one is made up of a different combination of emotional, social, and functional needs:

- **Surprise Me:** Search is fun and entertaining. It is extensive with many unique iterations.

- **Thrill Me:** Search is a quick adventure to find new things. It is brief, with just a few words and minimal back-button use.

- **Impress Me:** Search is about influencing and winning. It is laser-focused, using specific phrases.

- **Educate Me:** Search is about competence and control. It is thorough (reviews, ratings, comparisons, etc.).

- **Reassure Me:** Search is about simplicity, comfort, and trust. It is uncomplicated and more likely to include questions.

- **Help Me:** Search is about connecting and practicality. It is to the point and more likely to mention family or location.

De Graff also observes, "Emotions are the foundations of need states. The truth is, decision-making is not a rational process, but one driven mainly by how people feel. The rational brain layers on reasons for our choices only after they're made."

Before Google started this research, De Graff thought that one or two needs would dominate search behavior.

For example, he says that Educate Me seemed like a no-brainer given that search is all about exchanging information. But he discovered that search behavior is driven by all six "canonical" needs.

This approach to creating customer personas can transform not only digital advertising, SEO, content marketing, and social media marketing, but also video marketing.

For example, visit <u>Find My Audience</u>. This free tool helps you to go beyond demographics to find the people on YouTube who are your most valuable customers.

First, you need to select a type of audience. You have two options:

- **In-market audiences:** People actively researching or planning to purchase products or services like yours.
- **Affinity audiences:** People whose interests and habits relate to what your business offers.

Then, you need to select your category. For in-market audiences, you have 22 options: Apparel & Accessories, Arts & Crafts Supplies, Autos & Vehicles, Baby & Children's Products, Beauty & Personal Care, Business & Industrial Products, Business Services, Computers & Peripherals, Consumer Electronics, Education, Employment, Event Tickets, Food, Gifts & Occasions, Home & Garden, Media & Entertainment, Musical Instruments & Accessories, Real Estate, Software, Sports & Fitness, Telecom, and Travel.

For affinity audiences, you have 12 options: Banking & Finance, Beauty & Wellness, Food & Dining, Home & Garden, Lifestyles & Hobbies, Media & Entertainment, News & Politics, Shoppers, Sports & Fitness, Technology, Travel, and Vehicles & Transportation.

In other words, the Find My Audience tool enables you to do the following:

- Discover new audiences based on their interests, habits, and what they're planning to purchase.
- Get a free audience profile, with insights to help inform your video ad strategy.
- Use your insights to start a YouTube campaign that reaches people who matter most to your business.

Now, that's a way to execute the segmentation and targeting element of the M3 model that you can take to the bank.

How Will You Convey Your Product/Service and How Might That Differ by Individual Customer or Segment?

The sixth question that you need to answer is: "How will you convey your product/service and how might that differ by individual customer or segment?"

If you tackle this question using traditional marketing, then the answers you'll find are probably going to be ineffective and incomplete. But if you're using programmatic buying to drive your media and applying the latest advances in machine learning for data-driven creative, then automation can make positioning more effective and comprehensive.

So even if programmatic advertising isn't one of the top eight disciplines, the marketing competencies and capabilities required to execute positioning with a unified marketing and analytics platform are as follows:

- Organize audience insights
- Design compelling creative
- Execute with integrated technology
- Reach audiences across screens
- Measure the impact

Plus, if you segment customers by their intent, then positioning your product or service different ways to different groups becomes fairly straightforward. All you need to do is use a tool like Google's Director Mix to create multiple versions of a YouTube video ad that are customized to appeal to the different interests and intent of different shoppers.

For example, when soup sales were down in Australia, Campbell's Soup turned to Director Mix to create 1,700 variations of a single video. Users searching YouTube for "Orange Is the New Black," for example, were served ads with cheeky copy about prison food. Those searching for Beyonce's "Single Ladies" were asked if they needed "dinner for one."

With an average view rate of 55.43 percent, the "SoupTube" campaign garnered 1.67 million total views, generating a 6.9 percent lift in brand awareness—which is impressive for an already well-known brand like Campbell's. The use of Director Mix reduced production costs, and best of all, Campbell's "Simply Soups" saw a 55.6 percent increase in sales between May and July 2016.

If you have time, watch the video in Figure 1.12 to see how the campaign didn't give users one reason to buy Campbell's soup; it gave them thousands of reasons, while targeting specific audiences on YouTube.

What Is the Customer Journey, How Will You Understand and Improve It, and How Will You Support That with Content?

This brings us to the Execution stage in the M3 model. The seventh set of questions that you need to answer are: "What is the customer journey, how will you understand and improve it, and how will you support that with content?"

The marketing competencies and capabilities required to execute the customer experience element are as follows:

FIGURE 1.12 SoupTube Case Study for Campbell's Soup (**https://youtu.be/ NB11gG8NwC8**)

- Map your customer's journey from initial impression to final conversion.
- Identify all of the communication touchpoints in your customer's journey.
- Create content to impact perceptions and behavior through the journey.

Traditional marketers were taught the funnel was a linear customer journey—from attention to interest, desire, and action (AIDA). Their key levers to drive growth were reach and frequency using mass media. And they used demographics to approximate user intent and inform their targeting and creative.

But Elmo Lewis developed the AIDA model back in 1898, and William Townsend introduced the funnel concept in 1924. These outdated models no longer illustrate what today's customer journeys look like.

After observing several hundred hours of shopping tasks, covering 310 different journeys across 31 categories, Alistair Rennie and Jonny Protheroe, who work on Google's Market Insights team in the United Kingdom, discovered, "People don't make decisions in a neat, linear fashion. A lot happens between the moment they realize they have a need or a desire for something and the moment they make a purchase."

This is the gist of their 1,000-word article entitled, "How people decide what to buy lies in the 'messy middle' of the purchase journey," which was published in Think with Google in July 2020. And their article is actually a summary of their team's 98-page report, which is entitled, "Decoding Decisions: Making Sense of the Messy Middle."

Now, the "messy middle" is a big idea.

Their research found, "People look for information about a category's products and brands, and then weigh all the options. This equates to two different mental modes in the messy middle: exploration, an expansive activity, and evaluation, a reductive activity. Whatever a person is doing, across a huge array of online sources, such as search engines, social media, aggregators, and review websites, can be classified into one of these two mental modes."

But Rennie and Protheroe were focused on just the "messy middle" of today's customer journeys. They didn't examine what happens before the triggers or after the purchase.

Digital technology and mobile devices have put people in control. We all now expect an immediate answer in the moments we want to know, go, do, and buy. And all of these intent-rich moments are creating journey shapes as unique as each of us. In many ways, intent is redefining the old marketing funnel.

If no two customer journeys are the same, then how are you expected to understand where people are on the path to purchase and loyalty?

Well, the key step is the first one: Mapping your customer's journey.

And many people who work on mapping customer journeys have adopted Avinash Kaushik's "See, Think, Do, Care" framework to identify different stages (aka "audience intent clusters"):

- **See:** Anyone who could buy your product
- **Think:** Anyone who could buy your product showing some commercial intent
- **Do:** Anyone who could buy your product showing strong commercial intent
- **Care:** Your existing customers

Kaushik's framework has many benefits. But this framework was first published in July 2013 and then updated in July 2015. Since then, I've revised and extended it to incorporate new research that indicates there is a fifth stage.

For example, Justin De Graaf, whom I mentioned earlier, wrote an article entitled, "How consumer needs shape search behavior and drive intent," which was published in Think with Google in May 2019. He said, "The truth is, decision-making is not a rational process, but one driven mainly by how people feel. The rational brain layers on reasons for our choices only after they're made."

That's why I've added "Feel" to Kaushik's framework (Figure 1.13)—after "See" and before "Think."

FIGURE 1.13 See, Feel, Think, Do, Care Model of the Customer Journey

With the map of your customer's journey completed, you're ready to tackle the next two steps:

- Identify all of the communication touchpoints in your customer's journey.
- Create content to impact perceptions and behavior through the journey.

Since Chapter 5, which covers Content Marketing, will address these next steps in more detail, there's no need to elaborate on them here. But let me just give you this sneak preview: 83 percent of marketers say video has become more important in the last 2 years.

How Will You Be Found in the Places Your Customers Are?

The eighth question that you need to answer is: "How will you be found in the places your customers are?"

The marketing competencies and capabilities required to execute the distribution element are as follows:

- Digital public relations (PR)
- Earned media

Getting found in all the right places requires you to go beyond owned media and paid media. It requires you to identify other places that are called "earned media," which can be gained through publicity generated by digital PR, or organically, when content receives recognition and a following through communication channels such as social media and word of mouth.

If you have the time and interest in reading an article on this topic, then check out my post, **"What is digital PR (aka online PR) and why is it so damn important?"** It's more than 2,800 words long, so I won't republish all of it here (Figure 1.14).

Let me share a lightly edited excerpt of the key concepts.

Let's start with a definition: *digital PR* is a digital marketing discipline that uses press release SEO as well as digital media relations, blogger outreach, and influencer marketing to generate measurable results that are important to the success of a campaign or an organization.

Some people may mistakenly think that digital PR is just the early 21st-century version of traditional public relations, which was developed back in the early 20th century. But I'd argue that "PR" is experiencing a paradigm shift.

For more than 100 years, traditional public relations sent news releases to "the press" and engaged in media relations to generate publicity. But a funny thing happened in September 2002, when Google launched the beta version of Google News. When you did a news search, you could find press releases in the results along with articles from traditional news sources. This meant that "the public" as well as "the press" could find and read news releases that had been well optimized for relevant search terms.

FIGURE 1.14 What Is Digital PR (aka online PR), and Why Is It so Important?

In early 2003, SEO-PR was founded to seize this opportunity, and we pioneered several techniques, including adding campaign parameters to URLs so we could track custom campaigns in Google Analytics.

This innovation was a game changer because it generated website traffic, B2B leads, and B2C sales as well as publicity.

For example, Southwest Airlines and SEO-PR won the Golden Ruler Award for Excellence in Public Relations Measurement in 2005 for tracking $2.5 million in ticket sales in 2004 back to four optimized press releases. If you want more details, you can read our case study, which is entitled "You are now free to link PR and sales" and is posted on the Institute for Public Relations (IPR) website.

But press release SEO is just one of the key tactics used in digital PR. The other is digital media relations, blogger outreach, and influencer marketing. Together, they enable you to use a push/pull strategy to contact key people you know ahead of time and get contacted by key people you don't know after a newsworthy announcement.

This led to the development of an innovative digital PR tactic that put some newfangled "linkbait" on an old-fashioned "news hook." And, yes, Google considered this to be an ethical or "white-hat" practice.

In fact, Google's quality guidelines said, "The best way to get other sites to create high-quality, relevant links to yours is to create unique, relevant content that can naturally gain popularity in the Internet community. Creating good content pays off: Links are usually editorial votes given by choice, and the more useful content you have, the greater the chances someone else will find that content valuable to their readers and link to it."

That's why SEO-PR added blog outreach to our online PR services during this time frame. And we combined blogger outreach with press release SEO to generate publicity and build links for a variety of clients.

For example, we used some of the survey findings in the Harlequin Romance Report as linkbait for a campaign in 2007.

Harlequin Enterprises Ltd., one of the world's leading publishers of women's fiction, has polled more than 3,000 men and women across Canada and the United States and discovered that 55 percent of American men and 41 percent of American women had said, "I love you," in hopes it would lead to sex.

We offered influential journalists and bloggers a draft of our optimized press release in advance under a "news embargo."

This is another newfangled version of an old tactic that's been used for decades by traditional public relations professionals, who would ask journalists to hold a news story until a certain date in exchange for providing them with crucial information ahead of time.

This updated tactic enabled us to generate 11 news stories, 190 blog posts, and a mention in Jay Leno's monologue on the *Tonight Show,* as well as 202 natural links to the Harlequin Romance Report. That's what we were able to accomplish 15 years ago.

Today, we use SparkToro, the tool that I mentioned earlier, to quickly and accurately identify the places where our customers are, so our Digital PR efforts can be even better targeted and more effective (Figure 1.15).

Here's what this audience watches, listens-to, and reads

Podcasts They Listen-To	YouTube Channels They Subscribe-to
32.4% engage with The Growth Show	17.5% engage with HubSpot Marketing
23.6% engage with Marketing Smarts from MarketingProfs	16.1% engage with Moz
21.2% engage with Content Inc with Joe Pulizzi	14.5% engage with Search Engine Land
See all podcast results	See all YouTube results

Press Accounts They Read	
36.4% engage with Mashable	
33.0% engage with TechCrunch	
29.0% engage with Search Engine Land	
See all press results	

FIGURE 1.15 SparkToro's Data on What This Audience Watches, Listens to, and Reads

For example, SparkToro's database tells us that a signification percentage of the 117,949 people who talk about "digital marketing" listen to *The Growth Show, Marketing Smarts from MarketingProfs,* and *Content Inc with Joe Pulizzi* podcasts.

Digital PR isn't one of the top eight disciplines. But you will probably want at least a concept-level understanding of the tactics that were once called "online PR" and "linkbait" before you develop a digital marketing strategy for your organization in 2023 and beyond.

How Will You Actively Get Your Message in Front of the Right People?

The ninth question that you need to answer is: "How will you actively get your message in front of the right people?"

The marketing competencies and capabilities required to execute the integrated marketing communications element are as follows:

- Paid and owned media to promote your brand
- All forms of advertising and marketing

To actively get your message in front of the right people, you'll need an integrated marketing campaign that uses paid and owned media (as well as earned media) to promote your brand. This includes all forms of digital and traditional advertising and marketing approaches.

That's why we and the rest of our team need to learn how to master all eight of the disciplines that are considered core to OMCP certification. This includes these disciplines:

- Digital Advertising (including PPC, Social, Video, Display, and CTV)
- SEO (including local, publishing, and ecommerce)
- Content Marketing
- Social Media Marketing
- Conversion Optimization (including UX)
- Mobile Marketing
- Email Marketing

Since this is exactly what seven of the next eight chapters of this book are about, I won't elaborate about the integrated marketing element here.

What Data Do You Need to Support Your Marketing? How Do You Measure and Optimize Performance?

The 10th and final questions that you need to answer are: "What data do you need to support your marketing? How do you measure and optimize performance?" The marketing competencies and capabilities required to execute the data and measurement element are as follows:

- Define data sources/types (e.g., first party), metadata, schemas/taxonomies.
- Comply with data governance, privacy policies and procedures.
- Define what metrics will be used to gauge and optimize marketing performance.
- Provide reporting, analysis, and insights to improve performance and enable more efficient data-driven marketing.

This is why digital analytics is the eighth discipline. It may not help you to actively get our message in front of people, but it will let you know if the other seven disciplines are getting your message in front of the right people. That's why it's the topic of Chapter 2.

But Matt Bailey, who wrote Chapter 2, focuses on universal analytics because this is what the OMCA standards and the OMCA exam for certification focus on. And even though I'm a Wolverine and he's a Buckeye, I agree 42-27 with his decision. (If you don't get it, don't worry.)

Nevertheless, it won't hurt—and it may help—to have at least a concept-level understanding of the following data and measurement elements before you develop a digital marketing strategy for your organization in 2023 and beyond.

On October 14, 2020, Vidhya Srinivasan, vice president of measurement, analytics, and buying platforms at Google, introduced "The New Google Analytics." Called Google Analytics 4 (GA4), "It has machine learning at its core to automatically surface helpful insights and gives you a complete understanding of your customers across devices and platforms. It's privacy-centric by design, so you can rely on Analytics even as industry changes like restrictions on cookies and identifiers create gaps in your data."

GA4 also provides smarter insights to improve our marketing decisions and get better ROMI. As Srinivasan explained, "By applying Google's advanced machine learning models, the new Analytics can automatically alert you to significant trends in your data—like products seeing rising demand because of new customer needs. It even helps you anticipate future actions your customers may take. For example, it calculates churn probability so you can more efficiently invest in retaining customers at a time when marketing budgets are under pressure."

In addition, a deeper integration with Google Ads makes it possible to address longtime advertiser requests. Srinivasan explained, "Because the new Analytics can measure app and web interactions together, it can include conversions from YouTube engaged views that occur in-app and on the web in reports. Seeing conversions from YouTube video views alongside conversions from Google and non-Google paid channels, and organic channels like Google Search, social, and email, helps you understand the combined impact of all your marketing efforts."

However, GA4 doesn't help you show how you're delivering on your marketing strategy if you have the following business goals:

- Create brand awareness
- Build credibility/trust
- Educate audiences

If these are your goals, you need other tools to help deliver on your marketing strategy. And, as you will learn in Chapter 2, these other tools include surveys and qualitative research.

And as I mentioned earlier in this chapter, Google's Brand Lift solution measures the direct impact your YouTube ads are having on perceptions and behaviors throughout the consumer journey. With Brand Lift, you can answer the following questions:

- Do people recall watching my video ad?
- Are my target consumers more aware of my brand after viewing my video ad?
- Did my video ad move people to consider my brand or product?
- Are consumers more favorably aligned with my brand's message/identity after viewing my ad?
- Do consumers intend to purchase my product after seeing my ad?

Facebook also offers Brand Lift tests. So even if our goals don't involve increasing website traffic, website engagement, and conversions, you can still demonstrate that digital marketing is delivering on your business strategy. That should enable you to show that digital transformation is a self-guided, step-by-step journey, propelled by a self-sustaining flywheel instead of a grandiose project.

Why Do You Still Need to Add a Dash of Marketing Imagination?

Although adopting the M3 future-facing framework can help you "suck less, every day," you still need a dash of marketing imagination to continue "climbing two digital ladders of amazing success."

Why? Because "tackling the challenge of digital transformation" isn't paint-by-numbers. It is a real art.

Yes, an evolutionary approach is more likely to work than a revolutionary one. It will help you infuse agility into your plan, create marketing-driven growth for your company's bottom line, and future-proof your business so you're ready for whatever comes next. And what comes next may have already arrived.

On October 19, 2021, I wrote a news story for *Search Engine Journal* entitled, "YouTube Announces Live Shopping and CTV Product Updates." With permission from *Search Engine Journal*, let me share a lightly edited excerpt.

At *Advertising Week New York,* Tara Walpert Levy, Google vice president of brand and agency solutions, announced the latest live shopping and CTV product updates from YouTube. These announcements provide a clear picture of what's coming next in streaming and commerce.

As in-store and digital commerce continue converging, shoppers are seeking inspiration and advice from different sources.

"YouTube creators have been at the forefront of this shift, sharing helpful, credible, and entertaining shopping content that cuts through the noise," Levy says. She points out that 89 percent of viewers surveyed say they trust recommendations from YouTube creators.

In the video shown in Figure 1.16, Amy Lanzi, commerce practice lead North America, Publicis Groupe, explains how YouTube factors into consumers' shopping journeys.

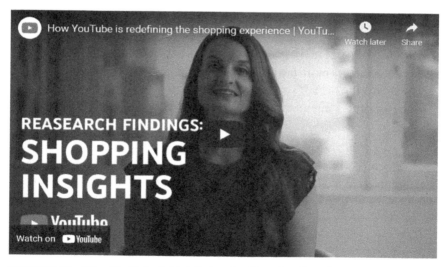

FIGURE 1.16 How YouTube Is Redefining the Shopping Experience

"Earlier this year," Levy said, "YouTube also started testing an integrated shopping experience that allows viewers to tap into the credibility and knowledge of trusted creators to make informed purchases on YouTube."

YouTube initially experimented with "shoppable" on-demand videos, and now the platform is testing "shoppable" livestreams, as well.

More recently, YouTube partnered with several top creators to test their new live shopping features, and has also tested shoppable livestreams with leading retailers on their channels.

In the video from Figure 1.17, you can hear from White and Jill Toscano, the vice president of media for Walmart, about how YouTube's partnership has allowed them to better understand and adapt to consumer needs.

FIGURE 1.17 Walmart Connects with Consumers by Adapting to Shifts in Behavior

Streaming households passed cable TV households in the United States for the first time last year. And according to Comscore OTT Intelligence, 40 percent of all ad-supported streaming watch time is currently taking place on YouTube.

Levy said that 60 percent of YouTube CTV viewers now watch video content with others, and that "people are connecting more deeply with each other by sharing the YouTube content that they love most on the big screen."

Brands have an opportunity here to extend the overall reach and impact of their advertising campaigns.

In addition, U.S. advertisers can fully measure their YouTube CTV video investments across YouTube and YouTube TV. This provides a more accurate view of true incremental reach and frequency in Comscore Campaign Ratings.

This helps to explain why "tackling the challenge of digital transformation" isn't paint-by-numbers. It is a real art.

That's also why marketers and their agencies that need to learn how to apply what they have learned are reading this and other news stories to pivot, zigzag, and evolve their digital marketing strategy when things change.

Why? Because things are constantly changing.

CHAPTER 2

Digital Marketing Analytics

By Matt Bailey

A *nalytics.* I've seen people literally cringe when that word is spoken. For some reason, analytics has become one of the most misunderstood, yet the most valuable of all digital skills. In this chapter, not only will I show you that analytics don't have to be intimidating, but I'll provide you with a working framework to apply in any organization. Because chances are, when going into a new position with your OMCA credentials, you may be one of the only people on your team with any formal training or understanding of analytics.

One of the reasons that analytics is so misunderstood is that most formal marketing education lacks even the basics of data measurement and analytics. It takes a while for the education system to catch up to digital marketing, and when it does, it's still years behind. Most marketers that I meet in large agencies, brands, or in the small to medium business (SMB) space have *never* had any analytics training.

The other aspect is that most analytics training courses get far more complicated than they ever need to be. Instructors quickly dive deep into predictive analytics or concepts that most markets will never need. Analytics becomes this out-of-reach idea that would be nice to know, but impossible to attain.

Let's take a different approach. It takes one singularly important skill to unlock analytics. And this skill is available to anyone but should be even more proficient for marketers. With this skill, analytics not only comes alive, but it transforms organizations.

The skill? Asking questions.

By the end of this chapter, you will know about the following:

- Aligning your analytics to organizational objectives and goals
- Defining key components of a useful KPI

- How data are collected
- Defining segments in analytics
- Important analytics terminology and concepts

My Analytics Journey

In the mid-1990s, I built a website to market and sell commercial real estate properties. Back then, this was a minor part of my real estate business, but the only way that I could reach an international audience. I learned so much from this experience. For starters, my background in journalism helped me in developing my website, writing content, and designing the pages. It was then that I realized that I was ranking highly in the search engines. I had learned SEO by applying the same techniques that were used to lay out newspapers and seeing the benefits as my rankings increased and business grew.

One night, I sat down to work on the website, but I only had 2 hours available. It was at that moment that my analytics journey was born with THE QUESTION: "What is the most profitable thing that I can do with my time?" But I didn't have an answer to that question. I realized that I must have the answer in order to prioritize my sales and marketing activities! Otherwise, it was all guesswork and gut instinct. I researched and added analytics to my site and connected it to my sales tracking. What I found astonished me and changed my entire marketing career. I found that big numbers lie.

I was getting thousands of visits a month from search engines, which also contributed more than 95 percent of my conversions (visitors who completed a lead form). If I were making marketing decisions based on those numbers, then I would increase my efforts at rankings—because those numbers were huge! But that finding wasn't answering the question. THE QUESTION was one of profitability, not visits, and not conversions.

Digging deeper, I connected the search-driven leads to sales to find how much revenue I could attribute to search. And wow, was I in for a shock! Search, which created hundreds of thousands of visits, which contributed significantly more visits and leads than any other source—created no revenue. That's right. None. Zero. Zilch. Big numbers lie.

When I dug into the 2 percent—those that came from other sources— that's when I found my eureka moment. People who came from links on other sites—which was a result of my PR campaign to gain more visibility— converted at a lower rate, but those conversions turned into sales. Those 2 percent of link-clicking visitors were responsible for 90 percent of sales. I finally had my answer to THE QUESTION.

What was most profitable? Old-fashioned public relations and networking.

- Getting my press out to other websites in the industry and creating relationships
- Getting my links on other websites that reached more qualified prospects
- Working leads from these qualified sources more than search leads

As I said earlier, this changed my approach to digital marketing from then on. To quote Peter Drucker, "If it cannot be measured, it cannot be managed." It was all about asking and answering THE QUESTION. But as I was to find out over the next 20+ years in digital marketing, most companies don't even know what THE QUESTION is.

THE QUESTION is what drives the organization. It is the central business outcome from the strategy. For example, there is a world of difference if the goal of the organization is to increase leads as opposed to increase profitability. Each goal requires a specific set of measurements to answer and address that goal. If an organization's goal is to increase leads, then the accompanying measurements will focus on performance data that surround that conversion point, such as sources of leads, numbers of leads, and conversion rates.

Conversely, if an organization is focused on increasing profitability, then measurements will not only focus on performance, but on the financial aspects of each channel, of campaigns, and even business processes that can be optimized to increase efficiency and reduce spend.

The goal of the organization defines the measurements that will be needed because it is in the context of answering the question. Because of this, analytics is not the same for every organization. Based on your or your organization's goal, you'll need to define the data you need and then analyze it according to the intended outcome. This is what makes analytics unique, relevant, and exciting.

Company goals define analytics, not the other way around. If the goal is to increase leads or to reach a certain number of leads entering the pipeline per month, then you have defined the most important measurements to evaluate the success of that goal, the number of leads gained each month. You'll know if you are successful by comparing the number leads gained to the number of leads desired. Simple, right?

However, if you want to implement a company goal to reduce the cost of a lead, then what you need to measure (and where you go to find the data) changes substantially. Now your analysis requires you to track the process of gaining the lead, tracking the investment through each source, channel, and campaign, while developing metrics to compare the cost per lead. Once that is done, then decisions must be made about where to spend the budget to maintain that lower cost per lead.

Analytics Start with Goals

Let's start with a very simple table and flow to establish analytics.

In the first column of Table 2.1, I start with defining the primary goal or objective of the organization. In this example, I use increase revenue. Now I start building the expectations and the comparative metrics. For any measurement to be useful, it must have a comparison. If increase revenue is my goal, then I must know the answer to these questions: (1) What is the current revenue? (2) Did revenue increase? (3) By how much?

What you have now is the beginnings of an analytics measurement model. I've defined the business outcome, then I defined the two questions that are essential for answering the objective. This also gives you the foundation of a simple dashboard that will provide the immediate information that you need to assess the progress toward the goal.

The next stage is to examine the primary goal further and examine the ways that it can be realized. In what ways can the organization increase revenue? If you really think about this stage, you'll realize that this isn't just a marketing question. It's a business question that may bring you back to the four *P*s of marketing (Product, Price, Place, Promotion), as each of these has an impact on revenue!

TABLE 2.1 Marketing Analytics Measurement Model; Stages 1 and 2

Business Objective	Activities That Increase Revenue
	Increase Leads
	Average number of leads/number of leads (baseline)
	Leads gained (compare)
	$ impact on revenue
Increase Revenue	**Increase Lead to Sale Rate**
What is the current revenue?	Current lead to sale rate (baseline)
Amount of revenue increase/ decrease	Measured lead to sale rate
	+/- sale rate – why?
	$ impact on revenue
	Increase Customer Purchases/Purchase Amounts
	Average/cumulative/YTD purchases/purchase amounts (baseline)
	Increased purchase and purchase amount
	$ impact on revenue

Usually at this point, I have to keep marketers focused on this question. Too many times, marketers want to immediately jump into making videos for TikTok, without making the time investment into formulating a strategic approach. They get to the social media fun, but to do it correctly requires the thoughtful groundwork of planning and defining measurable results.

Now what increases revenue? Initially, I can propose three events that increase revenue: increasing leads, increasing the lead-sale rate, and increasing the number of sales and the average amount of purchases. While I've presented this in a B2B context, you could easily apply this to other types of business. For an ecommerce business, it can be increasing the number of customers, increasing the average sale amount, increasing the number of sales, and decreasing customer churn. All these activities increase revenue. Once these are defined, you then identify the relevant measurements for each.

Once you start to develop a linear view of the activities you are also defining the relevant measurements required for each stage. The last point in each of the activities is there to refocus the measurements back to the primary business objective—what is the impact of that activity on revenue? That important detail can't be left out because it answers the question! What you'll start to notice at this stage is that the more you define the important measurements, you should know where to go to gain that information. It won't always be in your analytics. In fact, through this activity, some companies realize that they aren't capturing the critical business data that answer these questions!

For those who report data, this will streamline your approach and create a clear dashboard of critical information. I've heard many times from marketers that because they don't know what data are important, they just include all they can find!

In this case, if you are creating the report, you can disregard the charts, tables, and extraneous data that don't report the impact on revenue! Focus on the relevant measurements that answer the big question first: Did you increase revenue? Then, if the management or stakeholders want to know how or why, you can provide that data. But for most cases, when you report data, they only want an answer to the question. Be sure that you know the question before you create that report.

The next stage of this process (shown in Table 2.2) is to develop the strategy to meet the objective. Match the corresponding strategy that will meet the activities needed to increase revenue. For example, to increase leads, you need to implement a customer acquisition program. To increase the lead to sale rate, you need to optimize the nurturing process through the CRM and sales contacts. To increase the number and value of sales, you need to develop promotions and positioning for upsell, cross-sells or other incentives. Again, you list the relevant activities in this stage and the corresponding measurements that can be applied.

Then, you finally get to the marketer's dream—start talking about channels, content, and media. But you still have to be structured about this. The

TABLE 2.2 Marketing Analytics Measurement Model, Stage 3

Business Objective	Activities That Increase Revenue	Strategy
	Increase Leads	**New Customer Acquisition**
	Average number of leads/number of leads (baseline)	Inbound/content marketing
	Leads gained (compare)	# leads gained by channel
	$ Impact on revenue	$ revenue by channel
		# leads gained by campaign
		$ revenue by campaign
Increase Revenue	**Increase Lead to Sale Rate**	**Nurture (CRM and Sales)**
What is current revenue?	Current lead to sale rate (baseline)	
Amount of revenue increase/decrease	Measured lead to sale rate	
	+/- Sale rate – why?	
	$ Impact on revenue	
	Increase Customer Purchases/ Purchase Amounts	**Promotions and Positioning**
	Average/cumulative/YTD purchases/purchase amounts (baseline)	
	Increased purchase and purchase amount	
	$ Impact on revenue	

next stage is again defining *how* the strategy will be executed. In this stage I recommend defining the media or content that needs to be created for the activities that will drive the strategy. For example, for an inbound strategy I will define the primary media or content as webinars and research papers that act as lead magnets. In this case, I use webinars and research papers while also including the relevant measurements that tie back to the objective. As you can see in Table 2.3, the media and content measurements can easily be expanded, but here I am focusing on maintaining a clear line back to the business objective.

The next stage (shown in Table 2.4) gets to the tactical marketing activities that consume most of a marketer's time and attention. These are the activities

TABLE 2.3 Marketing Analytics Measurement Model, Stage 4

Business Objective	Activities That Increase Revenue	Strategy (What)	Media and Content (How)
	Increase Leads Average number of leads/number of leads (baseline) Leads gained (compare) $ Impact on revenue	**New Customer Acquisition** **Inbound/content marketing** # leads gained by channel $ revenue by channel # leads gained by campaign $ revenue by campaign	**Webinars** # webinar registrations # attended #leads generated $ estimated value of leads **Research Papers** # of new leads $ estimated value of leads
Increase Revenue What is current revenue? Amount of revenue increase/decrease	**Increase Lead to Sale Rate** Current lead to sale rate (baseline) Measured lead to sale rate +/- Sale rate – why? $ Impact on revenue	**Nurture (CRM and Sales)**	
	Increase Customer Purchases/Purchase Amounts Average/cumulative/YTD purchases/purchase amounts (baseline) Increased purchase and purchase amount $ Impact on revenue	**Promotions and Positioning**	

of developing a campaign that will target an audience, drive clicks, result in conversions, and meet the objectives of the campaign. It is this stage where massive amounts of data are produced because each channel and tactic create an overwhelming amount of information. At this stage, simply define the most important data you need to answer the questions in the previous stage. For example, from the co-branded email campaign, how many webinar registrations were captured? Then, how many of those registrations became leads?

TABLE 2.4 **Marketing Analytics Measurement Model, Stage 5**

Business Objective	Activities That Increase Revenue	Strategy (What)	Media and Content (How)	Channel and Tactic (Where)
	Increase Leads	**New Customer Acquisition**	**Webinars**	Email (co-branded+list)
	Average number of leads/ number of leads (baseline)	Inbound/ content marketing	# webinar registrations	Search Ads
			# attended	Display Ads
	Leads gained (compare)	# leads gained by channel	#leads generated	Social Ads
	$ Impact on revenue	$ revenue by channel	$ estimated value of leads	
		# leads gained by campaign	**Research Papers**	SEO—Organic Search
			# of new leads	Email (co-branded+list)
		$ revenue by campaign	$ estimated value of leads	Social (Organic and Paid)
Increase Revenue	**Increase Lead to Sale rate**	**Nurture (CRM and Sales)**		
What is current revenue?	Current lead to sale rate (baseline)			
Amount of revenue increase/ decrease	Measured lead to sale rate			
	+/- Sale rate – why?			
	$ Impact on revenue			

Business Objective	Activ-ities That Increase Revenue	Strategy (What)	Media and Content (How)	Channel and Tactic (Where)
	Increase Customer Purchases/ Purchase Amounts	Promo-tions and Position-ing		
	Average/ cumulative/YTD purchases/ purchase amounts (baseline)			
	Increased pur-chase and pur-chase amount			
	$ Impact on revenue			

The data produced by each channel and tactic are important—for those people working on those tactics. It is not always relevant or important to the decision-makers in the organization who are setting the strategy. They want to know the "bottom line" of the results that were produced. Maintaining a clear view of each stage provides a clear view of the activities in play and their impact on the purpose. At any stage and at any time, you can view this chart and the corresponding measurements and know which areas are lagging and which areas are producing the intended results. This is what creates a data-centric organization.

Where Do the Data Come From?

To navigate this complex world of overwhelming amounts of data, you need to know where they come from and the nature of the information. To put it in simple terms, the data start with people using your website or app. Their actions are captured, processed, and reported by a machine that sees every-thing in 1s and 0s. Literally, a computer is attempting to capture, understand, and communicate human behavior on a digital interface (website/app). Just think about how ridiculous that sounds. Yet, that's not the end of it! We now, as humans, are attempting to decode those charts, graphs, and reports that are given to us by these machines. See Figure 2.1.

Your job is to decode the data into meaningful information that explains what the humans (the visitors) were attempting to do on your websites and how that translates into business objectives! If that sounds overwhelming, it is! You are attempting to understand (on a machine) what data machines gather about human behavior (while they are on a machine), and there is nothing simple about that!

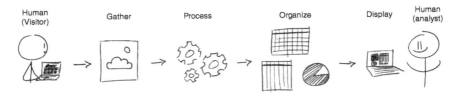

FIGURE 2.1 The Analytics Collection, Processing, and Reporting Process

Gathering the Data

The first step is to capture and collect visitor activity on your website. In the past, the server where a website was hosted would maintain a log of every page request. Of course, this was called the log file. Every request would be collected and timestamped. A page request, while sounding simple, could be highly complex. An HTML page is simply a file that contains a set of instructions and text. These instructions also provide the links to find the other necessary elements to assemble the page. Images, scripts, forms, and other elements are kept in separate files but assembled in the browser when someone requests the page. The HTML acts as the base canvas with the instructions of where to find all the necessary elements, how to assemble them, and how the page will function. Each request to the server is called a "hit." So, if a page is requested (one request) that has 10 images, 7 scripts, and 2 forms, it generates an additional 19 requests (or hits) to the server. Each of those requests is logged and timestamped in sequential order.

As you could imagine, once you start getting thousands of visits a day, the file would grow substantially. As the Internet became busier and more people going online, maintaining these log files on servers required more space than hosts were willing to provide. The response was to create a hosted version of the log file and provide analytics from the data. Now, the hosted service needed a method to gather the data because it wasn't connected to a website's hosting server. So began JavaScript tagging.

Just a warning that this next paragraph is going to get technical. There are three methods of implementing JavaScript tracking:

- The first is through an inline HTML tag. It is used to track a single click or a download, and it is *not recommended*. It increases download time for the page, which can negatively impact your rankings.

```
<a OnClick="ga('send', 'social', 'Linkedin', 'Share',window
.location.href);">...</a>
```

- Next is embedded JavaScript, which runs on the visitor's browser. It is identifiable by the `<script>` tag (the `<script>` tag does not include `src`):

```
<script>
Window.dataLayer = window.datalayer ||[];
Function gtag(){dataLayer.push(arguments);}
Gtag("js",new Date());
Gtag("config", "UA-123456");
</script>
```

- Finally, External JavaScript uses the `<script>` tag and includes `src`, which enables it to run in the background, apart from other scripting commands. This is used by Google Tag Manager to collect visitor data:

```
<script async src=https://www.googletagmanager.com/gtag/
js?id=UA-123456-xx></script>
```

What Data Does Analytics Script Collect?

That's the billion-dollar question. Google realized that the data they collect was their biggest asset because they use it to match advertisers to visitors based on the visitor's browsing history. Google's annual revenue from selling advertising will be more than $300 billion by the time this book is published.

For starters, when a page is requested, there is an exchange of information called the HTTP protocol. (Hey, recognize that!?!) Before the page is loaded into the browser, your computer engages in a very formal exchange of introductions. This is first initiated by the HTTP header, which transmits this data:

- Cookies (Google): For Google Analytics to track the user between sites
- IP address
- Device type
- Operating system and version
- Browser and browser version
- Referrer: URL of the current page with the link
- Language: Language and region of the requested website
- Date and time: Every request is timestamped
- Host: Domain name of the requested file

  Other data are also collected:

- Screen resolution
- Screen size
- Screen colors

- Client size
- Viewport size
- Performance data
- Plugins
- Top sites (bookmarks)

Other data are also utilized in Google Analytics. Some may be captured in analytics, some by other methods, as Google also owns the Chrome browser, which also transmits user data to Google. You know that these tags collect a massive amount of data, and Google does not offer a list of the full amount or types of data collected by its analytics script.

The development of cloud computing provided a perfect method for capturing and analyzing all this data. To be usable, these data have to be collected and processed, and it takes tremendous computing power to process millions of lines of activity to organize, synthesize, and report the data. Analytics providers employ *data sampling* to balance the computing time with the need for immediate access to standard reports. For large sites, it would simply take too long to crunch 100 percent of the data and provide it in an on-demand format. Sampling the data extrapolates the trends from the sample to provide the standard reports. Analytics owners can change the settings to choose a higher amount of data to be sampled. Obviously, if you see that 10 percent or less of your data are being used to create the reports, you know that there will be some major inaccuracies. For example, changing the preferences to greater precision rather than a faster response will create a larger dataset for sampling, but also take a bit more time in creating the report.

How Accurate Are the Data?

Let's just get this out there. There is no such thing as 100 percent accuracy in analytics.

While the data collection methods look impressive and capture a lot of data, there is still a lot of processing and interpretation that must be done with the raw data. Remember, you're dealing with humans and human behavior. How many times have you switched devices when researching a vendor or shopping? Let's say you start shopping while at work, maybe looking for a gift for someone. You cover a lot of ground by searching on Google for gift ideas and browse four or five websites. Later, at lunch, you think about one of the ideas, and you take out your phone and type in one of the websites that you remember. Of course, the ad for that brand is the first result, so rather than scrolling down, you click the ad, go to the site, find the product and spend time reading more about it, maybe even looking at a few of the videos about the product. Now, later that night, you are at home, and you decide to purchase. You go to your home computer, because you might feel more comfortable with the checkout procedure on the big screen, as most people of a certain age do. You type in the website URL, go directly to the website, then to the product, and you've completed the checkout in only a few minutes.

To you, this seems normal and nothing out of the ordinary. That's because you're thinking of this in human terms. In machine terms, here is a typical interpretation of your behavior in analytics:

- **New visitor:** Source: Google (Organic search), IP address xxx.xx.xx.xxx, device:desktop, pages viewed=12, time on site=6:25
- **New visitor:** Source Google (Paid Search), IP address: yyy.yy.yy.yyy, device:mobile/iPhone, pages viewed=3, time on site=3:20
- **New visitor:** Source: Direct, IP address: zzz.zz.zz.zzz, device:desktop, pages viewed=3, time on site=2:45, GOAL: Checkout purchase

In machine terms, you appear to be three separate visitors. This is because analytics is tied to the device. By tracking the device type, IP address (location), browser types, and identifying information this separates activities when using multiple devices. Now this can be overcome by personalizing each device for tracking. This is exactly what Google attempts to do when you login to your Google account on different devices. Google (and Facebook) attempts to unify your devices to know what you use, when you use it, and combine that data into a unified capture of the person rather than the devices. So, how do you share everything that you do to provide a complete record of your online activities to Google? Then use Google's Chrome browser on your devices, while logged into your Google account, and using websites with Google Analytics installed. Google will record everything that you do and track as much data as they can from your browsing behavior! If you aren't comfortable with this, you can mitigate the data collection by using different browsers while logged out of your accounts.

Analytics programs run on algorithms, just like search engines. The algorithms are simply rules applied to the interpretation of the data. Primarily, these rules define how to interpret certain events or data and classify it accordingly. As an example of this, have you ever left your computer overnight while your browser and a dozen or so tabs were open? Well, the analytics algorithm must figure out when exactly you left the website. This is the timeout. Some timeouts are after 20 minutes of inactivity (inactivity is defined as the time elapsed since the last request made to the server). How do you come up with a time-on-site calculation when there is no definitive exit action? All time-on-site calculations are based on estimates of behavior and the algorithm's rules to calculate this metric.

But what about the next morning? You awaken your computer, click on the browser, and the tabs reload all the web pages? According to the analytics algorithm, you've started another session! Even though you might only reload the tab and then not get to that website for another hour, you've since timed out again. Once you begin interacting with the website in that tab, you'll start another session, which will count the pages you request and the time on site. If you finally convert by purchasing something or filling out a form, the analytics will suggest that you did this on the third or fourth visit, which were generated by a direct visit to the website. But in your mind, it's been the same visit, with a few hours or days in between each interaction that was originally generated from a search query.

This is the issue with accuracy. It's machines and algorithms attempting to classify and report human behavior on websites, which is completely unpredictable. Every analytics program has its own method of addressing these behavioral question marks, which is why you'll never find agreement among different analytics providers. They all have different algorithms that interpret the behavior according to their rules.

Accuracy in Attribution

Here's the final way that accuracy is up for interpretation. Let's take the earlier example of multiple visits to a website. But let's also assume that the analytics has tracked these visits as being from the same visitor. It would look like this:

- **Visit 1:** Source: **Google (Organic search)**, IP address xxx.xx.xx.xxx, device: PC, pages viewed =12, time on site=6:25
- **Visit 2:** Source: **Google (Paid Search)**, IP address: yyy.yy.yy.yyy, device: iPhone, pages viewed=3, time on site=3:20
- **Visit 3:** Source: **Direct**, IP address: zzz.zz.z.zzz, Device: PC, Pages viewed=3, time on site=2:45, GOAL: Checkout purchase

The default setting in just about every analytics program is called last-click attribution. This means that the source of the visitor who met the goal in that session gets 100 percent of the credit for the conversion or the goal completion. Because of this, Google Analytics 4 changed drastically to report first touch, or first user medium, which favors search and paid search channels.

In this example, the goal completion was the last session, which the visitor initiated by going to the website directly. This means that a direct visit gets 100 percent of the credit for the sale or conversion. Do you think that is right?

The visitor first found the website through organic search, then performed a brand name search and clicked on the ad in the second visit, and then decided to purchase in the last visit. So, which source should have the attribution? Should the first since it was responsible for getting the visitor there in the first place? Should the second, because it showed that the visitor remembered the brand name? Or are you correct in giving the final source the full credit?

The answer will depend on your question. If you are evaluating the effectiveness of your marketing in driving customers, then you will want to focus on those first-touch sources and measure their effectiveness in ultimately driving conversions. In this case, you would change to a first-click attribution model. This would change the data completely to emphasize the sources and channels that are responsible for the first interaction with those visitors that would later become customers.

However, if you are evaluating multi-channel effectiveness in attracting, nurturing, and converting, then you would want to see all the channels that influence the outcome—from beginning to end. You would accomplish this by using a linear attribution model that gives each source equal credit for the conversion. This would change the data again, enabling you to see which channels contribute the most toward engaging visitors and nurturing them to become customers or leads. Without an understanding of the attribution models and how they affect the data, most beginners to analytics are making decisions based on last-click data, which neglects the first-touch channels that are instrumental in gaining new visits or influencing their decisions.

Additional Data Sources and Tracking

When marketing through third-party platforms, such as Facebook, Instagram, LinkedIn, or even email, you may not receive all of the data you need. There are additional methods of capturing tracking, such as UTM code, which appends to a link and provides clearer data about the visit. In addition, your analytics data may need to be supplemented with additional platform data, such as Google Ads, Facebook, and others.

UTM Codes   UTM codes are additional tracking codes that you can append to your campaign links. You can identify specific campaigns and campaign channels and view them as separate line items in your analytics. By the way, UTM stands for Urchin Tracking Module, used by Urchin Software Corporation. Urchin was acquired by Google in 2005 and rebranded as Google Analytics.

You implement UTM codes in your campaign links manually, and you can use one of the many UTM Builders available online. The UTM code in a link looks like this:

```
https://mydomain.com/landingpage?utm_campaign=freetrialoffer
&utm_medium=social&utm_source=linkedin
```

- `utm_campaign=freetrialoffer`: Identifies the campaign
- `utm_medium=social`: Identifies the type of medium, such as email, social, display, etc.
- `utm_source-linkedin`: Identifies the specific source where the link will be placed

Other UTM codes provide even more information, but these are the basics that are used in most campaigns. When evaluating your visits from different sources, these campaigns will show alongside the sources, providing a specific comparative view of your campaigns compared to regular traffic.

This is especially helpful to track activity and keep it separate from other types of campaigns or other sources. Tracking links in email campaigns enables you to see what people are clicking on and how they interact with your site after the click-through.

Platform Data   Analytics tracks the visitors to your website and what they do while they are there. The limitation to this is when you use other platforms to drive visits to your website. There is a lot of campaign activity that takes place on the other platforms (Facebook, Instagram, TikTok, Snapchat, LinkedIn, Pinterest, email, etc.) in order to get the visit. Analytics tracks the visitors once they get to your site and usually reports which platform delivered them, but much of the data of what they did on that third-party platform is not in your analytics.

Each third-party platform that you use generates its own measurements. Creating campaigns on Facebook and Instagram, Google, LinkedIn, TikTok, or even sending emails through an ESP (email service provider) creates measurements that are specific to each platform. Those measurements won't necessarily pass through to your analytics, so they need to be integrated or tracked as part of your overall campaign measurements. At least with Google, you still take manual steps to integrate your Google Ads with your Google Analytics. Otherwise, your campaign data are in two separate sources. Integrating the two enables you to see the initiation of the campaign data alongside the website activity that results from that visit.

The importance of this is to know which platforms are not only delivering visitors to your website, but also to measure the effectiveness of that platform in delivering visitors that convert and provide business value. The platforms themselves can't report conversions; they only report activity metrics such as views or impressions, likes or approval actions, shares, and comments. If you are buying ads on the platform, you'll get additional metrics such as CPM (cost per mille), click-through rates, and costs. These are activity metrics that provide feedback about the "engagement" of people on the platform, but they need to connect with your website or app analytics to track the ultimate business outcome of sales, leads, or other conversions.

Analytics Compared to Surveys and Research   Analytics is different from other sources of business data. When conducting research, organizations typically rely on surveys, questionnaires, focus groups, or even interviews of their target market. These are all legitimate forms of research and provide great data that can be used to formulate strategy, adjust targeting or messaging, or even create new products.

Analytics is different because it records behavior in real time. While someone may say that something is important, or that they have a preference, we often find that their actual behavior online is amazingly different. Analytics captures what people actually do rather than what they say they will do. It also captures the transaction rather than the intention. For example, when asked, "How did you find our website?" people may respond that they found the site from search, from social media, or from a friend. Analytics will report exactly how and when the first visit was generated. It does not rely on memory, influence, or the environment of the survey.

I always like to point people to the book *Everybody Lies* by Seth Stephens-Davidowitz. Basically, people lie in nearly every aspect of life. But they lie even more in surveys, polls, questionnaires, and interviews. The only place where people tell the truth is the search bar on Google. And in analytics.

Competitive Intelligence   I've always found it interesting that there is a persistent fear that competitors are always doing better. I've met too many business owners or managers who start with that assumption. Because the competitor's website has the latest bells and whistles, because it's prettier, and because it has that new AI chat thingy—they must be doing better than us! So, to answer a typical question about analytics: no, you can't see other company's analytics. Unless you have been given access, it isn't possible.

I've had to explain this numerous times. You can't judge how successful a business is simply based on the design, attractiveness, or function of a company's website! You can find many tools online that will provide some external, objective measurements, such as estimated visits, rankings, links to the website, and words they are bidding on. But again, those are all external factors. You have no way of knowing how many sales or leads they are generating. You don't know how much they are following up on those business leads, or even if they are competently managing them. Even more to the point, you don't know their profit margin. They could be outspending you significantly to get those leads, but then losing money in the long run. You just don't know.

Navigating Data: Concepts and Terminology

When people log into their analytics, I've seen their heads spin. They are confronted with an overwhelming amount of charts, graphs, and data tables, along with a new language. The language of analytics! In this section, I break down the language and terminology of analytics into understandable concepts and discuss how it applies to marketing campaigns. Remember, you are ultimately attempting to understand people and their behavior! The terms you encounter will be attempting to describe some form of human interaction or behavior.

The ABCs of Analytics

Now let's get into the basics of understanding data. To build your foundation of understanding any analytics program or report, just follow the ABCs.

A: Acquisition	Where did the people come from?
B: Behavior	What did they see and do?
C: Conversion	How much is it worth?

This is analytics and the purpose of analytics at its core. You are answering questions of WHAT happened, WHY it happened, and HOW to make decisions from what happened. You can only get to the data by breaking it into the essential elements of what you want to know.

A: Acquisition   Acquisition tracks where people come from. Here are the primary channels visitors use:

- **Search (organic and paid).** These are people who made a search and clicked on your website in the results. They either clicked on the organic results or on a paid ad if you are running a campaign.

- **Direct.** This means that the visitor typed in your website address in their browser or has it bookmarked in their favorites. With autocomplete in the browser, it makes this method much easier for people to remember the websites they visited.

- **Referral.** These visitors clicked on a link to your website while on another website. If a blog or a news site mentioned you and had a link alongside your business name, people who clicked that link are called *referrals*. Think of it like a word-of-mouth referral. Similarly, someone recommended your business by linking to it.

- **Social.** This category covers nearly every social media platform that is known in analytics.

- **Email.** Any email campaigns you send with analytics tracking will show the subsequent websites visits generated by the email.

- **Other.** Sometimes, referrer data aren't passed to analytics. If the referrer can't be determined, it gets dumped into the catch-all of Other.

- **UTM campaigns.** If you set up UTM links, they will show up in your acquisition reports alongside these categories.

Channel Types

CHANNEL TYPE	VISITS	ACTIONS	ACTIONS PER VISIT	AVG. TIME ON WEBSITE	BOUNCE RATE
Direct Entry	1,309	3,806	2.9	37s	13%
⊞ Search Engines	1,187	2,960	2.5	40s	12%
⊞ Social Networks	108	317	2.9	51s	12%
⊞ Websites	78	381	4.9	2 min 32s	12%
⊞ Campaigns	26	66	2.5	47s	38%

FIGURE 2.2 Matomo Analytics. Acquisition: All Channels Report. **https:// matomo.org/**

The measurements associated with acquisition are shown in the first columns: channel type and number of visits.

B: Behavior Behavior measures what people do on the website. However, I find it much more interesting to base any judgment of behavior on what people saw and how it affected their behavior. Evaluating behavior without knowing what people were looking for or what they saw is only half of the equation, because this helps us find *intent*—the reason for the visit in the first place!

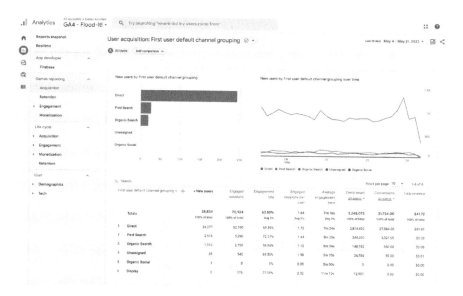

FIGURE 2.3 Google: G4 Analytics, Acquisition: All Channels Report (**https://Analytics.Google.com**)

Top converting channels

Main traffic channels	Visitors	Sessions	Events per session	Average session time	Goal conversions ▾	Goal conversion rate
Partners	485 _18.07%_	502 _25.1%_	19.95 _100.97%_	10m 13s	157 _25.18%_	20.32%
Social	490 _28.36%_	513 _25.65%_	18.97 _96.05%_	9m 46s	139 _22.46%_	17.35%
Video	246 _14.24%_	249 _12.45%_	20.86 _105.61%_	11m 27s	85 _13.73%_	24.5%
Organic	241 _13.95%_	246 _12.3%_	19.26 _97.47%_	10m 3s	71 _11.47%_	19.11%
Other paid	215 _12.44%_	219 _10.95%_	19.54 _98.92%_	9m 56s	66 _10.66%_	21.92%

FIGURE 2.4 Piwik Pro: Acquisition Channels (**https://piwik.pro/**)

Figures 2.2, 2.3 and 2.4 are examples of different analytics programs and their reporting of behavior. The terminology of each is slightly different, but centers on the same idea:

- **Actions/Events.** These are actions that the visitor performs, such as page views, link clicks, downloads, goals, and out clicks.
- **Bounce Rate.** A bounce is a single page visit. It means that there was only one page viewed and the visitor left the site. (In strict analytics terms, it means that they did not request another page or file and timed out.) The bounce rate tells you how many visitors out of 100 only had a single page visit. So, if the bounce rate is 33 percent, then (on average) 33 out of 100 visitors only saw a single page.
- **Pages per Session.** This is another average based on the number of pages that have been requested by the visitor during an active session. Pages per session is being phased out of newer analytics applications and being replaced with actions or events, as many interactions can happen in a single page.
- **Average Session Time/Average Engagement Time/Average Time on Website.** This is an interesting metric. As mentioned, it is based on the timestamped requests made from your browser. When you request a new page, it is timestamped, and so on for each additional page. When you stop making requests, the session times out, and the calculation is made to come up with length of the session. In the Average Engagement Time column in Figure 2.3, the averages are shown based on the source of the visit. You can compare the behavior of visitors based on their source. When comparing many different types of websites, there are some generalizations that can be made, such as visitors from direct and email tend to have longer sessions. Visitors from social and display ads tend to have

the shortest sessions. Of course, this isn't a rule; it's a generalization that is based on the behaviors of visitors from each source. People tend to behave differently based on their source, and it is something to find and evaluate for your business.

FIGURE 2.5 Piwik Pro: Custom Reports—Events (**https://piwik.pro/**)

Actions, or events, are replacing the page view metric, and analytics programs are adapting to allow businesses to create their own reports and events based on their unique website, app, or purpose. In this example in Figure 2.5, Piwik Pro provides a list of the events on the right that can be added to a custom report. This way, site owners or managers can adapt the event to their specific purpose.

C: Conversion   Conversions are the goals that have been set for visitors to reach. I like to define conversion as getting the visitor to do what you want them to do! Conversions encompass many actions, and they are based on what you define for your business. You'll find that the terms *conversions* and *goals* get used interchangeably. Google Analytics attempts to make a differentiation by labeling *conversion* as the main category, which is made up of *ecommerce* and *goals*. In Google Analytics, ecommerce conversions are tracked when integrating your ecommerce website and the Google Analytics ecommerce tracking code. All other conversions in Google Analytics are considered *goals*. Conversion reporting provides the goal-based conversions such as Total Conversions, Conversion Rates, Conversion Value, and Revenue Reporting.

Establish Goal Values　A goal here can be an ecommerce checkout. Google Analytics won't track a checkout action as a goal unless it is set up manually. In fact, all goals are set up manually in the Admin section. In some cases, you may find that your ecommerce software or customer relationship management (CRM) software are tracking the same information. Both types of systems are including more analytics into their tracking, which might reduce dependence on Google Analytics in the coming years.

> **Note**
>
> The goal conversion rate shows how many visits resulted in a goal completion. As it is a percentage, think of it as how many out of 100 are completing any goals. If it is a 1 percent conversion rate, then, on average, it takes 100 visits to get a single conversion.

Goal completions are the manually created goals for your business website. These are based on important tasks that you decide are worth tracking, as they show a contribution toward business value. These include email subscribers, form completions, video views, contact forms, downloads, etc. Anything that shows or can be tracked to business value can and should be tracked as a goal.

What's the Impact of the Goal Completion Value?　Finally, goal value. This is one of the more difficult functions to define, and it is typically neglected by most companies—at their own loss. Here is why this column is so valuable.

As an example, how much is a new email subscriber worth to your organization? There are a few methods that you could use to determine this.

First, what would it cost you to purchase a list of emails? (Not that I would ever recommend this.) Of course, any purchased list would be trouble. Those names have not opted-in to receive emails from you, and they most likely do not know your brand or business. But buying a low-quality list like this might run you about $0.10 per email.

Second, what is the average value of a subscriber? This is easier to figure out because it is information that should be measured and calculated within your organization. When sending your emails, do you track the revenue produced? If so, then you should have an average revenue per subscriber calculation, and it should be well known!

Third, start somewhere! For many in the industry, they recommend a value for a new subscriber somewhere around $20 or more.

What this goal value reflects is the economic value to an organization when a visitor completes a task-based action. It does not mean realized revenue, as an ecommerce report would; rather, it is the estimated value produced. B2B organizations track leads, and they usually have the estimated value of a lead in their calculations. When a visitor completes a lead form on the website, they can attribute a value to that lead. To use this example, if you have an estimated value of $10 of revenue per lead, it will accumulate a running total in the Goal Value column.

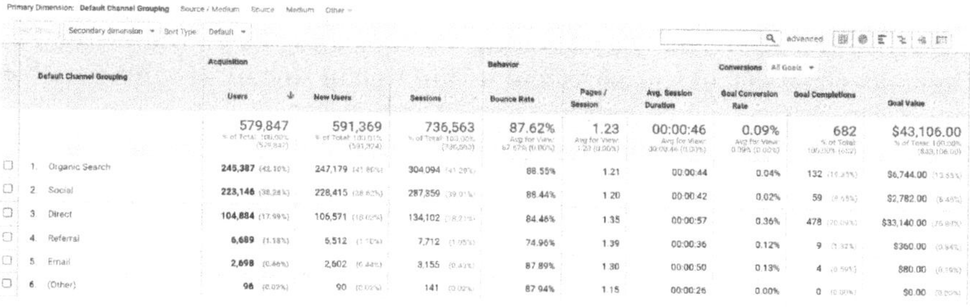
Primary Dimension: Default Channel Grouping Source / Medium Source Medium Other

Secondary dimension Sort Type: Default

Default Channel Grouping	Acquisition			Behavior			Conversions All Goals		
	Users	New Users	Sessions	Bounce Rate	Pages / Session	Avg. Session Duration	Goal Conversion Rate	Goal Completions	Goal Value
	579,847	591,369	736,563	87.62%	1.23	00:00:46	0.09%	682	$43,106.00
1. Organic Search	245,387	247,179	304,094	88.55%	1.21	00:00:44	0.04%	132	$6,744.00
2. Social	223,146	228,415	287,859	88.44%	1.20	00:00:42	0.02%	59	$2,782.00
3. Direct	104,884	106,571	134,102	84.46%	1.35	00:00:57	0.36%	478	$33,140.00
4. Referral	6,689	5,512	7,712	74.96%	1.39	00:00:36	0.12%	9	$360.00
5. Email	2,698	2,602	3,155	87.89%	1.30	00:00:50	0.13%	4	$80.00
6. (Other)	96	90	141	87.94%	1.15	00:00:26	0.00%	0	$0.00

FIGURE 2.6 Google Universal Analytics, Acquisition Channels (**https://Analytics.Google.com**)

Referring to Figure 2.6, the source of Organic Search has generated 132 goal completions. This is the sum of all goals defined by the organization, each of which may have a different estimated value. For example, Organic Search generated $6,744.00 of Goal Value from 132 goal completions, while Direct generated $33,140.00 from 478 goal completions.

Viewing goal value or the revenue created enables a complete view. Rather than basing judgments on the number of visitors, the conversion rate, or numbers of conversions, value provides feedback about the impact of the conversion because not all goals may have the same value. For example, gaining a subscriber may have a value of $20, whereas a visitor who completes a lead form may have a value of $150 per lead. While these are reported as two goal conversions, they have very different values to the organization.

Segmentation Is the Key

Using the ABCs gently brings you into the application of segmentation. Why? Because your visitors are not a herd of cattle. They don't all enter at the same page, they don't all visit the same pages, and they don't all want the same things. Looking at the big numbers, such as the number of visits or the number of sessions views your visitors as a large herd of cattle because it simply lumps those distinguishing factors into one number. What you need is *segmentation*.

Segmentation is the separation of your visitors based on common factors. For example, where did they come from? Google? Bing? Email? Facebook? Another website? Did they type the site into their browser? Simply breaking down how people came to your website is one of the first levels of segmentation. By breaking apart the sources of visits, you can start to develop an understanding of how people find the website.

Another method of segmentation is evaluating the landing page—or entry page of the visitor. This is where you really learn that people are looking for very different information, as they land on the page that they hope answers their question. You can also segment by new visitors or returning visitors, customers or noncustomers. Basically, any distinguishing factor can be used to segment people so that you can examine those factors to find insights into that group, your marketing, or your processes. See Figure 2.7.

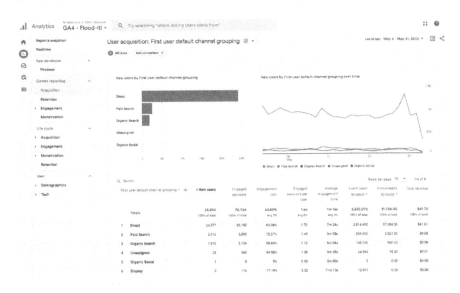

FIGURE 2.7 Google G4 Analytics, New Users by First User Default Channel (**https://Analytics.Google.com**)

This report automatically segments visitors by how they first found the website. Rather than simply looking at reports of aggregate data, you can find more value by separating visitors. You can explore this even further by adding more dimensions.

A dimension is simply adding another segmentation factor. How would you narrow down the segment of organic search? By the source of that search—the search engine that brought those visitors. By adding Source, you will see the segmentation progress to a secondary level of detailed information. The Primary dimension is Channel, and the Secondary Dimension is Source.

You can now see which search engines generated visitors to the website and which contributed to conversions. You can measurably count which search engines are sending valuable visitors that act and contribute to the goals of your business.

KPIs and Metrics

One of the most misunderstood terms in analytics is the *key performance indicator,* or KPI. I've found this in almost every organization, regardless of size.

A KPI is the measurement that influences the next step in the process, or tracks toward the outcome. It is not a final measurement, as it indirectly influences the outcome. For example, click-through rate is a great KPI. Click-through rate measures the percentage of people who see an ad and click on it to go to the landing page, giving you a quick measurement of the appeal of the content you've published and its influence in moving people to the next stage. *It does not directly impact the conversion rate* or the conversion itself; it only measures the rate that people are clicking on an ad to a landing page. It is a measurement along the pathway and holds indirect influence on the outcomes.

A metric is a number without context, or without a story. If I talk about having 2,000 visits to a website, that's a metric. When a number is used without the context of segment, source, behavior, outcome, or influence, then it is a metric. A metric is a measurement that is independent of an actionable outcome. The difference between these terms is the action that you can take to influence the outcome.

Analytics in Context

Instead of a list of terms and definitions, I find it easier to present them in context of a campaign. For this context, I am going to use a typical sales funnel, which provides a visual progression from one stage to the next.

In the diagram shown in Figures 2.8 through 2.13, you'll see the progression of a typical campaign or account on the left. The funnel itself is divided into two types of measurements: Performance and Financial. Finally, on the right are the action or causal factors related to that phase of the campaign.

Stage 1: Impressions

At the top of the funnel is the method of acquiring visitors to a website (see Figure 2.8). In this case, it could be any type of paid media campaign. In most cases, when starting a campaign, you have to decide on the size and type of audience you will target, along with a corresponding budget to reach that audience.

FIGURE 2.8　Analytics in Context: Impressions

CPM, or cost per mille (*mille* is Latin for 1,000), is the standard method of buying "impressions" or "views."

Note

I use quotes around these two terms as they are usually unknown factors within an organization. Most people think of impressions or view as a human who saw the ad. Some will be closer in defining it as ads that have been loaded on the page, but they are both thinking in human terms. Advertisers that sell ads based on CPM, like Facebook, define a view as anything greater than 0 pixels that is displayed for more than 0 seconds.

This is why terminology is so important and needs to be related throughout an organization. Everyone needs to know how these terms are defined and use a shared, negotiated meaning.

When you see a campaign that is marked as $40 CPM, that means that you will be paying $40 for every 1,000 impressions or views. If a campaign reaches 100,000 impressions, you will be charged $4,000.

Now is also when I stress the importance of a baseline, average, or a comparative metric: 100,000 impressions and $40 CPM might look okay, but you need to have a comparison to know for sure!

When you have a baseline to compare with, you'll immediately know if a campaign is on track. By asking how many impressions are expected or what a typical campaign averages, you might be able to catch if the impressions are significantly higher or lower than expected. If you do find that the expected number of impressions is very different than the actual performance, what can you do?

Causal Factors　There are two causal or influencing factors at the impression level for paid advertising:

- **Targeting parameters:** If you are using too many targeting parameters, then the size of the available audience may be restricted. A smaller audience means fewer impressions. Similarly, without targeting parameters, you could be targeting a wider audience than intended, causing more impressions.

- **Targeting:** The audience you are targeting could be a high-value or high-demand audience with a lot of competition. To reach your target audience, you may have to increase your CPM to compete with the other advertisers.

There are also causal factors influencing the impressions for organic social media marketing:

- **Activity:** How frequently do you post on this social platform? Infrequent posting will result in lower impressions on your content.
- **Relevance:** Is the content you are posting relevant to the channel or audience? Are you using relevant hashtags, and are followers interacting with your content, which would increase its reach?

This applies to any top of funnel or traffic driver. Identify the key factors that influence the goal for each stage. This enables you to catch anything that departs from the expected performance and suggested actions that could correct the campaign in its early stages.

Stage 2: Engagement

I don't like the word *engagement*. It has become a meaningless, catch-all term for rationalizing campaign activity, and it rarely provides any insight into actual economic benefit to an organization. It is made even worse by the so-called engagement metrics that lump separate actions into one measurement that is supposed to provide meaning, which it doesn't. It actually obscures meaning. See Figure 2.9.

FIGURE 2.9   Analytics in Context: Engagement

The problem with engagement and engagement rate is that it combines multiple metrics into a single metric, thereby stripping it of any meaning. Typically, engagement rate measures the number of likes, comments, and shares and any other trackable action into a single measurement. Even worse is when a cost per engagement is applied, making an even more meaningless metric.

The issue is that these actions are not equal! Given a choice, I am sure that any marketer would choose to have more shares than likes or comments. Shares mean that people are presenting your content to their network, friends, and followers. Likes simply show that someone took the least committal action to support the post—you don't know why; you only know that they did. A share shows loyalty, enthusiasm, and an active recommendation of your content and your business. Plus, it has economic value!

Rather than relying on the deceptive "engagement rate," focus on each individual metric and learn from it.

Applause Rate Starting with likes or approvals, this is called the *applause rate*. First, get your benchmark or average. Look at all the posts you've made over the past week, month, or quarter. Divide the number of approval actions gained by the number of posts made in that time frame. You now have an average.

For example, if you made 40 posts in a month and received 763 approvals (likes) on those posts, you are averaging 19 approval actions per post. Here's what you can do with this information now that you have an average. You can evaluate those 40 posts and group them by how many generated 25 or more approvals and how many generated 10 or fewer approvals. (Use whatever numbers make sense to contrast the performance.) You can now evaluate the common factors in the highly performing content, and you can evaluate common factors in poorly performing content. Common factors could be images used, the types of images, content, offers, time of day, events, etc. As you can see, it's not always a simple answer. As an example, with one client we found a consistent correlation of custom vector graphics gaining more approvals than stock photography.

Conversation Rate The *conversation rate* does a similar measurement for comments. Do the same math by dividing the number of comments generated by the number of posts made in that time frame. Get your average and then analyze the high-performing posts against to the average, and the low-performing posts against the average. Find the common factors—typically the common factor might be the content you are sharing, especially if it has any controversial or opinionated element attached to it.

Amplification Rate My favorite of the engagement metrics is *amplification rate*. This is because engagement rate ties directly to an economic impact. First, do the math, dividing the number of shares generated by the number of posts made in that time frame. Get your average, analyze the highly shared posts against the average, and find the common factors.

Next, calculate the added bonus of economic impact. Some platforms make this easier than others but track the shares of your content and see if you can find the impressions or views generated from each of the shares. Once you have the total amount of impressions or views generated by the shares, apply this to your average CPM. If you know the average cost to reach 1,000 impressions or views in a campaign, or even specifically to that platform, you'll be able to show an economic value of those shares! This is the value of earned media.

Causal Factors   What are the causal factors for this thing called engagement? At this stage it is simply the ability to capture someone's attention and move them to interact. What are the factors of a typical ad or post that gets a viewer's attention as they scroll through a feed or a page? It is the combination of the PHD: Picture, Headline, and Description—the three elements of nearly all social and ad content you'll find. If your ad is not attracting likes, comments, or shares, then you can bet that it suffers from a single issue: it is boring. No one interacts with boring posts or ads. Nothing has captured their attention or was worth their time to stop as they scrolled the page.

Primarily, it is the image and headline that get noticed. If you are producing content that isn't getting noticed, then change your approach to images and headlines. Those are the primary factors that people will view and decide to pause and look further.

Stage 3: The Click

This is where you finally reach a trackable clickable action with direct impact on a business objective (see Figure 2.10). The click-through on an ad, a post, or link is not only a KPI for the campaign, but also the measurement of the effectiveness of the ad or post in influencing someone to act! This is the summary measurement of the campaign's ability to persuade action and movement to the next stage.

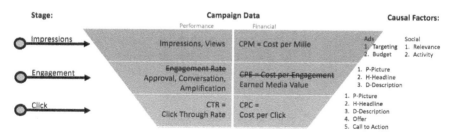

FIGURE 2.10   Analytics in Context, Click

The performance side of this stage is the click-through rate, which is self-explanatory. It is the rate at which people click the ad compared to the number of impressions or views. To reach this number, you divide the number of clicks by impressions and multiply by 100. This gives you the rate of clicks. If you have a 2 percent click-through rate, then it means that about 2 out of 100 people who see the ad or post click-through.

The causal factors provide immediate feedback for a lower than average click-through rate. If people are seeing the ad, interacting with it, and not clicking on it, then it is simply entertainment. You've not provided a compelling need or reason for them to act. This culprit is your offer and call to action, but it may also go back to the picture and headline. Evaluate the message of the ad or post. Is it clear? Are you presenting a clear solution to the audience's need? If not, the click-through rate will suffer.

The financial side of the click provides another layer of feedback. The cost-per-click (CPC) is found by dividing the number of clicks by the campaign cost. For example, if you spend $10,000 on a campaign that generates 1,200 clicks, then your average cost-per-click is $8.33. Most times, this number ends up on a report right next to the click-through rate and is not applied properly. To apply the CPC properly, it needs to be compared to another CPC calculation, the CPC generated by other channels.

Take the average CPC and compare it to the average CPC of similar campaigns on other channels. It may look like this example:

Google Ads	$3.25 CPC
Facebook	$5.75 CPC
Instagram	$4.50 CPC
LinkedIn	$8.95 CPC

By comparing the average CPC generated by other campaigns, you can start to see the trend and effectiveness of your campaign. If maximizing the efficiency of your spend is an important part of the campaign or objective, then this measurement is a critical factor in how you may decide to spend your budget. The CPC is a comparative measurement for the financial aspects of a campaign, allowing a quick assessment of the efficiency of the campaign. However, it is not the ultimate measurement of success! It is a KPI. This KPI is a step along the way to the goal of the campaign—the conversion. It only informs you of the factors that influence this stage and this milestone.

Stage 4: Conversion

This is where the sales pitch is made—on the landing page. It is also where the causal factors multiply exponentially. You've probably noticed that the closer that the visitor gets to a decision point, the causal factors that influence each stage increase. The landing page is no exception. Of course, if you need to improve the conversion rate of the landing page, you'll see that I've only listed a dozen factors that influence the conversion. There are many other factors, which is why conversion rate optimization is a skill unto itself and addressed in another chapter of this book. See Figure 2.11.

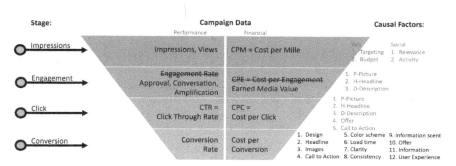

FIGURE 2.11   Analytics in Context, Conversion

The click was simply getting them to the page that does the heavy lifting of persuasion. The conversion is the intended action for the visitor, a registration, subscription, account creation, lead form, or a sale. All your work to this point was simply getting people's attention and arousing their curiosity and interest. Now you make the case for commitment.

The conversion rate is the overall judgment of your campaign's ability to attract and convert leads, subscribers, or customers. Divide the number of conversions from the amount of clicks or page visits and multiply by 100. For example, 100 conversions generated by 2,000 clicks yields a 5 percent conversion rate. About 5 people out of 100 decide to convert. But is that good or bad? It depends. You might find some industry trends or averages, but these numbers are so unique to your company and your approach that it is difficult to find a reliable comparison. The best conversion rate comparison is your own. Are you doing better today than yesterday? This quarter compared to the same quarter last year? This campaign compared to another campaign? There you go!

Comparing your campaign to other campaigns is a great way to apply this measurement to compare your effectiveness across a variety of channels. It becomes even more compelling when you factor in the average cost per conversion, be it a registration, lead, or sale. This now provides you with tangible monetary evidence of the campaign, and it is most effective when measuring the cost of the conversion against the other channels you are using.

You can compare your cost per conversion to previous campaigns, and you can compare it to other campaign sources:

Google Ads	$10 Cost per conversion
Facebook	$25 Cost per conversion
Instagram	$14 Cost per conversion
LinkedIn	$18 Cost per conversion

Your analysis and decisions of this comparison would be based on your business objectives.

This is vitally important if you are tracking the efficiency of a campaign. If your goal is to maximize your budget, then these numbers are important because they show you how you can adjust your budget to accommodate a lower cost per conversion. However, if you are only concerned with generating leads or customers, and budget or cost per lead is not a concern, then you would be primarily concerned with the numbers of leads or conversions produced by each channel and make your decision based on the production of the channel, not the economic efficiency. The data you need and how you will use it ties back to the organizational objectives and goals for the campaign.

Stage 5: Nurture

Regardless of capturing leads or making sales, nurturing is process of building and encouraging a relationship. Either you are persuading a new customer to be a regular customer or qualifying a lead through additional communications. The nurture process is very similar, and of course, hundreds of factors now influence this relationship-building or lead vetting process.

This stage measures the follow-up and development of the new conversion (see Figure 2.12). Depending on your organization, it will look different from others and is unique to your process. Creating measurements, associating them with action, and showing the economic impact are all vitally important at this stage.

Unfortunately, this is where I find many B2B marketers stretched to their limit and being asked to measure things that don't exist. For many B2B marketers, their primary task is to gain leads. For them, the financial metrics don't come into play because they are simply generating leads and handing them off to the sales team. They can track the source of the lead, but once it is handed off, the lead enters another system that the marketer will never see, and the tracking ends.

FIGURE 2.12 Analytics in Context, Nurture

What puts these marketers in a bind is when management wants them to start measuring the quality of the leads rather than just the number of leads generated, and that's a big problem. First, no one typically defines quality—they just want it measured. Second, the conversion trail was broken. If an organization has multiple data silos that do not communicate—there is no centralized data source—then that question is impossible to answer. For B2B marketers to be able to measure the quality of a lead (according to the source or campaign that generated the lead), the marketer must be able to track that lead through the nurturing and qualification process (Market Qualified Lead—MQL, Sales Qualified Lead—SQL), all the way to the ultimate sales and agreement and the value of the sale produced. If marketers are not able to see that information, then they cannot produce a simple quality measurement.

Tracking at this level also poses an issue of the "chain of custody." If you watch any crime dramas, then this term will be familiar to you. For the B2B marketer who hands off the lead, the custody of that lead and the associated data now belong to the sales department. Any assessment of "quality" must include the quality of the sales content, the frequency of contact, the sales-person responsible for follow-up, and any other interactions. This leads down a path that many people don't want to deal with! However, CRM systems are answering this data dilemma as they become implemented across organizations and unify the data.

The Final Stage: Customer Lifetime Value or Lifetime Customer Value

Regardless of what you call it, customer lifetime value (CLV) or lifetime customer value (LCV), this measurement is the sum of the customer experience with your company. It is based on three primary customer measurements (see Figure 2.13):

- The average value of a purchase
- The number of purchases per year
- The average length (years) of customer retention

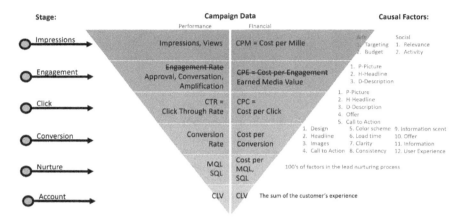

FIGURE 2.13 Analytics in Context, CLV

Capturing this number and the data involved provides a complete end-to-end view of the life cycle of the customer. As CRM systems are able to capture more and more data, the connection from account-level analysis all the way back to the acquisition, campaign, or other attributable sources is becoming easier. This provides the data necessary to close the loop on the true value and efficiency of channels and campaigns. If tracking to this level is the desired objective of your organization, then utilizing the analytics combined with a CRM enables a clearer picture of the efficiency and profitability of campaigns, channels, and offers.

CHAPTER 3

Digital Advertising

By Brad Geddes

D igital advertising is placing ads across the web. These can range from banner ads alongside content, video ads seen when streaming video, native advertising that fits in the content users are engaging with, to ads they see in search results.

The most common form of digital advertising is known as *pay-per-click*, or PPC, because it is one of the most effective advertising methods.

Consider your average day. There are times you do not know the answer to a question such as the weather, the next show time at your movie theater, how to use a service, or which product to buy.

When people do not know an answer to a question, they turn to a search engine to find more information. They enter their question or search term into a search engine, and suddenly they have many sources of information from which to choose, and some of those sources are ads.

Across the globe, billions of times each day people repeat this process: searching for information, finding their answers in ads, and becoming customers of search advertisers. From an advertising perspective, this is an amazing reach. Your ads can be viewed almost anywhere in the world, while reaching the vast majority of Internet users with a single advertising method.

The reason this advertising channel is so effective is that the user told a search engine what they were trying to learn so the advertiser can always create ads relevant to their needs. Users are currently seeking information, so they are only seeing these ads at the moment when they are receptive to learning more information. This powerful combination of immediacy and relevancy has propelled search advertising to be one of the most effective advertising channels in history.

Search engine advertising often extends beyond search to other aspects of the web. Google owns YouTube, so advertisers can use their Google Ads account to place ads on YouTube. Many search engines also have display networks, which consist of content publishers like newspapers, bloggers, forums, and other sites or apps that are ad supported, in which their ads can be displayed.

The reason it is called *PPC advertising* is that the advertiser is only charged if a searcher clicks on the ad. If the searcher interacts with other options on the search page, the advertiser is not charged. This means advertisers only pay when they have attracted a new potential customer to their website.

By the end of this chapter, you will know the following:

- How PPC advertising works
- How to develop a digital advertising strategy
- How and why to track conversions
- How to determine the best bid for your account goals
- How to find keywords that describe your business
- How to write a compelling ad
- How to target your advertising to the proper audience
- How to monitor your data
- How to create PPC reports

What's in a Name?

In some companies, you will hear search advertising referred to as PPC advertising. In other companies, you will hear the term SEM or search engine marketing. Yet, in other places, you might hear SEA or search engine advertising. While the names differ, in all cases, they are referring to advertising with search engines.

The other confusing jargon words are *search terms* and *search queries*. Both terms represent what a user types into a search engine. A *keyword* is a word or phrase that you put into your account that can represent multiple search terms or search queries.

For instance, you might have the keyword *men's shirts* in your account. This singular keyword might match these search terms or search queries: shirts for men, men's shirts, blue men's shirts, or XL blue men's shirts.

The Nuts and Bolts of PPC Advertising

From a conceptual perspective, PPC advertising is simple. An advertiser chooses keywords, which represent what users might type into a search engine. Then the advertiser creates ads for those keywords, which is what users will see if they type in one of your keywords. The advertiser chooses a landing page, the page the users will see after clicking an ad. Finally, the advertiser sets a bid, what they are willing to pay for a click on a specific keyword.

When users conduct a search and click on the advertiser's ad, they go to the advertiser's landing page, and the advertiser pays the search engine for that click.

Where PPC can get complicated is when you start digging into the nuances of how these features all fit together. If you sell both shoes and shirts, you will want a different ad for each of those products, and hence you will need to break your keywords down into various groups so that your ad is still compelling for both of those searches. If you have physical locations, then you might only want to serve ads around those actual locations.

The next section looks at how Google Ads, one of the most popular search engine advertising platforms, is structured so that you can see how the pieces properly fit together.

Account Hierarchy

The building blocks of an account are called *ad groups*. These are composed of both keywords and ads. The keywords represent the user's search terms. If your keyword matches the user's search term, then your ad can show. The ads persuade the users to click on your ad to visit your website. As each ad group should contain keywords and ads that are related to each other, each time you introduce a new product or idea to your account, you will have a new ad group so that the keywords and ads within the ad group are always related to each other (see Figure 3.1).

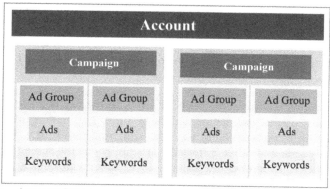

FIGURE 3.1   Account Structure

Ad groups are housed in a *campaign*. A campaign is where you define most of the settings for how the ad groups are displayed. These settings contain items like the geographies for where the ads will be displayed and the budget for those ad groups, among other settings.

If you want to show a set of ads in New York and a different set of ads in London, you create two campaigns, one for each geography.

An *account* represents a single advertiser and contains their advertising campaigns. At the account level, you are mostly defining who owns the account.

Settings are inherited downward. For instance, at the account level, you define how you are billed and pay the search engine. All the campaigns, and thus ad groups, within the account use the same billing method.

At the campaign level, you define the locations where your ads will be shown. All the ad groups within that campaign use those location settings. You could have one campaign that shows ads in a particular city and another campaign that shows ads in an entire country.

If there are conflicts in the settings, the most specific setting is used. That means a keyword or ad trumps the campaign settings. For example, you could have a bid set at the ad group level, the bid representing what you are willing to pay for a click. If you also have a bid at the keyword level, since the keyword is more specific, the keyword bid trumps the ad group bid.

The next section looks more closely at each of these account settings.

Account Settings: Access and Billing

A Google Ads account represents an advertiser. There are only a few account-level settings.

- The first is account access. You can have multiple users access your account, and their information and permission levels are set at the account level.

- Then you have billing and currency. This is how you will be billed and the currency in which you will set bids. It is best to set bids in the same currency that you take on your website.

Whenever someone clicks on your ad, a timestamp is set for that click. You can run reports and segment data by time. At the account level, you define your time zone, which is used for these timestamps. It is best to make sure your website and other software you employ use the same time zone. If your analytics is set in one time zone, your website in another, and your PPC account in yet another time zone, it will be incredibly difficult to line up the data for any single day.

You do have other account-level settings, such as notifications, and some additional preferences; these are the primary settings. In most PPC accounts, the currency and time zone often cannot be changed in an account once they are set. However, the other settings can be adjusted.

Campaign Settings: Define Your Targets

Your campaign consists of ad groups, and it is at the campaign level where you decide how those ad groups will be displayed, along with the budgets and bid technique. Unlike some account-level settings, most of these can be changed after a campaign is created.

The first setting is the networks where your ads will be displayed. You can have a campaign across search, display (content sites where users do not search), video (such as YouTube), or even shopping (such as Google or Microsoft Shopping).

For new advertisers, you will want to start with search only or shopping campaigns. This means that your ads are only shown on search results. This is a powerful advertising technique. While the display network contains millions of sites and apps where your ads can appear, the targeting for these networks goes beyond keywords into defining audiences, such as user behaviors or characteristics, or into the types of content where you want ads to appear.

Rarely will you want a campaign to target multiple networks at once, such as both search and display. Since your targeting methods and ads can vary across networks, it is best to limit your ads in a campaign to a single network.

Once you have defined the network, then you want to define the devices where your ads should appear. Devices can range from desktops, to tablets, phones, and even connected devices like TVs.

Next, you decide the budget. You will define a daily budget: how much a specific campaign should spend per day. Note that most search engines may spend more or less than your daily budget on any single day; however, they should not eclipse your daily budget times the days in the month, for a given month.

Then you define the locations, which are the geographies where the ads should be displayed. There are many options for defining geographies from a radius around an address to multiple countries. In addition, you can target multiple locations at once. You can have ads served in Chicago and California in a single campaign. You can also exclude locations where you do not want your ads to appear.

For instance, say you are selling insurance in the state of Illinois. Chicago makes up a large number of people in the state. Therefore, you might want one campaign to target Illinois but exclude Chicago and then another campaign to only target Chicago. That would let you write different offers in your ads or set different budgets, for Chicago versus the rest of the state.

Last, you define your bid method. This is how bids will be set for your keywords. The options range from manually controlling all your bids to using automated bidding for setting how much you are willing to pay for a click based on various criteria. As these options can be complex, the chapter covers bids and bid methods later.

While you can use additional settings at the campaign level—such as the time of day or the days of the week when you want your ads to appear or how you define geographic targeting by user interest—the listed settings are the primary ones to understand when creating a campaign.

Ad Groups: A Collection of Keywords and Ads

At the ad group level, you may define bids if you are using manual bidding or advanced features. However, your ad group's purpose is to create a cohesive user experience. Using keywords and ads that are related helps create a seamless user experience with your keywords, ads, and website.

A *keyword* is a word or phrase that is placed into your account. A search term or search query is what the user types into a search engine. When the user's search term matches your keyword, then an ad from that ad group can be shown to a user.

An *ad* is a piece of content that may contain text, and sometimes images, that are displayed to a searcher/user. The goal of the ad is to persuade the user that you have the solution to their question (what they asked the search engine) and direct them to click on your ad to go to your website.

When your keywords and ads in an ad group are related, you can create a wonderful experience for the users that shows them you know what they are looking for and that you have the solution that will help them best accomplish their goal.

The majority of your time in building an account will be researching keywords, breaking them up into ad groups, and then writing compelling ads that match the keywords in an ad group. The magic of *relevancy*, showing ads that are relevant to users so that they find your advertising useful, is found at the ad group level and how ad groups are created.

Bidding: How Much Do You Want to Pay for a Click?

Whenever someone clicks on your ad, you pay the search engine. You are rarely the only advertiser for a keyword, so you need to look at how bidding works in the real world.

Most search engines use an auction to determine how the ads are ordered on search pages and what you are charged for a click. If the highest bid was always placed in the top position, then a lot of irrelevant ads would show up for users, as advertisers would pick many irrelevant keywords just to show their ads more often. A search engine's goal is to always show relevant results to the users, so they use a special auction process to ensure the ads that do show are relevant.

This example looks at how Google Ads performs its auction. Google uses an algorithm that looks at three factors to determine an advertiser's ad rank. The ad rank numbers are used to order the ads from highest to lowest ad rank. So, your ad rank number, which you will never see, is only useful in comparison to other advertisers in the same auction.

The first item is your *bid*. How much are you willing to pay for any click?

The second item is your *quality score*. Your quality score is based on three factors. The first quality score factor is your expected click-through rate, which is how often someone is expected to click on your ad. The second factor is your ad relevance, which looks at how relevant your ad is to the search term. The last factor examines your landing page experience, which is determined by how nice of an experience users will have on your site, including speed and the relevancy of content.

The last item used in the auction is your ad extension's impact on the auction. Ad extensions are additional pieces of data that you can include with your ad to give the users more information about your offers, locations, and additional ways of interacting with your ad, such as getting driving directions or making a phone call.

Google examines these three items—your bid, quality score, and ad extensions—and then determines your ad rank. Google then does this for every advertiser for a given auction. Once the results have been calculated, the highest ad rank is placed in position one, the second highest in position two, and so on.

You may pay less than your bid. When you set a bid, it is called your maximum cost per click or *max CPC*. This is the most you are willing to pay for a click. However, you only pay one penny more than needed to beat the ad rank of the person below you. This is called the *actual CPC*, which is the amount you paid for a click.

This auction can lead to some confusing situations where you are paying less per click than an ad that appears below yours. For instance, if company one has an exceptionally high bid but a low quality score, and company two has a high quality score and a much lower bid, once the auction is done, the company with the more relevant ad could show up in the top position and pay less per click than the company appearing below them.

By using this combination of bid and relevancy metrics, the search engines are trying to ensure that users have a valuable experience with their advertisers when searchers do click on search ads.

Conversions: Determining the Value of Your Clicks

To understand the value of your clicks, you can use *conversion tracking*. Conversion tracking allows you to track business objectives on your website and tie them back to keywords and ads, so you know the value of a click.

The most common conversions that are tracked are the following:

- Ecommerce checkouts
- Filled lead forms
- Contact forms
- Downloaded whitepapers
- Scheduled appointments
- Phone calls
- In-store visits
- Newsletter subscriptions

You can count each conversion and, optionally, count the value of a conversion. For instance, not all ecommerce checkouts are for the same amount. Therefore, you can pass the value of the shopping cart back to the search engine so that you can see the actual amount of money a searcher spent on your products.

Tracking conversions allows you to see how much you are paying for a click and the value of those clicks so that you can set bids based on how much you are willing to pay for any conversion.

The Feedback Loop   By tracking conversions, you can evaluate how often your keywords, ads, and ad groups are converting clicks into customers. This creates a feedback loop where you can look at your total conversions and cost per conversion and then adjust bids based on how much you want to pay for a conversion.

You can evaluate your keywords and ads to see if some keywords are not producing conversions. Once you have this information, you can pause keywords or change the ads and landing pages associated with those keywords to see if the new combinations will produce conversions.

In addition, conversion tracking allows you to test keywords, ads, and landing pages to see which combination gives you the best result.

By using a feedback loop based on your conversions, you can fine tune your PPC account to ensure that your advertising is meeting your advertising objectives.

When you are involved in PPC advertising, you will find there is a lot of jargon to learn. With keywords, bidding, and conversion tracking, here are the most common ones you will come across:

- **Impression:** Each time your ad is displayed, you receive an impression.
- **Click:** When someone clicks on your ad, you receive a click.
- **Conversions:** When someone takes the desired action on your website, you get a conversion.
- **Max CPC:** How much you are willing to pay for a click.
- **CPC:** Your actual cost per click.
- **Average CPC:** The average amount you are paying for a set of clicks.
- **CTR:** How often a searcher clicks on your ad after it is displayed. This formula is your clicks divided by your impressions (each time an ad is displayed, you receive an impression for that ad).
- **CPA:** Your cost per acquisition or conversion.
- **ROAS:** Your return on ad spend. This is a formula of your conversion totals divided by your advertising costs.
- **Conversion rate:** How often someone converts after clicking on your ad. This formula is your conversions divided by your clicks.

These acronyms are used throughout PPC help files and discussions and are good terms to memorize.

Targeting Beyond Search

While most companies start with search advertising due to its effectiveness, you can advertise online many other ways. Many of these can be accomplished in your search engine PPC account.

Shopping Ads   Google Shopping, Microsoft Shopping, Amazon, Walmart, and many others allow you to place ads on their sites, within product search results, or even on search pages where the search term is likely to represent a product.

For instance, a search for running shoes on Google or Microsoft is usually done by someone looking to buy shoes, and thus it can trigger shopping ads to appear on search pages.

These ads usually show an image of a product, a price, and ratings. Figure 3.2 is an example of a search for running shoes on Google.

With Google Ads and Microsoft Ads, a few more steps are needed to create these campaign types; you need to create a Merchant Center account to house your product information and then connect them to your PPC accounts.

These types of ads can be managed in your Google Ads and Microsoft Ads accounts. The products are managed similar to keywords, where you can target various geographies, set bids, manage budgets, and track conversions, just as you can with typical search accounts.

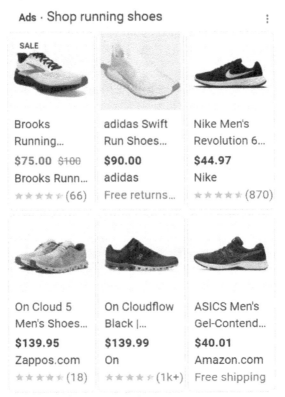

FIGURE 3.2 Shopping Ads for Running Shoes on Google

Programmatic Advertising Programmatic advertising is the automated buying of ads to show on content sites. Millions of sites and apps make their living by showing ads, and the ads they often show are automatically bought by software systems on behalf of advertisers.

These ads usually contain a combination of images and text to help highlight the products and services. These graphical components help to draw attention to the ads so that people reading the content of a page view and interact with the ads.

Many programmatic vendors will help you run ads across a large variety of sites; however, one of the largest is the Google Display Network.

With the Google Display Network, you are expanding the reach of your PPC ads beyond search. There are targeting options beyond keywords you can use to reach your target market. The most common technique is known as *remarketing*. With remarketing, you are making a list of users who visited your site or conducted some action on your site and then you can show ads to those users across the display network based on their behavior.

Often you will hear the terms *programmatic advertising* and *display advertising* used interchangeably. If someone is focused on PPC accounts, they will use the term *display advertising* based on Google's name for their programmatic network. If someone is not a search marketer, they are more likely to say *programmatic advertising* because that is the common term used for the automated buying of ads on display sites and apps.

Video Advertising   When you are watching a YouTube video and an ad pops up before, during, or after the video, these are video ads.

Video ads are what they sound like, videos. Because video ads contain both a visual and audio component, they are great for storytelling, demonstrating a product or service, or showcasing your brand.

The targeting for video ads can be highly varied as with programmatic or display advertising and is covered later in this chapter.

How PPC Fits into Your Company

As you learn digital marketing skills, it is useful to think about how these positions fit into different company sizes to prepare you for your career in marketing and ensure you are finding the right environment for how you want to use your skills.

PPC for Small Companies   With small companies, managing PPC is rarely a full-time job. PPC is either managed part-time by someone who has another role in the company, or the company has a full-time digital marketing individual.

A full-time person in digital marketing at a small company is going to wear many hats. They are often going to manage PPC, SEO, content marketing, and the company's social media channels.

This means that there are few meetings to coordinate messages across channels and ads or keywords rarely need approval from different departments such as legal or branding. Due to the lack of coordination and review, these accounts can be very flexible and changed quickly when the need arises. If you see a new opportunity, you can take advantage and be one of the first advertisers with new ads or keywords for the situation.

The biggest disadvantage of working in small companies is a lack of resources and traffic for testing. You often do not have an external person to bounce ideas off of or quickly create a new image or landing page.

PPC for Medium-Sized Companies

In mid-sized companies, digital marketing is now a full-time job. If the company is a digital focused company, managing the PPC accounts could be a sole job focus. In these instances, often a team of two to five people will manage all the marketing and website. It is also common to see some of the advertising managed in-house and other ads coordinated with external vendors for other management, such as the website or video ads.

In other cases, like with small companies, the role includes managing other advertising channels or coordinating with outside vendors.

Unless it is a highly specialized business, the focus of these accounts is to carve out a niche to compete with larger companies. Since PPC is based on relevancy as much as budgets, medium-sized accounts can do very well with PPC advertising if they are focused on specific products and services.

The biggest disadvantage is usually a lack of resources. You have more resources than a small company, such as someone who can create images, but you rarely have the resources to create your own video ads.

PPC for Enterprise Companies

Enterprise companies usually have entire teams for each digital marketing area. Usually, there is a PPC, SEO, website, and social team. Some companies also have teams dedicated to analytics or business intelligence. Each team can range in size from just two or three people to more than 20.

The focus of these accounts can range from branding to revenue generation to impression share. *Impression share* is the percentage of times your account displayed an ad compared to how often it could have displayed an ad. Impression share is used by enterprise companies to measure their search visibility. They often have large resources and can coordinate messages across channels.

The biggest disadvantage is the speed of implementation. Creating a new ad might involve both a legal and a brand team review. You will spend time in meetings making sure everything is perfect before it is launched.

You will have the resources to do anything you can get approved. When it comes to tracking, testing, and third-party software implementation, enterprise companies have the money and resources to make it happen.

Agency Life

The other job possibility is working within an agency. Advertising agencies handle accounts of all sizes and types. You will get to see how many distinct types of accounts are set up and managed.

Many agencies are specialized and only manage certain types of accounts, such as small business, dentists, lawyers, or ecommerce.

The advantage of working at an agency as compared to in-house is the total number of accounts you get to experience and manage. The downside is that you are beholden to your clients and how fast or slow they implement changes.

It is useful to work for a year or two both in-house and at an agency. When you work in-house, you understand meeting flows and why it sometimes takes a long time to accomplish tasks. When you work with agencies, you get to see a wide range of accounts and companies. Working for an agency and an in-house company lets you see the other side of marketing life and be a better manager and communicator.

You will likely find that you prefer one of these over the other, and by getting experience at both, you can find the job role where you excel and enjoy your work.

Digital Advertising Strategy and Planning

Before you can plan an account, you first need to understand how people make decisions. This is often called the *buying funnel* or *sales funnel*—see Figure 3.3. You may see it represented with different steps and processes; however, the overall concept does not change.

- The first step is *awareness*. Users must be aware of your company or products before they can decide if this is something that will interest them.
- The second step is *interest*. You want to make users interested in your products or services and how they can make their lives better. If you are successful in attracting users' interest, they will want to learn more.
- The third step is the *learning* phase. Users will research your product or service to see if it fits with their vision of what they need. If they are interested, they will progress to the next step.
- The fourth step is *shopping*. Users look around to determine where they want to buy the product or engage the service.
- Next, they may finally *buy* the products or services. Then you have retention. Can you sell to them again, or upsell another product or service? If the product is subscription based, how long does the user stay as a customer?

FIGURE 3.3   The Sales Funnel

Not all customer journeys are the same. In some cases, a user might progress through the entire funnel after a single search. In other cases, especially with expensive purchases such as TVs or vacations, there could be many searches across several weeks of time before a decision is reached. Understanding how users convert to a specific company or product set is useful to understand, as that will help you determine what you want to track along with where you want to advertise throughout the funnel. However, that is an entire exercise and something you should examine more in your future.

Search is known to be highly effective in the learn-to-buy phase. Awareness and interest are often covered with the display or video ads. Retention is often covered with remarketing and audience advertising. While you can cover the entire funnel in a PPC account, because this chapter focuses on search, it focuses more on the bottom of the funnel.

Before you build or plan your PPC account, you need to determine the account's goals. What do you want the account to achieve? What will your boss or client consider a successful account? How much budget do you have for the account or individual account goals? How will you track these success metrics?

Paid search allows you to advertise in any aspect of the conversion funnel, from awareness to sales to retention, so you must have specific goals in mind to determine how the account will be measured.

By first determining the account's goals, you can ensure you are building an account that will have the best chance of succeeding.

Setting and Managing Goals

A *goal* is something that you can measure that is tied directly to the business goals. The most common tracked goals are as follows:

- Lead forms submitted
- Ecommerce checkouts
- Contact forms submitted
- Phone calls
- Schedule appointments
- In-store visits
- Driving directions
- Whitepaper downloads
- Newsletter subscriptions
- Apps installed

The first step to setting goals is to determine what you consider a successful account and what you want it to accomplish. You can track multiple goals. For instance, service companies often track phone calls, contacts, and scheduled appointments because all three of these are ways that users can contact them. In this instance, a scheduled appointment is more likely to result in a sale (or maybe an actual sale) than a contact form or a phone call. Therefore, you would value it higher than the other goals. Not all goals are equal, and you can prioritize goals.

Once you decide what you want to track, the next step is to determine how much you want to pay for that goal if there is no direct revenue involved, such as a phone call. Often your client or boss will just have a number in mind, such as $50 per phone call or $20 per contact form.

In other cases, you will have to do some rough math. If the goal is $50 per new customer and 20 percent of all calls turn into customers, then your goal is $10 per phone call (that's $50 × 20% = $10).

When a conversion results in direct revenue, such as an ecommerce checkout, your goals might be based in a cost per conversion or *ROAS*, which stands for return on ad spend. The formula for ROAS is revenue/cost × 100.

For instance, if you spend $100 to make $100, then your ROAS is 1. Sometimes ROAS is expressed as a percentage, and the ROAS would be 1 or 100 percent. A 100 percent ROAS means you have broken even; you spent as much to obtain the sales as the sales were worth. Often ecommerce companies want a much higher ROAS since this formula does not consider salaries, cost of goods, rent, etc. So, it is common to see ROAS targets of 300 percent to 1,000 percent as advertising goals.

Once you determine how much you want to pay for a conversion or your target ROAS, you need to determine how many conversions a company wants per month. For instance, some companies can handle unlimited leads, so they are only constrained by their budget. A small one-person company, such as an electrician, might only want 10 or 20 contacts a month because they do not have the time to do more than a few jobs each month.

By looking at the cost per conversion goal and how many goals you want each month, you can determine the budget. If someone wants 20 calls a month at $50 per call, then the budget would be $1,000 (20 × $50 = 1,000).

If a company has multiple goals, you might need to consider the different values for each conversion in setting up and managing the account. Once you have determined the goals, you need to track them.

Conversion Tracking

Most search engines have a script you can place on the website that will allow you to track actions that take place on a website. These scripts allow you to define conversion actions in the search engine's PPC account so you can add or change them in the PPC platform whenever something needs to be updated.

In some cases, advanced implementations might be necessary. This is the case when revenue is being tracked and you need to tie the actual products being sold back to the conversions. In these cases, you will often use the company's developers or analytics team to implement these changes.

Some conversions will come from an external source, such as phone call tracking. Because the user is calling a number and that interaction does not happen online where the data can be tracked, then third-party tracking systems that specialize in phone call, SMS, or other types of tracking are often employed.

In the case of Google Ads, many advertisers are using Google Analytics. Any goal defined in the analytics platform can be imported into Google Ads, making advanced tracking quite easy once Google Analytics has been deployed on the website.

Unless it is a small client, the PPC manager is often defining what needs to be tracked, but other resources in the company are putting the actual tracking in place.

Attribution Management   When you have goal tracking in place, if someone clicks on your ad and does an action you are tracking, then in the PPC platform, you will be able to see the campaign, ad group, keyword, and ad that was clicked and led to that conversion.

What if someone clicks on two different ads before they convert? What if a user clicks on your search ad, then goes to your website directly, then clicks on an organic link, and then clicks on another ad, and then they finally convert?

In these scenarios, you might want to divide the credit for the conversion across multiple actions. For instance, if someone clicks on an ad and reads the site, and later they see another ad, click on it, and convert, how much credit should each click receive? If you were to give each click 50 percent of the credit, then each click, and the associated data points such as the keyword and ad, would have one-half of a conversion.

By default, most search engines use a *last-click attribution model*. This means that all the credit for a conversion is given to the last keyword and ad clicked. There are many more models. The more common ones are *linear*, meaning all the conversions are divided equally among the clicks, *position based*, which weights the first and last click more than the middle ones, and *time decay*, which weights the clicks that occurred closer to the conversion heavier than those that occurred early in the conversion process, or *data-driven attribution*, which uses machine learning to decide where to give credit for each click.

While going through the entire scope of attribution is well beyond what you need to know to start advertising, it is a good concept to understand

and discuss with your clients. It is quite common for users to search for a generic keyword (i.e., running shoes), look around a site, visit a few more sites, and then search for the brand and type they want (i.e., Nike Vaporfly) and convert.

If you are using last-touch attribution, then the brand terms get all the credit, and it could appear the term *running shoes* is not doing well. However, the brand term may never have been searched if the user did not first discover the shoe type from their initial search. Attribution management solves these types of problems.

Note

A common PPC mistake is only using last-touch attribution, as this tends to overweight brand terms and misses the customer's journey from initial discovery to the clicks that resulted in the final conversion.

Tracking Mistakes to Avoid Tracking conversions is fundamental to an account because you are blind to your advertising results without it. However, you should be aware of several common mistakes to avoid when setting up and evaluating conversion data.

Each visit or click should not be a conversion. You will sometimes see conversion tracking incorrectly set up and defined where every site visit or click is a conversion. Having liberal conversion tracking so that most clicks are a conversion does not let you evaluate good versus poor clicks.

With both attribution methods and conversion tracking, you can define time frames for how long a window is open from the time of the first click to the conversion where you still want to track conversions. For example, if someone clicked on your ad 6 months ago and converts today, do you really want to count that click as part of the conversion process? When you are looking at these time frames, you want them to be consistent across your tracked conversions. If you have phone calls set at 60 days and lead forms at 30 days, you will have inconsistent data.

That consistency should apply to your attribution method. You rarely want one conversion action to use a different attribution method than another conversion, as this leads to inconsistent conversion data.

Do some test conversions to make sure the conversion tracking is working properly. Poorly implemented tracking could double-count conversion, or some conversions could have been missed across the site.

Lastly, ensure you have enough data when making decisions with your conversion data. A common mistake is having too little data, conversions, clicks, or impressions when determining ad tests or the effectiveness of a keyword or ad.

In the end, you want to believe and trust your data. Your conversion data informs you about the success of your entire account from search terms to keywords to ads and everything else. If you do not believe your conversion data, then you will be paralyzed as to the proper course of action to take in improving the account. If you have good conversion data, then you can be confident that when you make decisions, they are based on data, and you have a data-driven PPC account.

Bidding Methods

Once you have conversion tracking in place, you need to determine how you want to set bids for your account.

Every ad group must have a bid. You can have different bids for each ad group. Optionally, each keyword can also have a bid. In cases where there are multiple bids, such as group and keyword, the most specific bid is used. If a search term matches a keyword that does not have a bid, the ad group's bid is used. If the search term matches a keyword that does have a bid, then the keyword's bid is used instead of the ad group's bid, as the keyword is more specific.

You set the bid method at the campaign level. That means that each campaign can choose a bid method that is best for the goals it is trying to achieve. You can use the same bid method for all your campaigns if you want. Just note that it is a campaign-level setting, so as you are considering your goals and account structure, if you want to use a different bid technique for some keywords or goals than others, you can do so by using multiple campaigns.

At a high level, there are two types of bid types you can employ—manual and automated.

Manual Bidding With manual bidding, you are setting the max CPC (the maximum cost-per-click) that you are willing to bid for every ad group and optionally every keyword. Because setting manually can take up a large amount of time, most accounts do not want to manually bid.

The most common reason for manual bidding is when you are using a third-party or in-house bid system that is setting the bids. While the bidding is still automated, from the PPC platform's perspective, you are manually setting them even though a machine is doing it, and you are not relying on the PPC platform's automated bidding.

The other reason companies use manual bidding is when there are unusual circumstances that the bid systems do not understand. This could be an unusual event, a sudden flash sale, or when tracking data have been inaccurate and you need to take over the bidding for a period before turning back to automated bidding.

Automated Bidding The most common bid methods are automated bid methods built into the platforms. These bid systems often rely on your conversion tracking data to set bids, so the more accurate your tracking data, the better they can do bidding on your behalf.

While various platforms have different automated bid systems, here are the most common ones you will come across.

- **Max Clicks:** The platform tries to get the most clicks for your budget. It does not care about the quality of the clicks, only getting the most traffic possible. This is often employed in brand new campaigns to jumpstart the data or short-term events when you need a lot of visitors to know about something.

- **Max Conversions:** The platform tries to get the most conversions for your budget. The system does not care how much any conversion costs. This is common for accounts that want leads or contacts and have small budgets where they do not have enough data to use one of the more constrained options.

- **Target CPA:** The platform tries to get you the most conversions possible at a specific CPA target. You define the conversions you want the platform to use for bidding and the CPA for any conversions and the system tries to hit your numbers. This is common for mid-sized and larger budgets for lead generation accounts. You might be an insurance company that is willing to pay $200 per contact regardless if the contact comes from a contact form, request a quote form, phone call, chat, or SMS contact.

- **Max Conversion Value or Max Revenue:** The platform tries to get you the most revenue possible based on your budget. To effectively use this bid method, you are passing ecommerce checkout revenue back to the search engine via your conversion tracking implementation. This is common for small-budget ecommerce companies.

- **Target ROAS:** The platform tries to hit your ROAS targets, such as 300 percent. As with Max Conversion Value, you need to pass revenue data back to the search engine to effectively use this bidding technique. This is a common bid technique for mid-sized and larger ecommerce companies.

Last, you can sometimes override bids with bid adjustments or bid modifiers. These are often campaign-level bid changes that allow you to bid differently on a specific device, such as a mobile phone, for a certain audience, or a location. For example, you might learn that the quality of your mobile leads is lower than your desktop leads. Therefore, you want to bid lower on phones than on computers for the same keywords. By using a bid adjustment, all your bids will be lowered for that device. Not all bid adjustments are compatible with all bid methods. Before employing these bid adjustments, you will want to make sure the platform will use a specific bid adjustment type for your bid method.

The world of PPC started with manual bidding. When automated bidding was devised, it was quickly adopted for many reasons. Manually controlling all your bids is a highly time-consuming and math-filled process that needs to be repeated frequently. If you use automated bidding, you can save yourself a massive amount of time that you can put toward keyword research, ad testing, and other account management actions that have more beneficial long-term returns on your PPC account than just changing bids.

Now that you understand the high-level settings from the types of campaigns to tracking to bidding, it is time to dive into building ad groups that follow these settings and that are the building blocks of the entire accounts.

Researching and Creating Ad Groups

Creating effective ad groups is the basis of a successful PPC account. The goal is to have highly related keywords and ads in an ad group so that when users type a search term into a search engine that matches a keyword in your ad group, they see a compelling ad related to their search term. If searchers click on your ad, it leads them to a page on your website that is connected to their search term where they can convert.

The majority of your account creation time will be spent at the ad group level in both researching keywords and creating ads. A point to remember is that only an ad from the ad group that contains the keyword that matched the search term will be shown to users. The search engines will not show ads from ad groups that do not contain matching keywords to the searcher.

An effective way to create ad groups is to first write a compelling ad. The ad should be answering a singular question from the user. If a user is searching for car insurance, the ad should not be about general insurance or home insurance; it should be about car insurance. You can sometimes be even more specific in your ad group creation, such as when a user searches for car insurance in California to then show an ad and landing page that talks about the benefits of your car insurance for people who live in California.

When creating ad groups, you need to balance creation and management time with what is possible. For instance, if you sell shoes, you could create an ad group for every color and size of a shoe so that when a user searches for a size-eleven men's black dress shoe, your ad echoes both the color and the size. However, if you sell thousands of shoes that come in a variety of colors and sizes, the number of ad groups you are selling grows so large that it will become incredibly difficult to build and manage an account of that size.

Therefore, you should first do keyword research to understand how often various words are searched and then make a list of ad groups to create. If the number is unstainable, then you need to find ways of combining ad groups so that you can manage the entire account.

The other item to keep in mind with ad groups is relevancy. A user has told you what they are looking for in their search term. If you show an ad that is not relevant to the search term, then users will not click on the ad because it does not appear to answer their search question.

A good exercise to undertake for your first few ad groups is to first write an ad that has a singular purpose. It represents a specific product or service that you offer. Then choose a page of your website for that product or service so you know the offer that a user will see after clicking on your ad. Then, look at your keywords. If the ad and landing page do not accurately reflect that keyword, the keyword needs to be in a different ad group. See Figure 3.4.

For instance, say you are a plumber. These might be some good starting ad groups:

- Plumber
- Plumber near me
- Emergency plumber
- Kitchen remodeling
- Unclog drain
- Fixing pipes
- Flooded basement
- Leaky sinks
- Fix garbage disposal

Having too many keywords in a singular ad group with a generic ad is one of the most common mistakes new advertisers make. For instance, if it is a frigid day outside and the pipes in your basement freeze, which causes them to burst and flood your basement, what do you do?

Most people turn to a search engine. The search term might be flooded basement or emergency plumbing. Consider if you saw the two ads shown in Figure 3.5.

Which ad would you click? The ad that mentions weekend work and emergency plumbing would get many more new customers than the ad that just says you are a plumbing service. The emergency plumbing ad is more relevant to the user's search term and fixing their problem.

Search engine advertising is all about being able to answer the user's question and providing them the proper direction so that they can get their answer, which is often buying your product or engaging with your service. Always ensure your ads are relevant to your keywords and the user's search term.

To properly build ad groups, you first need to learn about keywords, as they are the most common targeting method you will use in a paid search account.

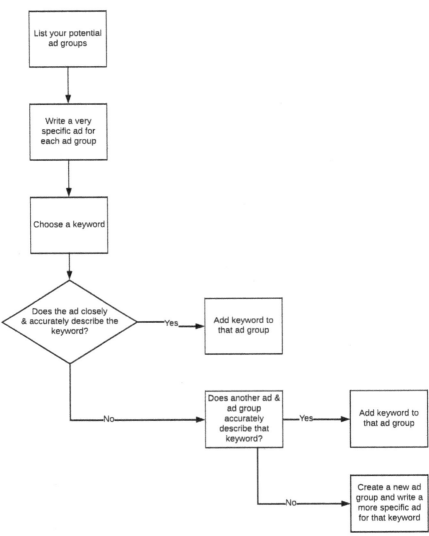

FIGURE 3.4 Ad Group Organization

Emergency Plumber Service
Call 24/7 for immediate assistance.
We work weekends!

John's Plumbing Service
Servicing the Chicago area
Call for an appointment today!

FIGURE 3.5 Emergency Plumbing Ads

All About Keywords   A keyword is a word or phrase that is placed in your ad group. A keyword could be a singular word such as *plumber* or a longer phrase such as *plumbers near me*. While the second instance is a three-word phrase, in your PPC account, it will be counted as a single keyword.

A keyword's purpose is to show an ad if the keyword matches the search term, the words a searcher typed into the search engine.

We use the word *matches* very specifically since there are multiple ways a keyword can match to a search term. These are known as match types, and you will look at them in-depth later in this chapter. Before jumping into match types, the next section looks closely at the types of keywords that exist and explains how to find them.

Types of Searches   Not all searches are the same, and not all searches can be monetized. There are several types of searches that users conduct.

One type of search is *navigational*. These are searches conducted to find a specific website or page of the web, often one that a user has visited before. Considering that some of the most common search terms are Facebook, Amazon, Google, and Gmail, a user is looking for that specific website and is not likely to visit another site other than the one they have in mind.

The most common search type is *informational*. There are more informational search queries than all the other types of search queries combined. Popular searches such as weather, time, or date are difficult to monetize, as a user often finds what they are looking for on the search result page without having to visit another site. However, you can monetize informational queries if the user is in the informational phase of the funnel. Search queries such as these are often someone who will make a purchase in the future:

- Best paint to use on a deck
- Plasma vs LCD TVs
- Why use a CRM system
- Best neighborhoods in Chicago

When you advertise with these types of words, you are introducing someone to your brand and how your products fit their needs. These words rarely result in a conversion and are often contributors to conversions, as the user needs to learn more before they are ready to convert.

Lastly, there are *transactional* searches. These types of searches are conducted by someone who does intend to convert and has progressed through the buying funnel. They are commonly product terms and brand names. Examples of these keywords include the following:

- 56" Sony LED TV
- State Farm car insurance quote
- Start Salesforce trial

There are also ambiguous queries that do not fall directly into any category. A search for *best board game Reddit* is both an informational and navigational query, as the user wants information on a board game discussion on Reddit.com.

Types of Keywords   Transactional and explicit keywords fall into one of four categories.

The first is by far the most frequently used words used in PPC accounts, *explicit* keywords. These keywords directly describe the product or service. If you see the word, you know what someone wants. Examples include the following:

- Chicago plumber
- Laptop memory
- Dermatologist

Next, there are *problem* keywords. They describe the condition the product or service solves and can include words such as these:

- Flooded basement
- Acne
- Can't run Excel

There are also *symptom* keywords, which describe the problem directly:

- Broken pipe
- Oily skin
- Slow computer

Lastly, there are *product names and part numbers*. These are the second most common keywords used because they are often direct exports from product or service lists:

- P-1011 ½
- Mint Souffle Cleanser
- 512 MB DDR2-533 So Dimm (a computer memory chip)

Together, these tell stories. If it is wintertime in Chicago and the pipe in your basement freezes and breaks, you need a plumber to come and fix it. The pipe that burst was a P-1011 ½.

If you consider how your potential customers search, you can start to think of the keywords that they would use to find your company. Do not just think about the product and service names, but also what happened to the user that they would need your product. What problems does your service solve? By thinking through the entire story from the product, conditions, symptoms, and solutions, you can often produce long lists of keywords that can help you jumpstart your keyword research process.

Keyword Research   Once you have created a campaign and determined its settings, you need to populate it with keywords and ad groups. While doing some mental exercises will help you with your initial list, you will want to use keyword research tools to round out the keywords you are using in your account.

The most popular keyword research tool is free and found in your Google Ads account. It is called the Keyword Planner.

With this tool, you have two options for researching keywords. The first is to input a starting set of keywords. You will then be given a list of additional keywords based on your inputs. The second is often a great starting point for users, whereby you have the option to put in a website or web page and Google will suggest keywords based on that page.

If you were to input the website **Nike.com** into the tool, you would see results like those shown in Figure 3.6.

	Keyword	↓	Avg. monthly searches	Three month change	YoY change	Competition	Ad impression share	Top of page bid (low range)	Top of page bid (high range)
	Keyword ideas								
☐	air force 1		1,220,000	0%	-18%	High	–	$0.48	$1.32
☐	nike air force		823,000	-18%	-18%	High	–	$0.46	$1.43
☐	nike blazer		823,000	0%	+83%	High	–	$0.34	$0.94
☐	airmax nikes		673,000	+22%	0%	High	–	$0.45	$1.36
☐	nike out		550,000	+22%	-33%	High	–	$0.15	$6.57
☐	running shoes nike		201,000	+22%	+22%	High	–	$0.34	$1.50
☐	snkr s		165,000	+22%	-45%	Medium	–	$0.01	$0.69
☐	vapor max nike		165,000	+22%	-33%	High	–	$0.61	$1.83
☐	nike sweatpants		165,000	-33%	-18%	High	–	$0.34	$1.14

FIGURE 3.6   Keyword Tool for Nike

This tool will show you a list of keywords and how often they are searched. In addition, you can see the competition levels, suggested bid amounts, and if you are using that keyword already, how often you are showing for that term.

Your goal is to consider the number of searches for a keyword and their costs, along with your budget. If you are adding words with very high search volumes and high bids, you might be adding words that can spend your entire budget by themselves and your other words might never get impressions. Choosing keywords is a balancing act between how much any keyword could spend along with your budget.

If you have a small budget, you will often want to start with more specific keywords that have low search volumes but are more likely to convert than more general keywords.

In these tools, you can start to add keywords to a keyword plan along with the ad groups where they should appear. Once you have added keywords, you can get an estimate of how much they will cost monthly and revise your plan before saving it to your account.

If you are building a large account, it can be useful to export this data to a spreadsheet program and organize your ad groups in the spreadsheet. Most PPC platforms have ways of importing data from spreadsheets to create your keywords and ads so that your work is not wasted.

In addition to the platform keyword tools, many third-party tools offer keyword research. These tools are often subscription based but can let you do additional research or competitor monitoring.

Another place to look for keyword inspiration is your analytics data. Often analytics data will show you what someone is searching for on a website and might include data on what people were searching for on a search engine to arrive at your site.

If you are involved in SEO efforts, you will have a Google Search Central account that helps you monitor your website's SEO data. This is another place where you can see what users are typing into search engines that are showing your website and can be a useful source of inspiration to find keywords.

Lastly, you can use your own PPC data. You will choose keywords in your account, and these keywords will match the user's search terms, what the searcher typed into the search engine. You have access to some of the search terms in your account. Reading the search terms can provide you with keyword ideas, especially ones where you are showing ads but do not have them in your account.

In most countries, you are allowed to use any word as a keyword, even trademarked words. These words just trigger an ad. However, you are generally not allowed to use a trademark within the ad unless you own that trademark. This combination helps combat customer confusion over who owns the brand. In some countries you are not allowed to use a trademark as a keyword or within the ad unless you own the trademark or you have been given explicit permission to use the trademark. It is always good to check with your local laws or your lawyer before using trademarks in your PPC accounts.

We keep using the phrase *matched to* and that phrase is used very specifically. You do not have to find every single search term that users will type into a search engine and add it as a keyword. There are several ways in which your keywords can match a searcher's search term. The next sections examine how these matches work.

Keyword Match Types

Keyword Match Types   If you had to find every single word and phrase that a searcher was inputting into a search engine, you would often need millions of keywords to cover some basic ideas. Many search terms are misspelled, in singular or plural form, or have words in a different order than you choose.

For instance, if you were advertising a hotel in New York City, these terms have all the same idea even if they are different sets of words:

- NYC Hotel
- Hotels in NYC
- Hotel in New York City
- New York City hotl (misspelled)
- And the list goes on

Luckily, you do not have to find all these combinations due to the way match types work. When you choose a match type, you are telling a search engine how closely or far away from your keywords you want the intent or idea of the search to be.

An exact match keyword is when the search term and your keyword should be the exact same idea. The examples of NYC would all apply to the exact match version of the keyword, NYC hotel.

A search for *cheap NYC Hotel* or *pet friendly New York City hotel* would not show an ad for the exact match keyword *NYC hotel* since the search term contains additional ideas such as price and pet friendliness. For keywords to match to search terms that contain your keyword's idea, you use a *phrase match*.

With phrase match, you are telling a search engine to match your keywords to search terms that contain your idea but may have additional ideas in the search term, if your base idea is included. This can be useful when you are selling products that come in a large variety of sizes and colors. You can use the base keywords to reach all the users who are adding information to the search term.

When you want your words to show for a wide variety of ideas that are similar to your keywords, then you can turn to *broad match*. With broad match, the search term must be similar to your keywords but does not have to be directly related to them. For instance, if you had the broad match NYC hotel, you could show an ad for these terms:

- Staying in NYC
- NYC vacations
- Hotels near Javits Center

In most PPC platforms, you can see some of the actual search terms that are matching to your keywords. Some of these terms will accurately reflect your products and services, and you can add them as keywords if they are not already in your account. Other terms will not be good fits for your account and in those cases, you can turn to negative keywords.

Negative keywords are words that you can add to your account. When the search term contains one or more of your negative keywords, it will stop your ad from showing. A negative keyword can be a single word or a phrase. If you use a negative keyword phrase, all the words must be in the search term, but not necessarily in the same order.

Technically, there are ways of using negative keyword match types to stop ads from showing for only specific combinations of terms, but that is a much more advanced concept and can quickly become confusing, so we leave that for another day. Just know it is possible if you come across those specific situations.

As a general rule, the more specific the keyword and match type, the higher the click-through rate and conversion rate will be as the matching search terms will be very similar to your chosen keywords. However, these restrictive match types will also have the fewest impressions since they cannot match to a lot of different search terms. The broader the keyword and match type, the lower the conversion rate and click-through rates are since these keywords can match to many search terms, of which some will not be highly related to your products and services. Broader match types usually receive more impressions than exact match keywords since they can match to a larger variety of search terms.

A keyword's job is to match to search terms where you want to show an ad. That is all a keyword really does, decide if you want to show an ad or not. The ad is what persuades users that you have the information they are looking for and to come to your website to become your next customer.

Therefore, the next step to completing ad groups once you have chosen and organized your keywords is to create ads in those ad groups.

Creating Compelling Ads

Once a search term matches your keyword, your ad can appear to the searcher. The ad's purpose is to persuade your potential customers to click on your ad and take your desired action on your website.

Not all clicks are created equal. You often do not want to persuade everyone to click on your ad as not everyone will be interested in or eligible for your offerings. In these cases, you need to pre-qualify users so that you are only attracting the correct type of audience.

For example, if you are an accounting firm that only serves other businesses and not individuals, you would not want clicks from individuals who are searching for accounting firms. In cases like these, you would want to mention that you are a business-to-business firm so that you only get the clicks from the searchers who might become customers.

Persuading Users to Take Action   When you are creating ads, there are a few basics of ad copy creation to keep in mind, and the next sections look at each of these items individually.

Relevance   You want your ad to be relevant to the search term. This relevancy lets a user know you understand what they are looking for and that they should look deeper at the rest of your ad.

Often this involves echoing your keywords or the search terms within the ad line. Do not just write the keyword as the headline as it creates a boring headline. You should write supporting text for such ad lines.

Here are few examples:

- Hire a Boston Plumber
- Your Fiji Dream Vacation Awaits
- Don't Get a Headache, we'll manage your taxes

In ecommerce, you are often adding supporting lines that might be about shopping, discounts, or prices. If someone is searching for a new TV, these are more appropriate ecommerce headlines:

- Buy New TVs at our site (replace "our site" with your company name)
- 10% off Brand New TVs
- Watch your favorite shows in High-Definition

Note that there are character limits for different ad copy elements, so not all these examples would fit for every single line. The goal here is to spur ideas for writing a compelling ad.

Features and Benefits   A *feature* is a list of true facts about a product. These are common lines in the shopping phase as a user wants to compare different features about a product or service.

A *benefit* is why the feature is useful. These show the user how a product or service will make their life better.

For instance, say you are selling laptops and a certain model has a 9-hour battery life. In a comparison chart, this is a simple average battery usage of 9 hours. There is nothing interesting about that fact. The same can be said for weight, screen size, processing speed, memory, and so forth.

To make a feature a benefit, you just finish a sentence about the feature. The laptop has a 9-hour battery life so you can work all day without having to hunt for a power outlet. By adding some text that explains why that feature is useful, you turn a feature into a benefit.

The higher the shopping funnel (often during the awareness and interest stage), the less users know about the products to care about individual features, so the focus should be on benefits. As the user starts to learn about a product, then you want to focus on benefits, how the product or service will benefit them, and begin to introduce features. Comparison shopping is all about feature comparison. However, people buy something based on what it does for them, which is a benefit.

This is why you should consider the funnel in your marketing and ad copy creation so that you are giving the searcher what they want at each funnel stage.

Calls to Action   A CTA or call to action tells users what to do after they click on your ad. Common calls to action include buy, sell, hire, book, download, learn more, and so forth. These are common CTAs and often lose their meaning unless they are flavored with additional text.

- Schedule a time for your New Look
- Find your new Dream Condo
- Call to Claim Your Free Consultation
- Start a 21 Day Free Trial
- Subscribe to powerful marketing tips

By adding some text around your call to action, you can make the ad lines more attractive to searchers.

Additional Ad Lines   A USP or unique selling proposition is what makes your product unique. When someone is searching, there are many options on the search results page. Why should a searcher do business with you and not another company?

While USPs such as "M&Ms melt in your mouth and not in your hands" or "A diamond is forever" are well known, your USP usage does not always have to be an iconic statement. Your goal is to make your products more appealing to customers than your competition.

Authority statements also work well. Over 100,000 trademarks filed. More than 50,000 vacations booked. Thousands of satisfied customers. #1 Rated. Bestselling author. These statements highlight your expertise and value that any searcher can tap into by working with your company.

With all these ad techniques, the end goal is to show a user you are relevant to their search term and can assist them with their needs. If the user is qualified for your business, you then want the searcher to click on the ad to visit your website.

You will not showcase every element in every ad. The next section looks at how to put these options together when you create an ad.

The Ad Copy Elements Across the various paid search engine platforms, there are different ad types. The most common, and what you will create with both Microsoft Ads and Google ads, are known as RSAs or *responsive search ads.*

There are several components to these ads.

The final URL, which is sometimes called the destination URL, is the specific web page that a user will go to after clicking on your ad. The web page where a user is delivered is known as the *landing page,* or the first page a user sees after clicking on your ad.

The final URL should rarely be your homepage. The power of search comes from a user being able to search for anything and then seeing search results that deliver them to web pages that contain the information they are seeking. Your ads should send a user to the most specific page on your website that contains information about that product or service and gives the user a chance to take an action, such as buying a product or contacting you.

In ecommerce terms, if users are searching for a specific product, then the ad should go to that product page. If users are searching for a category of products, such as running shoes, then they should be taken to a category page.

The next ad copy component is known as *paths* or *display paths*. These are appended to the final URL in the ad to give a user an idea of the type of landing page they are going to see on your website. Note that these are for marketing and persuasion purposes, so these pages do not have to exist.

For instance, if you see a URL of IBM.com, where are you going? IBM's website has millions of pages on it. If a user were to see these URLs, they would have a much better idea of their destination:

- IBM.com/Watson
- IBM.com/AI/Consulting
- IBM.com/Data/Analytics

By adding just a little bit of text in the display path, you can convey a lot of information to the user about the type of page they will see after clicking the ad.

The headlines are what will appear in larger text at the top of the ad. These are the most prominent parts of an ad and are often around 30 characters in length, maximum. These lines are where you highlight your ad relevance, authority, USPs, and calls to action. You can create a list of headlines in the ad.

Finally, there are descriptions. This is much longer text, often 90 characters in length, where you can explain more about the products and services for the keywords in that ad group. See Figure 3.7.

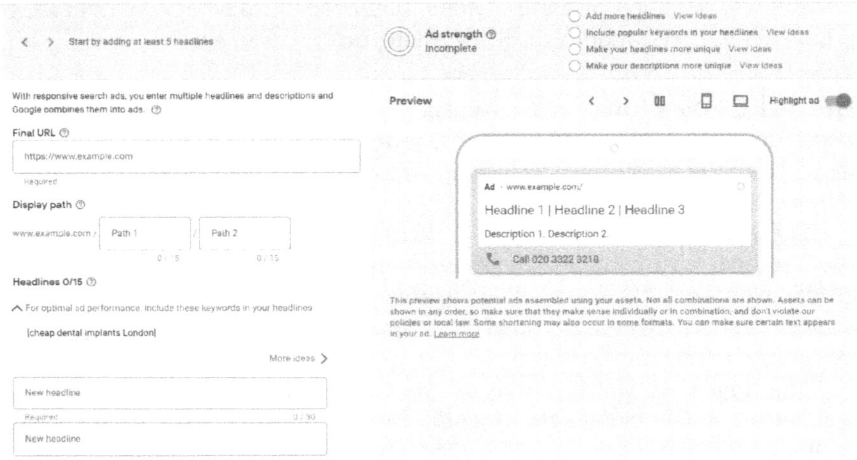

FIGURE 3.7 RSA Creation

The way that responsive ads work is that you create several headlines and descriptions known as *assets*. Then the search engine will render an ad with one to three headlines and one or two descriptions from those assets to show to the user, along with your paths and final URL. The search engines use artificial intelligence that looks at the searcher's search term and other factors to create an ad that should be compelling to that user.

If you have not given a search engine very many assets to work with, it is constrained in its ability to create ads. As you make RSAs, you will see suggestions as to how to make them more compelling to users and a score known as *ad strength*, which is a measure of your asset numbers and the diversity of those assets from each other.

While the search engines prefer you give them lots of ad serving control in the form of many assets, there will be times you want to restrict how ads are served. This could be due to legal or branding considerations. In these cases, you can use a technique called *pinning* to ensure that an ad line is always displayed in a particular position. While pinning is a more advanced concept, for larger companies or those in regulated industries, it is often a must-use additional option.

As you are creating ads and thinking about various ad combinations, you will often have more ideas than can fit within an ad. This is where testing comes into play. You can create multiple ads and test them to see which results in the best metrics for your company. Testing is covered later in this chapter.

When a keyword matches the search term, your ad can be displayed. Your ad is built based on that search term in real time using the assets you gave the ad. If the user finds your ad compelling, they will click on your ad to go to your landing page. Your landing page needs to meet the user at their stage of the funnel and then give them the option to progress further into the funnel so they can ultimately convert on your website.

Ad Extensions   Ad extensions allow you to add information to your ads. These features can either add options beyond clicking on the ad, such as phone numbers or driving directions, or add information to your ads.

The most common ad extensions are *callouts* and *sitelinks*. A callout extension is a few pieces of short text that give more information about your offer to the user. A sitelink is like a callout except each one can link to its own landing page. In the plumber search ad shown in Figure 3.8, Faucet Repair, View Coupons, Your Products, Water Damage Cleanup, and Plumbing Services are all sitelinks. If you were to click on one of the sitelinks, you would go to a different page of the website than if you had clicked on the ad.

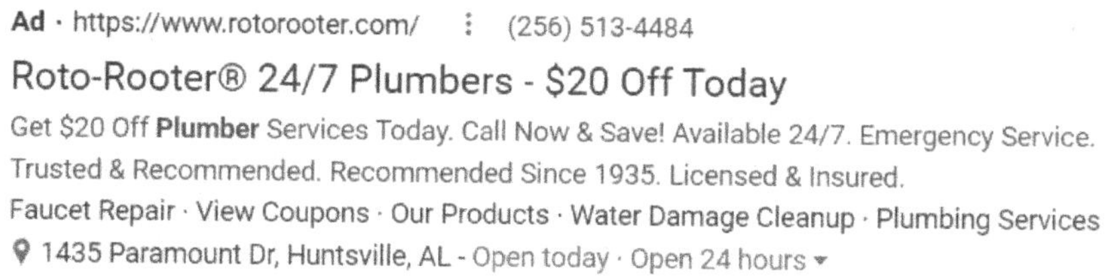

Ad · https://www.rotorooter.com/   ⋮   (256) 513-4484

Roto-Rooter® 24/7 Plumbers - $20 Off Today

Get $20 Off **Plumber** Services Today. Call Now & Save! Available 24/7. Emergency Service. Trusted & Recommended. Recommended Since 1935. Licensed & Insured.
Faucet Repair · View Coupons · Our Products · Water Damage Cleanup · Plumbing Services
📍 1435 Paramount Dr, Huntsville, AL - Open today · Open 24 hours ▾

FIGURE 3.8   Ad with Callouts, Sitelinks, and Location Extensions

In addition, you can also call the company. If this search were done on a mobile device, clicking on the phone number would load the phone dialer. This is known as the call extension.

You also see the company's address and if they are open. This is the location extension. Clicking on this extension will load a maps application on a phone or a maps page on a computer and will let you get driving directions to the location.

Ad extensions are often created at the account or campaign level. Since settings are inherited downward from account to campaign to ad group, within an account, if you create an extension at the account level, it will be used in every campaign and ad group in the account. If you want to show different information and options by campaign, which is common with sitelinks and callouts, then you would want to create them at the campaign level so you can showcase different information for each campaign.

While there are many ad extensions, you will want to use the appropriate ones for your company to highlight more information about your offer as well as give the user any conversion options that fit with your advertising goals.

The examples covered so far have focused on keyword targeting within search results. However, you can use several other targeting methods with search terms, or instead of search terms, to show relevant ads to users across the web. The next section dives further into these additional targeting methods.

PPC Targeting Options

Targeting methods are techniques you can use to dictate when, where, and how ads can be displayed. Some options can be used in conjunction with other targeting options, which often constrain how an ad is served. Other targeting options can replace the keyword in how an ad is triggered to be displayed.

Targeting Conditions   Targeting conditions allow you to constrain how ads are displayed. These are generally campaign-level options that affect all the ad groups in that campaign.

The most common of these is known as *geographic or location targeting.* With location targeting you can decide geographic conditions for how the ad is displayed. The most common use of geographic targeting is to list a location, which could be a country, state, metropolitan area, city, country, or even a radius around a specific location, of where the user must be in order for your ad to be displayed. This is how you can make sure that only users in Munich or Italy see your ads. This is useful for businesses that serve specific locations.

The other geographic targeting does not look at the user's location, but instead looks at the region where they are interested. For instance, if a searcher lives in Chicago, but is searching for hotels in London, the user's interest in London is a more important characteristic of their search intent than where they live. These options for geographic targeting look at a user's interested geography instead of their physical location. This is commonly used in the travel industry.

Regardless of the options you choose, you must define a geographic target for your campaign, which can range from one or more countries to a single ZIP code, for the PPC platform to know where your ads can be displayed.

Another common ad serving restraint is called *ad scheduling* or *day parting*. This is usually an optional feature and tells the search engine when you want the ads to show. If your business is only open Monday to Friday, you can have your ads only running during the weekdays. If you have a call center that only answers the phone between 8 a.m. and 5 p.m., you can set your ads to only show during those hours.

Some platforms also offer *demographic targeting*. These characters often include age, gender, income levels, education levels, and other user characteristics. Not all platforms support all these options, and you will find that even if they are supported, they may be supported in some countries but not in others, based on local laws or available data.

These targeting condition options can work with search keywords or non-keyword targeting options. The next section looks at ways beyond search that you can show ads to users.

Audience Targeting

An *audience* is a collection of users who have characteristics or behaviors in common. You will define the conditions for these audiences using your customer data, your analytics data, or data provided by the search engines.

The most common type of audience targeting is known as *remarketing*. With remarketing, you define behavioral conditions on your website that when a user does those behaviors, they are placed in an audience list. Then you can show ads to these specific users across display and video networks.

For instance, if a user comes to your website, adds an item to his or her shopping cart, begins the checkout process, and then stops and does not check out, you could make a list of abandoned checkout users. If someone were to buy from you, you can make a list of users who bought once and show ads to them to persuade them to buy again from you. You can simply have a list of all users who visited your website. You can place users in these lists based on any conditions you set within your analytics data.

People who have been to a website before know what experience they had with it. If they see an ad and click on it, then they are considered a qualified user and are more likely to convert than someone who has never been to your website before. This is a useful advertising targeting option to expand where your ads are shown from not only search to the display network. This is by far the most common audience targeting usage.

Sometimes remarketing is called *behavioral marketing,* as you are advertising to users based on their behavior. Other times you will hear this called *retargeting*. In most cases, the overall process of defining website behaviors that place a user into an audience and then serving ads to those years is the same process regardless of the name being used.

Another common type of audience targeting is known as *affinity audience targeting*. Affinity targeting shows ads to people based on long-term passions, interests, and hobbies. These users could be interested in classic cars, vacations, photography, gardening, or have some other common interest. Because these users may not be in the market for a product or service, your goal is often to introduce your brand to them so that when they are ready to engage with your company, you will come to their mind as a place to investigate.

In-market audiences are those currently looking for a solution. These audiences have a wide range, from someone who is in the market for a new car or home to someone who is researching new software for his or her company. The common characteristic for in-market audiences is that they are currently evaluating product or service solutions and actively engage in research. Since these users are in the market for a solution, you often want to get them deep into your sales funnel quickly and not spend a lot of time trying to introduce your brand to these users.

Customer match is a specific type of audience that you define from your customer data. You can create lists of users from your data, such as loyal shoppers, frequent buyers, people in a loyalty program, and so forth. Then you can serve ads specifically to these users. The goal of your customer match marketing can be highly varied as a list of loyal shoppers might want to see ads of your current specials, while you might want to show ads reminding people about your brand to a list of people who have not bought from you in a long time.

Regardless of the audience targeting being used, the PPC platforms will try to find patterns among the data. They can then use these patterns to find other users with similar characteristics to these patterns. The PPC platforms create lists of these additional audiences, which are known as lookalike or similar audiences. You can then use these additional audiences to try to expand your reach to these new potential customers.

Contextual Targeting   Not all users are known, and in some cases, you cannot advertise to specific audiences based on local privacy or other laws. In these cases, or if you want to explore new targeting options, you can turn to contextual targeting.

Contextual targeting shows ads based on the content of a website or web page. If a user is reading an article about how a company switched CRM systems and found new customer insights, and you are a CRM provider, this is a good page to place your ad since the user is currently engaged with similar content.

With contextual targeting, you define the type of content where you want to place your ads. Some of these contextual options might be extremely broad topics, such as software solutions, and others can be highly specific, such as classic car collectors.

You can also use keywords in your display campaigns instead of choosing topics. In these cases, the search engines are trying to match the theme of your keywords to the overall content of a web page. The keywords used are treated as broad match regardless of the match type you select when targeting the display network because your keywords are a general guideline for the type of content contained on the web page or app where you want your ads to appear.

Once you define the type of content where you want your ads to appear, when a user is on a site that matches your contextual targeting options, your ad can appear. Remember that campaign settings such as geography, time of day, and budget also apply to these ads. Therefore, you could show your ad only if a user is on a web page that has the type of content you want to target and is in your specific geography.

Maintaining Display Relevance   When you are using audience and contextual targeting, your ads appear across the display network. While these options may sound broader than search, you still want to maintain the relevancy of your targeting method to the ads your users see.

What this means from a PPC perspective is that each targeting option will often be in its own ad group. Then you create an ad that is specific to that ad group based on the audience or content that is triggering your ad to be displayed. You would not want to show the same ad to someone who abandoned his or her shopping cart as a user from a lookalike audience who has never been to your website before. By making each targeting method its own ad group, you can ensure that your ads are relevant across the display network.

The display network has more distractions than search since users are not primarily visiting websites for the ads, but the contents of that page. To better enhance the ad display, graphical components are often used.

There are two common display ads, which are banner ads, also called image ads, and responsive display ads. A *banner ad* is an image you provide to the search engine that has specific size requirements. You need to make several images in varied sizes to show across the web because different sites have allocated different sizes to ads on their site.

Responsive display ads are similar to responsive search ads except you also provide images that can be displayed in the ad. The search engine will then use a combination of your text and images in rendering the ads. With responsive ads, you can create a single ad and the search engine will render the ad in the appropriate size for where it will be displayed.

Creating Your First PPC Account

Once you understand how an account is structured, how ads are created, and the targeting methods, you are ready to create a PPC account.

When creating an account, you want to consider these items:

- Your advertising goals
- Budget and how it might be segmented by goal or geography
- Targeting information, especially location
- Any legal or brand considerations

While you can get more in depth in account creation, this introductory chapter keeps it simple. Say you are a remodeling company serving a single city. You will remodel any room in the house, and the most common rooms are bedroom, kitchen, and bathrooms. However, some people like to remodel their living rooms, offices, or other rooms in the house.

Once you have this basic information, you need to put conversion tracking into place. As you are trying to get leads, your most common conversions are going to be phone calls and website contact forms. You may have some additional options, such as SMS, that you also want to measure.

Then you need to determine your campaigns. Since you are a remodeling company in a single city, you only need a single search campaign unless the company wants to spend most of its budget on kitchen remodeling and a little bit of its budget on the other rooms. To keep it simple, this example assumes they want leads for any remodeling job and not for specific rooms.

When you think about the sales funnel, you know that users think about remodeling for a while before engaging with a company because they want to see how others have remodeled their rooms, research design ideas, and explore the pricing options from multiple companies. Therefore, you want a remarketing campaign to remind users about your company and persuade them to come back to your site to finally convert. This reminder campaign will be a remarketing campaign.

Since you have two campaigns, you need to split your budget between the two campaigns and set up the appropriate location targeting and pick a bid method. As search is your primary new customer driver and remarketing is a reminder, you will use 90 percent of your budget on search and 10 percent on remarketing. As your goal is to get new customers and you do not have a huge budget, you will use the max conversions bid strategy.

Once these campaigns are created, you need to create ad groups for each campaign. Your remarketing campaign might be simple with a single ad group with a remarketing list and a responsive display ad.

This search campaign will be more complex. At a minimum, you will want to make an ad group for each room in the house that can be remodeled. You will then do keyword research for each ad group and create a responsive search ad for each ad group that talks about remodeling for that specific room.

As you choose your keywords, you want to consider your match types. If you run a small company without a huge budget, you might limit your search term options by using exact and phrase match.

Lastly, you want to create ad extensions. Since you only have two campaigns that have the same goal, getting a user to contact you, you can create account level extensions. Some extensions cannot be created at the account level, so you will create those at the campaign level.

Once you finish building the account, it can be made live so that you are actively advertising across the search and display networks. Once that happens, you need to ensure you are achieving your goals by monitoring your data and making adjustments to your account.

PPC Analysis and Reporting

After you build the account and make it live, you will start to accrue statistics for how well your account is performing. You need to monitor the data to make changes and create reports about how the account is performing for your client or boss. This section turns to the third phase of PPC account management—analysis and reporting.

Monitoring Your Data

You will want to watch, and potentially improve, several common pieces of data in your PPC accounts. While most data stem from the ad or keyword, as you look at higher levels in your account, you will see the aggregate amounts. For instance, each time your ad receives a click, a click is associated with the ad, the keyword that triggered the ad, the ad group that contains that ad, and the campaign that contains that ad group. This makes it easy to take a high-level look at your data at the account or campaign level and then drill down into ad groups, keywords, and ads to the data associated with just that level of the account.

The next sections look at the most common data that are analyzed.

Click-Through Rate   Each time your ad is displayed, it receives an impression. When the ad is clicked, you will see a click in your account. The ratio of clicks to impressions is known as click-through rate or CTR.

If your ad receives 100 impressions and 5 clicks, you have a CTR of 5 percent: 5 clicks / 100 impressions = 5% CTR.

This metric is used to see how often your ad is being clicked. To improve your CTR, you must ensure that your ads are relevant to the keywords in the ad group and test the ads.

Conversion Rate   Each time a user clicks on your ad, visits your site, and takes one of your desired actions, you receive a conversion. The ratio of clicks to conversions is known as the *conversion rate,* often abbreviated as Conv. Rate or CR.

If your ad receives 100 clicks and 3 of them turn into conversions, you have a 3 percent conversion rate (3 conversions / 100 clicks = 3% Conv. Rate).

This metric examines how effective your keyword, ad, and landing page work together to convert a searcher into a customer.

One of the most effective ways of increasing conversion rates is to look at your search terms report. Your search terms report will show you the search terms that users are typing into a search engine that trigger your ads to show. If you see search terms that are not doing well, you can add them as negative keywords to keep your ads from showing on those terms.

You can examine your ads to make sure they are appealing to the correct types of people and test ads to see which ones get higher conversion rates. Last, another common way of increasing conversion rates is to try new landing pages or test landing pages to see which ones users are more likely to convert after visiting.

Conversion Data   The numbers that most executives focus on have to do with conversions, as that is the ultimate account goal. The total number of conversions is useful for reporting along with the costs and revenue of those conversions.

For lead generation sites, you are often focused on the CPA or cost per conversion. This is how much you spent in advertising compared to the number of conversions you received.

If you spent $1,000 in ad clicks and received 25 conversions, then each conversion cost you $40. CPA = the cost of ads / conversions. $1,000 ad spend / 25 conversions = $40 CPA.

Ecommerce companies are focused on ROAS or return on ad spend. If your ad cost was $1,000 and turned into $3,500 in revenue, your ROAS is 350 percent. ROAS = (revenue / cost) × 100 and expressed in a percentage: $3,500 revenue / $1,000 ad spend = 3.5; 3.5 × 100 = 350. When expressed as a percentage, this is 350 percent. On occasion, you will find that some people do not express this as a percentage and will have a ROAS number of 3.5 instead of 350 percent. These mean the same thing.

Increasing total conversions comes from increasing your conversion rates or increasing the total number of clicks you receive by either adding new keywords or increasing your click-through rates, assuming your conversion rate for these new clicks stays the same.

Increasing ROAS or decreasing CPA means either increasing your conversion rates or lowering how much you spent per click, which is composed of your bid and your quality score.

Quality Score   Your quality score is based on how good of an experience the search engines think a user will have with your ad and website based on the keyword being used. Three factors are associated with quality score. Each of these factors is given a rating of above average, average, or below average.

- The first factor in quality score is your expected CTR. This factor is based on how good of a CTR you are expected to achieve for a keyword. Increasing your CTR can improve this quality score factor.
- The second factor is ad relevance. This is an examination of your ad to keyword's relevance. If you see below-average ad relevance, it means the ad is not working well for that keyword. You can either adjust the lines used in your ad or move a keyword to a new ad group and write a more specific ad for that keyword.

- The last factor is your landing page experience. This factor is based on your site's speed and relevance to the user. If you make your site load faster, it can help increase your landing page experience. In addition, you can adjust the content of a web page to ensure it is related to the keyword and the ad so users can find the information they are seeking.

Improving any of these quality score factors can increase your quality scores, which can raise your ad position (where you are displayed in the search results) or lower your CPC. If your CPC decreases, your CPA should also decrease.

Click Fraud   Not all clicks are performed by searchers seeking information. There are nefarious bots and people who try to click on your ads so they can make money in the process by serving these ads or so you run out of budget, causing your ads to stop running.

The search engines have many click fraud mechanisms in place to stop this type of behavior. However, they might not catch every fraudulent click. If you suspect this behavior is happening, you can use third-party software or look deep into your web analytics and even server data to find patterns that you can turn over to a search engine for them to investigate.

While click fraud is not a huge issue these days and the search engines do automatic refunds on these clicks, it is worth noting in case you come across some anomalous data and want to further investigate this possibility so you can get a refund on your ad costs.

Testing Ads and Landing Pages

Testing is an essential part of PPC management. If you have three ideas for ads, which one gives you the best result? If you have two pages where you can send traffic for a keyword, which one converts the best? These are the types of questions that testing can give you.

Within an ad group, you can have three active responsive search ads. That means you can create multiple ads in an ad group to see which one gives you the best results. When you are testing in an ad group, this is usually called *single ad* group testing or *A/B testing*. If you create three ads in an ad group to test three different ad ideas, it is generally still called A/B testing.

You can also test themes across ad groups. If you want to know if your ads should show discounts or prices, you might not want to know that for just one ad group, but for many ad groups. In those cases, this is known as *multi-ad group testing,* as you are including multiple ad groups in your tests. It's also called *theme testing*, as you are testing discounts versus prices as two different themes.

With theme testing, you will set up the test in every ad group you want to include in the theme and then aggregate the ad data across all the ad groups at once. This can often lead to insightful information that your boss and clients are happy to hear when you share it.

Testing landing pages is also a good idea. You can send some traffic from an ad group to one page and the rest of the traffic to a different page. This will allow you to see what landing pages produce the best results.

With testing, one of the key factors is to believe your data. It is better to have too much data and take some time to decide than to decide quickly with little data. Ideally, running a test for one to three sales cycles, the length of time a user goes through the funnel, will give you good data to evaluate. If you are uncertain how long the sales cycle is, you can just run a test for a month and see if you have enough data to achieve statistical significance.

Testing ads and landing pages is a major component of increasing your click-through rate, conversion rate, and quality scores. It is one of the most powerful actions you can take in your account and should be done on a regular basis.

Reporting

You will need to run reports with the search engines for two reasons. The first is for your further analysis to find areas where you might want to make account changes, such as looking at conversion rate trends by day or hour to see if you should use *day parting*. For larger data sets, you might find it easier to compare the information in a spreadsheet program than within the search engine interfaces. The second reason to create reports is to provide your client or boss a summary of the advertising outcomes.

Within the search engines, you can modify the columns you want to evaluate and download. You can even save different column sets so that you can quickly change your views to additional types of data. Figure 3.9 shows how to modify columns in Google Ads.

Once you have adjusted your columns, you can simply adjust any date range for the data and download it to your local computer. If you need more custom exports, you can also filter data, such as only showing keywords that have at least one impression or conversion. This process makes every screen in Google Ads and Microsoft Ads a report.

Predefined Reports

Within the search engines, you can utilize many predefined reports. These types of reports can range from time of day, to competition, conversions, and other types of analysis based on what you need to examine.

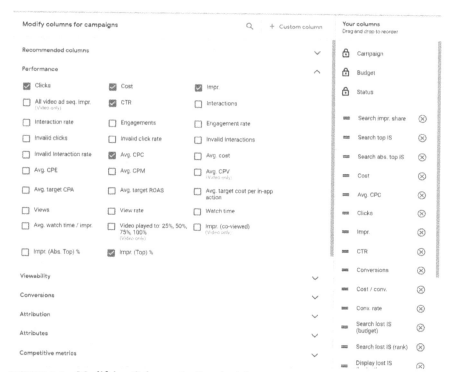

FIGURE 3.9 Modifying Columns in Google Ads

For instance, if you have a physical store, you might want to know your conversion rate based on the distance someone is traveling to reach your store to see if you want to expand or restrict your current radius targeting (see Figure 3.10).

In addition, you can create and save your own reports that use metrics from across your entire account so that you can combine any data points together to see a summary of your data.

In other cases, you might need a dashboard report to give to your boss on a weekly or monthly basis. Dashboard reports often express numbers in charts and graphs so it is easier to comprehend or compare data. You can customize and save your own dashboards and reports in the search engines. Once they are created, you can access and download them as needed to give reports to your clients or boss.

The most common data included in reports are similar to the metrics you want to monitor:

- Impressions, clicks, CTR, cost
- Conversions, conversion rate
- CPA or ROAS

Distance 🖉
Unsaved

Distance from location extensions	↓ Clicks ▼	Impr. ▼	CTR ▼	Avg. CPC ▼	Cost ▼	Conversions ▼	Cost / conv. ▼	Conv. rate ▼
Within 40 miles	27,846	2,760,770	1.01%	$1.69	$46,973.43	1,558.09	$30.15	5.60%
Within 35 miles	27,759	2,758,717	1.01%	$1.69	$46,895.43	1,533.75	$30.58	5.53%
Within 30 miles	27,612	2,751,586	1.00%	$1.69	$46,650.30	1,531.75	$30.46	5.55%
Within 25 miles	27,316	2,732,203	1.00%	$1.69	$46,112.34	1,522.85	$30.28	5.57%
Within 20 miles	26,902	2,706,566	0.99%	$1.68	$45,311.09	1,503.76	$30.13	5.59%
Within 15 miles	25,728	2,609,181	0.99%	$1.68	$43,130.10	1,476.30	$29.21	5.74%
Within 10 miles	20,584	1,979,943	1.04%	$1.67	$34,285.57	1,268.51	$27.03	6.16%
Within 5 miles	8,439	775,178	1.09%	$1.65	$13,922.37	631.55	$22.04	7.48%
Within 1 mile	284	15,100	1.88%	$1.38	$392.20	20.82	$18.84	7.33%
Within 0.7 miles	198	6,478	2.34%	$1.43	$282.51	18.33	$15.41	9.26%
Beyond 40 miles	33	763	4.33%	$0.67	$22.17	7.54	$2.94	22.86%

FIGURE 3.10 Distance Report

Some companies will want this broken down by device, others by network, and others by conversion types. You will want to have a discussion with your client or boss to determine the type of data they want included in a report.

Summary

In a digital world, advertising across the Internet is a fundamental part of every company's marketing process. Most of these companies start with search due to the 3Rs of PPC.

The first R is *relevance*. A search is how users look for answers. By providing ads only on search terms that are related to your business, you can ensure that the ads are relevant to users and your business objectives.

The second R stands for *reach*. The Internet is prevalent across the globe. Google by itself is the most used search engine in the world; when you include other search engines such as Bing, Baidu, Yandex, and others, almost everyone uses a search engine to find information. By just using search marketing, you have an amazing reach across users to show your ads. Once you add in other networks, such as video or display, you can reach users throughout your entire marketing funnel just by using the major PPC platforms.

The last R stands for *ROI* or return on investment. You can measure goals and revenue with search advertising. You can easily change your marketing by adding keywords, making changes to your ads, and performing tests to ensure you are getting a return on your investment. Search is one of the most measurable advertising methods that marketers can employ, and if something is not working, it is highly flexible and easy to change.

When users are searching, they are seeking answers and ready to trust the experts. When your ad is assisting a searcher to find the answer to a question, it is not viewed as an ad, but information that is helping them make an informed decision. By helping searchers find their answers, you can find new customers. They are searching; you just need your ad to be there.

CHAPTER 4

Search Engine Optimization

By Matt Bailey

S earch engines transformed the world. *First of all, they transformed the Internet.* Prior to search engines, you had to go to online directories, find a relevant website in the listings, go to that website, and navigate to the information that you needed. Search engines turned everything upside down by providing a single interface to access relevant information online—based on the words you used to search, called *keywords*.

It seems strange that this was only a few decades ago, and now search is an essential part of daily life. Could you even go a day or two without using a search engine?

Search also transformed business. Now, instead of relying on advertising to influence people to consider your company or organization (outbound marketing), people use search engines, actively looking for providers or destinations when they want them (inbound marketing). It has changed the velocity of business, as people now have the tools to find products, services, businesses, and information when they want them, based on how they describe their need.

Search engines created new industries, opportunities, and growth. With this newfound power, people search and find products from around the world. They find local providers. They can access information in a moment's notice.

Search transformed us. With mobile devices, we now carry the information of the world, available at a moment's notice. We use this power to search for everything. Nearly every decision we make, big or small, is informed by search. We use it to find things near us, from pharmacies to restaurants to entertainment. And having this power has only made us impatient—we demand speed and even faster access and results.

By the end of this chapter, you will know the following:

- What search engine optimization is and why it's important
- How search engines work

- How search results are influenced by location, search history, and other factors
- What keywords are and why they matter
- Why links are critical to good search engine optimization (SEO)
- How website architecture affects SEO
- How technical optimization assists search engines
- How to apply SEO for local or international organizations
- All about search engine algorithms and updates
- How to measure SEO rankings and results

Defining Search Engine Optimization

Search engine optimization (SEO) is the practice of optimizing the code and content of a website to be more accessible to search engines and more relevant to searchers. By creating and developing content that is more relevant to searchers, search engines rank a website higher in the search results. This increases a web page's visibility and potential for gaining visitors from the *search engine results page (SERP)*. In less eloquent terms, you optimize websites to get higher rankings. Why? To increase visits, which will increase business.

One look at the SERP and you'll realize that this is no easy task. There is a lot of competition. And to make matters even more interesting, the results change based on what you are searching for and where you are.

In this example search for a mechanical keyboard shown in Figure 4.1, it provides several different results. First, there are Shopping Ads. These are developed from ecommerce feeds directly into Google for product display.

Next is search engine advertising results. Advertisers create text-based ads that appear based on the search terms entered by the searcher. This is notated by the small "Ad" next to the URL of the result. As you can see, most of the prime space on the results page is advertising.

Next are Top Stories, which come from Google News and highlight recent news stories that are relevant to the search.

Finally, we get to the "organic" results. They are called organic because they are produced by the search engine algorithm without any financial consideration. The algorithm bases the rankings on credibility, authority, relevance, and many other factors. (I'm not sure why people call what is produced by a computer "organic," but it was an early term that stuck.)

Search engine optimization is concerned with influencing the organic results. They are not influenced by paid or human intervention. They are produced by the relevancy calculations of an algorithm, which you can influence but not control.

FIGURE 4.1   Google Search Engine Results Page (SERP) (**www.google.com**)

The Value of SEO

Regardless of the organization, being found for information that is relevant to you increases your credibility, visibility, and visits.

For any business, being found in the results can mean an instant boost in website visits or walk-in traffic, both of which contribute to increased sales or leads. As the world uses search to find information, being found in those searches contributes greatly to a business's profitability.

Being found in the search results is one of the most reliable channels for gaining new customers. SEO is also one of the highest ROI activities that a business can develop because once rankings are attained, they continue to bring in visitors for many years afterward, even years after a long-term SEO campaign is ended.

For many, search engine visitors are the most active and the most qualified visits to the business because they were searching to solve a problem or find information, and when they find the solution, they convert. *Conversion* is the action that fulfills a goal of the website, such as a purchase on an ecommerce website, a registration, subscription, or a completed lead form for a B2B business. When someone searches, they are taking an active step to solve a problem or find information, and they are more likely to complete the task when they find the best result.

Search is an in-the-moment answer to a need or task. People are actively searching, which makes them more qualified, more motivated, and more loyal to the solutions they find. Time and time again, search visitors tend to be the most profitable, most loyal, and produce the highest customer lifetime value compared to other channels. This is from the power of intent, timing, and relevance provided by search engines.

For any business model that relies on being found by searchers with questions or informational needs, search is critical to their operations. Publishers, nonprofits, and content producers all rely on being found for their work and information, making search engines an indispensable part of the world's economy.

How Search Engines Work

To understand how to do search engine optimization, you must first know how search engines work. For starters, when you search, you are not searching the real-time results of live websites. What you actually search is the database, or *index*, of the search engine.

To apply their ranking algorithm to billions of web pages, they must first download these pages to their servers. This retrieval process is carried out through a *spider*, also called a *bot,* or *crawler.* This software program "crawls" the links from page to page. It searches for and follows links and downloads the content of pages.

The search engine creates a map of the linking between pages and websites and the content that is contained on each page. This is where websites are assessed for credibility and authority. It is also where Google changed the game. Prior to Google, search engines ranked websites mainly based on the on-page content and how well the keywords in the content matched the keyword in the search phrase.

Of course, this led to abuse, mainly through the practice of "keyword stuffing," which attempted to place as many keywords on the page as possible to appear more relevant. This also led to a theory called "keyword density," where the keyword should be a certain percentage of the words on a page. The SEO tactics of the 1990s were a wild and word-of-mouth game of reverse engineering the search engine algorithms and competing with other webmasters for the same keywords.

PageRank: Google's Game Changer

Google started as a small search engine that quickly gained attention among SEOs and the tech industry. The results were fast and distinctly relevant compared to other search engines. The difference was that Google did not just evaluate on-page keywords but also relied on its first algorithm, called PageRank. Developed by founders Larry Page and Sergey Brin, PageRank evaluated the links between websites. Not just the link between your site and another site, but also the links to that site and beyond. PageRank changed relevancy by examining the relationships between websites. While it has since been deprecated, it served as the basis for ongoing development and evaluating influence factors.

What PageRank and future algorithms added was a mathematical method of assessing credibility and authority as humans do. When people make decisions, they not only rely on information, but on the credibility of that information. For example, I trust information from friends and family as they hold high influence on my decisions. However, for a medical issue they may have influence, but not expertise and credibility. In that case, I would seek a doctor who has expertise in a specialty, thereby gaining a more credible source.

SEO Is Not an Exact Science

When you search, remember that you are searching pages and information contained in the database, or the *index* of the search engine. This is important because it sets the stage for many of the technical and optimization tasks in SEO. Your efforts in SEO will influence the results, and the more factors that you optimize, the more influence your website may gain in the form of rankings.

However, this is not an exact science. I like to say that SEO is a combination of art, science, and weather forecasting. You can create the ideal conditions for good rankings and a great user experience, but that work never guarantees results.

SEO's Three Primary Areas

SEO is made up of three primary areas: content, links, and structure, as shown in Figure 4.2.

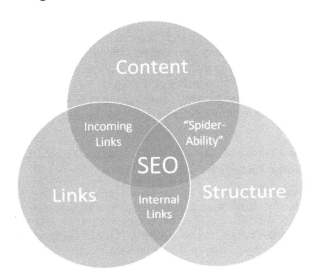

FIGURE 4.2   Three Elements of Search Engine Optimization

Content   Content is the information that people see on the page. This is where on-page SEO tactics, such as keyword optimization, HTML mark-up, and content structure, take place. The content that you publish on your website will also drive the incoming links from other websites, as people link to content that they like, trust, and recommend.

Links   Links are the primary navigational device. External links from other websites make your site more visible and provide credibility. Incoming links from other websites are one of the most important factors for increasing your rankings. Internal links are helpful for website visitors because they direct people to the information they need. Your navigation is the backbone of your website's information, enabling people and search engines to navigate the pages of content.

Structure   The structure, or architecture, of the website focuses on how the website is built, such as the organization of the content, the hierarchy of the content structure, the programming code, and server settings that make the website fast, accessible, and "spiderable" by search engines. *Spiderable* or *spiderability* is the how accessible and crawlable your website is for the search engine spiders.

These three areas, working in concert with each other, create the ideal conditions for search engines to find, assess, and rank your website. Optimizing a website involves each of these three areas. However, many times the tactics that you need to work on aren't clear. Experience is a wise teacher in SEO, as you develop a combination of an artist's eye, a scientists' framework, and a weatherperson's ability to predict the weather (and still get it wrong).

Keyword Research: How Do You Describe a Need?

What fascinates me about SEO is the study of keywords and how people describe their intent. Having a background in journalism, sales, and marketing, I was amazed to see this kind of information available. I have run surveys, focus groups, opinion polls, and user testing, which all provided good information, but they each have their failings. Believe it or not, people are not completely honest. They can be swayed by the pollster and others in the group, and some would rather keep their real opinions to themselves.

As Seth Stephens-Davidowitz (2017) writes in his book, *Everybody Lies*, "A major reason that Google searches are so valuable is not that there are so many of them; it is that people are so honest in them. People lie to friends, lovers, doctors, surveys, and themselves. . .. The power in Google data is that people tell the giant search engine things they might not tell anyone else."

Keywords provide a unique insight to the searcher's mind that other research methods aren't able to capture. Search keywords are in-the-moment steam of consciousness. Searches for urgent problem-solving solutions will provide much more insight as you see motivating factors, urgency, priorities, and time frames.

A great example of this is dog obedience training. Typically, people will search for dog obedience training as a keyword, but these are people who have a plan and are researching options. Comparatively, consider the urgency when people search for "how to stop my dog from jumping on people" or "stop my dog from barking at night" and other behavior problems. These types of searches expose real issues and problems where people are not only looking for solutions, but they are experiencing the pain point that will motivate them to act!

This is the beauty of keywords.

The Importance of Keyword Research

The value of this research is to first understand your audience and what they need. By using the same words they search for in search engines within the content of your website, you increase your relevance, which increases your visibility in the search results. Reflecting the same words, concepts, and ideas as the searchers on your pages increases the likelihood that they will find you.

Words   The first level of research is simply finding the words and phrases that your audience or customers use when searching for a solution or idea. In the early days of SEO, this was the biggest problem, as companies would create beautiful websites and add their corporate content. However, they would leave out the content that described their products and how those products solved problems. Instead, you would find generic corporatized phrases such as "enterprise application solutions" without any explanation of what the actual product or service was. If the words your customers used were not on the website, you would not be found.

My rule is to simply call things what they are.

Intent   Learning the needs of industry provides a depth of intent. For example, if I am selling car insurance, I can compare the number of searches for teen driver insurance to classic car insurance. I can determine a likely market size and learn the specific nuances of each group. These are two different groups—teen drivers and classic car owners—each with different needs, expectations, and budgets. Learning how they describe their needs enables you to create better content that matches the intent of each type of search.

Problems/Solutions   The next thing you learn from keywords is how their audience uses those works within context. People search when they need to find information, usually to make decisions. When people start using precise words and highly descriptive situations, you can learn the context of those searches and learn more about your audience. The more you relate your content to their needs, the more you enhance your rankings and conversions.

These additional words provide amazing insight into the thinking process, external factors, timing, location, and hundreds of other factors that make up the search phrase typed into a search engine. Learning the contextual words and how they affect or influence the search provides you with a unique insight into the mind of the searcher.

Buying Cycles   When learning the words people use, you quickly find that there may be a buying cycle (or a decision cycle) based on the types of words that are used and the depth of explanations. Typically, early in the buying cycle there are many *short-tail keywords*. Short-tail keywords are one- to two-word keywords or phrases that are very general. An example of this is a search for "cars." As a single word, it defines a very broad category, yet it contains no clues as to the need, intent, or nature of the search. The searcher could be shopping for cars or looking for pictures of cars. You do not know, but these searches are typically at the beginning of a decision cycle and will be refined as the searcher realizes that the results do not provide the information they need. While short-tail keywords tend to be the more popular, they are also more general and do not produce many conversions, if any.

However, when the searcher starts using *long-tail keywords*, which are phrases of four, five, or more words, you can begin to see defined intent and contextual signals. Toward the end of the decision cycle, searchers are looking for more detail and have specific questions. These keyword phrases are full of descriptive factors and attributes, providing rich feedback on the needs of the searcher. Long-tail searches are typically at the end of the decision cycle, so when searchers find exactly what they want, they tend to convert at a very high rate.

Trends   Depending on the industry, people search for things that may have dramatic shifts throughout the year. In addition, the words used in the searches may change in different seasons. In a research project in the hiking industry, I found that "hiking survival" was a popular term all year. "Hiking destinations" were researched in the winter months. Hikers usually researched and purchased equipment in the early spring before their outdoor adventures. But it wasn't always the hikers themselves. In October, November, and December, "hiking gifts" increased. What I found is that these searchers were usually friends or family members who want to get a gift for a hiker.

As you can see, you learn much more than a simple keyword.

Researching Keywords

Keyword research tools are prevalent online, and there are many choices. You can start as simple as talking to customers or subscribing to keyword research tools and SEO management software. Most SEO tools and software offer free trials but require a subscription to access multiple languages and full features.

Customer Research   First, interview your customers and talk to your salespeople. What problems did you solve? How do customers explain or describe your product, service, or solution? Look through emails, correspondence, call logs, and your interactions with the public to find the words they use.

Seed List   Starting with these words enables you to develop a seed list. These are the dozen or so words that you start with that describe your business. Now if you have a large ecommerce website, you have most of this ready to go with product names and descriptions. You'll take this list and use it to start your keywords research in multiple tools.

Keyword Research Tools There are multiple places online to get a sense of how people search and the words they use. **AnswerthePublic.com** (see Figure 4.3) is a great place to start. By adding a keyword, you'll find how people search and the questions they ask.

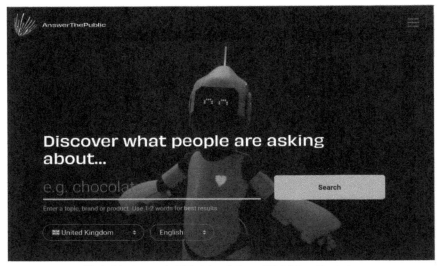

FIGURE 4.3 Answer the Public (**www.answerthepublic.com**)

Answer the public is a great resource because it focuses on keywords within the context of questions. This is important because of the growth in *voice search*. People are using Siri, Alexa, and other voice-activated assistance to search for information audibly. When people use these technologies, they are asking questions rather than using a few choice keywords, as they would if typing into the search bar. As a result, the questions are more specific, contain ideal keywords, and provide greater context and insight into the motivation of the searcher.

There are also dedicated keyword research tools such as **Wordtracker.com** (see Figure 4.4). When searching for keywords in Wordtracker, you'll see related keywords listed in order of volume, or popularity. This is the estimated amount that the word has been searched on in the past 12 months. You can also see a trend chart that shows the change in demand throughout the year.

These tools also provide calculations on the difficulty rating to rank for these words and the competition level. They allow you to research entire industries, create keyword projects, and explore your niche. Keywords are not just limited to Google. You can explore the keywords used at YouTube, Amazon, and eBay.

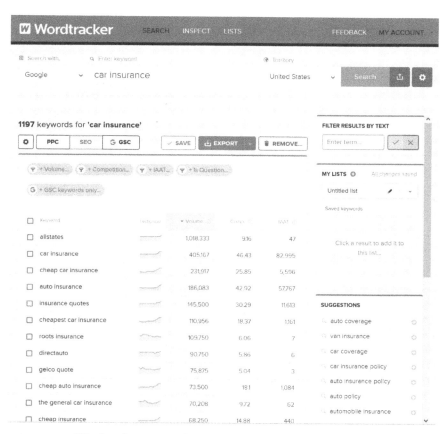

FIGURE 4.4 Wordtracker Keyword Research Tool (**www.Wordtracker.com**)

SEO Software   Another source of keyword data is from a full-suite SEO Software tool. SERanking, Ahrefs, SEMRush, Moz, Majestic, and Serpstat are the main tools used by the SEO industry.

In the example from SERanking in Figure 4.5, I am researching the keyword "car insurance" and can gain a significant amount of information. I can immediately see the difficulty score, estimated search volume, cost-per-click (CPC), related keywords, websites that are ranking for that term, and the volatility of the top 10 rankings.

SEO software provides in-depth keyword research tools and position tracking in the search engines. They will track your performance and that of your competitors. Some will also provide in-depth competitive analysis that will report the keywords used by your competitors in SEO and paid search.

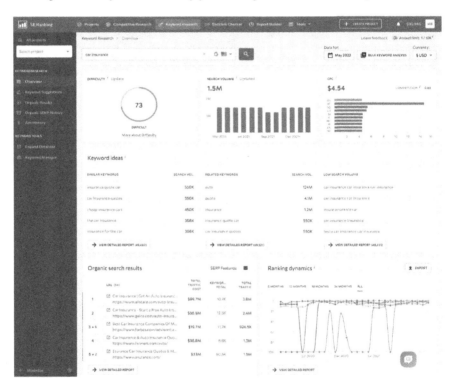

FIGURE 4.5   SERanking, SEO Management Software (**www.seranking.com**)

Caution

At this point, it is important to take a moment and explain a few important factors to know when researching, analyzing, and reporting keyword counts and ranking reports.

- **The keyword counts from any tool are just estimates based on limited data.** Regardless of where you get your keyword research data, all search volumes are estimated—Google does not share much data. The data that are shared are merged with other limited data sources and extrapolated through an algorithm. You are not seeing real traffic numbers!

- **Rankings reports are not reliable.** The rankings reported in any of these tools are based on an application programming interface (API) into the search engine. This means that the ranking reports are from a database set up specifically for ranking queries. What you see could be very different, as rankings are influenced by the location of the searcher and their search history. Two searchers in the same place could see variations in the ranking results. The results that are reported are a generic result and should mainly be used as an indicator of influence on the results.

Google Trends   This research tool (see Figure 4.6) provided by Google is an insight into Google search data, without revealing actual keyword counts. All comparisons are relative and provided on an index of 0–100, which bears no relation to the actual keyword demand—just the relationship among the keywords you are exploring.

While estimated search counts can be greatly out of proportion in SEO tools, I use Google Trends to compare keywords and get a comparison from the search giant itself.

For example, in comparing my "teen driver insurance" to "classic car insurance," I can see the difference in demand specifically in Google.

"Classic car insurance" is searched for three times as much as "teen driver insurance." However, you can also see that I added "vintage car insurance," which came up in the research as well, to compare "classic" to "vintage." This helps me understand and verify the word choices and explore other descriptive adjectives to use in my marketing content. Just because the word "vintage" isn't as popular doesn't mean I should exclude it from my use in optimization. It should be integrated to provide additional contextual content that is relevant to a potential customer.

Interestingly, Google Trends also provides a map to show where the highest percentages of searches are done, compared to the population of a state, country, or region. In this example, the darker states are those that have higher concentrations of searches as a representation of the population. This can be used when targeting geographically based audiences in paid campaigns.

Implementing Keywords into On-Page Optimization

I've noticed an interesting trend in SEO courses. Instructors and videos teach about the importance of keywords but then leave out one of the most important factors, which is also one of the most asked questions, "How do I integrate keywords into the page content?"

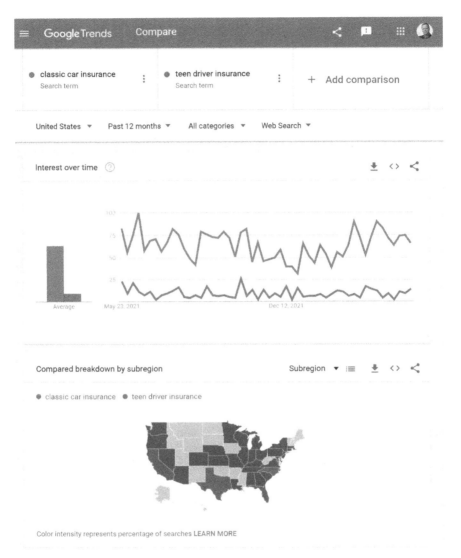

FIGURE 4.6　Google Trends (car insurance) (**Trends.Google.com**)

Let's start by looking back at the search results because this provides a clear place to start.

In the search results, every website looks basically the same. This is because the results are coming from the search index, and information from the page is being used to create the "snippet." The search results take elements from the pages and display them in a uniform context.

For the search "What do sea turtles eat?" I find the results shown in Figure 4.7.

What do sea turtles naturally eat?

- Loggerhead: Hatchlings are omnivores (meaning they eat both animals and plants) but adults are carnivores, favoring crabs, whelks, and conchs.
- Green: Fully grown sea turtles are herbivores and like to hang around coral reefs to scrape off seagrass and algae.

More items...

https://www.worldwildlife.org › stories › what-do-sea-turtl...   ⋮

What do sea turtles eat? Unfortunately, plastic bags. - World ...

ⓘ About featured snippets • ▣ Feedback

People also ask ⋮

Do sea turtles eat jellyfish?   ⌄

What are 5 things sea turtles eat?   ⌄

What are three things sea turtles eat?   ⌄

Feedback

https://www.seeturtles.org › sea-turtle-diet   ⋮

Sea Turtle Diet — SEE Turtles

What a **sea** turtle **eats** depends upon the species. Some are omnivores, **eating** a variety of plants and animals, while the hawksbill and the leatherback are ...

https://seaturtlespacecoast.org › what-do-sea-turtles-eat   ⋮

What do sea turtles eat?

Mar 23, 2021 — **What do sea turtles eat**? ; Green: algae, seagrasses, and seaweed ; Leatherback: jellies and other soft-bodied invertebrates like tunicates and sea ...

https://oliveridleyproject.org › FAQs › Sea Turtles FAQ   ⋮

What do sea turtles eat? | Olive Ridley Project

Feb 5, 2022 — Olive ridleys are omnivorous, mostly **eating** jellyfish, snails, crabs, and shrimp but they will occasionally **eat** algae and seaweed as well. Read ...

FIGURE 4.7   Google SERP (**www.google.com**)

Even though there are four sites listed in the results, they look the same. The *snippet* is made up of three primary page elements. (The dates listed are the date that the page or article was published.)

At the top is the *URL*, the uniform resource locator, or the address where the page is located online.

Next is the *Page Title*, and it is easy to identify because it is blue and in a larger typeface.

Finally, the *description* is pulled either from the text on the page or from the meta-description tag in the page's code. The description provides additional context to help searchers evaluate their choices.

When looking at the page shown in Figure 4.8, the Page Title is viewable in the tab. The Page URL is in the address bar.

Farther down in the page, you'll find that the content appears in the SERP description in the expanded listing. The expanded listing is when the search engine pulls additional content into the first result, such as information, products, additional pages or page links, reviews, or other types of content.

Step 1: Optimize SERP Factors   The search engine results page is the first thing that potential visitors will see about your website. This is where you present your best information and persuade them to click! The most important element is the Page Title. It is presented in the SERP in big, blue letters, and is most likely the only thing that people will read! Focus your attention on creating a highly descriptive sentence or phrase that answers a searcher's questions.

There are many options here, but it is best to keep the title around 50–60 characters (including spaces). You can create longer page titles, but the entire title may not be seen by searchers on mobile devices. It is a matter of preference, and there is no specific standard. The most important thing is what the searcher will see and how it will persuade them to click your result.

Next, use a keyword in the page title. I recommend that it be used in the context of the information. I have seen websites simply repeat the keyword and related phrases in the page title. This is a clear attempt to boost rankings. Similarly, others may recommend adding keywords separated by hyphens or bars. From my experience, I like a short, clear title in a sentence format that simply explains the content of the page. This method is the most contextually relevant and the easiest for a human to read.

Next, the URL should provide a description of the content, but also reflect the organization of the website, as in this example URL:

```
https://www.worldwildlife.org/stories/what-do-sea-turtles-
eat-unfortunately-plastic-bags
```

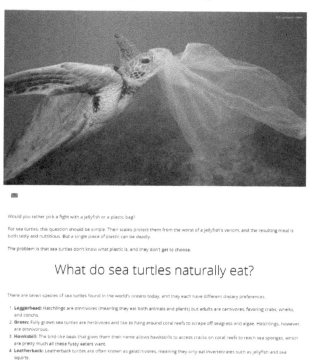

FIGURE 4.8   Page Structure and Elements of **worldwildlife.org (www.worldwild life.org/stories/what-do-sea-turtles-eat-unfortunately-plastic-bags)**

You can see that the article is located in the "Stories." The article heading is being used in the URL. Many times, this is the default setting for many websites and blogs. Each word of the title is used and separated by a hyphen. At one time, many SEO professionals would have cautioned against the use of so many hyphens in the URL, but now it is so commonplace because of the default publishing settings on content management systems (CMS), such as WordPress and Wix.

Finally, the description. In this case, the content is being pulled from the page. You can use a *meta-description* to provide a more in-depth description of the content of the page, and the search engines may use this, but not always. The key is that you can use this to provide more information to the searcher, as the content in the meta-description code does not affect rankings.

Step 2: Page Structure Now, examine the structure of a page. The content on the page will be read by humans and search engine bots. How will you communicate which content on the page is most important? This is done through markup. This is also where my journalism background prepared me for SEO.

The most important element on the page is the *headline.* In HTML markup, this is denoted by an H1 tag.

```
<H1> Place headline here</H1>
```

Like a newspaper, the headline is the largest text on the page. It is larger, bolder, and more contrasting to the background, enabling people to read it quickly and gain a summary of the content. Then, the content on the page should be organized into subtopics and displayed in a readable format. People avoid large paragraphs of text, so you can make reading easier by breaking up the content into smaller sections and headings that make it easier to scan. You do this through additional markup.

Subheadings are used to provide content organization and structure, and they are denoted by H2, H3, H4, etc. Links to additional resources are typically blue and sometimes underlined (links should look like links). Using bullet points increases the readability of the document, and bolding important words will grab the reader's attention. Writing impactful, descriptive sentences as subheadings, paragraph headings, captions, bullet points, and page links engage the readers and allow them to quickly scan the content and locate important information.

For the search engine, they need the markup to inform the context. Without markup, all text appears the same in the code. Using markup shows the search engine which content is the most important, such as headlines, headings, bold text, and more. When you place keywords in the headings using markup, you are showing the search engines the importance of these key concepts.

Here's the dual purpose of SEO: by making the content easier to read for humans, you are optimizing the content for search engines! See Figure 4.9.

Step 3: Other On-Page Optimization There are many other areas of on-page content that can be optimized. The key here is that you are not simply stuffing keywords into the content anywhere you can. Rather, you are creating a highly contextual development of content.

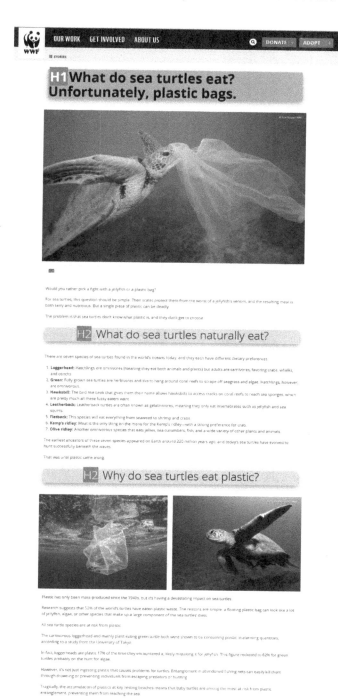

FIGURE 4.9   HTML Markup Showing Headings (**https://www.worldwildlife.org/ stories/what-do-sea-turtles-eat-unfortunately-plastic-bags**)

Content   You should also be using alternative versions of words such as synonyms, phrases, and contextualized descriptions. As an example, if you were creating a page about the sport of Cricket, you would employ many of the terms used in the sport, such as bowl, inning, wicket, batting, bowling, batsman, boundary, century, dismissal, fielder, and googly, to name a few. In creating this article, you wouldn't simply repeat the word *cricket* over and over. Instead, you would make it easy to read and understand by employing synonyms and descriptions that flow naturally for the reader.

This is the purpose of the context and using a full vocabulary of descriptions. Your keyword research should provide many of the additional concepts and related terms, and here is where you employ this variety to provide the most comprehensive and descriptive content.

Journalists often write in the inverse pyramid format, meaning that the pyramid is flipped and larger at the top. This style focuses the most important information at the top of the page or article, and the least important details toward the bottom of the page. It helps readers gain the important information quickly, but also provides the necessary details to those who reach the end of the article.

Alt Attributes   The images used in your pages need to be optimized not just for search engines, but for accessibility. Many visitors to your page may not see the images. Some people browse with images off, some use screen readers to access content, and others may only have low bandwidth connections that are unable to load high-resolution images. In these cases, the images may not appear on the page. For cases like these, two important attributes are used in the image code.

First is the *alt attribute*, which is the description of the image, such as what it contains or displays. Search engines rely on the alt attribute element to understand the content of the pages. The second image attribute is the *title attribute*, which is used as is the formal caption or title of the image.

File Names   Next, consider the filenames of all elements on the page—the page filename, images, videos, documents, PDFs, and other elements. For example, an image filename will carry a code; depending on the source, such as a stock photo or one taken with a camera, it may look like DSC1113338.jpg. A few seconds of optimization changes the image filename to explain the image using a keyword within a descriptive phrase.

Consider this when adding pages or blog posts to your website, as the page name will appear in the URL. When searchers see the keyword in the URL, it adds to their evaluation of relevance and can increase your click-through rate.

Microformats or Schema   Schema is an accepted data format that is understood and handled universally across search engines, browsers, devices, and operating systems. For example, an address schema (see Figure 4.10) is understood as an address in the search engine, the browser, apps, and operating systems. This enables users to see an address on a website while using their mobiles and be able to click the address, have it open in maps, and get directions.

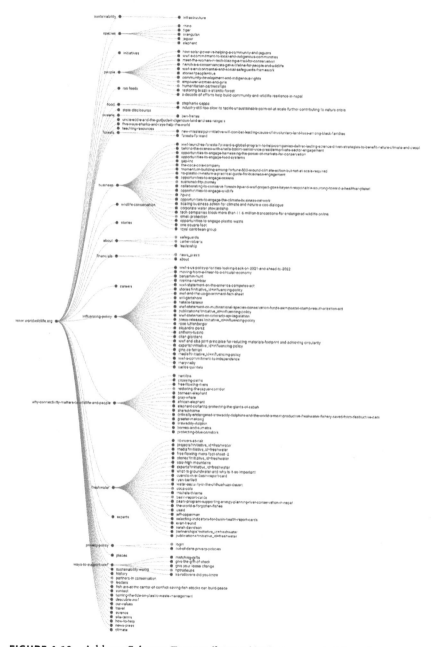

FIGURE 4.10   Address Schema Format (**https://schema.org/address**)

The coordination among different systems universally recognizes the format, function, and content of the markup. Google suggests the use of schema as much as possible to make it easy for crawlers and systems to easily identify, classify, and republish this information. Author pages and articles can benefit greatly from very simple HTML markup and schema techniques. These properties can be used for contacts, reviews, events, authors, locations, articles, and many other common features of websites. References for types of data and their formats can be found at **Schema.org**.

Interlinking Pages   While visitors may be at your page to seek information or answers, you can further assist them by providing them links to related articles, videos, or content that might be important. Using links in the content or as an additional sidebar providing contextually related information can help visitors dig deeper into your content. They also develop strong interlinking structures on your website to enhance the contextual structure and broaden keyword relevance.

Linking to other websites enhances your credibility. Creating an original article based on research, quoting authoritative articles or research, and linking to your sources can boost your own site's relevance. This is called *content curation*. By developing content that builds or centralizes relevant information and providing a link to those sources, it can increase your own authority on a topic.

In the sea turtle example, the World Wildlife website was first in the results for the topic of sea turtles and what they eat. Yet this page has numerous outgoing links to highly relevant research, studies, and news articles on the same topic.

Building Credibility with Links

The second factor in SEO is the *link*. The links coming into your website are indicators of your credibility and trust. When a website links to your website, it is because they are recommending your content, citing you as a source, or providing your information to their audience. Really, just think of the last time you linked to something. It probably served some purpose of recommending content to others.

Links serve many purposes because they are the fundamental building blocks of the Internet. WWW stands for "World Wide Web," which refers to the web of links that connect everything online. For starters, links make your website discoverable. While you can submit a new website to Google, Google also states that they prefer to find a website through their spiders and having links to your website enables this to happen. Second, links give you credibility. When someone links to you, it is because they are recommending something relevant. Third, links provide visitors. When links to your site are in the content of another site, people click on those links and are immediately transported to your page!

Links Replicate Human Judgement

Before using links, search engines relied on the content of the page to deter-mine relevance. As mentioned, Google changed this with the PageRank algorithm, which employed links to determine relevance when choosing from hundreds or even millions of similar pages. Using an external factor that is largely out of direct control of a website owner meant that a better assessment of influence and credibility could be established.

Similarly, when you make decisions about companies or people that you will work with, you rely on external factors to inform your decision, such as ratings and reviews, recommendations from friends or family, consumer information, news, and other sources that help formulate an opinion. In this same way, links provide that external judgment factor. People don't link to every website; they link to ones that they recommend, so it creates a level of trust.

Gaining Links Is About Quality, not Quantity

Of course, when the SEO world learned about links, it started a free-for-all. Websites were doing anything to increase the number of links coming from anywhere, simply to boost their incoming link numbers. However, it doesn't work that way. One quality link is worth more than millions of low-quality links. But first, you must be able to define a quality link!

Popularity   A link from a popular website is one of the desirable factors. A recognizable website that is visited often can provide a great boost when a link is made. Gaining a link on a popular site may also provide a branding benefit, as people will see the link mentioned in the content and could also result in visitors coming from that link! News and information sites are excel-lent examples of popular links from credible, established, and popular sites.

Relevance   The second factor in measuring links is the relevance of the linking website. For example, is the site that is linking to your site related in some way? A news site can provide a great link, but an industry-related website can provide a highly relevant link. Contextually, they provide content and information within a specific subject matter and can be seen as more authoritative because of the depth of content. Gaining a link from this source enhances your credibility by being associated in the same industry.

Influence   It is not simply the link from one site to your site. Linking algorithms measure the influence of websites beyond the first level of links. They evaluate the links of the site that is linking to the site that is linking to you—and beyond! Evaluating the extended link networks, they find the sites that may not be the most popular, or the most relevant, but the most influential. These indirect clusters of influence impact the amount of credibility and authority attributed to your site.

Link Structure

There are many methods of creating a link, and some provide more relevance than others for both search engines and humans.

First, here is a basic link as seen on a page and the associated HTML instructions to create the link:

```
Link: http://example.com/links/
Link as written in HTML <a href=http://example.com/
links/></a>
```

The <a> tag defines a hyperlink. *Href* specifies the URL, which follows. The </a> tag closes the hyperlink instructions.

Next, you can make the link more interesting. Instead of publishing the URL of the link, you can use anchor text. By making it more interesting, you are also increasing the relevance of the link because you've made it more friendly to humans by using text, words, and yes, keywords!

For example, I'm sure that you've seen links that say, "Click here." However, those don't have any keywords, and they aren't that helpful. Instead, use anchor text that describes what the visitors will find, receive, or see when they click the link.

```
Link: Best Math Games for kids
HTML:   <a href="http://example.com/mathgames">Best Math Games
for kids</a>
```

By placing text between the brackets and describing the link, you create a higher level of relevance of the link. This anchor text increases the relevance because it makes a more readable presentation, especially if the link is contained within content.

An image link is a bit more complex because it needs to link to the source of the image and the destination of the link and to provide alternative text in case the image is not visible.

```
<a href="http://example.com/mathgames"><img src="/images/
img_math.png" width="120" height="80" alt="math games
website"/></a>
```

The website still gets credit for the link, even though the link is an image. The alternative text (or alt text) provides the context and description of the link.

Link Attributes

Attributes have been added to links over the years to combat link spam. *Link spam* became a problem alongside the popularity of blogs. Blogging software allowed people to leave comments, along with a link to their website, which was great when people would leave legitimate comments and conversation. It was not so great when people and bots posted links to their affiliated pharmaceutical site. This became a significant problem as automated bots left thousands of comments on blogs, attempting to spam the comments with links.

In 2005, Google created the rel=nofollow link attribute to identify untrusted links. (The rel attribute is short for relationship, which discloses the relationships of the link between two websites.) Soon, the nofollow attribute was used as the default link method in nearly all social media and blogging software. The rel=nofollow attribute means that Google will not assign any influence or credit from your site to the linked site. It isn't a negative signal, but simply that you do not trust the source.

```
<a href="https://example.com" rel="nofollow></a>
```

The second attribute expanded on the nofollow link, as some SEO practitioners attempted to create false relevance by purchasing links on other websites. By purchasing links from a relevant website, they could artificially increase their relevance. However, any time a link is exchanged for money, Google considers the link to be paid advertising. This means that the paid link should be attributed differently from an "organic" or editorial link.

For a paid or sponsored link, rel=sponsored is the preferred method of providing this attribution.

```
<a href="https://example.com" rel="sponsored">anchortext</a>
```

Building Links

To build high-quality links to your site, there are a few things to avoid. First are link exchanges, which is simply exchanging your link on another site for their link to be placed on your site. There are times where this may be acceptable, such as a local network or related industry. However, as a regular practice it will gain little and may send your customers to other places!

Avoid any link-building tactics or link-building offers that are automated. Of course, some software sends out millions of emails with link-building efforts, and many people will sell link-building services. If I can see that the service or the offer are automated, I recommend deleting the offer and moving on. I can't stress enough how dangerous it is to use an automated software to build links.

Avoid buying links on other websites without using the rel=nofollow or rel=sponsored link. Purchasing links for the purpose of increasing rankings can get you caught up in a quality update and possibly demote your site in the rankings.

Avoid any offers of developing hundreds or thousands of backlinks. Remember, this is a quality game, not a quantity. One great link is worth more than thousands of low-quality links. This leads to the downside or the risk of responding to low-quality offers or participating in link-building schemes. The downside is a penalization of your website, which can reduce your rankings and visibility. Or, at worst, being de-listed from the search results completely. Once this happens, you can recover, but not without a lot of work to clean up and regain your reputation!

Another popular technique is *guest blogging*, which has its advantages and disadvantages. It's been abused over the years and has created some penalties. I personally do not like this form of link building, as people offer to write for your website or blog to get a link from your website. However, if you pay them for the article, the link needs to be attributed as a sponsored link!

As an opinion, I simply find guest blogging offers to be off-target and mass marketed. I see too many offers going to businesses, agencies, and other companies, simply because they have an established blog with a high trust factor. Guest blogging pitches typically do not present a relevant offer that shows their value, or why my readers would even care. In addition, most guest bloggers attempt to get as many links back to their site in a single article as they can. To me, writing for a media site and gaining an author link is going to carry more weight and provide better return than pursuing hundreds or thousands of blogs. As I mentioned, this is only my opinion, and you'll easily find people who disagree with my assessment, but that's the beauty of SEO. You don't have to do everything, just the things that are the most effective and the things that work for you and fit your approach.

Verify Your Name, Address, Phone, and URL   One of the first link-building methods is to search for websites that mention or list your business or organization on their page. First, verify that your business or organization's name, address, phone number, and website URL are accurate. Second, ensure that they are consistent! These primary fields need to be consistently formatted across every listing, entry, mention, and directory. This includes your website URL. Inconsistency in the business name, the address, or the URL may cause search engines to create duplicate entries or confusion about which version is the actual one. Machines may not process the different formats as a human would understand them.

Once you've verified that the information is accurate and consistent, then see if there is a link. If your business is listed, but it does not contain a link, ask for one. You may have to complete a form or contact the website manager. These are typically the easiest links to gain and provide a good foundation.

Directories and Associations   The next level of links focuses on Internet directories, industry directories, business listings, and local associations. These are benefits of joining organizations or finding industry resources. In the early days of SEO, directory links were the primary place to start, and I still find them to be an overlooked method of establishing a good link base. Search for relevant directories and ask any membership organizations if they publish a directory of members. Many times, the link and listing are a benefit of this membership.

Prospecting Competitor Links   This is where SEO software tools became valuable. You can use these tools to track your competitors and see the websites that are linking to them. I like to look for the links from articles or resources that are publishing lists of vendors or businesses. These are easy to get into, and many times there is a link to the author of the article where you can approach and ask for inclusion in the page or in the next article. Sometimes, this tactic simply uncovers many links that you can't replicate, such as a media link where the story is specifically about that business.

Prospecting Podcasters   One place that is growing in popularity is to be a guest on a podcast, or even start your own! Podcasters create pages on their website for each show and link to the guest's website. The podcast also promotes the guest interview through email and social media. In response, guests will also reach out to their audience and promote their interview on the podcast. Multiple links are developed and created based on one event, which benefits all involved.

Create Amazing Content   I'll admit, it sounds like I am jumping ahead here. But this is what drives most high-quality links! Original content such as research, studies, analysis, articles, stories, and videos naturally attract attention and people link to them, curate them, and republish them. I work with a company that specializes in developing original research. They partner with companies in a specific industry and use the content to attract leads by registering to access the research. They also find many media and industry influencers who will use the research to create articles and additional content, which provide links back to the original source.

Digital Public Relations Finally, I have found the most effective method of develop high-quality, popular, and relevant links is to develop a public relations (PR) campaign. Using press releases, compelling stories that are developing with video and images, and a clear pitch is an effective method of gaining links in news search, search results, media sites, industry news, and beyond.

This method takes work, as you develop an appropriate pitch to take your story to reporters, editors, podcasters, bloggers, and others. The pitch is what attracts attention and makes the case to publish your article, information, research, or story to the wide world. However, the work is worth it, as a great PR campaign can create valuable links, gain immediate visibility in search and news results, increase visits, and make a significant economic impact.

The Pitch The pitch is how you approach others to persuade them to act, in this case, to include a link to your site through any of these means. Remember that no one is under any obligation to give you a link! It is on you and your ability to present a compelling reason to publish your article or to give you a link. How you approach and ask for this largely determines if it is read and considered or deleted without a thought.

Your pitch should first show familiarity with the person or source that you are approaching. Have you read their material? Find a unique perspective that they have given, or a recent article, and quote it. Showing that you have done the most basic research first will provide a good first impression. Second, how will your information or link help their audience? You need to focus on their benefits, not yours. Third, realize that most editors, writers, and website owners receive dozens of pitches like this a day. Usually, they send it to spam without a thought. How will you stand out and make an impression?

Website Architecture and Technical SEO

In larger organizations, the content is developed by the marketing team, and they rarely, if ever deal with the technical aspects of running the website. The larger the organization, the less marketing manages or influences website architecture or technical challenges. This means that the marketing team needs to build influence with those who manage the technical aspects of the website to make changes that can increase search engine compliance, crawling, or optimization.

Conversely, in smaller organizations, the management of the website is integral to the marketing team, website manager, or owner. Thus, the responsibility for managing all areas of SEO increases dramatically. Not simply limited to creating content for rankings, the owner or manager must also ensure that the architecture of the website is developed properly, the server settings enhance crawlability, and that considerations are made for managing search engines and their requirements.

Architecture

The organization and structure of a website helps visitors navigate their way through the content, and it enables search engines to develop a contextual map of the content. Typically, the home page is a very general presentation of the organization at a high level. The main navigation contains links to the primary categories of content. Then, each category breaks down the content even further, becoming more detailed and descriptive.

The organization of your content pages should work together to present highly relevant categories of information. This enables the detailed pages to focus on the long-tail, detailed keywords. As the visitor moves toward the main categories, the keywords become a bit more generalized.

This also helps to develop a URL format that can be consistently applied throughout the website. In WordPress, these are called *permalinks*, where the format is developed from the domain, or the root level, of the website.

- Domain/root: www.domain.com/
- Category: www.domain.com/category
- Subcategory, if needed: www.domain.com/category/topic
- Posts or pages: www.domain.com/category/topic/Optimizing-your-website/

Screaming Frog is one of the essential SEO tools for evaluating a website structure. It crawls (or "spiders") a website, just like a search engine, and provides feedback on the success or failure in accessing pages and content of the website. It also produces a visualization of the site's structure. Defining each category, subcategory, and the structure of the site assists the optimization and the website development. This helps by defining the filename of the pages and the content addressed on each.

In the example from worldwildlife.org shown back in Figure 4.10, Screaming Frog provides a visualization of the website's structure. You can see the primary categories that make up the second and third levels of content, with the subsequent articles, stories, and information farther down. The information is logically organized and supports the focus of the organization.

Duplicate Content

A typical problem that arises with websites is *duplicate content*. This happens as the content populates a web page from a database and the pages are repeated across the website. Content duplication takes many forms. It can be a complete page, duplicated many times with unique URLs, to duplicated products that are listed numerous times throughout a website because tagging and category options create additional versions of the same product page, entire categories, or the entire website.

Duplicate content creates a problem that inhibits your rankings. It is not a penalty, but a structural issue. The search engine is attempting to identify the most relevant page on your website. However, if there are duplicated pages, which page should the search engine choose to rank? Having duplicate pages reduces relevance because there is not a single page of information, but 2, 5, or 100 with the same content. Which page is the real page?

When the search engine sees the same page available at different URLs, it doesn't know which is the primary version of the page, called the primary URL. It may assign a version that you don't prefer, which can limit your rankings and negatively impact your incoming link benefits.

Canonical URLs

Canonical URL management deals with duplicated content by presenting the correct version or the correct URL to the search engine. The first method is the Rel=Canonical tag. This tag is placed in the header of the duplicated pages and points to the actual or primary page.

Another method of directing the search engine to the correct or primary page or directory is through a redirect. A server *redirect* is like a change of address, which forwards the search engine and a browser to the correct URL.

Another application of canonicalization is the main URL. If the website uses the www prefix as part of the URL, make sure that the URL without the www prefix redirects (or moves people) to the www version. If both versions can be accessed, this can create a duplicate content problem.

Redirects

Redirects are helpful and are overlooked many times in important transitions. Many businesses redesign their websites and go live with a completely new website and website structure yet forget to add redirects. In forgetting this, they lose the rankings of their old pages and quickly lose visitors to the website.

When a website is redesigned and the URLs of directories and pages change, a redirect maintains the old URL in the rankings and forwards both visitors and search engines to the new versions of the website's pages. There are many types of redirects, but two are used more than others. A *301 redirect* is considered a permanent redirect (or change of URL address) and is usually recommended. A *302 redirect* is a temporary redirect and can be used in some cases.

Robots.txt

The Robots.txt, as shown in Figure 4.11, is a text file that sits at the root level of your website's hosting server. This is requested by the search engines at the initiation of every crawl. The robots.txt file informs the search engines which content is off-limits and should not be indexed.

The Robots.txt file is not a security measure! Not all robots will follow these instructions. It is simply a protocol that excludes directories or files that are not important or critical for indexing. Some also use this file to manage duplicate content by listing duplicated files or directories for exclusion.

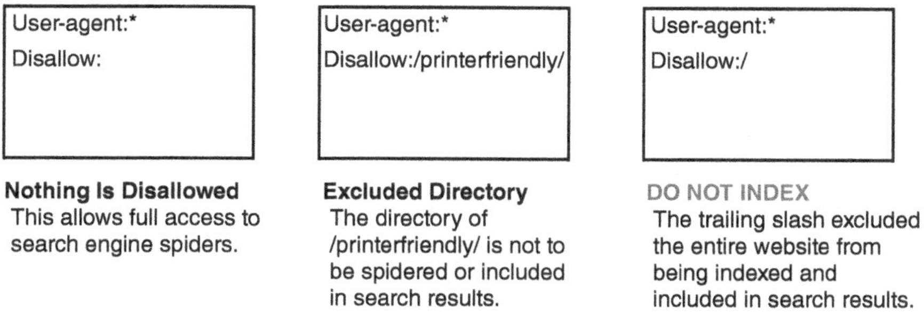

```
User-agent:*
Disallow:
```

Nothing Is Disallowed
This allows full access to search engine spiders.

```
User-agent:*
Disallow:/printerfriendly/
```

Excluded Directory
The directory of /printerfriendly/ is not to be spidered or included in search results.

```
User-agent:*
Disallow:/
```

DO NOT INDEX
The trailing slash excluded the entire website from being indexed and included in search results.

FIGURE 4.11   Robots.txt Formats

This little file has probably created more headaches for site owners than any other factor. This is because with one little slash, it can remove your website from the search results! In Figure 4.11, the difference between full site access and blocking the search engines completely is a forward slash.

Many times, developers will add this protocol to keep development sites from being indexed and ranking in the search engines. Yet when the site goes live, this file is often forgotten! This causes the site to drop out of the rankings because the search engine spiders are being instructed *not* to index the website. Each of the webmaster tools provided by Google and Bing will verify the format of your `Robots.txt` file and ensure that it is properly developed for your website.

Sitemaps

There are two types of sitemaps recommended for a website. The first is for humans, as it is useful to find a clear layout and directory of pages. You might see this kind of sitemap as part of a 404-error page to help people find the content they need; 404 is a server code for "page not found."

The second type is an XML file that is used by the search engines. Many content management systems, such as WordPress, offer this through SEO plugins. This file updates as you update your website, as it provides the search engine with an index of the available pages and files of your website, their URL addresses, and the timestamp of when the document was last updated. Using Webmaster tools in Bing or Google's Site Manager, you can verify that your XML sitemap is published and indexed by the search engines.

Speed (Load Time)

An increasingly vital factor in optimization is the speed of the website. Decreasing the load time of a page makes impatient people very happy, especially when they are using a mobile device. Google has created *Core Web Vitals* as measurements for response times and speed of your website.

Core Web Vitals measures three aspects of Page Speed:

- **Largest Contentful Paint:** Measures the time it takes for the largest image or text block to load on the page. The target is under 2.5 seconds.
- **First Input Delay:** Measures how quickly people can interact with your page. The target delay is under 100 milliseconds.
- **Cumulative Layout Shift:** Measures how much the layout of the page changes as elements load. Typically, ads are the culprit here, as they cause content to move.

These measurements are used by Google and other search engines to measure the user experience and responsiveness on a page. Having poor scores in these categories does not mean that rankings will suffer. These elements are only a small part of the overall ranking algorithm.

Hreflang Attribute

Another important attribute to include in the code of your pages is the *Language* attribute. If you have multiple versions of your site for different countries or languages, this attribute enables search engines to classify and present the searcher with the most relevant version of your page based on their country and language.

The hreflang attribute looks like this: `hreflang="fr-ca"`

The first element, fr, denotes the language of the document of page. The second element denotes the country. In this example, the country is Canada, ca, so the page's content would be designed for French-speaking Canadians. These are ISO language and country codes and can be found at https://www.w3schools.com/tags/ref_language_codes.asp.

Search Engine Algorithms

"Things change all of the time" is what I hear people say about search engines. And it's true! The algorithm is the foundation of the rankings, and it is updated more frequently than many people realize, as Google makes many daily changes to the algorithm. However, the competencies outlined in this book are central to digital marketing, and the core of these competencies has not changed in the past two decades.

The skills of SEO have been much the same as they were in the early 2000s, but the tactics have adapted to better website technology, content management systems, media types, and changing design factors.

The danger that some fall into is chasing the algorithm. By attempting to reverse-engineer the search engine algorithm, some fall into tactics that are designed to take advantage of tricks or schemes that create artificial relevancy. This is done to fool the search engines into ranking your website higher. The danger is that many of these tactics—as soon as Google identifies them—are penalized. This can mean losing visibility in the rankings or, worse, being completely dropped from the results. Best practices avoid anything that creates a false relevance as an attempt to fool the search engines.

Major Algorithm Updates

Occasionally there is a major shift or technology applied to the algorithm. It may be an addition to the current algorithm or a replacement. These major algorithm shifts create dynamic changes in the rankings and are tracked by many SEO professionals. Evaluating these major updates over the years enables people to see where the trend is going and how the search engines, especially Google, prioritize the content of their results.

As you'll notice, the updates are named like hurricanes, as they mark major shifts in relevance, quality, and spam. Yes, websites built and optimized specifically to fool the search engines are called "spam" as well!

Google Panda, 2011 One of the earliest and most impactful updates was the Panda update. For starters, this update targeted "thin" content that was very shallow or was duplicated across dozens or hundreds of pages. An example of "thin content" is a website attempting to rank for plumbing contractors and building a page for every city or town, then interlinking all the pages with the city name and the word *plumbing* as the anchor text. The text on the page would be the same, with only the name of the city changing.

This update also targeted websites that simply aggregated feeds from other websites and published them as their own. Other tactics were those that published duplicated or stolen content from other websites or had the same content repeated across the website (such as 200 how-to articles on the same subject). Google targeted sites that were built specifically for rankings and had little to no quality based on user experience or the content itself. This was one of the first algorithms that focused on identifying the authorship of content, as many sites were simply stealing or appropriating content and publishing it as their own.

Google Penguin, 2012 This update was targeted at sites developing false relevance from linking schemes. This targeted sites that were buying links or participating in link networks designed to inflate a backlink profile. Additionally, Google targeted websites that employed "doorway pages," which was a method of showing the search engine a false page designed for rankings but sending the searcher to another page.

Google Hummingbird, 2013 Hummingbird was a unique update in that it focused on the on-page content of websites rather than backlinks or spam. This algorithm was focused on a context-driven evaluation of the content. This marked a major shift in Google's search technology as the search phrase itself, rather than the individual words, was being evaluated for relevance. Previously, in a search for "mechanical gaming keyboard" the algorithm would attempt to find the best matches for the three words separately. This update was the first application to evaluate the intent of the phrase rather than the individual words.

This update showed a dramatic shift in evaluating the content of pages, as simple keyword repetitiveness was not going to be effective. Rather, the natural use of synonyms, contextual cues, natural conversational content, and long-tail keywords would be used to evaluate the page for relevance.

For example, think of the many synonyms for cars: autos, automobiles, vehicle, motor, wheels, motorcar, hybrid, SUV, and so on. Webster's lists 57 synonyms. In natural conversation, people use synonyms all the time, because using one word becomes repetitive and contrived. According to Google, "Synonyms affect 70 percent of user searches across more than 100 languages."

Google Pidgeon, 2014   Pidgeon was designed to enhance the local search results using distance and location. The emphasis started the development of enhancing the visibility of local businesses in the results.

Google RankBrain, 2015   After these major algorithm shifts, there was a change, as many of the newer algorithms were additions to the primary algorithm. In this case, RankBrain was added as an update to the Hummingbird algorithm. RankBrain was a machine-learning AI designed to learn words and concepts of rare or uncommon words. It was designed to understand the variations of different search phrases. In 2013, Google announced that 30 percent of search terms were phrases that had never been used before! Also, as new words, trends, and events happen around the world, Google needs to keep up with the increasing vocabulary. RankBrain was designed to learn these new words or phrases and connect them to meaningful results.

Google Fred, 2017   Fred was another update that targeted false relevance, specifically keyword stuffing, link schemes, and misleading backlinks.

Google BERT, 2019   While not an algorithm update, BERT (Bidirectional Encoder Representations) is a Google technology for natural language processing. The goal is to understand language nuance and idioms. As an example, think of the many ways that the word "like" is used in English:

- I *like* coffee
- This coffee tastes *like* dirt
- I feel *like* dancing
- My friend and I are *alike*
- It's *like*, you know

It's a single word with multiple meanings based on the context of the words around it. BERT was designed to pick up and interpret these meanings.

Google MUM, 2021   Another technology change, Google's MUM (Multitask Unified Model) is built on BERT architecture but is 1,000 times more powerful. This expands the language capabilities of the search results to reach across language barriers and find answers through accessing and translating information in other languages.

How to Handle Updates

Don't panic. If you are following best practices, then you should see very little or negligible changes to your rankings. Remember, the algorithms change daily and so will your rankings as the entire system is always in flux. You will find millions of articles complaining about and analyzing every update, and it is easy to get caught up in the drama of the game.

The goal of SEO is to influence the search engines to gain higher rankings, but you can't do this without creating a great experience for the searcher. By creating content that answers questions, informs searchers, and helps people, you will naturally develop relevance. By developing relationships and marketing your organization, you will build influential links that enhance your credibility. These factors result in higher rankings. Maintain this focus, and the shifts in algorithms and technology won't change your status much at all.

This is where additional disciplines enhance your ability to market your website, build links, and gain visibility. Through content marketing, conversion optimization, social media marketing, and more, you are actively building links and content that enhance your relevance.

Measuring SEO Results

Measuring and reporting the results of SEO efforts has grown over the years. I know a few SEO practitioners who maintain that their only job is to get rankings and nothing more! I simply cannot accept that. One of the goals of SEO is to gain rankings, of course. But the natural result of those rankings is to increase the visitors to a website. Then, I want those visitors to do something—to reach a goal, accomplish a conversion action such as subscribe, register, or purchase! Ultimately, SEO is a business-building activity and should be measured as such.

This means that rankings are not the primary measurement of success. They are an indicator, but not the final measurement.

The Problem with Measuring Rankings

Measuring SEO results by rankings is a moving target. Many factors prevent the objective measurement of actual rankings. The results are influenced by many factors, and two people can see very different results, even sitting next to each other or working in the same office. The next sections discuss just a few of the influences on rankings.

Localized Results   Primarily, search results are first delivered based on the searcher's location. The vast majority of searches are conducted on a mobile phone, so the search engines primarily provide results based on location and favor local businesses.

Search History   Another factor that influences the results is your past search history. This information enables Google to develop personalization factors and information or industry preferences based on your usual activity. While this will not heavily influence results, your history informs how certain phrases or concepts should be weighted in the results.

SEO Software Reports   Any SEO tool or software program has to query Google to gain rankings data. However, to comply with Google's terms of service, they need to have a token or an API access to Google. This enables them to query a certain number of times or a number of queries in a day and only from a designated server so that the ranking reports do not take up valuable resources from human searchers, and so that ads are not shown to reporting queries.

Because of this, the rankings are coming from a centralized server and not from servers that humans are using. The data may be out of date, may not be using the latest algorithm, or have not updated based on the last crawl. The rankings reports produced from these tools or software are good as a comparison and trending view of a website's progress or ability to hold consistent rankings. If you choose to track rankings daily or even weekly, you'll see many changes back and forth and predictable swings of one to four positions, gained or lost. For this stage of reporting, a level of consistency is the desired outcome.

Analytics Is the Objective Measurement

The primary result of gaining higher rankings is increased visitors to your website from the search engines. While rankings may show results of optimization, increased visits show that you have chosen the right words and phrases and that your marketing is influencing people to click on your results!

Any SEO should be first measured by the overall increase of visits to the website. Then, the increase of visits to individual pages, which reflect the focus on long-tail and more detailed phrases and information.

Acquisition   An acquisition report should compare your search engine visits as compared to other channels such as paid search, social, direct, email, and other campaigns. This provides a direct comparison of the effectiveness of search as a primary channel for generating qualified visits to the website.

Also, when tracking value, such as goal value or transaction value, this is reflected in the revenue and can show that search is one of the most effective revenue generators for your business website.

Landing Pages   When evaluating the results of optimization, evaluating the increase of visits to the landing pages is one of the most direct measurements of the results. Not only this, but the influence of that page on the revenue of the website shows the impact of developing a visitor experience that results in a measurable economic impact of your optimization!

Comparing time frames prior to optimization to the same time frame after optimization will provide the data you need to justify your SEO efforts. Depending on the impact of the SEO, if you see rankings increase, then you should see visits and goal completions increase as well. While you may not see the increases over days or weeks, you may see it more clearly when comparing years or quarters.

Revenue and Value   With Google's shifting of analytics toward a first-channel attribution model, you will see more and more the influence of search as a major contributor toward visits, revenue, conversions, and overall business impact. Search is a top-of-mind activity and the primary method of finding information.

Measuring rankings only reflects a first-step influence of your efforts. To truly show the full impact of search to an organization, reporting must start with the first-visit channel, showing how it influences ongoing visits through additional searches and direct visits, and how it confirms actions and economic impact at the end or through the decision cycle.

CHAPTER 5

Content Marketing

By Greg Jarboe

It's relatively straightforward to prepare for the OMCA exam. You have 75 minutes to answer approximately 70 multiple choice questions—and roughly 10 of those questions will test your concept-level understanding of the components and practices of content marketing.

But, it's significantly more complicated to prepare to be successful in this marketing discipline. Why? Because many of the competencies and skills required to qualify for employment in a supervised associate position in content marketing have changed significantly over the past decade, although some concepts have remained remarkably the same.

Content Marketing Context

When I started teaching content marketing in 2012, I'd began my online courses and in-person classes by answering these questions:

- What is content marketing?
- What are the benefits of content marketing?
- How does content marketing relate to search engine optimization (SEO) and social media?
- How is content marketing different from SEO and social media?

By the end of this chapter, you will have learned the answers to these questions, plus the answers to 20 more:

- What is the concept of content value?
- What is the concept of content relevancy?
- What is the concept of content engagement?

- What is the concept of content shareability?
- Why is video content important?
- How should content marketing be structured?
- Should you increase time spent talking with your customers?
- Should you revisit your customer/buyer personas?
- Should you reexamine the customer journey?
- What is a content marketing matrix and do you need one?
- Should you change your targeting/messaging strategy?
- Should you change your content distribution/promotion strategy?
- Should you adjust your editorial calendar?
- Should you put more resources into social media?
- Should you change your website?
- Should you change your products/services?
- What is a product-led content strategy?
- What are the benefits of product-led video content?
- Should you adjust your key performance indicators (KPIs)?
- Should you change your content marketing metrics?

What Is Content Marketing?

According to the Content Marketing Institute (CMI), which was founded in 2011, "Content marketing is a strategic marketing approach focused on creating and distributing valuable, relevant, and consistent content to attract and retain a clearly defined audience—and, ultimately, to drive profitable customer action."

More than a decade later, this is still the best definition of content marketing that I've seen.

Note that "valuable, relevant, and consistent content" is being used like a magnet to attract and retain "a clearly defined audience." But it also needs to be used like a screen that filters out disinterested or unqualified people "to drive profitable customer action."

What Are the Benefits of Content Marketing?

According to the CMI, content marketing has four key benefits:

- Increased sales
- Cost savings

- Better customers who have more loyalty
- Content as a profit center

The first of these benefits, *increased sales*, is also one of the goals that you can set in universal analytics to measure how content marketing fulfills your target objectives.

Content marketers can use Google Analytics to measure the number of conversions generated by a campaign, although "conversions" might mean making a purchase for an ecommerce site or submitting a contact information form for a marketing or lead generation site.

The second benefit, *cost savings,* is popular in organizations that want you to do more with less. And if you want to deliver cost savings, read my column in *Search Engine Journal,* which was published on Feb. 19, 2020. It's entitled, "Is a Super Bowl Ad the Equivalent of Lighting Money on Fire?"

If content marketers can demonstrate that their latest campaign lifted brand awareness, favorability, consideration, and purchase intent more cost-effectively than running a 30-second commercial during Super Bowl LVI (which cost as much as $6.5 million in 2022), then that should convince senior executives in the C-suite to increase their content marketing budget.

The third benefit, *better customers who have more loyalty,* isn't one that mass marketers will focus on because they ignore market segment differences and still believe, "Any customer can have a car painted any color that he wants so long as it is black."

However, content marketers who've analyzed their market opportunities, selected their target segments, and tailored their marketing mix are much more likely to appreciate the benefit of having better customers who are more loyal.

The fourth benefit, *content as a profit center*, sounds like "pie in the sky." But it's the goal of brands like Red Bull, which is often described as a media company that sells energy drinks rather than a beverage seller that publishes content.

Many content creators and social media influencers are also focused on content as a profit center. For example, YouTube's creative ecosystem supported 394,000 full-time equivalent jobs and contributed $20.5 billion to the U.S. economy in 2020, according to "The State of the Creator Economy" by Oxford Economics.

How Does Content Marketing Relate to SEO and Social Media?

The practice of SEO started back in the mid-1990s. (I know because I used SEO to optimize our website when I became the vice president of marketing at WebCT in 1999. Back then, the leading search engines included AltaVista, Excite, Infoseek, and Lycos.)

The term "social media" was coined by Chris Shipley in 2004. (I know because she asked me to speak at BlogOn 2004, which was the first "social media conference.") Interest in the search term *social media marketing* took off in 2008.

But interest in the search term *content marketing* didn't take off until 2011, which was also when the Content Marketing Institute was founded. (I know because I became the faculty chair of content marketing at Market Motive in 2012.)

Because content marketing was the new-new thing, I was frequently asked to explain how it related to SEO and social media marketing. And I often used a Venn diagram to illustrate the similarities, differences, and relationships between these basic digital marketing disciplines (Figure 5.1).

I'd explain that many SEO strategies and tactics are often focused on optimizing content on websites. However, many content marketing strategies and tactics are often focused on optimizing content on websites, blogs, YouTube, and other platforms, which have been blended into Google's Universal Search results since May 2007.

Yes, there is overlap. SEOs and content marketers can collaborate to optimize all of the short articles/posts (fewer than 3,000 words), videos, virtual events/webinars/online courses, research reports, e-books/whitepapers, and case studies on their organization's website.

And I'd explain that most social media marketing strategies and tactics are often focused on creating and distributing engaging and shareable content on Facebook, LinkedIn, Instagram, and YouTube. However, most content marketing strategies and tactics are often focused on creating and distributing valuable and relevant content on websites, blogs, and email newsletters as well as social media platforms.

FIGURE 5.1 Venn Diagram of SEO, Social Media Marketing, and Content Marketing

Yes, there is overlap. But social media and content marketers can collaborate to create a consistent stream of content that is valuable, relevant, engaging, and shareable as well as distribute it across more and different channels. Although, this often requires the teams to share a "war room" for product launches or industry tent-pole events.

How Is Content Marketing Different from SEO and Social Media?

Unfortunately, far too many SEOs, social media marketers, and content marketers are fighting with each other over their shares of a small but growing digital marketing budget. So, if you work for or get hired by one of these fractious organizations, then it's important to understand how content marketing is different from SEO and social media marketing.

Differences Between SEO and Content Marketing Let's start with the differences between SEO and content marketing.

Google's site quality algorithms have been aimed at helping people find "high-quality" sites by reducing the rankings of low-quality content since the first of 28 "Panda" algorithm updates rolled out in February 2011. This explains why interest in content marketing took off that year and is now essential to getting found in all the right places.

For example, content marketers should read the entire post entitled, "**What site owners should know about Google's core updates**," which was written by Danny Sullivan, Google's Public Liaison for Search, on August 1, 2019.

Sullivan provides a set of questions to ask yourself to ensure that "you're offering the best content you can. That's what our algorithms seek to reward."

His content and quality questions included the following:

- Does the content provide original information, reporting, research, or analysis?
- Does the content provide a substantial, complete, or comprehensive description of the topic?
- Does the content provide insightful analysis or interesting information that is beyond obvious?
- If the content draws on other sources, does it avoid simply copying or rewriting those sources and instead provide substantial additional value and originality?
- Does the headline and/or page title provide a descriptive, helpful summary of the content?

- Is this the sort of page you'd want to bookmark, share with a friend, or recommend?
- Would you expect to see this content in or referenced by a printed magazine, encyclopedia, or book?

Ask yourself, "Who is more likely to have the skills, education, and experience that's necessary to create quality content? The people in my organization's SEO department or the people on my content marketing team?"

Sullivan also said, "Beyond asking yourself these questions, consider having others you trust but who are unaffiliated with your site provide an honest assessment."

In addition, the various types of the universal or blended search integrations have created a variety of traffic-generating options for SEOs since May 2007. But, the vast majority of SEOs act like they're still living in the era of "10 blue links."

For example, most SEOs don't know how to optimize YouTube videos despite the fact that an analysis of Google Universal Search results by Searchmetrics in March 2018 found that at least one video integration was displayed for 22 percent of desktop and 23 percent of mobile search results. Oh, and YouTube had 92 percent of those video integrations.

And, according to other data from Searchmetrics, YouTube has steadily (and stealthily) increased its organic visibility in Google's SERPs over the past several years and surpassed Wikipedia for the number 1 spot at the end of 2019.

This knowledge should enable content marketers to get a seat at the table—and a larger share of their organization's small, but growing digital marketing budget.

Differences Between Social Media Marketing and Content Marketing

Let's now look at the differences between social media marketing and content marketing.

After the algorithm update known as the "Facebook Apocalypse" hit in January 2018, Adam Mosseri, who was then the head of Facebook's News Feed, explained, "Today we use signals like how many people react to, comment on, or share posts to determine how high they appear in News Feed. With this update, we will also prioritize posts that spark conversations and meaningful interactions between people. To do this, we will predict which posts you might want to interact with your friends about, and show these posts higher in feed. These are posts that inspire back-and-forth discussion in the comments and posts that you might want to share and react to—whether that's a post from a friend seeking advice, a friend asking for recommendations for a trip, or a news article or video prompting lots of discussion."

He added, "Because space in News Feed is limited, showing more posts from friends and family and updates that spark conversation means we'll show less public content, including videos and other posts from publishers or businesses."

Later that summer, Buffer and BuzzSumo teamed up to analyze more than 43 million posts from the top 20,000 brands on Facebook. They found that top business pages had increased their output from 72,000 posts per day in Q1 2017 to 90,032 posts per day in Q2 2018.

At the same time, the average engagement per post for the world's top brands had dropped from 4,490 engagements per post to 1,582 engagements per post. And it's worth noting that engagement on Facebook posts had dropped for all types of content.

- The average engagement per image had dropped from 9,370 per post in Q1 2017 to just 3,454 per post in Q2 2018.
- The average engagement per video had fallen from 5,486 to 2,867.
- The average engagement for links had plummeted from 2,577 to 763.

So, if you were the average social media marketer, then you were facing an existential crisis. (We talk about how to become an exceptional social media marketer in Chapter 6.)

That same summer, CMI and MarketingProfs surveyed content marketers for the 2019 B2B Content Marketing Benchmarks, Budgets, and Trends—North America report. And among the key findings were 15 noticeable differences between the most successful and least successful B2B content marketers. Following were among the differences:

- Ninety-two percent of the most successful content marketers (aka "top performers") agreed there was content marketing buy-in from highest levels in their organization versus 55 percent of the least successful.
- Ninety percent of the most successful B2B content marketers always/ frequently prioritized their audience's informational needs over their organization's sales/promotional message versus 56 percent of the least successful.
- Seventy-seven percent of the most successful used personas for content marketing purposes versus 36 percent of the least successful.
- Seventy-three percent of the most successful gleaned better insight from technology into audience behavior/preferences versus 40 percent of the least successful.
- Seventy-two percent of the most successful measured content marketing ROI versus 22 percent of the least successful.
- Sixty-five percent of the most successful had a documented content marketing strategy versus 14 percent of the least successful.

So, even if you were just an average content marketer back then, you had a pretty good idea of how to become more successful the following year.

Before we dive deeper into how you can become more successful in content marketing, let's make sure that you're prepared for the OMCA exam.

What Is the Concept of Content Value?

One of the concepts that you'll need to understand is "content value." In other words, what makes content valuable for a clearly defined audience?

Cassandra Naji, the Director of Learning & Development at Animalz, provides a clear explanation of this concept in a post entitled, "The Content Value Curve," which was published on the content marketing agency's blog on Oct. 11, 2021.

She said, "Content adds value to the reader by enabling that reader to do something or to think something; it can add tactical value (do something) or strategic value (think something)."

Naji added, "Generally, the more strategic value a piece of content adds, the less likely it is to add tactical value, and vice versa." Why? Because tactical and strategic content offer significantly different value to radically different audiences.

She explained, "Tactical content is situationally relevant. This kind of content is helpful for one person trying to solve a particular problem, but it isn't very interesting to anyone who doesn't have that particular problem." She added, "Tactical content reaches tactical readers or folks lower down the marketing food chain."

Naji continued, "Content adds strategic value when it equips the reader with a new conceptual framework, a new first principle, or a new perspective." She added, "Strategic readers—executives and decision-makers—need frameworks and first principles, not instructions on how to do their job."

What Is the Concept of Content Relevancy?

Another concept you'll need to understand is "content relevancy." In other words, what makes content relevant to a clearly defined audience?

Andrew Johnson and Colleen Jones of Content Science, an end-to-end content company, tackled this question in an article entitled, "Content Relevance and Usefulness: Why You Need It and 4 Ways to Achieve It," which was published Dec. 1, 2019, in *Content Science Review*. Their insights are based on content feedback from more than 100,000 people.

They said, "Content relevance is all about your audience's perception of your content's pertinence to topics, issues, needs, or interests. Content usefulness refers to your content's ability to help users make decisions or make progress toward goals."

They added, "Whenever a user visits your content, they have a specific goal in mind—even if that goal is just to learn more about you. How well your content helps them accomplish that goal is hugely important to how effective your content is overall."

They also identified customers and audiences who perceived the content they used was "relevant" as follows:

- Nearly three times as likely to report accomplishing their goals than users who felt the content was only somewhat relevant
- More than eight times as likely to report accomplishing their goals than users who felt the content was not relevant

They concluded, "Even more pronounced is the effect of the two dimensions together. According to our data, users who found content to be both relevant and useful said the content helped them accomplish their goal 91.5 percent of the time. That's more than 15 times as often as users who found the content neither useful nor relevant."

What Is the Concept of Content Engagement?

The third concept you'll need to understand is "content engagement." In other words, what makes content engaging for a clearly defined audience?

BuzzSumo, a content marketing platform, built machine learning models and used them to analyze 400,000 articles in order to find out what boosts content engagement on social media.

Here are their key insights:

- Facebook provides the most content engagement. But content that generates very strong engagement on one social networking site isn't necessarily going to see much engagement elsewhere.
- On Facebook, Likes made up 70 percent of content engagements. But Likes are highly correlated with Shares and Comments. So, if you can create likeable content, you can expect more substantive content engagement to follow.
- If Twitter is your main platform, then find influencers who can help amplify your content. Using these strategies can help you overcome some of the challenges of working with a platform that has a smaller user base.
- Tweaking content can turn a dial, not a switch. BuzzSumo didn't see any features making more of a 6 percent contribution to the probability of creating high content engagement, which means there's no magic formula for creating high-performing content.

What Is the Concept of Content Shareability?

The fourth concept you'll need to understand is "content shareability." In other words, what makes content sharable for a clearly defined audience?

Although "shareability" isn't included in the definition of content marketing, it is absolutely essential if content marketers hope one of their videos will "go viral."

Original research from more than 2 years of work, five different data sets, around 1,000 videos, nine individual studies, and a large team of researchers from the Ehrenberg-Bass Institute for Marketing Science at the University of South Australia found the following:

- Videos that display personal triumph appear most likely to deliver sharing success. But content creators rarely use personal triumph as a creative device.
- Weather/science/nature also achieved very good sharing rates. But these are also rare.
- Videos of babies outperform many other creative devices, but only when the video evokes intense emotions.
- Using poorly branded advertising is like throwing away your marketing budget.

Shareable content is also important for B2B marketers. Gartner research has found, "The typical buying group for a complex B2B solution involves six to 10 decision makers, each armed with four or five pieces of information they've gathered independently and must deconflict with the group."

Gartner has also found that customers who perceived the information they received from suppliers to be "helpful" were "three times more likely to buy a bigger deal with less regret"—even if that information is shared with other decision-makers in meetings instead of online.

Why Is Video Content Important?

You will also want to understand why video content has become so important. The reason is obvious: video now plays an increasingly important role in our daily lives.

In July 2019, the Google/Insight Strategy Group asked 12,000 people worldwide why they had watched what they watched in the last 24 hours. In March 2020, Think with Google published their findings in an interactive feature entitled, "**What the world watched in a day**."

The participants, ages 13 to 64, watched a wide variety of content, ranging from traditional media to online video. They chose their number

1 reason to watch from a list of 20. The following were the 12 most important reasons:

- Helps me relax and unwind
- Teaches me something new
- Allows me to dig deeper into my interests
- Makes me laugh
- Relates to my passions
- Is inspiring
- Makes me forget about the world around me
- Keeps me in-the-know
- Addresses social issues that are important to me
- Has high production quality
- Helps me be efficient
- Is on a network or platform I like

If you analyze these responses, then you'll notice a pattern: traditional,
TV-era indicators of quality are less important to viewers than they once were.
People are now placing more value on content that relates to their personal
interests and passions. In fact, the ability to teach people something new,
help them dig deeper into their interests, or relate to their passions are twice
as important as high production quality or being on a preferred network
or platform.

We discuss these findings again later in this chapter—in the section entitled "Content Marketing Strategy and Planning."

Organizational Structure

Although content marketing has evolved significantly over the past decade,
our ideas of organizational structure have mutated rapidly since March 11,
2020, when working remotely taught all of us that "work is what you do, not
where you do it."

In the "blended working future," we'll still need systems that outline how
certain activities are directed in order to achieve the goals of our organization.
But they can vary a lot.

For example, small organizations (1–99 employees) often have just one
person serving the entire organization's content marketing needs. On the
other hand, medium-size organizations (100–999 employees) generally have
small content marketing teams in the two- to five-employee range.

Even large organizations (1,000+ employees), which are the most likely to have both centralized groups and individual teams working throughout the organization, rarely have more than 6–10 employees managing content marketing.

So, how does all the work get done?

The latest data from CMI and MarketingProfs suggests that many companies are both outsourcing content marketing work and asking internal staff with other responsibilities to take on more. However, those who have dedicated internal content marketing resources tend to be more successful with content marketing.

Why? Because companies often outsource content creation to *content mills* (or content farms) that employ large numbers of freelance writers to generate a large amount of textual web content that was specifically designed to satisfy what they thought were Google's ranking algorithms or signals.

Ethical (white hat) SEOs have known since May 6, 2011, when Google provided more guidance on the "Panda" algorithm change, that Google's algorithms are aimed at helping people find "high-quality" pages and articles by reducing the rankings of "low-quality" content.

Unfortunately, many of the least successful content marketers didn't get the memo. There's nothing intrinsically wrong with outsourcing content creation. But you need to vet providers as carefully as you need to vet influencers.

The current challenges of outsourcing content marketing include finding partners with the following qualities:

- Adequate topical expertise
- Understand/can empathize with your audience
- Can provide adequate strategic advice
- Consistently deliver on time

And I'd bet dollars to donuts that the top challenge for content marketers who outsource next year and the year after will continue to be finding partners with adequate topical expertise.

Why? Because *subject matter experts* (SMEs) are worth their weight in printer ink, which is more precious than gold.

On the other hand, hiring new employees isn't a panacea either. Being new to an organization comes with a learning curve to become an SME in that brand, even if you're a content marketing veteran. So, there is no one-size-fits-all solution.

New employees who get hired might work in one of four different types of organizational structures:

- **"Flatarchy"**: There are no levels of management when you're a team of one.

- **Functional:** Employees are divided into specialized groups with specific roles and duties.
- **Divisional:** Various teams work alongside each other toward a single, common goal.
- **Matrix:** Employees are divided into teams that report to two managers—a project or product manager along with a functional manager.

So, who sets strategy and who owns implementation of content marketing at small, medium, and large organizations?

Well, this person could be the only content marketing specialist at a small organization, the first content marketing manager at a medium-size organization, or the new content marketing strategist at a large organization.

In the most successful organizations, this person needs the necessary skills, education, and experience to turn content marketing into a strategic marketing approach. In other words, this person could be you.

These key concepts and definitions should help to prepare you for the OMCA exam. But nothing could have prepared you to respond quickly and effectively to a global pandemic.

That's why the rest of this chapter goes well beyond "teaching to the test" to foster a holistic understanding of content marketing strategy, tactics, and metrics.

Content Marketing Strategy and Planning

Even in the digital marketing industry, which prides itself on agility and adaptability, the escalating menace of the novel coronavirus pandemic was something very different.

Collectively, we're pretty adept at devising new strategies and tactics when Google or Facebook rolls out a major algorithmic update. So, we were fairly well prepared to respond quickly and effectively to the coronavirus pandemic—as long as we recognized that COVID-19 wasn't an algorithm change.

In fact, it's still having a bigger impact on our organizations today because post-pandemic changes in consumer behavior are still changing content marketing strategies and plans more than the Google Panda and Facebook Apocalypse updates did put together.

This particular crisis represented a unique opportunity for content marketers to help craft their company or clients' coronavirus response—if they were bold enough to seize it.

For example, they needed to have a more favorable attitude to change than most of their colleagues in digital marketing to propose that their small and underfunded content marketing team would create and optimize several new blog posts that tackled a new set of topics that weren't in the editorial calendar that had been created in late 2019.

Why? Because it was safer to stick to the plan.

And they needed to overcome obstacles to get a seat at the table—especially at a time when many members of their organization's digital marketing team were working remotely. Once content marketers had a seat at the table, they needed to come up with innovative plans.

Why? Because there was no off-the-shelf solution.

Content Marketing Planning

So, what happened next?

CMI and MarketingProfs fielded their annual survey during the summer of 2020. They found: "Content marketers are resilient. Most have met the challenges of the pandemic head-on." The found the following responses to the pandemic:

- Increased time spent talking with customers: 30 percent of B2B and 26 percent of B2C marketers
- Revisited their customer/buyer personas: 25 percent of B2B and 18 percent of B2C marketers
- Reexamined the customer journey: 31 percent of B2B and 34 percent of B2C marketers
- Changed their targeting/messaging strategy: 70 percent of B2B and 63 percent of B2C marketers
- Changed their distribution strategy: 53 percent of B2B and 46 percent of B2C marketers
- Adjusted their editorial calendar: 64 percent of B2B and 54 percent of B2C marketers
- Put more resources toward social media/online communities: 40 percent of B2B and 43 percent of B2C marketers
- Changed their website: 40 percent of B2B and 37 percent of B2C marketers
- Changed their products/services: 26 percent of B2B and 25 percent of B2C marketers
- Adjusted their KPIs: 20 percent of B2B and 23 percent of B2C marketers
- Changed their content marketing metrics (e.g., set up new analytics/dashboards): 14 percent of B2B and 13 percent of B2C marketers

In other words, both B2B and B2C marketers totally overhauled the process for creating a content marketing plan from stem to stern. For some, 2020 was the year of quickly adapting their content marketing strategy. For others, it was the year to finally develop one.

As Stephanie Stahl, the General Manager of the CMI, said when the 12th annual B2B Content Marketing Benchmarks, Budgets, and Trends: Insights for 2022 report was published on Oct. 13, 2021, "Companies are waking up to the power of content marketing due in part to the pandemic. That's not some grand pronouncement from the Content Marketing Institute. It's a recurring refrain we heard from you (or content marketers like you) in our 2022 B2B research."

She then shared three of the open-ended responses in the latest survey to the question, "How does your content marketing look post-pandemic?"

- "Who would have thought that a pandemic would be the thing to finally bring content marketing out from behind the shadows and into the forefront of marketing communication?"
- "The pandemic reinforced the importance of our content marketing strategy. There had been a commitment to it, but now that commitment is company-wide and there is more collaboration between marketing and sales."
- "The pandemic allowed our content marketing approach to come front and center for the whole organization and our leadership team. We now understand the power of what content can do. Our challenge is to be able to tie it into a revenue center that generates leads for the firm."

A year later, the 12th annual <u>B2B Content Marketing Benchmarks, Budgets, and Trends: Insights for 2022 report</u>, which was published October 13, 2021, said: "The key theme that emerged was this: The pandemic awoke a sleeping giant—content marketing, that is."

It continued, "Without in-person events and face-to-face selling, many who had previously paid little attention to content marketing suddenly became aware of its power. More content marketers got a seat at the table and helped keep many businesses on their audiences' radar. Some discovered new audiences altogether."

And report concluded, "The research also confirmed what many of us already knew: Content marketers are some of the fiercest business pros around. In the most difficult of times, they get the job done—and many come through more creative and stronger than before."

So, you will want to adopt this new planning process—because it's been battle tested.

Increase Time Spent Talking with Customers

In the pre-pandemic era, the first step in the content marketing planning process was to define your purpose and set your goals. (I know because I've taught courses on the five core elements that belong in an effective or successful content marketing plan.)

But this approach often led many of the least successful content marketers to prioritize their organization's sales/promotional message over their audience's informational needs.

In the post-pandemic era, it's now more important than ever to avoid a product and sales orientation and embrace a market orientation and customer focus. And the best way to do that today is to increase the time content marketers spend talking with customers.

B2B salespeople will argue that they're already doing this. But research has found that they're talking with customers about different things than B2B marketers should focus on.

In fact, the B2B Institute at LinkedIn, in partnership with WARC and Lions, undertook a major study to analyze the effectiveness of 10 years of B2B marketing campaigns, and to replicate the Lions and WARC B2C study, The Effectiveness Code.

Following were among the key findings of **The B2B Effectiveness Code**:

- For B2B brands to grow, they require a better balance of short-term sales activation and long-term brand building. In addition, they need a greater focus on large audiences who aren't necessarily "in the market" today, as well as more use of emotion to connect deeply and powerfully with B2B purchasers.
- But their data showed that B2B marketing currently skews heavily toward short-term, rational, and tightly targeted campaigns that seek to drive immediate sales effects. Their data also found the use of long-term campaigning, broad targeting, and emotional creative work were largely absent from B2B marketing.

For B2C marketers, it's more challenging to increase the time spent "talking" with consumers. We can't hold more focus groups muffled by masks these days. But we can do the following:

- Use qualitative, quantitative, and digital techniques to gather customer insights.
- Design customer surveys, conduct market research, and analyze the data to identify or validate who our customers are as well as what they need and expect.

In Chapter 1, this is Step 3 in the process of developing a digital marketing strategy. But let me add this tactical advice: you can conduct a website survey that asks visitors three key questions—for free.

In a post entitled, "**The Three Greatest Survey Questions Ever**," which was published in July 2015 on Occam's Razor, Avinash Kaushik said these key questions are:

- What is the purpose of your visit to our website today?
- Were you able to complete your task today?
- (Conditional, if No) Why were you not able to complete your task?
- (Conditional, if Yes) What could we have done to make your experience delightful?

And, I might add, there's no better way for content marketers to get "a seat at the table" than by being the "voice of the customer."

Revisit Customer/Buyer Personas

In "the before time," the second step in the content marketing planning process was to define your audience and describe how they would benefit from your content.

But this approach often led many of the least successful content marketers to ignore market segment differences and try to appeal to the whole market with general interest content.

In "the after times," we now recognize the importance of breaking down our markets into segments and deciding which ones we will go after. And the best way to do that today is to create or revisit customer/buyer personas.

As you learned in Chapter 1, if you rely solely on demographics to create your persona, you'll often create content that is less relevant or engaging.

Why? Because consumer intent outperforms demographics.

For example, Vanessa Hensler, Lead Effectiveness Researcher for Ads Marketing at YouTube, wrote an article entitled, "**Consumer intent is better than demographic data for video ads**," which was published in *Think with Google* in August 2020.

She said, "When it comes to marketing, the use of demographics has always been a blunt instrument. To get the most out of your marketing spend and to increase engagement with consumers, ads must be relevant to what they care about, not just their demographic."

She added, "Relevance—creating ads that appeal directly to a shopper's interests and intent—drives brand lift and sales. A recent study conducted by Google and Ipsos found that video advertising based on consumer intent does have significantly more impact than advertising based on demographics."

The study measured brand lift data across 16 video ads relevant to four different life events: getting married, buying a home, moving, and home renovation. The YouTube ads were served using three different levels of alignment: demographics only, demographics with intent, and intent only.

The YouTube ads served in alignment with intent drove a 32 percent higher lift in ad recall and 100 percent higher lift in purchase intent than those served using demographics only. And the addition of demographics to intent didn't produce a significant incremental lift versus using intent alone.

Reexamine the Customer Journey

Five years ago, the third step in the content marketing planning process was to develop your story—the specific, unique, and valuable ideas that you would build content assets around.

But this approach often led many of the least successful content marketers to focus on telling an "authentic" story about their organization's "brand purpose" instead of crafting content based on the specific stages of the buyer's journey.

Today, we've also learned that we need to craft emotional as well as rational content for a journey that is often more like a sightseeing tour with stops, exploration, and discussion along the way—all moments when you need to convince people to pick your brand and stick with it instead of switching to a competitor.

This is why you need to totally reexamine the customer journey—because the map of the specific stages is probably far too linear. And even if it isn't liner, then the roadmap of the journey that different customer segments are taking is probably two-dimensional.

What's the alternative?

With permission from *Search Engine Journal*, the next section is a shortened version of the column that I wrote on Jan. 12, 2022, which tackled this question.

What Is a Content Marketing Matrix and Do We Need One?

According to the Content Marketing Institute's Video & Visual Storytelling Survey, which was published November 10, 2021, 83 percent of marketers say video has become more important in the last two years.

Videos were always a powerful tool in the storytelling arsenal. But maybe it's time to reexamine our content marketing matrix.

What is a content marketing matrix and do we need one now? Well, a content marketing matrix is a planning tool to help marketers generate ideas for the most engaging content types for their audiences.

A number of them have been created over the past decade, including one that I contributed to Guy Kawasaki's book, *Enchantment: The Art of Changing Hearts, Minds, and Actions* (2012).

Figure 5.2 shows what it looks like.

As you can see, my content marketing matrix has two dimensions:

- Awareness through to action on the horizontal axis
- Rational through emotional on the vertical axis

Content marketers are supposed to use the four quadrants—entertain, inspire, educate, and convince—"as a starting point" to review how their content can support the goals of their B2B, B2C, or not-for-profit organizations.

Do We Need a Content Marketing Matrix in 2023?
A decade later, I don't have a problem with using a 2 × 2 matrix "as a starting point."

But it reminds me of the scene in *Star Trek II: The Wrath of Kahn* (1982) when Captain Spock (Leonard Nimoy) analyzes the tactics of Khan Noonien Singh (Ricardo Montalbán) and observes, "He is intelligent, but not experienced. His pattern indicates two-dimensional thinking."

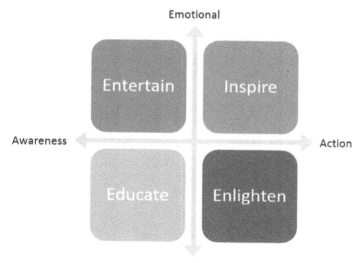

FIGURE 5.2 A Content Marketing Matrix

That's why I believe experienced content marketers need a three-dimensional matrix to compete successfully in a world where

- YouTube has more than 2 billion monthly logged-in users,
- 500 hours of video are uploaded to YouTube every minute, and
- video content is playing a starring role in all four quadrants.

I don't have a problem with putting "branded stories" (e.g., short films, series, documentaries, and inspirational videos) in the upper-left quadrant of the matrix. I've seen some entertaining short films "go viral."

I've also seen some inspiring, educational, and enlightening videos go viral too. In Chapter 1, we looked at how several major brands in the United Kingdom use nostalgic Christmas ads to build brand awareness and connect with customers on a deeper level.

(Note: This column is republished in Chapter 1.)

Viral Marketing: The Science of Sharing   Maybe it's time to share the secret of how to create branded video content that is more likely to go viral.

Actually, it isn't a secret. It is the subject of Karen Nelson-Field's book, *Viral Marketing: The Science of Sharing,* which was published in October 2013.

Back then, Dr. Nelson-Field was a senior research associate at the University of South Australia's Ehrenberg-Bass Institute for Marketing Science.

Today, she's the founder and chief executive officer at Amplified Intelligence.

Her book used original research from more than 2 years of work, five different data sets, around 1,000 videos, nine individual studies, and a large team of researchers from Ehrenberg-Bass Institute for Marketing Science.

Her research found that "an emotional response is important in driving further cognitive or behavioral responses. Reactions to advertising—or anything for that matter—are rarely purely rational."

The data she shared show the most engaging content types for your audiences are branded videos that can elicit intense, positive, emotional responses, using the following:

- Exhilaration
- Inspiration
- Astonishment
- Hilarity

Dr. Nelson-Field's book also reveals the following:

- On average, videos that elicit intense emotions are shared twice as much as those that evoke moderate emotions, yet more than 70 percent of all branded videos evoke moderate emotions.

- Branded videos that evoke feelings of exhilaration are shared more than any other intense positive emotion.
- While professional video creators may be aiming to create hilarious branded content, most are falling well short of the amateurs.

The most engaging holiday ads of 2021 indicate that Dr. Nelson-Field's findings are still valid today.

Unruly Reveals Top Emotionally Engaging Holiday Ads of 2021

Each year, Unruly tests holiday ads and measures the intensity of emotions, brand favorability, authenticity, and purchase intent that viewers felt while watching an ad, which all contribute to an overall "EQ Score."

Unruly is a global video and Connected TV (CTV) advertising platform. Content marketers can learn some important lessons from them about how to generate ideas for the most engaging content types for their audiences.

(It's worth noting that Dr. Nelson-Field worked with Unruly a decade ago to develop an earlier version of their methodology.)

In 2021, Unruly analyzed the emotional responses of approximately 9,700 consumers around the world to more than 50 holiday ads.

Carol Gillard, the vice president of marketing and communications at Unruly, observed several interesting trends:

- "As December 2020 approached, brands went out of their way to relate to the uncertainty of holidays amidst a global pandemic. Messages last year reflected the change in storied traditions and adaptability of consumers as they still attempted to bring cheer into their holiday season.
- "By comparison, many in the 2021 crop of holiday ads do not reference or allude to Covid-19, and instead seek to create nostalgia for Christmases past, and excite consumers about gathering and celebrating with their nearest and dearest."
- "Top-performing ads have high EQ scores (above 6 or 7) and demonstrate a combination of intense emotional response, brand favorability, and purchase intent by viewers."

Let's start with **_Wegmans Holiday Commercial 2021_**, which was ranked number 1 in the United States (Figure 5.3).

The video's description says, "The holidays are about sharing, caring, and enjoying great food. Watch as a little boy shows us that you don't have to be all grown up to be a big helper. Let's get back to happy, together."

The ad from Wegmans Food Markets scored 61 percent in Emotional Intensity, 53 percent in Brand Favorability, and 38 percent in Happiness, to get an overall EQ Score of 7.3.

FIGURE 5.3 Wegmans Holiday Commercial 2021 (**https://youtu.be/Xr6Yzzhez3E**)

Wegmans Food Markets selected Optic Sky, an advertising and digital experience production company, to produce this ad.

I asked Aaron Gordon, the CEO of Optic Sky, "What was your thinking/ strategy behind the Wegmans approach to holiday advertising at this particular time in history?"

Gordon said, "This holiday spot is part of the Wegmans 'Back to Happy' campaign. It's the first ad campaign Wegmans has run since the start of the pandemic, so it was important to consider the state of COVID-19 at the time. On one hand, it seemed as though we were making real progress; vaccines were finally available, the economy was rebounding, and schools and stadiums were opening back up. On the other hand, we knew that COVID was unpredictable."

He added, "The Wegmans internal creative agency decided to focus all three ads on the values they as a company share with their customers, who represent all walks of life. The Optic Sky team worked closely with Wegmans to create ads that evoke a warm, human, and nostalgic tone, while touching upon our shared yearning to leave the pandemic behind (as the campaign name, 'Back to Happy,' implies). Together, we emphasized our common humanity, love of family, and hope for the future with scenes of joy, sincere caring, and family meals."

It's the Most Wonderful Time of the Year | Frito-Lay ranked number 2 in the United States (Figure 5.4).

The video's description says, "Share more joy this Holi-LAY'S season with Jimmy Fallon and your Frito-Lay favorites." Frito-Lay's ad scored 55 percent in Emotional Intensity, 45 percent in Brand Favorability, and 36 percent in Happiness to get an overall EQ Score of 7.3.

FIGURE 5.4   It's the Most Wonderful Time of the Year | Frito-Lay (**https://youtu.be/0nznQReHNKY**)

The Whoopsery | Stories of Evergreen Hills | Created by Chick-fil-A ranked number 3 (Figure 5.5).

This video's description says, "Sam is back for another adventure this holiday season, and she brought a friend! After an unfortunate mishap while decorating Cece's family Christmas tree, Sam and Cece try to make it right and end up in a magical place called The Whoopsery."

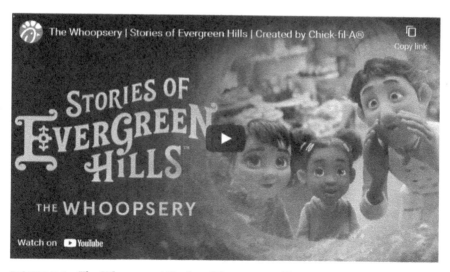

FIGURE 5.5   The Whoopsery | Stories of Evergreen Hills | Created by Chick-fil-A (**https://youtu.be/vvPRdk2i0_0**)

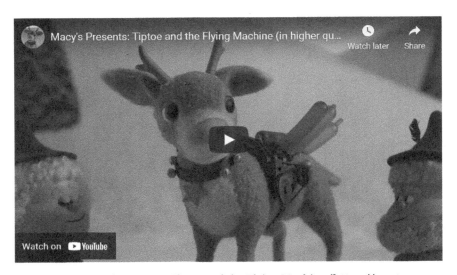

FIGURE 5.6   Macy's Presents: Tiptoe and the Flying Machine (**https://youtu. be/4Hry38CgPTo**)

Chick-fil-A's ad scored 56 percent in Emotional Intensity, 49 percent in Brand Favorability, and 36 percent in Happiness, to get an overall EQ Score of 7.1.

(Gillard noted, "Several top ads used animation, which is reminiscent of the iconic stop motion animation holiday movies of the 1960s and 1970s.)

Macy's Presents: Tiptoe and the Flying Machine ranked number 4 in the United States (Figure 5.6).

The video's description says, "This is the story of Tiptoe. A little reindeer with a big problem. She's absolutely terrified of flying. So her friends get together and teach her a very important lesson: if you believe in yourself, there's no telling how high you can soar."

Macy's ad scored 53 percent in Emotional Intensity, 48 percent in Brand Favorability, and 33 percent in Happiness to get an overall EQ Score of 6.9.

Finally, ***OREO "A Holiday Twist" :30*** ranked number 5 in the United States (Figure 5.7). This video's description says, "The holidays' favorite cookie #OREO #StayPlayful." Oreo's ad scored 45 percent in Emotional Intensity, 41 percent in Brand Favorability, and 29 percent in Happiness to get an overall EQ Score of 6.7.

Some content marketers are going to look at these top emotionally engaging holiday ads, scratch their heads, and say, "But those are YouTube ads!"

Yes, they are. And according to the Content Marketing Video Survey, repurposed ads (long-form versions of TV ads) are one of the video types that produced the best content marketing results in 2021. (Note: Repurposed ads ranked number 9, so eight other types of video got better results.)

FIGURE 5.7   OREO "A Holiday Twist" :30 (**https://youtu.be/AZFGaFIISSo**)

Besides, a content marketing matrix is supposed to help you generate ideas for the most engaging content types for your audiences. So, if you mistakenly think that you can't learn lessons from the top emotionally engaging holiday ads of 2021, then you've got to ask yourself: "Does this pattern indicate two-dimensional thinking?"

To transform this situation, we need to go beyond producing more videos in 2023. We need to make videos worth watching and create content worth sharing. And there are plenty examples of branded videos that are emotionally engaging even though they aren't ads. If you want to see one, just watch ***Google – Year in Search 2021***.

The description of Google's branded video (Figure 5.8) says, "In a year that continued to test many, the world searched "how to heal" more than ever. Whether they're taking care of mental health, honoring a loved one, or reuniting with family, people are finding ways to come back stronger than before."

Uploaded on November 22, 2021, it has more than 228 million views and over 178,000 engagements (e.g., likes, comments, shares).

And, if you mistakenly think that B2B videos have to be rational or boring, then check out ***"Zero Tolerance Machining" with the Wire EDM - Part 1 | US Digital #Shorts***. US Digital designs and manufactures motion control products for OEM manufacturers as well as end users. The description of their branded video (Figure 5.9) says, "Our machine shop can cut metal so precisely using our wire EDM that two parts fit together with virtually no gap between."

Uploaded on October 27, 2021, it has 42.6 million views and 1.7 million engagements.

FIGURE 5.8 Google—Year in Search 2021 (**https://youtu.be/EqboAI-Vk-U**)

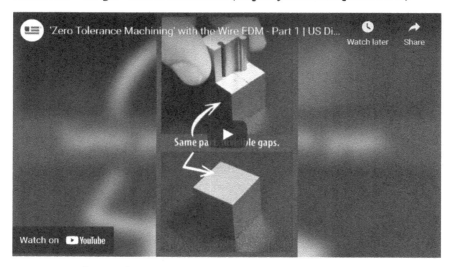

FIGURE 5.9 "Zero Tolerance Machining" with the Wire EDM—Part 1 | US Digital #Shorts" (**https://youtu.be/7OMTDW0vH0Y**)

The B2B Content Marketing Benchmarks, Budgets, and Trends: Insights for 2022 report produced by the Content Marketing Institute and Marketing Profs says, "The top content marketing-related area of investment for 2022 is expected to be video (69 percent). This makes sense, as business has shifted online, and marketers look for new/more ways to tell compelling stories to capture and keep audience attention."

All of this is—potentially—good news. Hopefully, most content marketers won't blow this opportunity by cranking out more branded videos that evoke moderate emotions.

I realize that eliciting intense emotions sounds risky. So, let me close with an excerpt from an interview in WARC's "Insights from the 2021 Creative Effectiveness Lions winners."

WARC asked Ann Mukherjee, who is chairman and chief executive officer at Pernod Ricard North America and was president of the 2021 Creative Effectiveness Lions jury, "What stood out to you about the Grand Prix winner, Nike's Dream Crazy?"

Mukherjee said, "We felt that Dream Crazy was the next chapter in advertising, helping the industry think about what's possible and redefining the roles brands can play in making a positive dent in the universe."

She added, "It's also important to remember that Nike was actually solving a business problem around its relevance to younger consumers. This audience does not only want to buy brands, they want to buy into brands. Nike took a risk because it understood that's what it took."

That's why we need to use a three-dimensional content marketing matrix "as a starting point" to generate ideas for the most engaging content types for our audiences. Then, we've also got to think outside the box (Figure 5.10).

FIGURE 5.10   Nike/Dream Crazy (United States) (**https://youtu.be/ WW2yKSt2C_A**)

Change the Targeting/Messaging Strategy

In response to the pandemic, 70 percent of B2B and 63 percent of B2C marketers changed their targeting/messaging strategy. Ironically, this wasn't even one of the steps in the content marketing planning process a couple of years ago.

As I explained in Chapter 1, strategy has also been "the elephant in the room" for digital marketing since 2019. And it may also explain why the CMI needs to keep reminding marketers they need to have a documented content marketing strategy.

Having a documented content marketing strategy is correlated with being successful, but correlation does not imply causation. Documenting your strategy only helps if it leads your team to create and distribute valuable, relevant, and consistent content that attracts and retains a clearly defined audience—and, ultimately, drives profitable customer action.

So, focus on creating a successful content marketing strategy first, before you harness the benefits of documenting it to accomplish the following:

- Align your team around a common mission/goals.
- Make it easier to determine which types of content to develop.
- Keep your team focused on documented priorities.
- Help your team allocate resources to optimize desired results.
- Provide clarity on targeted audience(s).

You'll need to start by making some scientific, wild guesses about the best targeting/messaging strategy for your brand and industry. Let's use Direct Line, one of the leading insurers in the United Kingdom, as an example. Start by mapping your customer's journey:

- **See:** People who could end up owning a car
- **Feel:** People who feel they might need a new car
- **Think:** People who think they might need car insurance
- **Do:** People who compare their car insurance options
- **Care:** Your existing customers whose car insurance is about to expire

Then, craft an overall message for each stage of the customer journey, identify some of the key communication touchpoints that you'll create in an ongoing content marketing program, and identify the KPIs that you'll use to measure the impact of these touchpoints on customer perceptions and behavior.

Table 5.1 shows how that might look.

TABLE 5.1   **Preliminary Targeting/Messaging Strategy Overview**

See	Feel	Think	Do	Care
See that your brand exists and provides car insurance	Feel that "You're On It"	Think you are more proactive rather than continuing to show how you can react to problems	Drive long- and short-term business impact	Care that you give people their money back and put things right when they go wrong
Short articles/ posts	Videos	Virtual events	Case studies	Email newsletters
Brand awareness	Favorability	Consideration	Purchase intent	Brand affinity

Finally, Table 5.2 is my hypothetical outline of the headlines of the key messages, which are tailored for each communication touchpoint in a targeted persona's customer journey.

The proposed headlines for the short articles/posts, virtual events, case studies, as well as email newsletters should be self-explanatory. But you might want to know a little more about the proposed content of the videos.

They build on Direct Line Group's "We're On It" campaign, which took home the top prize at the *Marketing Week Masters* in 2021 for driving long- and short-term business impact (Figure 5.11).

Direct Line took over a year to develop its new campaign. After delivering the brief to creative agency Saatchi & Saatchi in 2019, the brand launched "We're On It" in February 2020.

The successful campaign featured three characters—Bumblebee from Transformers, Donatello from Teenage Mutant Ninja Turtles, and Robocop— showing each of them being beaten by Direct Line in an emergency situation including a car accident or office break-in.

A hypothetical content marketing's targeting/messaging strategy matrix would leverage these characters to craft a tailored message for targeted persona during the "Feel" stage of the customer journey. This should drive even more long- and short-term business impact.

How do you measure that? Well, you could use Google Surveys once or twice a year to measure brand awareness, favorability, consideration, and purchase intent. You could also use Google Forms to conduct an annual or semi-annual customer survey to measure brand affinity.

(I'll examine other ways to measure results at the end of this chapter.)

TABLE 5.2 Hypothetical Targeting/Messaging Strategy Matrix

Personas	See	Feel	Think	Do	Care
Educate me	What car insurance do I need to deliver food?	Bumblebee encounters driverless cars	What factors impact the price of your quote?	Why they chose Direct Line	Can I drive any car?
Reassure me	Will car insurance go up next year?	Robocop examines the Smart Crossing	How would you cope without your car?	Why she chose Direct Line	Will my price be different if I choose to renew automatically?
Help me	How do car insurance deductibles work?	Donatello offers tips on how to get your parents off your back	How do you insure your electric car?	Why he chose Direct Line	Can I transfer my No Claim Discount (NCD) to another individual?
Surprise me	Are car insurance companies open on weekends?	Interview with Bumblebee on being beaten by one of the U.K.'s leading insurers	Who will sort out claims more efficiently than any other insurance providers?	Why my friends chose Direct Line	Can I add a temporary additional vehicle to my policy?
Thrill me	Will car insurance cover a blown engine?	Stories about Robocop in emergency situations	Who goes beyond what you would expect from an insurer?	Why I chose Direct Line	Are my spouse and I covered for business use?
Impress me	Which car insurance is best for new drivers?	Will Donatello be #OutHeroed again by The Fixer?	Which insurers are best at solving problems?	Why our kids chose Direct Line	How do you get a multi-car insurance discount?

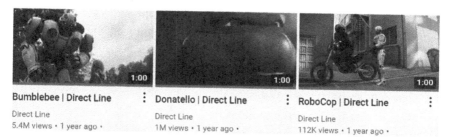

Bumblebee | Direct Line   Donatello | Direct Line   RoboCop | Direct Line
Direct Line   Direct Line   Direct Line
5.4M views · 1 year ago · 1M views · 1 year ago ·   112K views · 1 year ago ·

FIGURE 5.11   Direct Line's "We're On It" Campaign

Change the Distribution Strategy

In response to the pandemic, 53 percent of B2B and 46 percent of B2C marketers changed their distribution strategy. Ironically, this wasn't one of the steps in the content marketing planning process 5 years ago either.

This omission led many content marketers to mistakenly "assume" that employing "more" content marketing tactics as well as distributing their content through "more" channels would make them "more" effective. All too often, it didn't.

So, what's the best approach for creating a distribution strategy today? Well, the B2B and B2C Benchmarks, Budgets, and Trends reports for 2022 from CMI and MarketingProfs asked content marketers which content assets produced the best results in the last 12 months. Following were the top content assets:

- Short articles/posts (fewer than 3,000 words)
- Videos
- Virtual events/webinars/online courses
- Research reports
- E-books/whitepapers
- Case studies

CMI and MarketingProfs also asked content marketers which organic (nonpaid) social media platforms produced the best results in the last 12 months:

- Facebook
- LinkedIn
- Instagram
- YouTube

According to CMI's Video & Visual Storytelling Survey, which was mentioned previously, the following video types produced the best content marketing results in the previous 12 months:

- Interviews with influencers/subject matter experts
- Case studies or customer stories
- How-to videos or explainer videos
- Branded stories (e.g., short films, series, documentaries, and inspirational videos)

Sticking to what produced the best results in the past is like driving a car down a busy street by looking in the rear-view mirror. You have to drive slowly. So, if your distribution strategy isn't getting you where you need to go fast enough, then how should you change it?

Well, let me share a counterintuitive, strategic insight: creative effectiveness is the single most powerful force multiplier in your arsenal. Why? Because the lion's share of your success will be determined by the quality of your content. So, you should invest about twice as much of your time, talent, and treasure creating a consistent stream of valuable, relevant, engaging, and shareable video content as you invest in distributing it across more and different channels.

If you can't capture your audience's attention with the video content that you're creating, you need to identify the right partners who can.

Influencer marketing isn't one of the top eight disciplines. But you will probably want at least a concept-level understanding of how to do the following:

- Identify the right influencers.
- Find the right engagement tactics.
- Keep track of your influencers' activity.
- Measure the performance of your programs.

To identify the right social media influencers, use these three key criteria:

- **Reach:** Measures the total size of an influencer's online audience across all major social networks
- **Relevance:** Measures an influencer's contextual affinity to your areas of interest
- **Resonance:** Measures the engagement of an influencer's audience with their content

When it comes to reach and resonance, be careful. Some influencers are still using bad practices such as fake followers, bots, and fraud to inflate their numbers. However, Influencer Marketing Hub's free Instagram Audit Tool,

Fake Follower & Audience Credibility Checker, can help you spot fake or misstated accounts on Instagram.

Before you engage influencers, you need to invest a serious amount of time watching the videos they've created to ensure their relevance as well as their suitability. In other words, vet their content like your career depends on it—because it does. Once you've thoroughly vetted influencers, let go of control. This will ensure that social media influencers keep creating compelling content that resonates with their audience.

For example, Honey, a browser extension that automatically searches for coupons on more than 30,000 sites, sponsored Jimmy Donaldson, aka MrBeast, to create an "expensive" stunt on his popular YouTube channel to expose Honey's service to MrBeast's viewers.

(In January 2022, *Forbes* declared MrBeast the highest-earning YouTuber of 2021, hauling in $54 million from advertising, sponsorship deals, and spin-off products.)

The result of this collaboration was ***Would YOU Rather Have A Lamborghini or This House?*** Uploaded on Aug. 22, 2020, this 20-minute-long sponsored video got 122 million views and 3.2 million engagements (Figure 5.12). That's more views than a Super Bowl ad typically gets—at a fraction of the cost.

"... And i'm going to give this man a choice would you rather have a real lamborghini here's a clip of it ..."   More ⌄

YouTube · *MrBeast*   ⋮

Would YOU Rather Have A Lamborghini or This House?

FIGURE 5.12   Would YOU Rather Have A Lamborghini or This House? (**https:// youtu.be/s1ax8Tx_Jz0**)

To track each of your influencers, use Google's free **Campaign URL Builder tool** (`https://ga-dev-tools.web.app/campaign-url-builder/`), which allows you to add campaign parameters to URLs so you can measure custom campaigns in Google Analytics. Just enter the website URL, campaign medium, and campaign name as well as a unique identifier for each campaign source. You can even use Bitly to shorten the link. Then share the generated campaign URL with each of your influencers to use in any of the promotional channels that they want to be associated with this custom campaign.

We'll talk about other ways to measure the performance of your content marketing and influencer marketing programs at the end of this chapter as well as in Chapter 6, which tackles the challenge of measuring social media marketing.

Content Marketing Channel Management and Promotion

In the fourth step of the old content marketing planning process, I asked budding content marketers, "How will you structure and manage your operations to activate your plans?"

I answered my rhetorical question about "process" by urging them to create "an operational plan that enables your team or department to function as a media company."

Then, I told them to look at content marketing as a sustainable, ongoing operation, not as yet another form of campaign-based marketing. As they looked to structure those operations, I also recommended constructing the appropriate guidelines or "playbook" by including the following:

- The steps involved in your content marketing process and the order in which they should be executed
- The owner of each of those tasks and the other players who should be involved
- The brand and quality standards you have established and guidelines on how they should be maintained
- The primary content format and media channel you will concentrate on and the best practices that should be followed in their use
- Who your content creators/contributors are and how your team will be expected to support/manage their efforts
- What other resources you can access to facilitate your efforts (both internally and externally)

The vast majority of the budding content marketers that I taught had never worked in media companies, although many had worked in marketing communications (marcom) departments, where they'd learned how to produce sales brochures. Some of them used this playbook to crank out what could charitably be described as "brochureware."

And most didn't read Rebecca Lieb's book, *Content Marketing: Think Like a Publisher—How to Use Content to Market Online and in Social Media* (2011).

So most didn't learn what Lieb was also trying to teach: "Content marketing is no longer a nice-to-have. It's a must-have. It's imperative that businesses create content on an ongoing basis. They can't create just any old content, of course. It must be relevant and high quality. It also must be valuable and drive profitable customer interactions. And it must be about customer needs and customer interests, not ad-speak, which is all about the 'me.'"

Things slowly got better. A growing number of content marketers had started to "think like publishers" and were beginning to "function as media companies" before the World Health Organization (WHO) declared COVID-19 to be a global pandemic on March 11, 2020.

And you already know what happened next.

As a short article in the *McKinsey Quarterly Five Fifty* newsletter entitled, "The Quickening," which was published in July 2020, noted, "If you're feeling whiplash, it might be the ten years forward we just jumped in 90 days' time. How fast is the world moving around us? Consider how quickly ecommerce has replaced physical channels in three months. Or how consumers are reconsidering brand loyalties and the stores and websites where they shop."

Microsoft read the memo. Microsoft CEO Satya Nadella said on quarterly earnings call that month, "We've seen two years' worth of digital transformation in two months."

Adjust the Editorial Calendar

In response to the pandemic, 64 percent of B2B and 54 percent of B2C marketers in North America adjusted their editorial calendar. Hopefully, they did this after they'd changed their targeting/messaging strategy. Why? Because your editorial calendar is not your targeting/messaging strategy.

So, if they adjusted their editorial calendars without changing their targeting/messaging strategies first, then this was just a sad example of what the British call "panic stations," which is a short period in which there is a lot of confused activity because people feel anxious.

If you've never created an editorial calendar before, read the article entitled, "**7 Steps to a More Strategic Editorial Calendar**," which was written by Kelsey Raymond, the co-founder and CEO of Influence & Co., and published by CMI on Jan. 6, 2022.

She says, "Too many companies focus on the logistics of their editorial calendar—what days content is publishing, at what times, and at what cadence—and ignore the strategic elements. Anyone can schedule blog posts regularly, but the best content marketers create robust, strategic editorial calendars."

Her seven-step guide details how to build an effective editorial calendar:

- Determine who needs to be included.
- Identify goals for the quarter.
- Decide the content mix and publishing cadence to support those goals.
- Document your mix and cadence decisions on the editorial calendar.
- Brainstorm topics.
- Plan for flexibility.
- Measure results to determine the success of your plan.

She concludes, "Following a strategic approach to your editorial calendar is a never-ending process. But that ongoing work should be affected by your evaluation process. Review your key metrics toward the end of the quarter as you begin to plan for your next three months. It gets easier each time you plan the editorial calendar for the next quarter because you're simply tweaking your previous plan rather than starting from scratch."

The overwhelming majority of content marketers say that *video* has become more important to their organizations over the last 2 years. And future investments into video are expected to climb even further.

To up your video investment and make it the backbone of your overall marketing approach—like a lot of your peers are planning to do—you need a video content calendar.

You can start by borrowing a page out of the **YouTube creator playbook for brands**. In the section entitled, "Schedule your content," the playbook recommends building a channel calendar to map your programming strategy over the year. It advocates producing three types of complementary content in the following framework: help, hub, and hero content.

- **Help content:** What is your audience actively searching for regarding your brand or industry? What can serve as your 365-day-relevant, always-on, content programming (e.g., product tutorials, how-to content, customer service)?
- **Hub content:** The content you develop on a regular basis to give a fresh perspective on your target audience's passion points (e.g., verticalized content about a product line). This is often staggered throughout the year.
- **Hero content:** What content do you want to push to a big, broad audience? What would be your Super Bowl moment? A brand may have only a few hero moments in a year, such as product launch events or industry tent-poles.

This playbook was published in October 2015. I would argue that brands have added a fourth type of content to this framework in the past two years: hygiene content.

- **Hygiene content:** This is the Corporate Social Responsibility (CSR), Corporate Social Advocacy (CSA), Environmental, Social, and Governance (ESG), and Public Service Announcement (PSA) content that you create on an occasional basis.

If you would like some examples of each these four types of content, check out this very small sample of the 754 videos that YouTube uploaded to the brand's 10 channels in 2021.

To see an example of YouTube's help content, watch ***Creator Basics: How to Set Up and Customize Your Channel***. Uploaded to the YouTube Creators channel on May 13, 2021, this video got 1 million views and 15,400 engagements (Figure 5.13).

To see an example of YouTube's hub content, watch ***CMO X Creator Conversations – The Trailer | Season 2***. Uploaded to the YouTube Advertisers channel on July 14, 2021, this video got 13,600 views and 100 engagements (Figure 5.14).

Next, watch ***Join the BTS #PermissiontoDance Challenge*** to see an example of YouTube's hero content. Uploaded to the YouTube channel on July 19, 2021, this video got 58 million views and 146,000 engagements (Figure 5.15).

Finally, watch ***Wear a mask to stay protected during COVID-19*** to see an example of YouTube's hygiene content. Uploaded to the YouTube India Spotlight channel on May 3, 2021, this video has 54.2 million views and 403,000 engagements (Figure 5.16).

In other words, YouTube practices what it preaches. The 754 videos that the brand uploaded in 2021 got a total of 1.8 billion (with a "b") views and 8 million engagements, according to data from **Tubular Labs**. That's an average of 2.4 million views and 12,000 engagements per video.

Here's the key takeaway for you: don't sprinkle video into your marketing programs here and there; use these four types of complementary content to create a consistent stream of content that is valuable, relevant, engaging, and shareable. By upping your video investment and making it the backbone of your overall content marketing approach, you can begin using video strategically.

FIGURE 5.13   Creator Basics: How to Set Up and Customize Your Channel (**https://youtu.be/aKydtOXW8mI**)

CMO X Creator Conversations — The Trailer |
Season 2

13K views · 6 months ago ·

YouTube Advertisers ✓ 353K subscribers

What happens when you put YouTube's top creators and today's leading
marketers in a (virtual) room? Find out as Deborah Wahl ...

FIGURE 5.14   CMO X Creator Conversations—The Trailer | Season 2 (**https://
youtu.be/9MTzct0pnb0**)

Join the BTS #PermissiontoDance Challenge

57M views · 5 months ago ·

YouTube ✓ 32.7M subscribers

Dance your out to the new BTS song #PermissiontoDance only on YouTube
#Shorts. BTS will be spotlighting some of their ...

FIGURE 5.15   Join the BTS #PermissiontoDance Challenge

Wear a mask to stay protected during COVID-19

54M views · 8 months ago ·

YouTube India Spotlight ✓ 3.69M subscribers

FIGURE 5.16   Wear a Mask to Stay Protected During COVID-19 (**https://youtu.be/
BqAKBXvppfw**)

Put More Resources Toward Social Media/Online Communities

In response to the pandemic, 40 percent of B2B and 43 percent of B2C
marketers put more resources toward social media/online communities.
In Chapter 6, we analyze why many brands haven't seen a return on their
marketing investment—yet.

Red Bull is one of the exceptions to the rule. So, let's take a quick look at
how the brand quietly changed its video content marketing strategy.

Brands that already have a successful content marketing strategy are generally tempted to stick with what's working. You know what they say, "If it
ain't broke, don't fix it."

FIGURE 5.17   Felix Baumgartner's Supersonic Freefall from 128k—Mission Highlights (**https://youtu.be/FHtvDA0W34I**)

Back in the old days, Red Bull was known for creating monster hits, like _**Felix Baumgartner's supersonic freefall from 128k – Mission Highlights**_. The Red Bull Stratos space diving project, which took place on Oct. 14, 2012, was viewed live by over 9.5 million users, setting a record for the live stream with the most concurrent views ever on YouTube (Figure 5.17).

This 1:31-long video now has 47.2 million views, and 250,000 engagements, according to data from Tubular Labs. So, you might mistakenly think that Red Bull's current video marketing strategy is still built around creating similar hero content for massive tent-pole events that ignore market segment differences on YouTube. But you would be wrong.

Red Bull started putting more resources toward niche social media/ online communities more than 5 years ago. And their successful video content marketing strategy has been built on creating hub content that's different from their competition, which gets views from fans with a special interest in biking, motorsport, surfing, winter sports, music, gaming, or other events.

For example, Red Bull creates some of the best action sports clips and original series on YouTube. Sports fans can watch highlights from niche events like UCI Mountain Biking, Red Bull Rampage, Red Bull Ice Cross, Red Bull Straight Rhythm, Red Bull Soap Box Race, Red Bull Flugtag, Volcom Pipe Pro, and Red Bull Cliff Diving. Or they can discover the behind-the-scenes lives of athletes like pro mountain bikers Matt Jones and Danny MacAskill.

And Red Bull creates similar content on Facebook.

If we look at the data for 2021, here's what the switch to a strategy of creating hub content on YouTube and Facebook has produced: 2.7 billion views (with a "b") and 65.1 million engagements. That's the equivalent of making 57 space jumps a year—or more than one a week!

That's what I mean about dramatically changing what everyone thought a successful video content marketing strategy looked like. Red Bull has moved from making occasional "hits" to producing an ongoing stream of videos that get lots of views—and engagements—week in and week out from social media/online communities with special, not general interests.

How did Red Bull put this wildly successful video marketing strategy together? Well, the energy drink brand started uploading videos to Facebook in November 2007 and YouTube in April 2008. And they initially crafted content targeted at young men 18–24 years old who were looking for videos with a "stoke factor."

Red Bull's demographics are still 91 percent male, but the age brackets are as follows:

- Ages18–24 are 28.8 percent on YouTube and 19.1 percent on Facebook.
- Ages 25–34 are 32.1 percent on YouTube and 34.6 percent on Facebook.
- Ages 35–44 are 6.1 percent on YouTube and 19.5 percent on Facebook.

The demographics don't tell the whole story. Red Bull's social media/online communities are sports fans: people who enjoy watching, reading about, or participating in sports. They regularly spend a reasonable portion of their disposable incomes on sports-related purchases like sports programming, games, tickets, and sporting equipment. They're routinely the first in their offices to join a sports team. They often come to YouTube to watch sports highlights and commentary.

If this sounds like the target audience of a media company, then Red Bull functions as a media company. And if you ask Red Bull marketers what they are focused on, then you may be shocked—shocked to find they aren't focused on selling an energy drink.

But just for the record, Red Bull sold 7.9 billion cans of the energy drink globally for $7.2 billion (€6.31 billion) in 2020, the most recent year that data are available. In other words, Red Bull has been exceptionally successful because the brand does the following:

- Prioritizes their audience's informational needs over their organization's sales and/or promotional message
- Differentiates their content from the competition
- Crafts content based on specific stages of the buyer's journey

Change the Website

In response to the pandemic, 40 percent of B2B and 37 percent of B2C marketers changed their website. But this may not have generated the results their organizations were hoping for.

Barry Schwartz, the CEO of RustyBrick and Editor of *Search Engine Roundtable,* wrote in Search Engine Land's newsletter on January 12, 2022, "I've been following Google's algorithm updates for about two decades now and time-and-time again, the algorithm updates that Google gives us months or even years to prepare for, are often the ones that have the least amount of impact on rankings in Google's search results."

Recent examples include the page experience update, which was pre-announced in May 2020 but didn't start to roll out until over a year later. He added, "Google even told us the page experience update is a minor factor and you should not see significant changes from it."

Schwartz continued, "The same with page speed update, months of notice, little impact in reality. The list goes on and on, virtually all these long lead time search algorithm updates."

And he observed, "It is the updates Google does not give us huge lead time to prepare for that impact the rankings the most, like the core updates, the Penguin and Panda updates from the past, and most of the updates that go unconfirmed or unannounced."

So, why do so many SEOs spend so much time and effort working on updates where the outcome in ranking is so minor? According to Schwartz, "It is because we can act on these pre-announced updates because they require technical changes to our sites. Core updates and quality updates are about the content and quality of your site; there isn't one technical change to make. But again, there is no real meat in these pre-announced updates—so should we panic and put so much effort into working on them, when we can focus on overall site quality improvements?"

Let me answer his rhetorical question: instead of rushing to "panic stations," SEOs should keep calm and carry on creating new quality content for their sites.

This is an opportunity for content marketers to reach out to SEOs and invite them to collaborate on creating new quality content for their company or clients' websites. This will ensure you're offering the best content you can. That's what Google's algorithms seek to reward.

For example, let's imagine that you're a content marketer working on the Tim Hortons Roll Up the Rim campaign, an iconic annual tradition for Canadians from 1986 onward. Every year, Tim Hortons guests could reveal a tab printed under the rim of hot beverage cups that would either announce a prize win—ranging from a free coffee or donut to a free car—or a "please play again" message.

More than 80 percent of all Canadians have said they've played Roll Up over the years. Some things changed—prizes were updated and the odds of winning gradually improved—but the core game remained largely the same.

Then 2020 happened.

And like so many businesses and industries, Tim Hortons was pushed into a digital transformation of sorts. App Annie saw between 2 and 3 years of mobile usage habit growth squeezed into less than a year due to the pandemic. Fortunately, Tim Hortons had already been focused on building and developing a strong digital foundation over the last 3 years, such as the launch of Tim's Rewards and Mobile Order + Pay on our app. But in a matter of days, the brand was forced to take its digital plans to the next level.

So, how might content marketers and SEOs collaborate on creating content in this crisis? Well, you could use Google's free **Grow My Store** tool (`https://growmystore.thinkwithgoogle.com`) to boost your business in this ever-changing environment with a quick and easy evaluation of your retail website.

Here's how the tool works:

- It analyzes your retail site, gives you an overall score, and offers you detailed insights and recommendations to help you strengthen your business.
- It also lets you see how your site stacks up against retailers in your sector.
- It identifies areas of improvement so you can upgrade effectively.
- It accesses personalized market and consumer trends to reach new customers.
- It helps you grow with advice from Google's database of resources and curated tools.

For example, Grow My Store tells you the following:

- Of smartphone users, 87 percent consult their phone on purchases they are about to make in-store.
- Of in-store food and grocery shoppers in the United States, 47 percent say that remembering past sizes or items they've bought is a feature that empowers their shopping decisions.

- Of in-store food and grocery shoppers in the United States, 47 percent say that receiving promotions or deals specific to past purchases is a "nice to have" feature that empowers their shopping decisions

It would be "nice to have" Canadian consumer trends. But it is what it is. Reach out to the SEOs working on the Tim Hortons site and invite them to a Zoom meeting to brainstorm ideas that would enable teams to harness the surge in search interest in both the Roll Up the Rim and the redesigned Roll Up To Win contest on the Tim Hortons app.

Working together, you can create a comprehensive full-funnel strategy that captures interest with new audiences, helps connect new and existing customers, and informs, educates and drives consumers to partake in these Roll Up events.

That should get you a seat at the table.

Change the Products/Services

In response to the pandemic, 26 percent of B2B and 25 percent of B2C marketers changed their products/services. Um, okay. But, what can content marketers do—beyond supporting the launch of a new product?

Well, for starters, they can read "**A Complete Guide To Product-Led Content Strategy (With Examples)**," which I wrote on November 10, 2021. With permission from *Search Engine Journal*, let me share a lightly edited excerpt.

What Is a Product-Led Content Strategy?   "Product-led content is any type of content that strategically weaves a product into the narrative and uses it to illustrate a point, solve a problem, and/or help the audience accomplish a goal," says Dr. Fio Dossetto, who writes and publishes the *contentfolks* newsletter.

The problem with most product-led content is essentially that people just don't know how to craft content with their product as the star in natural, engaging ways.

Product-led content isn't an infomercial. It's not direct response copywriting. If it's a hard sell, then you'll lose the reader and your content will be ineffective. On the other side of the coin, there are marketers who are so afraid to appear promotional that they don't mention their product or service at all.

Neither approach will help you achieve your business goals.

A Time-Tested Solution to this Problem

So, let me share an outline that can help content marketers develop a good storyline so their product can be the star of the show in a way that is valuable, relevant, engaging, and shareable.

By the way, this outline can be found in Aristotle's *Rhetoric*. This ancient Greek treatise, which dates back to the 4th century BCE, is regarded as "the most important single work on persuasion ever written."

You could say it has withstood the test of time. Aristotle's five-part outline for a persuasive speech is as follows:

- Get your audience's attention.
- Explain a key problem they face.
- Identify a solution to their problem.
- Describe the benefits of this solution.
- Give your audience a call to action.

This outline still works more than 2,400 years later because it strategically weaves a product into the middle of the narrative after getting the audience's attention and explaining a key problem they face, which is the limited goal of most brand-building marketing campaigns.

FIGURE 5.18 Real Life Trick Shots 3 | Dude Perfect

FIGURE 5.19 Do You Love Me?

It does this before describing the product's benefits and giving the audience a call to action, which is the limited objective of most performance marketing campaigns. In other words, this product-led content strategy works because it transforms a product into a solution.

The Benefits of Product-Led Video Content (with Examples)

Your content marketing teams should want to watch and analyze the following two videos, so you can apply what you learn to your own product-led content strategy.

On February 25, 2019, *Real Life Trick Shots 3 | Dude Perfect* got 124 million views and 2.4 million engagements (Figure 5.18).

More importantly, it demonstrated that a video sponsored by Sam's Club could get 1,503 times more views and 4,528 times more engagements than the top video created by Sam's Club.

On December 29, 2020, *Do You Love Me?* demonstrated that Boston Dynamics knows how to develop a good storyline so their product can be the star of the show in a way that is relevant, engaging, and interesting to watch (Figure 5.19).

The video's description says, "Our whole crew got together to celebrate the start of what we hope will be a happier year: Happy New Year from all of us at Boston Dynamics."

You and I both know this is just another product demo. But it's a product demo video that got 35 million views and 1.3 million engagements.

Content Marketing Measurement and Control

In the fifth step of the old content marketing planning process, I asked budding content marketers, "How will you gauge your efforts and continually optimize your performance?"

Then, I added this word of caution: "Just because you can measure just about anything these days, doesn't mean that you should. Start by focusing on what you really need to know, based on what goals you are looking to achieve."

The unintended consequences of this approach was to put far too much time and distance between the topics of goals and measurement, which often led many of the least successful content marketers to select metrics to measure content performance that were not aligned with their organization's goals for content marketing. So, let me avoid this unplanned outcome in this concluding section on Content Marketing Measurement and Control by explicitly juxtaposing goals and metrics.

For their 2022 Content Marketing Benchmarks, Budgets, and Trends reports, CMI and MarketingProfs asked B2B and B2C marketers in North America what goals content marketing helps them achieve. Respondents said:

- Create brand awareness.
- Build credibility/trust.
- Educate audience(s).
- Build loyalty with existing clients/customers.
- Generate demand/leads.
- Nurture subscribers/audience/leads.
- Drive attendance to one or more in-person or virtual events.
- Generate sales/revenue.
- Support the launch of a new product.
- Build a subscribed audience.

These same marketers were asked which metrics have provided the most insight into B2B and B2C content performance in the last 12 months. Respondents said:

- Website engagement
- Conversions

- Website traffic
- Email engagement
- Social media analytics
- Quality of leads
- Search rankings
- Email subscriber numbers
- Quantity of leads
- Cost to acquire a lead, subscriber, and/or customer

Different marketers will have different goals and use different metrics as KPIs. But if the metrics that they use to get insight into their content performance aren't fully aligned with their goals for content marketing, then, "Houston, we have a problem."

That's why it's imperative to identify which metrics are linked to business outcomes instead of marketing outputs if you want to set up your content marketing initiatives for success.

Adjust the KPIs

In response to the pandemic, 20 percent of B2B and 23 percent of B2C marketers adjusted their KPIs. I would love to know which marketers adjusted which KPIs.

In Chapter 2 of this book, Matt Bailey defined "KPI" as a metric that helps you understand how you are doing against your objectives. But different organizations have different objectives, which is also why KPIs tend to be unique to each organization. So, let's apply what we learned about digital analytics to content marketing.

- If your goal is to "support the launch of a new product," then use "search rankings," "social media analytics," and "website traffic" as your KPIs.
- If your goals are to "generate demand/leads" or "drive attendance to one or more in-person or virtual events," then use "quantity of leads" and "quality of leads" as your KPIs.
- If your goal is to "build a subscribed audience," then use "email subscriber numbers" as your KPI, as you will learn in Chapter 9 from Michael Stebbins.
- If your goal is to "nurture subscribers/audience/leads," then use "email engagement" or "website engagement" as your KPIs.
- If your goal is to "generate sales/revenue," then use "conversions" and "cost to acquire a lead, subscriber, and/or customer" as your KPIs.

- If your goals are to "create brand awareness," "build credibility/trust," "educate audience(s)," or "build loyalty with existing clients/customers," then what are your KPIs?

To understand how you are doing against these objectives, you need to periodically conduct market research. There are several questions that you need to ask before you start gathering information, advises Nate Laban, the Owner of **Growth Survey Systems**. These questions (and some quick answers) include the following:

- **What audience are you targeting and can you access them?** (For example, Google provides different tools to help you access different audiences. If you are targeting Internet users, you should use Google Surveys, but if you are targeting a list of contacts, you should use Google Forms.)
- **Do your contacts need to be pre-screened?** (You can use screening questions to filter respondents to your survey. For example, respondents first see your screening question, and then those who select a threshold answer such as "Yes" or "I plan to" can answer the remaining questions in your survey.)
- **How many responses do you need?** (The number depends on how confident you want to be in your results. The U.S. population is 328.2 million people, so 384 responses have a margin of error of +/– 5 percent, and 1,067 responses have a margin of error of +/– 3 percent.)
- **Have all stakeholders agreed to the objectives?** (Do yourself a favor and make that boring bulleted list of research goals and then make sure all other stakeholders on your team have contributed and approved your goals before you start writing your questionnaire.)

You're ready to write the questions that your target audience will answer.

At the "See" stage of the customer journey, one of your KPIs should be "brand awareness." This metric measures the portion of a market that can identify a brand either when prompted (aided) or unprompted (unaided).

For example: When it comes to <category>, what brands come to mind?

At the "Feel" stage of the customer journey, one of your KPIs should be "favorability." This metric measures a target audience's feelings or attitudes toward a company or its products.

For example: How would you describe your overall opinion of <brand>?

- Very favorable
- Somewhat favorable
- Neutral

- Somewhat unfavorable
- Very unfavorable

At the "Think" stage, one of your KPIs should be "consideration." This metric measures how consumers weigh different factors in their minds while planning a purchase.

For example: Which factors are important when considering *<product category>*?

At the "Do" stage of the customer journey, one of your KPIs should be "purchase intent." This metric measures the respondent's attitude toward buying a product or service.

For example: Will you buy <brand> the next time you shop for <category>?

At the "Care" stage of the customer journey, one of your KPIs should be "brand affinity." This metric measures an individual's brand preference in a product category, which tends to retain loyal customers for longer.

For example: "How do you feel about <brand>?

- I love it.
- I like it.
- I'm neutral.
- I don't like it.
- I hate it.

There are other questions that you can ask your target audience at least once a year—or a couple of times a year if you're using a seasonal calendar to plan for the next 12 months.

For example, an article by Michaela Jefferson entitled, "**Inside the Grand Prix winning Direct Line campaign that delivered against all measures**," which was published in *Marketing Week* on October 27, 2021, reported that all three of the creatives that we discussed earlier "delivered recognition significantly above the Kantar norm of 33 percent. The ad featuring Bumblebee scored 62 percent, Robocop scored 55 percent, and Donatello scored 53 percent."

She added, "The brand also closely tracked performance against three brand associations which 'ladder up' to a perception of brand superiority, and improvements were again recorded across all three. Those associations were: 'are best at solving problems' (+3.8 points), 'goes beyond what you would expect from an insurer' (+4.7 points), and 'will sort out claims more efficiently than any other insurance providers' (+4.2 points)."

So, if you can measure ad creative with these metrics, you should consider using them as KPIs to understand how your content is doing against your objectives.

Change the Content Marketing Metrics

Finally, 14 percent of B2B and 13 percent of B2C marketers changed their content marketing metrics (e.g., they set up new analytics/dashboards) in response to the pandemic.

I can't tell if these data mean that content marketers set up new metrics in Google Analytics because their goals had changed or if they merely set up new dashboards. The first is critical if there've been changes in consumer behavior. And the second is useful if you set up an "action dashboard."

Much has already been written by other industry observers about how the global pandemic has dramatically changed consumer behavior. For example, it's no small feat to understand travel restrictions, rules, and exemptions as COVID-19 cases rise, fall, and rise again. So, it's hardly surprising that many travelers are now planning domestic trips instead of international travel.

Let me share a short excerpt from a post I wrote entitled, "Best video content marketing examples from the New Media Academy," which illustrates what you can do when consumer behavior changes.

In July 2020, I started teaching a series of courses at the New Media Academy in the United Arab Emirates (UAE). There were 22 content creators and social media influencers who were "students" in the New Media Academy's first Impact Digital Creator Program. I put the term "students" in quotation marks because these creators were already successful.

FIGURE 5.20   Let's Go—The Emirates (**https://youtu.be/G_cf-dPyeqg**)

The New Media Academy teamed up a year ago with Beautiful Destinations, the world's leading travel content marketing agency, to showcase the UAE's hidden gems in beautiful cinematic videos for the World's Coolest Winter campaign.

Check out this video, which is entitled, *Let's Go—The Emirates* (Figure 5.20).

Several of my "students" are featured in the video, including Fatima AlHashmi, the first Emirati Opera singer; Ghaith Al Falasi, an FIA certified race car driver as well as a self-taught off-roader and drift enthusiast; Abdullah Omar AlAli, an AlJazira jiu-jitsu player; Fahima Falaknaz, the first Emirati female boxer; and Chef Saud Al Matrooshi, the first Emirati chef at Emirates Flight Catering.

So, what transforms this case study into a success story? Well, the World's Coolest Winter, the UAE's first federal domestic tourism campaign, which was launched on December 12, 2020, and concluded on January 25, 2021, generated measurable results.

The country decided to promote domestic tourism because the pandemic had dramatically impacted international tourism. And the direct contribution of the travel and tourism sector to the UAE's gross domestic product (GDP) was AED 68.5 billion (USD 18.7 billion), which is equivalent to 5.2 percent of the country's total GDP.

The 45-day campaign generated the following:

- More than 2,000 media reports that reached over 20 million people across the world
- 215 million views on videos that captured the UAE's beauty
- 950,000 domestic tourists across the country
- AED1 billion of revenue for the hospitality sector within 1 month

Yep, that's what transforms this case study into a success story. So, if there've been changes in consumer behavior in your industry, that should prompt you to consider changing your goals. That means that you should consider setting up new metrics in Google Analytics too.

What are the benefits of setting up a dashboard in Google Analytics? Dashboards let you monitor many metrics at once, so you can quickly check the health of your accounts or see correlations between different reports.

Setting up an "action dashboard" is especially useful. To learn why, you should read the blog post entitled, "**Digital Dashboards: Strategic & Tactical: Best Practices, Tips, Examples**," which was published on Occam's Razor by Avinash Kaushik back on July 15, 2014.

He clarified the purpose of an "action dashboard" and explained how it should be used within an organization:

- **Dashboards are not reports:** Don't data puke. Instead, include insights, recommendations for actions, and business impact.
- **Never leave the interpretation of data to executives:** Always let them focus on your recommendations for action with the benefit of their wisdom and their knowledge of business strategy.
- **Don't skip anything:** When it comes to KPIs, segments, and recommendations, make sure you cover customer acquisition, behavior, and outcomes end-to-end.
- **Context is everything:** Great dashboards leverage targets, benchmarks, and competitive intelligence deliver context.
- **Create a meaningful dashboard:** The primary purpose of a dashboard is not to inform and not to educate. The primary purpose is to drive action!

Hopefully, this chapter has prepared you to be successful in content marketing as well as on the OMCA exam. This required me to go well beyond "teaching to the test."

Why? Because many the competencies and skills required to qualify for employment in a supervised associate position in content marketing are fundamentally changing.

Nevertheless, content marketing continues to be a strategic marketing approach focused on creating and distributing valuable, relevant, and consistent content to attract and retain a clearly defined audience—and, ultimately, to drive profitable customer action.

CHAPTER 6

Social Media Marketing

By Matt Bailey and Greg Jarboe

To our readers: This chapter is different. Greg and I decided to co-write this content, but as we talked about it, it turned into a podcast. We've edited down the important bits to meet the OMCA requirements, but we thought that presenting our content in a conversation format may help you get through a jam-packed chapter on a subject that changes frequently. Or you could tune in and listen to this chapter on the *Endless Coffee Cup* podcast (Figure 6.1). —Matt

What you'll learn in this chapter:

- Social media marketing terms and concepts
- How social media impacts business goals
- How social media integrates with other channels
- How to evaluate and use influencers to extend your message
- What content is effective in different channels
- How to plan content for different platforms
- Why you should track and measure social media

Welcome to the *Endless Coffee Cup* Podcast

MATT: Well, hello, dear listener, and welcome to another edition of the *Endless Coffee Cup* podcast. Today is something a little different. I have Greg Jarboe with me. Greg, welcome back to the show.

Defining Social Media Marketing

Featured Guest:

Greg Jarboe

Long time friends Matt Bailey and Greg Jarboe are partnering on an upcoming book from Wiley, *"Digital Marketing Fundamentals: OMCP's Official Guide to OMCA Certification."* The core of the book is defining each area of digital marketing and outlining the critical skills and knowledge necessary to achieve the OMCA Certification.

As a major part of digital marketing, social media becomes the most difficult to define. Greg and Matt discuss the definitive practices in social media, and define the difference between core skills and changing tactics.

CEO & Co-Founder, SEO-PR

FIGURE 6.1 Endless Coffee Cup Podcast, June 14, 2022

GREG: Matt, I feel like I've never left.

MATT: You know, I feel as though you've never left as well.

GREG: Well, let's hope that we give the audience something new.

Social Media Context

MATT: Greg, we have something new. We're going to talk about social media.

Term "Social Media" Coined in 2004

GREG: Well, I was actually in the room when the term was coined by Chris Shipley. This was back in 2004, and she was planning to launch a new event called BlogOn. She said, "Greg, I'd like you to be a speaker at the first social media conference." And I asked, "Chris, what's social media?" It was a term that she had made up. And I said, "Well, if nobody knows what the term means, then why do you expect anyone to attend?" So, I was there when she defined the term for the first time. It included blogs and social networks.

MATT: Hey, since we're at the beginning of a good discussion, I should provide our listeners with some background. Greg and I are writing a book along with other co-authors. It's entitled *Digital Marketing Fundamentals: OMCP's Official Guide to OMCA Certification.*

We're writing the chapter on social media marketing. As we were going back and forth about how we should do this with something that changes so quickly, I said, "Let's make a recording of us talking about it and put the edited transcript in the book."

GREG: And I said, "That's a brilliant idea." Except I had one fundamental disagreement. Your shorthand for what we are about to embark on was "Socratic dialogue."

Socratic dialogue assumes that we're going to be engaged in a rational discussion with deep insight and penetrating analysis and all that left brain stuff. Right?

But a different metaphor came to my mind. I don't know if you remember it, but back in the 1990s there was a comic strip called *Calvin and Hobbes.*

MATT: Yes, yes.

GREG: Calvin, the little boy, and Hobbes, his stuffed tiger, frequently play a game called Calvinball. No sport is less organized than Calvinball. There is only one permanent rule. You can't play it the same way twice.

The improvisational game can feature the Babysitter Flag, Corollary Zone, Invisible Sector, Opposite Pole, Perimeter of Wisdom, Pernicious Poem Place, or Very Sorry Song. That makes it a contest of creativity and adaptability rather than skill and stamina.

Scoring is arbitrary, whimsical, and capricious like, "Q to 12."

And the lack of fixed rules leads to frequent debates over who scored, where the boundaries are, and when the game is finished.

That is the right metaphor for social media marketing because it is hard to learn. And then next week, you have to learn the new rules, and you have to adapt. And if you adapt well, you have a chance of winning.

And that's hard to do. In fact, the only other player beyond Calvin and Hobbes who picked it up quickly was Rosalind, the babysitter.

MATT: Oh, I love the metaphor because I can't think of another industry where as soon as we can explain the rules, somebody will change them.

GREG: For example, in June of 2021, Adam Mosseri, the head of Instagram, declared, "We're no longer just a square photo-sharing app."

And he added, "Right now we're focused on four key areas: Creators, Video, Shopping, and Messaging."

MATT: So, once again, the rules changed in the middle of the game. There were winners, there were losers, and there were people standing there wondering what had happened.

So, it has nothing to do with your digital marketing skills, education, and experience. These decisions were made on high for the profitability of a company and they filtered down into algorithmic changes.

GREG: Yes, and then the boundaries shifted.

Key Definitions and Framework

MATT: Well, okay. In a Socratic dialogue, you start by defining terms. So, I love that you started out with your story of where the term was first coined. And now we face the question of how do we define social media?

GREG: There should be a "best if used by" date stamped on everything that we say.

Social Media Marketing Today

MATT: Yes. here's Wikipedia's definition.

"Social media are interactive digital channels that facilitate the creation and sharing of information, ideas, interests, and other forms of expression through virtual communities and networks."

GREG: That's not a bad definition. But I will tell you that when people use the term "social media" today, there are two definitions that float around. One includes Facebook and anything that they've acquired like Instagram. But somehow it does not include YouTube. Oh, no, no, no. YouTube's in a different category.

And that sort of made sense until 2015, when Facebook decided to adopt a "video first" strategy. And they started to cram features borrowed from YouTube, Snapchat, and TikTok into either Facebook and/or Instagram wherever they could.

And some industry analysts still said Facebook and Instagram were social media. But YouTube wasn't. Excuse me. YouTube is an online video sharing and social media platform. So, just what puts them in a different category? That's why you have to start off any discussion like this one with the question, "What do you include in your definition of social media?"

MATT: Well, okay. So, I'm going to throw out my definition. And when I was doing my master's degree just a few short years ago, a lot of content that had to do with social media was referred to—hold on, Greg—Web 2.0!

In university level content, they're still using terms such as Web 2.0, which is what we now call social media. Here's what I would say defines social media: it is content on a platform that integrates or allows community participation. It's posted content or information that allows a public response. It often produces this in a threaded view so that you can see subsequent comments, shares, or likes in an organized view. So, it's not always based on the entire site or page, but it's per post.

GREG: I agree. Somebody may post some content—a video, photo, or text—which gets a lot of comments or replies, shares or retweets, and likes or reactions. And, this can kick off a discussion among other members of their niche audience or broader community that goes well beyond what the person who initiated that thread may have had in mind. That's why Chris Shipley called it "social" media.

MATT: So, how do you define social media marketing?

GREG: I use *Search Engine Journal*'s definition. They say, "Social media marketing is the use of social media platforms to market a business's products or services, connect with existing customers, reach new audiences, and build their brand."

Areas Associated with Social Media Marketing Today

MATT: That is great. So, let's talk about what areas we associate with social media marketing. Businesses often ask, "What channels should I use?"

My response to them is, "What do you want to do?" That's the first question.

GREG: Yeah. Too many people jumped into social media because it was the new, new thing. Everyone else is doing it. So, I've got to go do it, too.

What are you doing? "Well, I'm trying to learn how to write in fewer than 140 characters." Okay, why? "Because it is new."

So, we all focused on the quirky little features that we had to contort ourselves to learn how to use as opposed to asking, "For what purpose, what reason?"

You're right. It's great to define your goals and objectives ahead of time. And maybe social media will fit into them and maybe they won't.

Content Marketing

MATT: So, how does that fit into content marketing?

GREG: Content marketing overlaps with social media marketing because there's some of the content that you can create that you might post on Facebook, you might upload to YouTube, or you might put on another social media platform.

You may have a message that you then tailor for the quirky, individualistic nature of a particular platform. That's fine. But guess what?

You can also communicate by posting new content on your website. This is where the blog comes back. If you consider blogs social media, then putting your content on a blog is part of a social media marketing campaign.

But the way Facebook has redefined things, there are a lot of people who not only forget YouTube is a social medium, but they also forget that blogs are the original social media, even before Facebook came along.

In fact, Facebook's biggest challenger—once upon a time—was Myspace. So, Facebook wasn't even the first social network that was out there. They just are the biggest surviving network that is out there.

Content marketing focuses on creating valuable and relevant content that can attract a clearly defined audience. And oh, by the way, the purpose of attracting that clearly defined audience is to make money one way or another.

Start by asking, "What is my audience interested in?" Then, "How can I get them to visit my website, visit my blog, visit my social media platforms, listen to my podcast, or listen to my executives speaking at events?"

And, you know what? Events—digital, in-person, and hybrid—are very effective content marketing channels and for some reason they aren't considered social media.

Content marketing starts off trying to attract and retain a clearly defined audience. And there are a lot of reasons why businesses and other kinds of organizations want to do that.

Finally, content marketing, in some ways, overlaps with social media marketing. But in other ways it's different and broader. And, okay, there's a lot of elbowing at the table when people are fighting over budgets. But at the end of the day, you've got to ask, "Did we move the needle when it came to achieving our goals and objectives?"

MATT: I see content marketing like a capstone activity because you need social, you need SEO, and you need some paid channels to get your message out. Content marketing requires these disciplines to do it well.

GREG: Well, it gets messy.

But show me who your brightest leaders are, put them in charge, and don't worry about the name of the team. If your content marketer is the director and your social media manager takes direction, that's fine.

MATT: If it's the other way around, if it's a social media director who is telling the content marketing manager what kind of content will resonate with an audience, then that's fine too. Just tell me who is strong or weak in your organization and structure it accordingly.

But content marketing and social media marketing are frequently confused, and people do need to define where they overlap, where they don't overlap, as well as who's playing the lead role, and who's following.

Reputation Management

MATT: I think that also goes along with reputation management.

I see that in local businesses. They want people to find their listing on Google, but they're concerned that people can also leave a review. What reviews are added, what people say—that is part of reputation management.

But that's the nature of social media itself. We're allowing community participation. And I forget who it was, but they said that if you allow anyone to say anything, someone's going to start complaining. And social media has really allowed people to comment now on anything.

Recently, we had a bad accident in my town. I went to the local paper online to see some details about it. Then I went to the bottom of the article and started reading the comments.

Greg, why do they add comments to the bottom of a well-researched article from a reporter who was on the spot? Why do we think it's a good idea to let the general public comment on an article?

GREG: Oh, I can answer that as a former editor of a local newspaper. It's because there are 57 percent fewer newspaper reporters and editors today than there were in 2008.

In the New England town where I live, our local newspaper suspended its print edition last month. And the online edition, which is called *Wicked Local,* rarely sends journalists to cover local events.

So, now we're using social media to crowdsource the news.

Disinformation

MATT: Wow. Which brings me to the big elephant in the room that is filling this vacuum. And it's not just the public who's asking questions, making comments, and leaving reviews. That's actually just a good, healthy conversation. What is more problematic is disinformation.

GREG: This is not misinformation, which may be spread without the sender having harmful intentions. We're talking about disinformation, which is the deliberate spread of misleading or biased information.

You see this more often than not in politics, although, frankly, there've been a lot of disinformation campaigns around COVID-19, which 75 percent of Americans believe has prolonged the pandemic, according to a survey by the Institute for Public Relations.

In late 2017, Facebook said that as many as 126 million of its users had seen content from Russian disinformation campaigns over the previous 2 years. And Twitter said that it had found 36,000 Russian bots spreading tweets related to the 2016 U.S. elections.

So, one of the problems is that anybody can post a comment. Okay. Are they a real person or are they a Russian troll? Or, heaven forbid, are they a bot that's just been turned loose?

And that is a much more problematic area for social media marketers.

MATT: Absolutely. It falls under the astroturfing label as well. We're going to make something look like it is a groundswell of citizen demands when in reality it's a bot farm, and it is creating a false sense that's something's important.

GREG: Yep. SparkToro and Followerwonk conducted a joint analysis in May 2022 and found 19.4 percent of active Twitter accounts were likely to be fake or spam.

Monitoring/Participating in Conversations

MATT: Well, this leads us to a discussion on monitoring conversations.

Some businesses have set up alerts just to see what people are saying about their brand, their product, or their CEO. They're using it more for crisis communications because they want to make sure that everything said about them is good. If someone complains, "We're on it."

The next level is actually participating in conversations where I'm not proactively going out and creating content, but I'm going to participate when the conversation rolls around.

But the danger of that is the so-called "1 percent rule." In Internet culture, the general rule of thumb pertaining to participation in a community states that only 1 percent of the users of a community will create original content, only 10 percent of users will like, share, or comment on a post, and 90 percent are simply lurkers. They're just there to read and watch, but they don't engage.

GREG: According to data from Tubular Labs, video content on YouTube and Facebook got a total of 5 trillion views in the last 90 days and 206 billion engagements, which includes likes, comments, and shares. So, about 4 percent of people who watch social videos, engage with them.

MATT: So, there's a danger to using social media as a primary listening device to get the voice of the consumer, or to pick the customer's brain to find out what they're thinking. What you're actually reading is the vocal minority.

GREG: And you can tell pretty quickly that vocal minority is disproportionately male. So, one of the things as you start digging into social listening, you're listening to a bunch of loudmouth guys who've got to express their opinions. And you're not listening to the more reasonable guys or, in a lot of cases, women who seem savvy enough to say, "I'm not going to get dragged into that mud pit."

MATT: Yup. I'll read it, but I'm not going to add my name to the comments. So, I think that it's important to remember it's a very vocal minority that are actually creating and commenting. If you want to hear directly from the types of audiences you care about, then you should be using other ways to acquire market intelligence.

GREG: And make sure you also use some audit tools to discover if the people who are making the loudest noise are real people or fake followers.

Influencer Marketing

MATT: Which brings us to the next area that often overlaps with social media marketing and that's influencer marketing.

GREG: Now, most marketers tend to target social media influencers. But

I would consider a journalist to be an influencer. But most marketers say, "Oh, that's PR. That's a whole different thing altogether."

MATT: Well, I love the distinction that's being made in the industry right now between the title "influencer" and the actual influence that they can create. I'd like to call them "a person of influence" rather than an influencer.

I was in a crisis communications lecture just yesterday, and they were talking about how part of your crisis communication plan is deciding when you bring in an expert. And that expert speaks to their level of knowledge. That is an influencer because they have established authority. They speak to that, and this assists the credibility of your response. So, an influencer is not always a want-to-be fitness guru.

GREG: Well, it can be a want-to-be fitness guru. It depends on the topic.

When most people talk about influencer marketing, they're talking about social media influencers. But, here again, you've got to be careful.

Most social media influencers learned early on that they got compensated better if they had more followers. So, guess what? Many found a way to pump up their fake followers.

Then, marketers figured out how to detect fake followers. And said, "Now we're going to look at engagement. That's our new metric."

And then many social media influencers figured a way to generate fake engagement metrics.

So, if you're going to work with influencers in your social media marketing campaign, then you've got to vet them. You've got to double-check that they're real. And, this is much more important, their audience is real.

Fortunately, a lot of tools and platforms have been developed that detect influencer fraud. As a result, the percentage of influencer accounts impacted by fraud has fallen across the board to less than 50 percent, according to "The State of Influencer Marketing 2022: Benchmark Report."

MATT: But that's still a huge percentage.

GREG: So, vetting them is becoming even more important as influencer marketing budgets continue growing.

The Influencer Marketing Hub says over three quarters of brand marketers out there have dedicated a budget to influencer marketing. And they estimate that brands will spend about $16.4 billion on influencer marketing in 2022.

That's big bucks.

That's why you've got to be able to measure what matters to make sure that the influencer is actually influential and that the influencer's audience is even remotely interested in your product, your service, your brand, or your cause.

Digital Advertising

MATT: Absolutely. There are so many more methods of measurement now that are assisting us to measure the true influence that is wielded by an individual who has a following.

The next section is digital advertising, which is interesting because I remember some of the conferences that we were at a couple of years ago, everyone was saying, "You've got to get on Facebook. You've got to build your audience. You've got to put hours into your organic posting."

And a few short years later, Facebook changed the algorithm, and they reduced their organic reach. So, if you are a brand or a business, you are now reaching about 2 percent of that audience.

And if you want to reach more of that audience, you've got to pay. You've got to boost your posts. You've got to use their network in order to reach the same level of audience that you were reaching before.

And this goes to what we were talking about before. The rules changed all of a sudden and all that work that companies put into developing that organic presence on Facebook pretty much evaporated overnight.

And, hey, you know what? It's the social networks being completely honest. They are money driven. And they're going to make decisions that enable them to create more revenue.

So, every platform adjusts their algorithms to favor certain types of content, reduce corporate content, and force you into using paid media to ignite earned media. Which is not a bad business model if they have the audience—like Facebook does.

They know all the demographic information. They know what you like. They know what you're looking at. They know what groups you're a part of. So, you can actually be a bit more targeted by advertising on these platforms to people that follow certain hashtags, follow certain personalities, or express that I like this content.

And now you can target them based on the hamster wheel of content creation, when you're trying to build an audience on a third-party platform. I'm just going to target my ad campaign on whom I want focus on.

GREG: But there's often a problem with targeting the people I want. Too many small businesses, medium-sized businesses, and even very large brands think they want a demographic audience.

"I want women who are 18 to 35."

Okay. Why?

"Well, because in the television era, the only information I had about an audience was its size and composition by gender and age. And I used to be able to pick TV shows to run ads against based on those factors. So, that's how I'm comfortable targeting."

Well, as you just said, when you get the social media, you can get a whole lot of information about people's intent and behavior.

And if they've been visiting 14 sites in the last 2 days looking at different cars, then guess what? They're interested in buying a car! And, oh, by the way, whether you're Facebook, YouTube, or any of the other social platforms, they can target these people too.

They can serve up audiences based on their affinities. You know, I'm an auto enthusiast. I'm passionate about cars. Or, based on their in-market behavior, I'm planning to purchase a motor vehicle.

If they're only using demographics to reach the people they want to reach, then they are stuck on a 20th century model of market segmentation.

It's time to wake up and smell the coffee, which seems to be the right thing to say on an *Endless Coffee Cup* podcast. And understand that you're not leveraging other information that's available for targeting that you should be using instead.

MATT: Absolutely. Regardless of their demographic, people have needs. And when we understand their needs and have a product that meets their needs, then I don't care what their age or gender is.

GREG: So, if you are using two-dimensional thinking in a three-dimensional world, you're going to get hit from below or above.

Social Media Marketing and Organizational Structure

MATT: There we go. So, the next thing we deal with is the organizational structure.

And how you deal with social media is going to be different based on the size of your team. You alluded to this before. Who's in charge? Where does it fall?

So, for organizations with small marketing teams of two to five people, where would we put social media marketing, Greg?

GREG: It's only going to be one person. So, you don't have any organizational structure problems at all.

This is a really typical example of what's actually going on in the real world out there. One person has to do it all, and they only have so much bandwidth, so they have to make trade-offs. They focus on what matters most because that's all they can do today.

MATT: What structure works best for organizations with mid-sized teams of 6 to 20 people?

GREG: You might have a centralized social media marketing group of two to five people that works with multiple brands, products, and departments throughout the organization. Or each brand, product, department might have its own social media marketing specialist.

If your group is centralized, then it may also be structured by social media platforms. But this can be problematic.

You wouldn't have wanted to be the Vine specialist when it was shut down in 2017. And you wouldn't have wanted to be the Google+ specialist when that was shut down in 2019.

So, try to get some cross-training because you never know if or when you'll be hit by the Calvinball and required to sing the Very Sorry Song.

MATT: What about organizations with more than 20 marketers?

GREG: Your organization may have six or more social media marketers. But it may also outsource some specialized social media marketing activities, like video production and social media advertising, to outside agencies and consultants. So, that will make your organizational structure even more like Calvinball.

MATT: So, when do I staff and when do I hire an outside agency to manage an ongoing social media marketing program or the launch of a new campaign?

GREG: Well, if it is crucial to your success, then you better have someone on your staff. If you've got something that's seasonal—that you want to dial up and dial back—then it is actually pretty handy to have an outside agency.

MATT: I find an agency is helpful because typically they've got all the tools in place. They have people who know how to use the tools. It's a great way to get experienced people very quickly. And, as you said, it can ebb and flow with the business.

The downside is the agency also has 20 other companies that they are doing this for. So, you're on a budget of time of what they can do for you.

GREG: Another downside of the agency is the hidden mark-up for renting one of their talented people instead of hiring a new person in-house.

MATT: What do you mean?

GREG: When you hire a person in-house, you generally give them an annual salary.

Then, you need to take their salary and multiply by 2.0 to get the fully loaded cost of a full-time person on your staff.

But if you hire an agency, you need to multiply that same person's salary by 2.7. Why? Because in addition to paying the person's salary and covering their fully loaded costs, you also have to pay the agency enough to provide it with a profit margin.

And I know this because I've worked on both the client and agency side.

But this only works if you've got enough work to do 12 months a year. If you've got 8 months of work a year, then the flexibility of the outside agency is a little more useful.

So again, the number is 2.0 versus 2.7. That's the difference between having the person in-house and paying for the same person at an outside agency.

MATT: That's a great metric.

GREG: Well, here's how to use it.

On June 19, 2022, Jim Puzzanghera wrote an article in the *Boston Sunday Globe*, entitled, "The world economic outlook turns grim as 'once in a lifetime' shocks take their toll."

He said, "The pernicious forces largely responsible for these problems also are rippling through economies across the globe, as war in Europe combines with continued pandemic disruptions to pile new hardships onto a world still reeling from the devastating effects of COVID-19."

Puzzanghera added, "Soaring prices for energy and food since Russia's invasion of Ukraine are slowing growth in nations large and small, sharply reversing the soaring economic gains of last year."

So, if you head up a big organization with more than 20 marketers, then having a mix of staff and agency people gives you a lot more elbow room. It's easier to dial back your agency than it is to lay off people. I know because I've had to do both.

MATT: Absolutely. That's never a fun part of the deal.

And then there are the social media platforms. They're still playing Calvinball.

GREG: You're right. And on June 15, 2022, Alex Heath of *The Verge* wrote an article entitled, "Facebook is changing its algorithm to take on TikTok, leaked memo reveals."

The leaked internal memo was written by Tom Alison, the head of Facebook, who revealed the platform plans to turn its main feed into a "discovery engine" for video content.

Apparently, the main feed will become "a mix of Stories and Reels at the top, followed by posts its discovery engine recommends from across both Facebook and Instagram. It'll be a more visual, video-heavy experience with clearer prompts to direct message friends a post."

So, we've just entered the Pernicious Poem Place and the score is Q to 12.

Social Media Marketing Strategy and Planning

MATT: This brings us to the next section: describing social media marketing strategy and planning. So, can social media impact your business goals?

How Social Media Impacts Business Goals

GREG: It should, but way too often it doesn't.

One of the things that a strategist should do at the beginning of any campaign, let alone during any ongoing program, is to ask, "What are we trying to accomplish?"

If you tell top management, "Our strategy is to send out 47 tweets a week," will they approve your plan? No, they won't. They'll want a strategy and plan that will move the needle.

So, the question you may be asked is, "How many tweets do we need to sell a car?"

That's a good question. And there's no answer. Why? Because there's no correlation between marketing inputs and business outcomes.

That's why you want to start with "My objective is to sell a car." Or pick a different product or service. Whatever it is, start with your objective. And then work backward.

According to Luth Research, one consumer journey included more than 900 digital interactions before a 32-year-old mother of two decided to lease an SUV.

Did social media help her during any of these shopping moments? If it did, then great!

So, what was the return on marketing investment for the money that you put into that social media campaign, social media advertising, or influencer marketing program?

Top management will probably know how much you spent. What they'll want you to do is "show a return" on your activities.

Did your strategy increase brand awareness, consideration, or purchase intent? If it did, then by how much? Did your plan generate high-quality leads? If it did, then how many?

Value of Influencers

MATT: We'll talk more about social media measurement later in this podcast. But how do you determine the value of influencers?

GREG: Actually, I wrote an article about that in September 2021 for *Search Engine Journal.* It's entitled, "How to Calculate the ROI of Influencer Marketing Campaigns."

The demand for the top celebrities and influencers is so great that Clear, a global brand, paid Cristiano Ronaldo, one of the most popular soccer players in the world, an estimated $619,497 to $1 million for a single Instagram post.

With so much money getting poured into reaching Ronaldo's 339 million Instagram followers, you can bet dollars to donuts that someone at Clear asked, "What's the ROI of our latest influencer marketing campaign?"

That's a great question—and it's one that all of us need to know how to answer.

So, how do you calculate your Return on Marketing Investment (ROMI)? The formula is [Incremental Revenue Attributable to Marketing ($) × Contribution Margin (%) – Marketing Spending ($)]/Marketing Spending ($).

So, let's say Ronaldo's #sponsored Instagram post cost $1 million, just so we can use a round number. And let's say that the contribution margin on Clear shampoo is 60 percent, which is just a completely unscientific, wild-assed guess.

If Ronaldo's post generated $5 million in incremental revenue, then you multiply that by 60 percent to get $3 million in gross profit. Then, you subtract the $1 million spent on influencer marketing and then divide the $2 million result by the $1 million spent on influencer marketing to get a ROMI of 2.

Like this: [$5,000,000 * 60% – $1,000,000]/$1,000,000 = 2.

In other words, every dollar that Clear spent on influencer marketing generated an additional $2 on the global brand's bottom line.

Now, how can you be sure that you can attribute $5 million in incremental revenue to Ronaldo's post?

Well, one way is to leverage the fact that Ronaldo was promoting the new Clear Men Legend Shampoo by CR7, which has a design, scent, and texture personally selected by Cristiano Ronaldo, who wears the number 7 on his jersey.

In addition, Clear Legend Shampoo by CR7 was only available at leading drug stores and supermarkets in Malaysia, Cambodia, Myanmar, Turkey, Kazakhstan, Uzbekistan, Azerbaijan, Greece, China, KSA, Gulf, Levant, Mashreq, Maghreb, Russia, Romania, and Greece.

All the marketers at Clear needed to do was track incremental revenue from this sub-brand and compare that to revenue from Thailand, Italy, and Portugal, where Clear Legend Shampoo by CR7 wasn't available yet.

Now, social media marketing strategists may not want to bet their jobs on the possibility that a celebrity or mega-influencer with more than 1 million followers can generate $5 million in incremental revenue with a single post.

Well, they'll be relieved then to discover that smaller influencers will probably give them an even better ROMI.

For example, micro-influencers with less than 15,000 Instagram followers might make around $100 per post, although it depends on the profile.

However, the calculation for your return on marketing investment remains the same.

So, let's say a micro-influencer's #sponsored Instagram post costs $100. And let's say that the contribution margin on your brand is 60 percent, which is as good a guess as I can make without knowing more about your product category.

If the post generates $1,000 in incremental revenue, then you multiply that by 60 percent to get $600 in gross profit. Then, you subtract the $100 spent on marketing and then divide the $500 result by the $100 spent on marketing to get a ROMI of 5.

In other words, every dollar spent on micro-influencer marketing would have generated an additional $5 for your bottom line.

Now, generating $1,000 in incremental revenue isn't going to get you a promotion. But let's say you identified 10 micro-influencers and were able to generate $10,000 in incremental revenue. Do you see where this is headed?

That's how you determine the value of influencers.

MATT: Which brings us to the new buzzword: *social commerce.*

GREG: Terrific. But before you jump on the social commerce bandwagon next week, ask yourself: "How many cars can we sell with that?" Or "How many bottles of shampoo?"

And once you use your business goals to determine if your strategy and plans will move the needle, then a lot of the silliness in social media marketing falls away. And some of the serious opportunities actually begin to emerge because there are times when social media marketing pays its way.

MATT: And it gets right back to what we talked about at the beginning. One of the biggest questions is, "How do I justify this? How do I rationalize the time and the investment that we're making in that?"

And you're establishing a very clear connection between business goals and marketing strategy. And without that, we're not going to impact anything.

But what I like is how social media is a distribution multiplier. If I'm doing content marketing, then social allows me to distribute content across a wide variety of channels in a wide variety of media. And I can target different networks based on what type of reaction I want. What do I want people to do?

For example, if I want someone to click-through, then I may not want to use Instagram because it doesn't allow me to put a link in the post. Whereas, I might use Facebook because I can put a link in the post. And I can put a strong call to action and make that happen.

GREG: And you can use Google's free Campaign URL Builder tool, which allows you to add campaign parameters to URLs so you can measure custom campaigns in Google Analytics.

All you need to do is:

1. Enter the URL of the landing page.

2. Enter Facebook, Twitter, or blog in the box for the Campaign Source.

3. Enter Ronaldo or microinfluencer_2 in the box for Campaign Medium.

4. And then enter a term like CR7 in the box for the Campaign Name.

The Campaign URL Builder tool will generate a campaign URL for you—and you can even use Bitly to shorten the URL. Then, all Ronaldo or a micro-influencer needs to do is use this URL in their post or tweet and the marketers at Clear can track the results in Google Analytics.

But this doesn't work for all products and services. A couple of years ago, there was a brand that came to us to launch an influencer marketing campaign for their jock itch solution. And we had to tell them that we couldn't identify any social media influencers talking about the jock itch problem, for obvious reasons. So, they were going to have to find a different way to market that product.

Social Media Channel Management

MATT: All right. So, before we tackle social media channel management, Greg, we have to share a little history of early social media channels.

Early Social Media Channels

What I think is interesting about the history is that there used to be distinctive categories of social media, and those distinctions are being eliminated or adopted by every other platform.

> **GREG:** I think the greatest example that we've seen recently is TikTok, which has forced Instagram to launch Reels and YouTube to launch Shorts.
>
> And before that, Snapchat had everyone ripping off their Stories idea.
>
> So, if you've got a really cool feature, you've got about a 3-week head start on your competitors, who are going to try to knock it off.

Social Networks

> **MATT:** One of the first categories was a social network, which I think would be more defined by building networks of people.
>
> Facebook and LinkedIn are the two big ones. I think it's interesting that when you chart the growth of both, LinkedIn has a slow, steady increase over the years, where Facebook had huge growth, and now seems to be in decline.

Video Sharing

> **GREG:** Another category was the video-sharing site. And in the early days, that meant YouTube and Vimeo.
>
> This is why some people still think Facebook and YouTube are in different categories. Well, they were until Facebook zigged. And even LinkedIn now says, "We have video too."

Microblogging

MATT: The next category was microblogging. The big examples were Twitter and Tumblr.

Twitter started out with a limit of 140 characters of text. Well, now I can upload video. I can upload images. And Twitter has doubled the character limit for tweets from 140 to 280. So, this is a great example of changing functionality to accommodate what people want to do.

Photo Sharing

GREG: Then there's the photo-sharing category. I used Flicker extensively when I was promoting the Search Engine Strategies conferences.

And then Flickr added short videos, but their user base revolted. "No, we're for photo sharing, not video sharing."

So, it is amazing to watch what's going on in Instagram now because they started off as a square photo sharing app. But now over 45 percent of Instagram accounts like, comment on, or share Reels at least once a week.

Blogs

MATT: And you mentioned earlier that blogs were considered a category of social media. And when WordPress came out in 2003, I was at a digital agency and the bread and butter of the company was building websites.

And when I saw WordPress come out, I was taking it and showing it to people. I said, "This is going to change everything." And today, 40 percent of the billions of websites on the Internet are on WordPress.

Platform Convergence

GREG: Now, that brings us to the blender. Is short-form video just a feature? Is it a category? The answer is: "It depends."

That means any good social media marketer needs to pay a little bit of attention to the lessons of history because, okay, maybe it doesn't repeat itself, but things come back again and again that seem awfully familiar. So, there are lessons you can learn, even if they aren't exact.

So, the poster child for evolving their definition of who they are and what they're about is Facebook. And some of that was forced on them.

MATT: Facebook's first crisis was in 2012, when it was just a desktop application. And the iPhone was turning everything into a mobile first world. And Facebook decided to pivot and become a "mobile first company."

GREG: Then, in 2015, Facebook decided to pivot and become a "video first company."

MATT: In 2021, Facebook changed its name to Meta Platforms.

GREG: And in February 2022, following the greatest single-day stock drop in recorded history, Mark Zuckerberg, the co-founder, chairman, and CEO of Meta Platforms, announced the company's focus would shift to growing short-form video.

Top Social Media Channels Today

MATT: That's why I'll call this next section the "spittin' facts" section because it's about the top social media channels "today," which is hilarious. We could have said this month, but here's where we are right now.

GREG: I know. In May 2022, Michael Stelzner of *Social Media Examiner* had just published the "2022 Social Media Marketing Industry Report."

Based on their annual survey, which was conducted in January 2022, the most commonly used social media platforms were:

- Facebook (90 percent)
- Instagram (79 percent)
- LinkedIn (61 percent)
- YouTube (52 percent)
- Twitter (43 percent)
- TikTok (18 percent)

But I wrote, "A Guide to Social Media Algorithms & How They Work," which was published by *Search Engine Journal* on June 23, 2022. And to ensure that I was including the top social media channels, I asked SimilarWeb for their latest data, which was for May 2022.

Spoiler alert: There were some surprising shifts in the latest data on monthly unique visitors, monthly visits, and monthly average visit duration.

MATT: What was the biggest surprise?

YouTube

GREG: YouTube.com got 1.953 billion unique visitors worldwide in May. The platform received 35.083 billion monthly visits that month, with an average visit duration of 21:41.

Now, some social media marketers may be shocked—shocked to find YouTube ranking ahead of Facebook. But SimilarWeb's data is only for desktop and mobile web channels. It doesn't include data for connected TVs, which became the fastest-growing screen among YouTube viewers in 2020.

This makes it imperative to know how YouTube's algorithm works.

MATT: So, how does it work?

GREG: YouTube's algorithm tries to match each viewer to the videos they're most likely to watch and enjoy. But with over 500 hours of video content uploaded to YouTube every minute, this is a Herculean task.

YouTube's search and discovery systems tackle this challenge by focusing on:

- What viewers watch
- What they don't watch
- How much time they spend watching
- What they share and like

Next, you need to learn that YouTube has multiple algorithms, including ones for:

- **YouTube Search:** Videos are ranked based on how well titles, descriptions, and video content match the viewer's search and which videos get the most engagement for a search.
- **Up Next:** The rankings of suggested videos are based on machine learning's understanding of which ones viewers are most likely to watch next. These videos are often related to the video a viewer is watching, but they can also be personalized based on the viewer's watch history.
- **Your homepage:** Videos are selected based on how often viewers watch a channel or topic, how well similar videos have interested and satisfied

similar viewers, and how many times YouTube has already shown each video to a viewer.

- **YouTube shorts:** YouTube wants both short and long videos to succeed. So, relative watch time is generally more important for short videos, while absolute watch time is generally more important for longer videos.

So, search engine marketers need to stop treating YouTube like a red-headed stepchild.

Facebook

MATT: What about Facebook? I know the platform isn't growing. They have the same target audience of the generation that started using it. The kids have moved on, so now I would call it the legacy social network.

GREG: Well, according to SimilarWeb, **Facebook.com** got only 1.620 billion unique visitors worldwide in May 2022. The platform received 19.739 billion visits that month with an average session duration of 10:05.

Now, Facebook's unique visitors started dipping worldwide in February 2022. But there was a substantial drop in unique visitors in Russia in early March, after Russia blocked Facebook in an effort to control the spread of information on the invasion of Ukraine.

This had a negative impact on Facebook's total unique visitors worldwide, which were already losing momentum. Nevertheless, the platform is still too big to ignore.

MATT: So, how does Facebook's algorithm work today?

GREG: Well, we thought that we knew how Facebook's News Feed ranking process worked until mid-June 2022, when a leaked internal memo revealed Facebook's near-term plans to restructure its main feed around video content, such as Reels and Stories.

MATT: So, what should social media marketers do next?

GREG: Read Matt G. Southern's article in *Search Engine Journal*, which is entitled, "Facebook to Restructure Main Feed around Video Content."

Then, follow Southern's expert, authoritative, and trustworthy advice: "The best way to prepare for this change, if Facebook is a priority for you and your business, is to get comfortable with creating and publishing more short-form video. While Facebook will continue to surface text and photo posts, they'll be ancillary to the main attractions of Reels and Stories."

Instagram

MATT: What about Instagram?

GREG: Instagram.com got 1.050 billion unique visitors worldwide in May. The platform received 6.497 billion visits that month with an average session duration of 07:51.

Now, Russia has also banned Instagram, but growth in unique visitors from other countries around the world has offset that. So, you still need to know how Instagram's algorithms work.

MATT: And how do they work?

GREG: In June 2021, Adam Mosseri, the head of Instagram, wrote a post entitled, "Shedding More Light on How Instagram Works." He revealed, "Instagram doesn't have one algorithm that oversees what people do and don't see on the app. We use a variety of algorithms, classifiers, and processes, each with its own purpose."

For the Feed and Stories, the key ranking signals are:

- **Information about the post:** How popular a post is, when it was posted, how long it is, if it's a video, and if it's attached to a location.
- **Information about the person who posted:** How many times users have interacted with that person in the past few weeks.
- **User activity:** What a user might be interested in and how many posts they've liked.
- **User history of interacting with someone:** How interested a user is in seeing posts from a particular person.

For Explore, the key ranking signals are:

- **Information about the post:** How popular a post seems to be as well as how many and how quickly other people are liking, commenting, sharing, and saving a post.
- **User history of interacting with someone:** (See above.)
- **User activity:** What posts a user has liked, saved, or commented on as well as how they've interacted with posts in Explore in the past.
- **Information about the person who posted:** (See above.)

For Reels, the key ranking signals are:

- **User activity:** Which Reels a user has liked, commented on, and engaged with recently.
- **User history of interacting with someone:** (See above.)

- **Information about the Reel:** The audio track, video data such as pixels and whole frames, as well as popularity.
- **Information about the person who posted:** (See above.)

Twitter

MATT: What about Twitter, Greg? In a video chat with Twitter employees, Elon Musk said in mid-June 2022 that he wants one billion users on Twitter. Is that even doable?

GREG: Well, according to SimilarWeb's data, **Twitter.com** got 979 million unique visitors worldwide in May 2022. The platform received 7.056 billion visits that month with an average session duration of 10.39.

MATT: How much of this traffic is coming from fake or spam accounts? I don't have a dog in the fight, Greg. I'm just getting some popcorn and watching this movie.

GREG: SimilarWeb's data does not screen for fake or spam accounts. Nevertheless, it's probably worth investing the time and effort to keep up with how Twitter's algorithm works.

MATT: And how does it work?

GREG: Like most social media platforms, Twitter has multiple algorithms.

Twitter says its "algorithmic Home timeline displays a stream of tweets from accounts you have chosen to follow on Twitter, as well as recommendations of other content we think you might be interested in based on accounts you interact with frequently, tweets you engage with, and more."

If users want to, they can click on the star symbol to see the latest tweets as they happen. But few people choose to drink water from a firehose.

If they want to, users can click on Explore and see trending tweets or ones about COVID-19, news, sports, and entertainment.

If users want to, they can click on More to see the topics that Twitter thinks they're interested in.

And like most social media platforms, Twitter's algorithms use machine learning to sort content based on different ranking signals. And it's worth noting that Twitter is currently involved in analyzing the results of its algorithms as part of its "responsible machine learning initiative."

So, here's what Twitter has said publicly about its Home timeline, trends, and topics ranking signals:

Relevance

- Users' previous actions on Twitter, like their own tweets and tweets they've engaged with.
- Accounts they often engage with.
- Topics they follow and engage with most.
- The number of tweets related to a topic.
- For trends: Their location.

Engagement

- For tweets: "How popular it is and how people in your network are interacting with [the tweet]."
- For trends: "The number of tweets related to the trend."
- For topics: "How much people are tweeting, retweeting, replying, and liking tweets about that topic."

Recency

- For trends: "Topics that are popular now, rather than topics that have been popular for a while or on a daily basis."

Rich media

- The type of media the tweet includes, like an image, video, GIF, and polls.

TikTok

MATT: What about TikTok? It's where all the cool kids hang out now.

GREG: According to SimilarWeb, **TikTok.com** got 690 million monthly visitors worldwide in May 2022. The platform received 1.766 billion visits that month, with an average session duration of 03:48.

This data doesn't include **Douyin.com**, which is counted separately. But **TikTok.com** gets about 98 percent of the unique visitors worldwide for both of the ByteDance apps.

So, you should probably learn how TikTok's algorithm works ASAP.

In June 2020, TikTok revealed how its recommendation system selected videos in a post entitled, "How TikTok recommends videos #ForYou." Little has fundamentally changed since then, except the U.S. government is no longer trying to ban the social media platform.

TikTok's For You feed presents a stream of videos curated to each user's interests, making it easy for a user to find content and creators they love. In other words, there isn't one For You feed for over one billion monthly active TikTok users. There are a billion For You feeds tailored to what each user watches, likes, and shares.

TikTok added, "This feed is powered by a recommendation system that delivers content to each user that is likely to be of interest to that particular user." And recommendations are based on a number of factors, including:

- User interactions such as the videos they like or share, accounts they follow, comments they post, and content they create.
- Video information, which might include details like captions, sounds, and hashtags.
- Device and account settings like their language preference, country setting, and device type.

TikTok also revealed: "All these factors are processed by our recommendation system and weighted based on their value to a user. A strong indicator of interest, such as whether a user finishes watching a longer video from beginning to end, would receive greater weight than a weak indicator, such as whether the video's viewer and creator are both in the same country. Videos are then ranked to determine the likelihood of a user's interest in a piece of content and delivered to each unique For You feed."

Pinterest

MATT: What are some of the other top social media channels today?

GREG: Well, **Pinterest.com** got 409 million unique visitors worldwide in May. The platform received 945 million visits that month with an average session duration of 05:29.

MATT: With Instagram declaring it is "no longer just a square photo-sharing app," this is probably the time to ask, "How does Pinterest's algorithm work?"

GREG: The ranking factors on Pinterest relate more to engagement metrics and social shares, but it also involves keywords. And Pinterest autocomplete provides ideas by automatically suggesting semantically related modifiers to a core keyword.

Pinterest's search feature then curates a user's "feed" based on what they're searching for and how those key terms are used in the pins being shared by content creators. Pinterest also categorizes and subcategorizes topics to make it easy to find keywords for your particular niche.

To optimize your pins, use:

- Long images: The optimal pin size is 1,000px by 1,500px, or a ratio of 2:3.
- Eye-catching colors: Catch users' attention with high-contrast colors.
- Enticing, keyword-rich titles: Entice users to click through to your content.
- Detailed descriptions: Include your target keywords in your descriptions.

Then, optimize your boards. Boards provide a great opportunity to tell Pinterest's search engine how you categorize your products and/or organize your content, which will only aid visibility.

Finally, aim for engagement, which can increase your pin's (and your profile's) visibility in search, increasing your traffic.

LinkedIn

MATT: What about LinkedIn? You can't leave them out.

They are the largest business-to-business (B2B) social network. If you're trying to do any B2B social media marketing, then LinkedIn is it. There isn't even a close competitor.

GREG: According to SimilarWeb, **LinkedIn.com** got 306 million unique visitors worldwide in May. The platform received 1.479 billion visits that month with an average session duration of 07:32.

So, social media marketers—especially ones at B2B organizations—need to know how LinkedIn's algorithm works.

MATT: So, how does it work?

GREG: In June 2019, Pete Davies, senior director of product management at LinkedIn, wrote a post entitled, "What's in Your LinkedIn Feed: People You Know, Talking about Things You Care About." He explained, "The more valuable the conversation, the higher in your feed the post will be."

MATT: How does LinkedIn's algorithm know if a conversation is valuable?

GREG: It uses the following framework:

- **People you know:** LinkedIn's algorithm looks at a user's connections and prioritizes whom they've interacted with directly through comments and reactions; the user's implicit interests and experiences based on information in their profile; explicit signals, such as whom a user works with; as well as who would benefit from hearing from the user.

- **Things you're talking about:** A lot of sophistication goes into understanding a good conversation. As a rule of thumb, the better conversations are authentic and have constructive back-and-forth.
- **Things you care about:** LinkedIn's algorithm also looks at whether the content and the conversation are relevant and interesting to a user. It considers a number of signals, including joining groups and following hashtags, people, and pages.

Cross-Platform Content Strategies

MATT: So, that leads us into how to develop cross-platform content strategies, which is a huge issue when you're launching a new product.

Launching a New Product Across Multiple Platforms

GREG: Well, it turns out, Matt, that you and I have both been involved in a launch, but we don't think we were working on the campaign. So, the case study that I'm going to tell you about is one that you know intimately, but you may think, "I didn't do that." However, we did.

And the case study is the launch of the New Media Academy, which is based in the United Arab Emirates (UAE). You and I are both instructors there. So, we helped to train some of the content creation community. We played a role. I'm teaching another module tomorrow.

MATT: Yeah, I taught one today.

GREG: Okay. So, interestingly enough, when the New Media Academy was launched in June 2020 during the beginning of a global pandemic they did a couple of things that were cross-platform. They created Instagram, Facebook, YouTube, TikTok, and Twitter accounts.

Basically, they were trying to inform potential students in the Middle East and North Africa (MENA) that they could learn about social media marketing and content creation.

Yeah, a couple of the instructors were English-speaking experts, but we were focused on putting our students on the path toward success in an ever-evolving digital landscape.

So, when they launched their YouTube channel, it obviously had zero views and no subscribers. Today, it has a total of 145 million all-time views and 1.7 million subscribers.

And when they launched their Facebook page, it obviously started from scratch too. Today, the videos on their Facebook page have 81.3 million all-time views.

Now, I don't know about you, but I think that's a success story.

How did the New Media Academy accomplish this in just 2 years? They re-launched the "El Daheeh" program, which is presented by the Egyptian YouTuber and content creator Ahmed Al-Ghandour. It aims to simplify science in a comic way (Figure 6.2).

The debut of "El Daheeh" increased subscribers to the channel from 9,000 to 323,000 in one night. It also added two million views in one day. By the end of the first week, subscribers to the channel had doubled to 650,000, and six million views had been added, which was equal to the total number of views the channel had achieved since its inception in the summer of 2020.

And the rest is history. The New Media Academy now has an audience that is theirs. This enables them to launch enlightening shows like "Ektisadiyat," which simplifies the world of economics, or participate in inspiring campaigns like "The World's Coolest Winter," which highlights the various tourism destinations in the UAE.

But the point is this: talking about yourself, "Hi, we're an educational institution. We offer courses," was okay. But putting your audience first, "Hi, we've got an entertaining nerd who pokes fun at science. We also offer courses," was the recipe for success.

And that's what we were teaching in the first Impact Digital Creator Program at the New Media Academy. We taught 22 content creators and social media influencers to start by asking, "Who is your target audience?" And continue by asking, "What content do they seek?"

Then, we asked our students, "Why will they love your content?" And we taught them that nobody will visit their social media account twice because they like it; they'll only come back if they love it.

Now, what you and I didn't realize at the time was that some of the New Media Academy's staff was also watching our modules. And later, some of the content creators and social media influencers who we'd taught joined the New Media Academy's staff.

And they applied the lessons that we were teaching. They experimented with new initiatives and learned that their target audience in MENA liked educational video content that "teaches me something new," but loved entertaining video content that "makes me laugh."

Our Productions

01/06

FIGURE 6.2   El Daheeh Is Here to Simplify Science in a Comic Way

So, that's why I think we were indirectly involved in launching a new product across multiple platforms without realizing that we were working on the campaign.

Engaging a Target Audience Across Multiple Platforms

MATT: But, I think I'd share some different advice for this new era of social media. You can't rely on your organic social reach.

The platforms want you to pay to reach audiences. So, you can't take what you've built on one platform and move it to another. And so the solution then becomes: build your own community. And then use social media to populate that new community.

So for me, I focus on my website, and I use social to drive people to the site.

Same with the podcast. That's my community. It's my destination. And the listeners I get are mine.

I think one of the greatest examples is Yoga with Adriene, a YouTube channel (Figure 6.3). Adriene Mishler is an actress, writer, international yoga teacher, and entrepreneur from Austin, Texas.

Now, the channel was already doing well in the yoga community. But once the pandemic hit, searches for yoga fitness just went crazy. It exploded in popularity.

Now, here's the thing. She has a YouTube channel, and it's her main social channel to expand her audience. During her videos, she

FIGURE 6.3 Yoga with Adriene

encourages comments and subscriptions. But she directs people to her website.

And on her website, you can get branded clothing and yoga equipment. You can sign up for her newsletter. You can also join her community on an app.

And it's estimated that this membership-based app drives more revenue than her YouTube channel, which has more than 1.2 billion all-time views and over 11.2 million subscribers.

So, she's created her own community on her own platform. And now she's moved people from being passive subscribers on YouTube to paying members of a community. And now she can do whatever she wants.

If YouTube's algorithms change, that won't affect the monetization of her app. And she uses YouTube now to build her audience and develop her own community independently. This is what's going to distinguish companies moving forward in the next decade with social media.

GREG: Strangely—and this is coming from a Wolverine—I find myself agreeing with a Buckeye. And if we're in agreement, then I need to go back and double-check my assumptions.

MATT: I think we're in agreement a lot more than we are in disagreement.

GREG: Well, if we disagree one day a year during "The Game" between the University of Michigan and the Ohio State University, then I think we've got the right balance.

MATT: So, we're in agreement on engaging a target audience across multiple platforms.

When I'm driving audiences to a destination, such as a landing page, I'm also going across platforms because I'm going to retarget them. I'm going to drive them from social media to maybe a blog or a website or some other destination where I'm going to engage with them. I'm going to try to get them to convert. And if they don't convert, then I'll switch to another discipline and do more ad buying to reach them and drive them back.

So any campaign is going to involve multiple platforms. And if I'm buying ads on LinkedIn, then I absolutely must do retargeting because your first pass with ads on LinkedIn never works. You get lots of interest, but no one converts. So, retargeting is absolutely essential to maintain that contact and bring people back because they're inundated with so many messages.

GREG: I agree.

Using Social Commerce to Sell Products Across Multiple Platforms

MATT: And here's where it's headed. It's all about the sale.

The platforms are all moving to get users to buy products right from the social site. So, this is not leaving their platform. It's leading into social commerce, which is growing.

But I like to caution people that social commerce has been called the "next big thing" for the past 12 years. So, every year there are headlines telling us to watch out for social commerce.

"It's going to explode!" And they've been saying that year after year after year. I think we're getting to a point where it is growing faster. But there's a level of caution to take there.

GREG: Well, there was an accelerant that nobody could have predicted called the global pandemic. All of a sudden a lot of people's behavior changed and started doing things online that they hadn't been doing as much online. So, the growth curve mutated quickly—almost as quickly as the virus. And more people are doing more things online now.

So, you should be testing social commerce. You should be trying to figure it out. But one of the things that a lot of social media marketers get wrong is they think that the process is push.

I'm going to push people to buy my product. And if I can only tack on this social commerce thing at the end of a post, then I can actually get you all the way to where the cash register rings.

I know, cash registers don't ring anymore. Pardon an old metaphor from an old marketer. But I don't think it's a push process. I think it's a pull process.

So, one of the things that Pinterest has done brilliantly is this: if I pin something to my board, then it's because I plan to come back and do something with it later.

It's my wish list. It's my planning tool. In other words, I'm providing the motivation here, not the marketer. And if you're aligned with the plans of your community, target audiences, or your business buyers, and if you're providing them with useful information to get them to the next step in their plans, then that's not push marketing. That's pull marketing.

Right?

MATT: Absolutely. And we could probably do an entire podcast on social commerce.

I'm looking at a headline right now that says social commerce is expected to grow to $1.2 trillion by 2025. But you don't get numbers that big without including China.

GREG: It's massive, but when you have an audience of 1.3 billion, everything becomes a big number.

MATT: China has something driving social commerce that isn't a big driver in other countries. It's Singles Day, and it's the biggest day for sales in the world.

China had their biggest Singles Day in November 2021. It's called Singles Day because it's November 11, which is 1, 1, 1, 1.

GREG: I did not know that.

MATT: Yes. And it's about going out and buying yourself a gift. It's a reward for yourself. Alibaba and **JD.com** racked up a record $139 billion in sales across their platforms on China's Singles Day shopping event in 2021.

GREG: That's bigger than the $10.7 billion spent on Cyber Monday that year.

MATT: Or the $8.9 billion spent on our Black Friday in 2021.

So, I always recommend: take these numbers for social commerce very lightly and be aware that they may be driven by unique holidays that don't occur month in and month out.

GREG: So, when your target audience interacts with a social medium, what are they looking for? Are they shopping for a product or do they just want to be entertained?

Are they there to dig deeper into something that interests them? That's okay. Are they there for product reviews? Well, they may look somewhere else. It's a complex process. And, yes, you want to be providing different content at every touchpoint that you can.

But again, focus on the customer first, as opposed to some kind of narrow model that tells you to "push on a string." Because you'll be more effective in moving things if you pull.

Reputation Management Practices

MATT: Well, the next part in our outline is reputation management. And the first level is just simply being aware that someone is saying something.

So, using a social listening tool or setting up Google Alerts can help you discover when someone is saying something about your company, your CEO, or your products.

GREG: Oh yeah. And, the most brilliant thing I think I've ever seen was the "US Air Force Web Posting Response Assessment." David Merrman Scott wrote about it in a blog post back in 2009. And, believe it or not, the United States Air Force has a flowchart that helps individuals decide how to participate in online discussions.

The flowchart was developed and revised by Captain David Faggard, chief of emerging technology at the Air Force Public Affairs Agency in the Pentagon in 2009 (Figure 6.4). That means it's public domain and may be used freely by social media marketers today.

Back then, Captain Faggard acknowledged, "We obviously have many more concerns regarding cyberspace than a typical Social Media user." He added, "I am concerned with how insurgents or potential enemies can use Social Media to their advantage. It's our role to provide a clear and accurate, completely truthful and transparent picture for any audience."

Social media marketers should take a look at the assessment tool and consider applying something similar in their own organization today. There are trolls, and there are haters. And sometimes, "Don't feed the trolls" is the right policy. But there are other times when someone has just alerted you to a crisis. Then, you need clear guidelines on when to respond and when to pass that on up the chain of command because this is one that they need to respond to.

MATT: Absolutely. And it always scares me when people say, "The youngest person on the staff is the one in charge of social media." I think this used to be a joke. I pray it's not the same way now. If an intern is running your social media, then an intern is managing your reputation or your crisis response.

And you don't want that. But that's where having that flowchart or your own policy is so key to how you do respond. And just some simple crisis management techniques are crucial.

GREG: And the majority of crises that you will face can be categorized as operational or reputational.

An operational crisis creates an actual or potential disruption to organizational operations. Examples include fires, explosions,

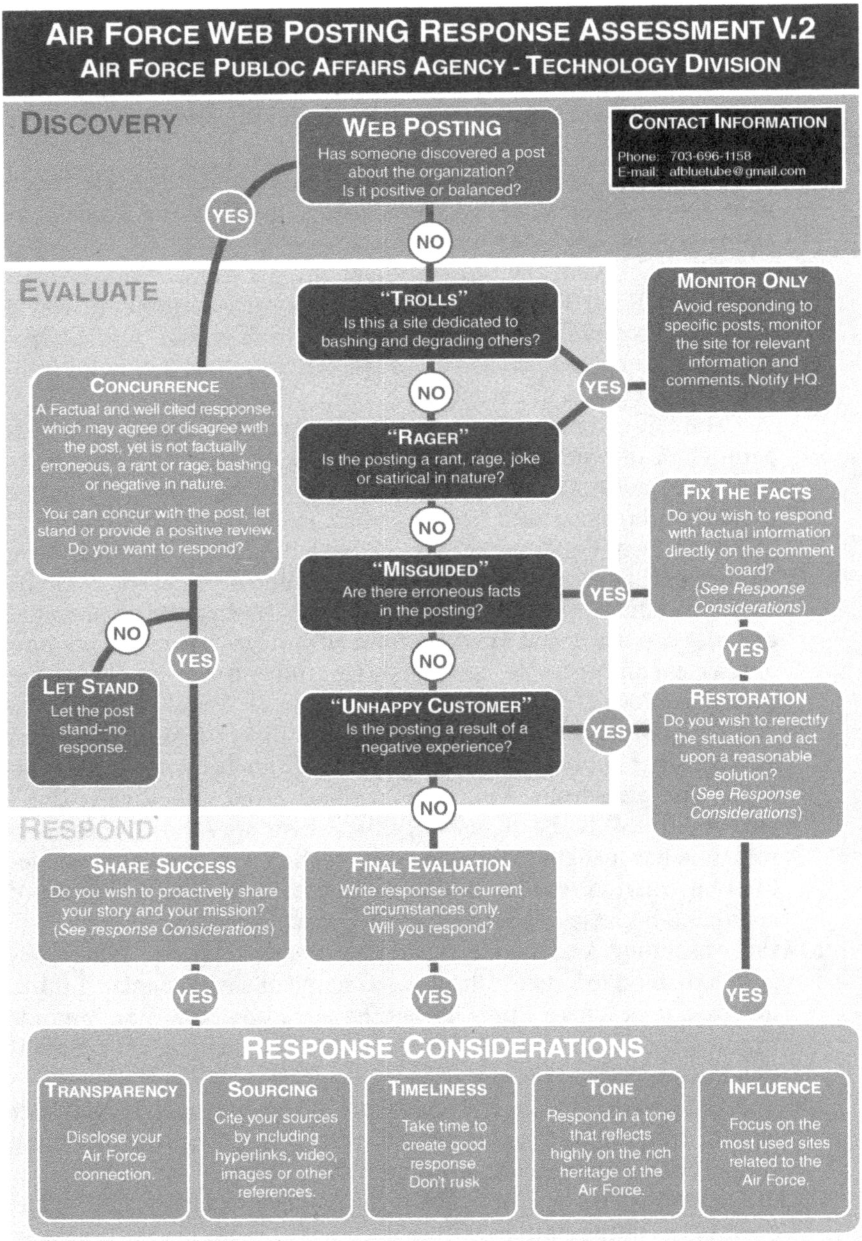

AIR FORCE WEB POSTING RESPONSE ASSESSMENT V.2
AIR FORCE PUBLOC AFFAIRS AGENCY - TECHNOLOGY DIVISION

DISCOVERY

WEB POSTING
Has someone discovered a post about the organization? Is it positive or balanced?

CONTACT INFORMATION
Phone: 703-696-1158
E-mail: afbluetube@gmail.com

(YES) (NO)

EVALUATE

"TROLLS"
Is this a site dedicated to bashing and degrading others?

MONITOR ONLY
Avoid responding to specific posts, monitor the site for relevant information and comments. Notify HQ.

(NO) (YES)

CONCURRENCE
A Factual and well cited responose, which may agree or disagree with the post, yet is not factually erroneous, a rant or rage, bashing or negative in nature.
You can concur with the post, let stand or provide a positive review. Do you want to respond?

"RAGER"
Is the posting a rant, rage, joke or satirical in nature?

(NO)

FIX THE FACTS
Do you wish to respond with factual information directly on the comment board?
(See Response Considerations)

"MISGUIDED"
Are there erroneous facts in the posting?

(YES)

(NO) (YES)

(NO)

LET STAND
Let the post stand--no response.

"UNHAPPY CUSTOMER"
Is the posting a result of a negative experience?

(YES)

RESTORATION
Do you wish to rerectify the situation and act upon a reasonable solution?
(See Response Considerations)

(NO)

(YES)

RESPOND

SHARE SUCCESS
Do you wish to proactively share your story and your mission?
(See response Considerations)

FINAL EVALUATION
Write response for current circumstances only. Will you respond?

(YES) (YES) (YES)

RESPONSE CONSIDERATIONS

TRANSPARENCY
Disclose your Air Force connection.

SOURCING
Cite your sources by including hyperlinks, video, images or other references.

TIMELINESS
Take time to create good response. Don't rush.

TONE
Respond in a tone that reflects highly on the rich heritage of the Air Force.

INFLUENCE
Focus on the most used sites related to the Air Force.

FIGURE 6.4 US Air Force Web Posting Response Assessment

Source: Developed and revised by Captain David Faggard, chief of emerging technology at the Air Force Public Affairs Agency, Pentagon

or a chemical release, which can disrupt your operations in some fashion. Crisis management initially was created to address operational crises.

A reputational crisis threatens to inflict serious damage on an organization's reputation. This includes irresponsible behavior by management or corporate messages that offend some stakeholders. These will cause stakeholders to perceive the organization much less favorably.

So, a key difference between the two types of crises is that an operational crisis typically creates some threat to public safety and/or stakeholder welfare, while a reputational crisis is far less likely to produce the same level of public safety or stakeholder welfare concerns.

So, a policy or flowchart can help you know what to do in a crisis.

Social Media Advertising

MATT: All right, Greg. Next on our agenda is social media advertising, which we've been forced into using over the past few years.

GREG: Do we have to make them richer than they already are? I'd prefer to focus on organic content. You know, the posts, videos, and photos that users, businesses, and brands share with each other on their feeds for free.

MATT: Yeah, that's a great point. At the conferences we attended years ago, I remember people saying, "You have to be on Facebook. You have to be on Twitter. You have to be on Instagram. You have to develop your organic presence."

And then the organic reach of these platforms started declining. Now, this didn't happen suddenly. The trend started in 2014 and continued year after year. But today, all that investment into creating an organic presence on these platforms needs to be written off.

And if you didn't see that coming, then you were blissfully blind.

My friend, they were going to monetize all of this because what the platforms had was an audience and data on the audience. And, so now your organic post is maybe reaching 1 percent or 2 percent of your audience.

Decline of Organic Reach

GREG: Well, according to "The Digital 2022 Global Overview Report," from *We Are Social and Hootsuite*, the average organic reach on Facebook is 5.2 percent and the average organic reach on Instagram is around 1.0 percent. Other research has found that Twitter's organic reach is only 0.045 percent.

MATT: I think that's still overestimating organic reach on Facebook.

GREG: Well, that's average organic reach. But that's not the average engagement rate. According to the "Social Media Marketing Benchmark Report 2022," the median engagement rate on Facebook has been dwindling steadily to less than 0.1 percent, and the algorithms of most social platforms are actively discriminating against posts made by business users.

MATT: And this doesn't factor in fake engagement by fake accounts that are run by bots. In the first quarter of 2022, Facebook removed 1.6 billion fake accounts.

GREG: Well, I wouldn't mind if the declines in organic reach were entirely driven by purges of fake or spam accounts. But there's something else at work.

Earlier, I mentioned that SparkToro and Followerwonk had conducted a joint analysis of Twitter accounts. And they found that 18.4 percent of "active" accounts are fake or spam.

But they also took a rigorous look at Elon Musk's Twitter account and found that 23.4 percent of his 26.8 million "active" followers were fake or spam.

But Mr. Musk's Twitter account had a total of 93.4 million followers at the time. That means 66.6 million were "inactive" accounts. In other words, they were older profiles that hadn't tweeted in the last 90 days.

And as we've learned about Twitter's algorithm, nonactive accounts are far less likely to see Mr. Musk's tweets. And that's an even bigger reason why organic reach is declining.

Now, this isn't nefarious, but it's still problematic.

So, one of the things that social media marketers need to focus on is metrics. And I know we're going to spend a lot more time talking about measurement at the tail end of this.

But whether you're trying to increase your organic reach, or you're buying advertising to promote your posts because you're trying to beef up your numbers, one of the things that you really need to think about long and hard is, "How are you measuring your results?"

And if you are only using the metrics that the social media platforms provide you, then you can get in trouble fast.

MATT: I think you've nailed it right there. If I'm just using the platform numbers, then all I'm doing is measuring "platform reach and engagement."

GREG: And you're getting sucked into what the platform wants, which is to sell more ads. And so the metrics are all built around, "Do you need more? Okay, you've got to spend more."

MATT: Oh, absolutely. And it also means buying more reach and engagement on the platforms, which may or may not drive more people to a destination.

Marketers need to view social media as a way of building their community, not on these platforms, but driving people to a destination where they become yours, where they sign up for something and you get their email address.

GREG: Right. So, one of the things that social media can teach us is what works and what doesn't—whether you're creating organic content or crafting an ad.

And one of the things you learn quickly is that "corporate propaganda" doesn't work. This should be obvious, right? But, I can't tell you how many brands and businesses are still using social media to push out their corporate propaganda.

Avinash Kaushik, the Digital Marketing Evangelist at Google, lamented this tendency in a post entitled, "Stop All Social Media Activity (Organic) | Solve for a Profitable Reality." It was posted back on June 17, 2017, on his blog, *Occam's Razor*.

Avinash said, "Businesses of all types, including Google, got on amazing platforms like Facebook and started pimping. All that their collective imagination could manifest in a Utopia-possible environment was: 'LOOK AT ME! I AM SO PRETTY!! BUY NOW!!!' Stuff that is a turn-off."

So, that doesn't work. What does?

Creating and Targeting Social Media Ads

With a video ad, start by getting the viewer's attention. Hook them right from the get-go. Of course, there are many ways to do this. You can open with a close-up or start in the middle of the story.

And storytelling works. People will remember your stories long after they've forgotten the three key reasons why they should buy your product or service.

And don't think of your viewer as passive. Work to educate, inspire, or entertain them. Humanize your story to help them relate. Lean into emotional levers with storytelling techniques, such as humor or surprise.

Then, it's okay to work your brand identity into the story. And ask them to take action.

MATT: One of my first lessons in social media advertising was on YouTube.

We developed a video campaign on YouTube for a library levy. And it wasn't too popular in the community. So we decided, "Let's go to YouTube. Let's start informing people."

This was one of the earliest campaigns I did. We targeted women with children because women with children were much more sympathetic to funding the library. But older people, who don't have children, did not want their taxes to go up to fund a library that—in their mind—they don't use.

So, we created a video ad campaign that targeted women with children. One of the things I loved about YouTube advertising was I could see what video people were watching when our ad appeared.

But as the data started coming in, I started seeing a lot of ABC songs, learning the alphabet, and Minecraft walkthroughs. Having children that same age, I realized, "Oh no, the kids are watching YouTube on mom's account. They've got the iPad in their lap and they are being entertained. Kids are watching the ads that we wanted their mothers to see."

A more recent example that I'll never forget was when I turned on my connected TV and immediately saw a video ad on YouTube TV that grabbed my attention. It was about pets and dogs specifically. And I watched this 3-minute ad well past the skip button. I was hooked.

A great hook made me stay past the skip button. And a great story. The only way they could have done that was by targeting me, what I searched for, my interests, my behavior. That showed me right there that this legacy 30-second ad thing? Throw it out the window.

GREG: Oh yeah. And believe it or not, before the legacy 30-second ad, there was the legacy 60-second ad. The whole arbitrary "You have to tell your story in 60 seconds."

Oh, wait. Nobody could afford that anymore. So, then you had to tell your story in 30 seconds. Oh, wait. You can't afford that anymore. So, 15 seconds is the new standard.

When you're selling television time, everything had to be arbitrary in order to fit into the hour-long or half-hour-long programming concept.

On social media, your story can be as long as it needs to be until it gets boring. Right? And people will watch it as long as it's interesting. And as soon as it gets boring, they're out of there, which is not television behavior, but it is social media video viewing behavior.

It's interesting that a lot of people in social media advertising think, "You've got to keep it short." Why? "Because the attention span of a goldfish is only 8 seconds."

If your target audience is a goldfish, then that's great. But guess what? There are people who will binge-watch episode upon episode of TV shows for hours, if they're interested.

To be an effective producer of social video advertising, don't ask, "How long should my video ad be?" It should be long enough to reach a point.

If you need examples, look at the organic video content being produced by YouTube stars, Instagram influencers, and TikTok creators.

They're making videos worth watching. They're creating content worth sharing. Now, they often make short-form videos, but many of them also create long-form content. But no matter what the duration of their videos are, their content is entertaining, inspiring, educational, or enlightening. And that is changing people's hearts, minds, and behavior.

And if you can even come close to doing what they're doing, then you can be successful. And if you can't come close, then maybe you need to move some of your social media advertising budget into influencer marketing. Why? Because sponsoring people who can create enchanting content may get you further, faster than running more social video ads.

Targeting by Intent, not Demographics

MATT: What I like about social media advertising is the ability to target by needs. Or to set up my targeting regionally. I use those options instead of targeting demographically.

Dr. Augustin Fou was on the show a couple months ago, and I loved it when he said, "Why would you target men instead of women? You've already excluded half your audience."

And the more you target by age, you're excluding more and more people. So, you're excluding people who might need and want to buy what you offer.

I love that aspect of targeting, especially on Google and YouTube, which are built on behavioral targeting, because they know what people are looking for. They know what people have searched for in the past week.

I'm targeting based on need or behavioral aspects because this is what grabs your audience much more than focusing on their gender, age, or all that demographic stuff.

GREG: Gender and age was the only data that television could provide marketers back in the 20th century. So, that's why most traditional marketing is focused on demographics.

And, that's okay. If that's the only data you have, then as Erasmus observed back in 1500, "In the land of the blind, the one-eyed man is king."

But one of the more powerful ways to tap into what your audience is actually, already interested in can be discovered with a free tool that YouTube offers. It's called Find My Audience. Now, that's a cryptic name. And it helps you find in-market segments—people who are actively researching or planning to purchase products or services like yours.

How does YouTube know this? Like you said, they know what you've been searching for on Google. They know which videos you've been watching on YouTube. Oh, by the way, they know what websites you've been looking at on your Chrome browser. So, they know that you're in the market for a car. They know when you're planning to travel. They know if you're in the market for 20 other products and services.

They can serve up that audience, so you can advertise to people whom you don't have to take from "0 to 60." They're already traveling at 55-miles-an-hour on their customer journey. So, you just need to accelerate their pace the rest of the way.

YouTube's Find My Audience also helps you to target affinity segments—people whose interests and habits relate to what your business offers.

You can target travel buffs—people who enjoy traveling for pleasure and planning vacations. They often spend a considerable amount of time online, researching the locations they want to visit and planning their trips. While traveling, they immerse themselves in the cultures of their destinations and love experiencing the local cuisine, entertainment, history, and sites. They often come to YouTube to scout their next trips.

They may not have traveled for pleasure or vacations during the global pandemic. But they're already planning to do a lot of "revenge travel" as soon as it's safe.

The planning process may be a little longer and interest in travel insurance is higher than it used to be. But guess what? Whether you're advertising air travel, hotels and accommodations, or trips by destination, you can target travel buffs even before they start researching or planning to purchase travel-related products or services.

You can see what videos they watch, which channels they visit. You can target those specifically with your advertising. You now are leveraging what customers want to do anyway. You're just helping them complete that journey by providing them with information about your brand or your service.

MATT: One thing I love showing people is Google Ad Settings. And I'm amazed how many people don't know this is there.

If you go to **adssettings.google.com**, you will see how Google sees you as a consumer. There will be some basic demographic information there, but you'll find probably 30 to 40 behavioral categories.

This is based on your activity on Google services, such as Search or YouTube, while you were signed in. Greg, if your ad personalization is on, and you use Google Search to find the results of "The Game," or you go to YouTube to watch the highlights often enough, then Google estimates that you are interested in American Football. Then you will be included in the American Football affinity group. Now, you're going to see ads that target this affinity group on Google services, such as Search or YouTube, as well as on websites and apps that partner with Google to show ads.

It's not always completely accurate. It's based on your activity.

For example, Google Ad Settings had me down for cats, but I don't like cats. I can't stand cats. But we were trying to find a home for a cat, and because I was on cat adoption sites, the next thing I saw was ads for cat stuff. It's because I was visiting these sites.

So, I go into Google Ad Settings. I say, "Ah-huh, they think I like cats." And I can turn that off. But it is amazing sometimes that, based on your YouTube watching, they'll just assign you to a group. And, then all of a sudden, I notice I started seeing ads for horror movies.

And it's because I watched a clip from an old movie years ago that I was showing to someone. And because of that single activity, it said, "You love horror movies." So, it's not always accurate, but it might answer some questions.

GREG: I have looked at my Google Ad Settings and, yes, American Football is one of them. And I have no problem with that whatsoever.

But it also told me that I'm "35 to 44 years old." Heck, I have kids who are that old. So, how could they possibly make that assumption?

Well, I also have grandkids, who come over and watch YouTube Kids on my laptop. So, is that the behavior you were talking about earlier, Matt? Does Google think I let my grandkids watch a little too much stuff on YouTube? Does Google think I behave like an irresponsible parent, when I'm actually an irresponsible grandparent?

MATT: Greg, I think the age is from when you signed up on Google. You had to give your birthdate. So, did you put the wrong date as your birthday?

GREG: No, But, here's another possibility. Back in 2011, my Google+ account was created by someone who is a generation younger than I am. Maybe he put in his birthday.

MATT: Let's go with that.

GREG: Okay. I like that explanation better than being considered irresponsible by Google.

MATT: But things are constantly changing tactically on these channels. The biggest anticipated changes are the rise of TikTok and short-form video content. These changes are pushing other channels, especially Instagram, to announce new features, new ad formats, and new layouts on a weekly basis.

When you look at all the changes in advertising on social platforms, it's on you to keep up with the latest tactics. But from a strategic standpoint, it's all about your objective. And you really have to plan a series of ads to tell your story because your average social media user doesn't want to watch the same ad over and over again. So, you need to prepare a progression of ads.

That's really the more strategic view.

Social Media Measurement and Control

GREG: Yes. And we're walking around it, but I think we are going to have to go right to measurement. Because if you aren't measuring what matters, then you never know if your old ad has worn out its welcome or this particular message just didn't resonate on social media.

Avoiding Vanity Metrics

So, there are a couple of vanity metrics that the platforms give you—and they've been giving you for years—that you need to question or you get into trouble. Are we ready to get into trouble?

MATT: Let's do it. I like starting with the vanity metrics. Let's start with what not to do. And then we'll get into what to do.

GREG: Well, one of the metrics that you've got to question is "Followers." Now, YouTube calls them Subscribers. Facebook initially called them

Fans and now calls it Page Likes. But Instagram, Twitter, and Linked In call them Followers.

So, different platforms have different names for it, but the number doesn't measure how many people you're reaching. Why? Well, all of the social media platforms have adopted algorithms because they can't show everybody everything posted by an account that they followed, liked, or subscribed to once upon a time. They show you some of them.

So, those old numbers—your Followers, Page Likes, and Subscriber—were devalued. As we mentioned earlier, the average organic reach on Facebook is 5.2 percent, if you're lucky. And it's around 1.0 percent on Instagram and only 0.045 percent on Twitter.

It's an even harder thing to get real metrics around how many people you reached when you run social media advertising campaigns across multiple platforms. What happens if the same person sees your video ad seven times? Do your metrics tell you that you reached seven people, or do you realize that all you reached was one person who got very annoyed?

MATT: Maybe they were a big fan.

GREG: Yeah, right. So, one of the vanity metrics you've got to question is Followers.

Another one that I see people getting into trouble with again and again, is "Views." People keep saying, "Look how many views my social video got."

Well, how do you define a view? Because YouTube defines it as up to 30 seconds long. Facebook and Instagram define a view as anything over 3 seconds long. And TikTok says, "As soon as the video starts playing, that's a view."

So, a "view" is not a "view" is not a "view." You're comparing apples to kumquats and grapes. So, that's another vanity metric that you need to question.

MATT: There's one more vanity metric. And that is "Impressions" on a lot of platforms.

When I am teaching analytics to marketing teams, I will give them a multiple choice option, "Define an impression," and I give them five options.

I get a pretty consistent distribution of responses. That tells me the team doesn't have a single definition of an impression. After I point this out, I ask, "What made you select that?"

I point out that as a human, we are thinking of an impression in a human term, which is I physically saw it.

However, several years ago, the Media Rating Council (MRC) created a standard definition of viewable ad impression: "At least

50 percent of an ad must be in view for a minimum of 1 second for display ads or 2 seconds for video ads."

Here's how YouTube and Facebook calculate an impression for a video ad: When "50 percent of the ad's pixels" are viewable for "2 continuous seconds." Facebook's definition of an ad impression is anything greater than 0 pixels that is shown for more than 0 seconds!

So not everyone in the industry adopted the MRC's viewable ad impression measurement guidelines. That's a big problem. Because when consistent advertising viewability standards aren't used, marketers may come to inaccurate conclusions about the effectiveness of their ads, which could lead to misguided buying decisions and suboptimal results.

And when I'm reporting up the ladder, when I say, "a viewable ad impression," what are they thinking? They're thinking less and less in digital terms and more and more in human terms.

Viewability has proven to be a valuable metric for brand campaigns. Research has found a consistent relationship between how long an ad is viewable and increases in awareness and consideration.

Other research has found viewability is as important for performance outcomes, such as conversions, as it is for brand outcomes. So, it may sound obvious, but video ads that have a chance to be seen are the ones that drive business results.

So, it's important to understand the vocabulary and have an organizational definition so that we all know what it is we are buying, reporting, and making decisions about.

GREG: Yeah. And those are things that you do not want to take for granted and just use because they're convenient and available. You really need to think about and adopt metrics that matter. So, maybe we should begin to segue to, "How do I get out of this predicament?"

MATT: So, what do you measure?

GREG: Well, let me tell you about an organization called the Global Video Measurement Alliance (GVMA). They were formed in 2019.

They are developing cross-platform standard metrics for social video, including ones that are significantly better than "Followers" and "Views."

For example, the GVMA developed a new metric called de-duplicated "unique viewers." Instead of using Followers, Page Likes, or Subscribers, you can use this new metric to measure reach more accurately. It also enables you to leverage the power of de-duplicated viewership to make better content and media decisions on both platforms.

Another new metric developed by the GVMA that you'll want to adopt is "quality views," which uses a 30-second view as a qualifier.

Any video shorter than 30 seconds is counted only if it is watched to completion.

Now, these are relatively new definitions. They have not been widely adopted as industry standards yet. But I would certainly encourage social media marketers who are serious about solving the problem of vanity metrics to pay attention to the GVMA. They are tackling the biggest problems of social video audience measurement.

And it's worth noting that Tubular Labs, which helped to establish the GVMA in 2019, expanded their Audience Ratings suite in 2021 by adding ecommerce measurement capabilities. These provide a unique view into how product-related social video viewing influences online sales through Amazon.

Measuring Brand Lift and Engaged-View Conversions

MATT: We both think that "Impressions" is a vanity metric. So, what should you use as a key performance indicator (KPI)?

GREG: There are different answers to your question, depending on whether you're launching a brand-building campaign or running and performance marketing campaign.

For brand-building campaigns, YouTube, Facebook, Instagram, Twitter, TikTok, Pinterest, and LinkedIn all offer "Brand Lift" studies to advertisers. These measure the impact of video ads on metrics that matter like brand awareness, consideration, and purchase intent.

They work by dividing the people into randomized test and holdout groups and showing your video ad to the larger test group, but the smaller holdout group doesn't see it. Then, they conduct surveys comparing the performance of these groups over time.

To measure the impact of organic social video campaigns, you can conduct one brand lift study before a campaign is launched and a second one after it ends. Or for ongoing social video programs, conduct periodic brand lift studies—at least one per year and up to one per quarter.

For performance marketing campaigns, Google Analytics 4 (GA4) offers a new metric called YouTube Engaged-View Conversion (EVC) events. An EVC event indicates that a user has watched a YouTube video for at least 10 seconds and has completed a conversion event on your website or app within 3 days of viewing the video.

This new metric is a game changer. Why? Because 70 percent of YouTube viewers say that they bought a brand as a result of finding the brand on YouTube. But YouTube video viewers have strong intent to continue watching the content that they're in the middle of watching. As a result, they're very likely to stay on the platform when they encounter an ad as part of their viewing experience.

Measuring Conversation, Amplification, and Applause Rates

MATT: Absolutely. I'm really excited about that. I think that's going to be great.

And there are other social media metrics that we should use as KPIs. They've been hidden in plain sight since October 2011, when Avinash Kaushik first defined them in a post on his *Occam's Razor* blog entitled, "Best Social Media Metrics: Conversation, Amplification, Applause, Economic Value."

The definitions have evolved over the years, but here's what each one measures and how it's calculated:

- **Conversation rate:** Indicates how many Comments/Replies on average each of your posts has received (e.g., Conversation rate = # of Comments/ # of Posts)
- **Amplification rate:** Indicates how many times on average each of your posts was Shared/Retweeted (e.g., Amplification rate = # of Shares/ # of Posts)
- **Applause rate:** Indicates how many Likes/Likes each of your posts has received on average (e.g., Applause rate = # of Likes/ # of Posts)
- **Economic value:** Shows how much economic value each visit from a social network brings to your site by completing your site's goals (e.g., Economic value = Per session Goal value, which is calculated by Google Analytics when you assign a monetary amount to each completed activity, called a conversion, that contributes to the success of your business)

You and I have both been training marketers to use these metrics as KPIs since our good friend Avinash came up with them. And I absolutely love that he came up with three different metrics for measuring the real active engagement of users with your social media pages.

GREG: Avinash is the Digital Marketing Evangelist at Google, so you'd assume that the vast majority of marketers would be using these "best social media metrics" by now. But they aren't.

Why? Because they make most social media marketing activities look like a total waste of time and money. So, most marketers stick with vanity metrics and hope that no one notices.

But it turns out that we need to adopt Conversation, Amplification, and Applause rates as KPIs. Why? Because the social media platforms are using them.

For example, Facebook freaked everybody out in January of 2018 when they announced what the industry called the Facebook feed apocalypse. That's when they acknowledged that their engagement metrics were a little whacked. They needed to readjust them.

What they did was decrease the impact of Reactions in their algorithm, increase the impact of Comments, and maintain the impact of Shares. So, even Facebook was using these metrics to make adjustments in their algorithm. And you should also focus on them if you want to create content that gets higher engagement and interaction rates going forward.

MATT: And if your posts aren't engaging your followers, then you shouldn't expect your social media accounts to generate much economic value.

Comparing the Economic Value of All Your Social Media Accounts

GREG: And economic value is already an important metric. Increasingly, it will become your most important KPI. Social media marketers are going to have to struggle with this ugly transition between now and then.

But guess what? You're struggling in the right area.

After Willie Sutton, a famous bank robber from the 1930s, was arrested, a reporter asked, "Willie, why do you rob banks?" And he said, "Because that's where the money is."

So, if you're not measuring economic value, then learn how to. Because that's where the money is. And one of the things that may require you to do is connect the dots.

As Matt said eloquently at the beginning of this podcast, you need to think beyond your social media platforms. If people need to come to your website before they can buy your product, generate a lead for your sales force, or do something that can be monetized, then figure out how to create a conversion event in GA4. And, then:

- Link your property to Google Ads to make YouTube Web EVCs available in your GA4 reports.
- Activate Google signals to see conversions from users who are signed in to their Google accounts.
- Add a monetary value to each conversion event.

Finally, use Predictive Audiences to target "likely seven-day purchasers" or create a remarketing campaign to re-engage users based on their behavior on your site.

Now, this won't be easy to learn at first. But it will eventually enable you to compare the economic value of all your social media accounts. So, when the often predicted social commerce trend finally takes off, you'll be in a strong position to measure what matters.

Social Media Reporting

MATT: In my training, I do an informal poll asking people what their frustrations are about analytics. And especially when I get a lot of social media managers, their number-one frustration is having to justify what they do. The problem, as we've just gone through, is they're bringing platform metrics to analytics.

They're not connecting these dots. They think they're reporting on their activity. "Here's how busy I am. Here's how many posts I made." And if you want to be ignored at an important meeting, then talk about engagement.

No one sees the economic value of a Comment, Share, or Like. And until you're translating all of this into dollar signs, nobody cares.

GREG: Yeah. I run into exactly the same phenomena. So, here's how I explain this in onsite and online courses that prepare professionals for OMCA certification: too many people are measuring inputs. You know, how many hours I spent working on this project or program.

And more people need to start measuring outputs. That's where the Conversation, Amplification, and Applause rates come in.

But ultimately, you want to begin measuring outcomes. And that's where the economic value comes in.

So, inputs? Who cares? Outputs? Nice. Not thrilling, but nice. It tells social media managers what they need to do next to be more effective. But outcomes? That's what executives are paying for. That's why they've given you a salary and a budget for your social media marketing campaign or program.

So, move from inputs to outputs. And then move from outputs to outcomes.

Selecting KPIs Tied to Your Business Objectives

MATT: Well, that requires a better understanding of KPIs.

Now, Greg, I don't know if you saw the report entitled, "Media KPIs That Matter," which was published in 2021 by the Association of National Advertisers (ANA). The most important KPI for Media was Return on Investment (ROI)/Return on Ad Spend (ROAS).

And ROI/ROAS is an outcome metric that's directly tied to business growth. It's used to calculate: "For every dollar spent, what is the expected return?" It guides marketers on whether their advertising investment paid off this quarter. Measurement of ROI/ROAS can be done via marketing mix modeling, which is often used to optimize advertising mix and promotional tactics. This metric was not only ranked first in importance, but also fourth in use. It was identified as a top new/emerging KPI for media.

And I went through the list of most important KPIs saying, "Five of the top six are outcomes. That's great." Then, I looked at the second list of *most used* KPIs and only one out of the top six was an outcome.

And the most used KPI was CPM (Cost per Thousand). And here's where my nerdiness comes out because I said, "CPM is not a KPI. It measures efficiency, not performance." And the second most used KPI was CPC (cost-per-click), which also measures efficiency.

So, it blows my mind that most social media marketers don't know that a key performance indicator (KPI) is a metric that helps you understand how you are doing against your objectives. And efficiency is nice. Not thrilling, but nice. But your KPIs should be tied to outcomes.

GREG: Yeah. And that reminds me of a story that I told on one of your earlier podcasts. It was about my father, who was the director of marketing at Oldsmobile.

Now, some of our listeners are too young to remember what an Oldsmobile was. It was a car. It had been around for more than a hundred years. And my father became the director of marketing back in 1988, before many of you were born. So, you may not have heard about his classic advertising campaign, which declared, "This is NOT your father's Oldsmobile."

And that was really ironic for me because it was my father's Oldsmobile.

The campaign's slogan became a meme. But sales went down.

So, my father asked his ad agency, "How are we measuring success?" And their answer was gross rating points (GRPs).

So, my father asked, "How many GRPs do we need to sell a car?" And the agency couldn't answer his question because there is no correlation between GRPs and sales.

So, I learned the hard way from my father's unsuccessful ad campaign that you need to measure what matters. That's not inputs or even outputs. What you need to measure are outcomes.

MATT: Well, I think you hit the nail on the head because that story is so good at showing what can happen when you use the wrong metrics as KPIs.

GREG: And beyond ROI/ROAS, there are other metrics that matter, including customer satisfaction and lifetime value that you should focus on.

This is why so many social media marketers fail to get a seat at the big table. They often measure inputs and sometimes measure outputs. But they rarely measure outcomes.

Using "Action Dashboard" Versus "Crappy Dashboard"

MATT: This gets to the final topic in our outline: The "action dashboard" versus the "crappy dashboard."

One of the reasons that most dashboards are "crappy" is because they are data dumps that provide few insights and little analysis of key trends. And they rarely recommend what actions or next steps should be taken.

To create an "actionable" dashboard, you need to take your engagement metrics for Conversation, Amplification, and Applause and do an analysis of your best/worst posts. Then, you need to uncover the best and the worst topics and keywords for successful posts. And discover which types of content perform the best—videos, pictures, or text.

Or you can compare your social media stats against your competitors and against industry average results. Do this both in absolute and relative metrics (per 1,000 followers).

Or you can analyze how user activity on your social media accounts has changed over time and compare the percentage of increase or decrease for each metric by week or month.

GREG: And you need to have the courage to let your executives know if corporate propaganda doesn't work. Why can you afford to make this kind of career-damaging move? Because, if you do, then you will become more successful and valuable to your organization. And if you don't, then your job will remain pushing corporate propaganda into social channels.

MATT: Right. And then compare the performance and economic value for all your social media accounts. Then find the most effective content and platforms for your business.

Then, you should recommend what needs to be done next. Most executives actually want insights tied to action recommendations. This is what gets you a seat at the big table.

So, you've got to know which KPI to use at every stage of the customer journey, so that you can measure brand lift in the early stages and conversion events in the later stages.

GREG: Otherwise, you end up trying to measure a fish by its ability to climb a tree.

MATT: I like that metaphor.

GREG: Well, it's attributed to Albert Einstein of all people.

But one of the things that you need to understand about the customer journey is it's a process. It's not a one-time event. And if you try to move people to the next stage too rapidly, or you ask for the order too soon, then they feel pushed.

So, the process may be longer and more convoluted than the old sales funnel model. But your ability to interact with people as they return again and again for different information is building a relationship. That is really where social media can shine.

Reporting

MATT: The final topic that we need to talk about is reporting. "Whom are you reporting to?"

If I'm reporting information to a product manager, then they will typically have access to as much data as I have. So, I can share more data, graphs, and tables because they know how to read these. They will understand the opportunities and can respond to the threats.

But if I am reporting up to the C-level, I do not use dozens of platform metrics. I get straight to economic impact. I have less data and more analysis, more recommendations, and more focus on the customer or company because that's what they want. C-level executives want you to be quick, concise, and to the point.

And if you can speak in dollar signs, then you've made them happy.

GREG: Absolutely. So, when you are the social media manager, you'll want to go beyond reporting inputs, and report outputs, which product managers will love, because they are like Rosalind, the baby-sitter who picked up Calvinball quickly.

So, you can report the Brand Lift and Engaged-View Conversions generated by your new YouTube ad campaign, as well as the Conversation, Amplification, and Applause rates for your ongoing social media marketing program. They'll know what you're talking about.

But down the road, when you become the director of marketing, you'll want to go beyond reporting outputs and report outcomes, which top management need to know, because they have to make decisions about the organization's performance and growth.

So, your report will also include recommendations like moving some of your budget out of social media marketing on Facebook and into social media advertising on YouTube and influencer marketing on TikTok. Why? Because this will give us more bang for the buck.

MATT: That's a great way to end this social media marketing segment, Greg, because I don't think enough people focus on outcomes.

So, thank you again for your time. This has been one of the more fun podcasts, which has turned into a series. Hopefully, we are still relevant in 3 days or 3 weeks.

GREG: Yes, we should stamp this with a "best if used by" date of today.

CHAPTER 7

Conversion Optimization

By Kim Krause Berg

I dialed up the Internet for the first time in 1995 to see what the fuss was about and was introduced to two surprises. One was email. The other was communities of people. In one instant, the entire world was at my fingertips, and I wanted to know more about everyone with a keyboard. I dove into the web headfirst before I knew how to swim. This helped me learn that communication is vital. So is trust. And no ALL CAPS.

My first job was building and promoting websites for a magazine publisher back in 1997. This was when search engines and directories were so numerous that it became its own field, called search engine optimization (SEO).

I founded an online community in 1998 for web designers and SEOs, which is how I learned the importance of understanding website user experiences from many countries.

Communication with people around the world became a new skill. Australians will tell you like it is. The United Kingdom can be counted on for wry humor. Americans were boring but learned quickly.

Everyone saw the potential to generate revenue from their kitchen table.

The Internet provided new opportunities for businesses to expand their reach and small businesses to launch. Imagine two teams meeting on a large football field. The corporation with a staff of web designers, content writers, and graphic designers building online empires were ready with data and skills on one side of the field.

And then there was the rest of us. Same ball field. Outmatched.

How do you compete online when you're a startup or new and jumping in? Well, by the end of this chapter, you will know that and more:

- Some simple conversion guidelines
- Key areas important to conversion
- What persuasive design is
- Understand your customers and their intent
- How to design for people with disabilities
- Basic conversion opportunities and considerations
- How to create calls to action
- The value of user personas

Build It and They Will Come

This is what we thought would happen in those early days.

Maybe it was because there was less competition or experience with building websites. I remember how long it took to learn nested tables in HTML. The most common homepage design literally linked to every page without a menu because we thought that *if we didn't put it there, nobody would know what we had* on the website.

Oh, and text links were expected to be the color blue.

The art of web conversions evolved because we were building websites people didn't *want* to come to.

Why was that?

Our customers learned that some websites were difficult to use. This created website abandonment, which provided helpful data used to help determine how to improve web page design. Today this is called *KPIs*, for key performance indicators.

In 25 years, regardless of the size of the business, the same issues occur that prevent people from completing a task on a website or mobile app. When a task is measurable, such as adding an item to a shopping cart, there is no room for error.

If a flutter from data indicates "something bad is happening," certain steps can be performed to find out if there is a functional or design bug. Split A/B testing with distinctive designs can contribute possible insight into user behaviors.

You may be thinking to yourself that your site meets every performance recommendation for speed or responsive layout and there is not a single grammatical error anywhere. Today's testing tools provide tremendous support for making those improvements.

But sales are still not where you want them. Downloads are slowing down. Rank and referrals are taking a hit.

Now what can you do?

Conversions optimization techniques have changed because computers did. Advanced SEO audits include user experience and information architecture audits because we learned how these areas affect conversions.

As the technology changes from desktop to mobile devices, user experience designers and digital marketers look for new ways to make us click. Human experience is the last place companies look for clues.

There are five areas for new conversions opportunities. In every website audit I perform, the most often neglected is *Who*. This is followed up with *Why*.

People are unique. If you fail to understand the core source for conversions, they simply will not meet your expectations.

To persuade anyone to use your website, mobile app, make a purchase, follow a link, join your community, or make a connection, there is one basic rule of thumb: *never make assumptions about your visitors.*

Easy Conversion Guidelines

Conversions optimization is directly related to the neurosciences. How we behave and think, choose, make decisions, plan, and comprehend our world is a researcher's dream. We learn from their data.

Don't Design for Yourself

It's important to accept that there is no one way to convert a click. This is because people are unique and unpredictable. Well, unique at least. After years of studying humans and computers, and human behavior and the Web, we may have figured out some common denominators.

For example, how we learn has a direct influence on how we search, browse, and make decisions online.

How customers purchase from one company may not be how customers buy from others. One retailer may find that their customers require many design ideas that require shipping free samples first, while another one has so many five-star ratings that customer confidence is already a sure thing.

What persuades one online visitor may not work for the next one. The worst approach to conversions design is designing for yourself.

Many companies do it anyway.

Study User Behavior

I'm a visual learner. I didn't know that until I needed to learn how to design a property we moved to into a small horse stable for my retired racehorse.

For starters, we had woods and a house. No barn. No pasture. One horse. One husband and a pile of contractors.

The only way any of them could communicate to me where the electric, water, fences, and barn would go was to make drawings. And even with that, I still had my horse friends review the layout.

Could we expand to get another horse? Was there room for a riding ring? Can we get water out to the new barn before winter comes?

- There was the immediate need.
- There was the future need.

There was me not wanting to carry buckets in knee-deep snow. It didn't take long for the contractors to know that to persuade me to agree to anything required knowing the following:

- **Cost.** How much will it cost? (Cost matters for conversions.)
- **Time.** How long will it take? (Amazon learned this early on.)
- **Security.** Will the fencing be secure? (Privacy and security for transactions and data can make or break conversions.)
- **Brand loyalty.** When can I add another horse? (Scheduled shipments, upsell, future enhancement discounts, dreamer enablement tactic.)

There are other key areas important to conversions:

- Relevancy
- Trust
- Customer service
- Ease of use
- Competitive pricing
- Brand reputation
- User interface design

Determine Who Performs Conversion Optimization

Companies develop methodologies that work within their vertical and business culture. A team approach delivers the most chance for success because frankly there's much to explore and understand.

Stakeholders answer to someone, and usually they want to know how much to invest to improve revenue opportunities.

Stakeholders rely on *marketers*, who may be responsible for writing content. I discuss this later, but for now, let me assure you that every conversion is tied to words. Those words must be in the right place at the right time, say the right thing to the right person, and be accessible to anyone who wants to know what the content is. This is one of the areas for web and mobile conversions where failures are high.

Like I said, communication is the key to conversion survival.

Usability and user experience (UX) designers must understand conversion design. This is everything from color use and button placement to patterns and designing for cognition.

Mobile developers have a similar path as UX, but the code is different. Mobile devices manage user experiences differently depending on the operating system. Downloadable mobile apps render on small screens, requiring innovative designs to make call-to-action prompts visible and tappable.

Anyone with a title that includes *analyzing data* produces spreadsheets and tracking information that help gauge performance. When they meet with marketing people, they help devise or revise game plans.

Persuasive Design for Conversion

What does it mean when someone recommends persuasive design? At first it may seem odd to think that a web or mobile page can lead anyone around with clever tricks, but that's the beauty of conversions design. The goal is to remove pain points.

Instant Feedback

If you are using a keyboard, press the Tab key. Do it several times. What do you see? If the page you are clicking on was designed to provide instant feedback on sense of place, each link reached with the Tab key would be highlighted upon activation.

Sometimes the designer will put a border around the link and a colored background. If it is a button, the colors may switch. If a screen reader is being used, the words are highlighted to help with orientation for sight-impaired people. On a mobile phone, accessibility settings can indicate wherever the cursor is by highlighting it and adding audio.

In other words, we create these design touches because we want to know where we are, where we're going, and hey, is there anything else cool in here?

Being Responsive Is About Meeting Expectations

A polished, functioning, successful website supports your marketing investment and so it is important to focus on increasing user engagement and flow by making your pages responsive to your site visitors.

Make every task easy to find and use, provide feedback, create a clear information architecture using terms your target users understand, and minimize distractions.

Calls to action, tasks, navigation, content, images, page layout, and forms design lead visitors to interact with the web page. Success or failure impacts ROI (return on investment) and KPIs.

Before you design for conversions, take a look under the hood for the parts you should focus on:

- **Calls to action**, also known as CTAs, are the points in your content where you invite a website visitor to take action. This may be in the form of a button or a text link. For mobile apps, sometimes filling out a form field activates something. Typically, CTAs stand out visually so that they capture attention. For people using a screen reader, there is no visual prompt, making the text itself more important.

- **Leading tasks** are often the main actions on a page. There can be several, from finding a contact page to searching for a product. The "moneymaker" tasks should be easy to find and follow to avoid user frustration.

- **Desirability and momentum** are critical, coveted human responses to every web page that contains a task, even if that task is to simply provide content to read or listen to. The goal is to create reasons to read and inspire the need to want more. These responses are tied to persuasion and incorporated into what is known as persuasive design.

- **Information architecture** works in tandem with search engine optimization and site structure for web and mobile applications. It's so important that journey mapping is recommended as part of the mockup and design process.

For navigation and conversions to function and grow over time, the crucial element is understanding how your users think. Couple that with how you know they behave online when searching, purchasing, and using their devices. To ignore anyone is to lose potential revenue.

Information architecture supports revenue tasks.

Taxonomies are simply the words chosen for a specific type of website. For example, you are familiar with "About," "Contact," and "Blog." Everyone understands what they refer to and what happens if they go there. The challenge is giving a tour of your particular place online. Do you sell fitness or exercise equipment? If you sell boots, where are the clearance men's boots in width EEE?

Do you know how to structure the navigation for the guy with big feet? What else is he looking for? Do you have related items? A newsletter? Maybe Mr. EEE has a favorite brand, and the only reason he found your shoes is because the others were sold out.

Findability is your friend.

Structure is related to navigation. Having each page layout be consistent helps reduce pain points. Headings structure is an accessibility guideline recommendation because of how screen readers can be asked to sort through content. Both search engines and assistive devices are programmed to place higher importance on H1 headings because they are used for page titles, followed by H2, H3, and so on, with keywords for easy subject scanning.

Desirability, Momentum, and Conversions

What makes people stay on your website has everything to do with how they feel when they get there. Proper navigation means that users can move forward and backward and side to side with ease, always knowing where they are within the site. For mobile apps, this design approach is sometimes ignored, making it difficult for mobile users to complete tasks.

Avoid High Bounce Rates

From the perspective of the user experience and conversions, issues can be traced to the lack of a guidance system. When there is no sense of place built into the navigation, and it's built for forward momentum only, one page at a time, browsing and item searches are the first casualties.

Whether the page appears as an embedded text link or is located in a navigation menu, the task is to go to a page and read or perform a task. For many users, the activity stops there for the following reasons:

- There is no incentive to conduct a task.
- The page opened a new window, and they are lost. (New windows are a risk on mobile devices and screen readers.)

- There is no sense of place, and they are lost within the website. Where was that cool discount code?
- There are too many choices (too much content, too many links, and so on), and they are overwhelmed. If you want to kill conversions, overwhelm and overstimulate your visitors.
- Related content is not found.
- Pages are too long to read.
- There is redundant information.
- There is no incentive provided to create momentum to "click for more."

Conversion Optimization Strategy and Planning

We're entering an era where web pages are expected to render on mobile devices. From there, the next step is downloading a mobile app to continue the relationship between company and customer.

The basic principles for conversions design are the same, but the challenges for web designers, mobile developers, and digital marketers increased. Everyone is chasing new target markets that have learned to become dependent on mobile.

One of those lucrative areas are people with disabilities who are far more independent thanks to advances in technology that come with their mobile devices.

Another growing target market is the aging population. They may have more cognitive or eyesight issues, but they are often better off financially and ready to buy gifts, read hot novels, and search for natural organic products.

The old saying "take the time to walk a mile in someone else's moccasins" is helpful when putting together a strategy for marketing to people we don't know. Picture a team with a gigantic whiteboard brainstorming. The first ideas begin with what we know. Then we explore.

Awareness, Interest, Desire, Action

I'll let you in a secret. There is one sure way to convert anyone on a web page to act. When you present your amazing solution or product, introduce it, and get out of their way.

Copywriters often follow a particular pattern:

1. Introduce new product or service in the first sentence of a paragraph.
2. Describe a benefit or drop a juicy morsel about it in the next sentence.
3. Link to the product or service in the next sentence, so that the sentence literally cradles the object you want them to do something about. (The anchor text is important here.)
4. Continue to throw out juicy morsels and teasers in the next sentence or two, then end the paragraph.
5. Continue with a new heading for different content.
6. Hope they clicked the link in the previous paragraph.

So, what's wrong with this approach? Most notably, there is too much information surrounding the linked text. That link is the conversion sweet spot, but what often occurs is contrary to what you want:

- It does not contain action-oriented anchor text. (Think verbs.)
- It contains a product name that is new and unfamiliar. (No confidence.)
- It cannot be easily seen.
- Too much distracting information surrounds it, so the reader literally jumps over the call to action to continue reading so they don't miss the content after the link.
- Some readers scan the entire page's content first. They take it all in and may not return to the paragraph with the link.
- Unconsidered cognitive behaviors might interfere with the click response you're looking for. Memory, cognitive impairment, emotional distress, and age are several factors to consider.

For awareness, interest, desire, and action to activate into a strong conversion point, less is more.

Advocating for Your Website Visitors

Business owners know their products or services inside and out. They created them. They built something from scratch and watched it grow. They hire creatives and marketers and follow every SEO technique recommended to them. What they don't fully understand is who their customers are. They believe they do. (They truly do!) Remember: never assume to know what your website visitors are looking for.

Understanding Customer Intent

When considering a digital marketing strategy, the most successful results occur when everyone agrees on whom they are marketing to. The other agreement must be what the look and feel of the website or mobile app will be.

I'm Too Young and Sexy for My Shades
In one real-life example, a seller of brand-name sunglasses couldn't understand why sales were not meeting expectations. All of the SEO efforts were intact. The web page layouts were fine for an ecommerce website. They were stumped.

The brand had a line specially created for young people wanting to look cool and tough. The two main colors on the product pages were black and blood red. In fact, some of the images contained street language, and the overall design was intended to present a feeling of turf, fighting, and anger.

For a young person to walk down the street wearing these cool shades, they needed a credit card to buy them. No other payment methods were accepted. Which meant they had to be old enough to own a credit card.

The target market for that particular product line ran from high school age to early 20s with no credit history. They would need to convince a parent to buy them the sunglasses.

Maybe dad might. Mom, not so lucky. Adding other payment options would help sales. So might gift certificates and birthday lists.

Unexpected Cosmetics Demos
The beauty products industry is hot and highly competitive. Brands today live or die by customer loyalty and must watch and listen to what their customers say and do.

So, it was a surprise to one brand to see video demos of its products created by men. Thought to be targeting women, some of the more fascinating demonstrations and expertly created videos were by men demonstrating expert applications of everything from eye liner to how to hide acne with foundation.

Realizing that the company had a bias built into their web page content, they went back to review and adjust for inclusion.

Services Are Not One Size Fits All
Before COVID-19 created personal deliveries to your home, some home services were already experts at it. Plumbers, electricians, roofers, and building contractors with a website plan for how their customers want to be serviced.

- Is it an emergency call? What would a landing page look like for the customer who is concerned about a flooded basement?
- Is routine maintenance an option, and if so, how is it structured?

- What type of payments are accepted?
- If the business delivers or makes house calls, what does the truck look like? Do they wear uniforms?

You might be surprised at the variables in customer preferences. The more you know their number-one desire, the more conversions will follow because your web pages will be designed to connect with their needs.

Creating User Personas

User personas are a technique developed in the early days that was used to help understand target markets. The goal is always about learning human behavior as it relates to websites since this is how we reach people in today's information age. A tremendous volume of research and data are used to create them.

Could you be a user persona? What is your story?

Today, user testing in person or with software applications developed for interviews provides better accuracy. We can interview customers. We can use video interviews combined with user testing software to go through web pages or test software during the development phases. Some companies use focus groups.

The first personas I worked with were printed booklets containing imaginary stories of pretend people. I referred to them as "user characters" because when I put them to use, it was like acting in a play.

An exercise in persona creation is simply an aid used by design and marketing teams to ask questions and sort out practical solutions.

Nothing beats true user testing, but defining certain human characteristics, considering how people use computers, and understanding user behavior in various circumstances is valuable for user experience design and writing marketing content.

The Willow Harrington sidebar is one example to start you thinking about conversion optimizations for a specific set of people.

If you were to sit down with Willow and ask her to shop for clothes for herself, and then shop for clothes for her daughter, you might learn there are differences in her choices.

Would she purchase for herself and a child from one store? Does she search with a cell phone or a laptop? Is she super-organized while job hunting online? How does she research career options?

What if Willow is living at home because she depends on a wheelchair to get around sometimes?

What has changed in your thought process? What did you miss? She asked about customer service. This is a good clue. She's independent

Willow Harrington: My Story

My name is Willow Harrington and I live on my parents' farm in Tennessee even though I'm 28 years old. I haven't found a job yet, but I went to college to learn how to be a teacher. My parents are good people but getting older. I am a single mom of a 5-year-old daughter. Long story. I figure I'll be home schooling her because COVID-19 is making it hard for kids to go to school. I'm pretty smart and do most everything with my cell phone. I want a Mac but am using a PC laptop until I can afford one. It can be pretty stressful taking care of a kid, living with parents, trying to find a job, and helping around the farm. My eyesight is pretty bad, so I need to wear glasses and increase the text on computer screens. We get the Internet out here, but boy, it's really slow sometimes! I sometimes need my wheelchair to get around because of some health issues that tire me out, but if you know me, you know I never give up. Nothing stops me from fitting in wherever I go.

Image (insert picture)	Persona Type Young single female with child.
Name Willow Harrington	Background Self-starter who grew up on family farm. Wants a better life for herself and daughter. College-level education. Needs her wheelchair sometimes but is fairly independent.
Quote "Never say never."	Worries/Fears Worried about job prospects, discrimination and supporting a child. Biggest threat is losing a parent.
A Day in the Life of (Describe her day.) Does she multitask? Grow her own vegetables? Spend time with her child? Socialize with friends?	Online Behavior Does she carry her cell phone around with her? Use social media? Order products online? Belong to any communities for people with disabilities?
Pain Points/Health Poor eyesight, stress, anxiety, could lose a bit of weight. Always dealing with severe arthritis in her spine.	Goals and Dreams Become a teacher. Get married. Leave Tennessee to travel and explore the country.
What Would Make My Life Easier Fast Internet. Downtime. More money. Customer service. Why do they make it so hard to find!	What Influences Me Friends and family. TV. *Virgin River* show. People who treat me like I'm disabled really tick me off.

Image (insert picture)	Persona Type
	Young single female with child.
My Favorite Brands	
Affordable anything. Levi	
jeans. Jeep cars.	

and refuses to pity herself. ("Leave Tennessee to travel and explore the country.")

She has a cradle for her mobile device attached to her wheelchair and sometimes can't access websites that are not designed to flip to landscape mode.

In fact, most of us never stop to consider how people use computers.

This is why creating personas contributes to gathering requirements for marketing and design. We are missing opportunities by not listening to customers or inviting them to ask us for help when they may require assistance.

Of course, Willow isn't real. I made her up based on what I see when conversions testing fails to pinpoint any obvious cause for low conversion rates.

It's always tied to simply being human.

Designing the Landing Page

For PPC projects, the landing page is the main moneymaker, and therefore the most scrutinized page to be designed. For that reason, there is rarely one design per campaign. There are several.

This is because of what Tim Ash introduced in his landmark book, *Landing Page Optimization,* as the four stages for decision-making:

- Awareness (attention)
- Interested
- Desire (decision)
- Action

And then he added a fifth post-sale stage called "Permanent Satisfaction," which drives repeat sales.

Amazon figured out how to simplify repeat orders by creating the "Buy Again" filter, making it easier to search for an item that met with customer satisfaction. When you add in a "Buy Now" button, the entire process takes seconds because all of the information is already in the database.

> ## Designing for People with Disabilities
>
> The Web is not designed for everyone to use, and nowhere is this more evident than web and mobile pages for people with disabilities or impairments.
>
> Universal design principles were developed in 1997 to make environments accessible to all people, regardless of age or disability. Principle 3, Simple and Intuitive Use, makes sense for conversions design. So does Principle 4, Perceptible Information. Enhancing conversion rates may be as simple as being practical with the use interface.
>
> The Americans with Disabilities Act (ADA) has been around since 1990 but doesn't automatically apply to websites or mobile apps because they didn't exist back then.
>
> Some major companies work hard to develop technology that can be used universally. IBM, Google, Microsoft, and Apple each have policies addressing design for inclusion.
>
> It's so much part of web design that the World Wide Web Consortium (W3C) backs the writing of Web Content Accessibility Guidelines, or WCAG. These guidelines are the foundation for laws in various countries and applied in the United States for government and educational web properties for what is known as Section 508.
>
> In other words, conversions are directly tied to people's ability or inability to use websites and mobile apps. When we don't build what they are able to use, they shun the brand.
>
> In verticals where competition for customers is high, developing mobile apps for inclusion means thinking creatively. For example, how might a blind person make a check deposit with their cell phone camera? Did their bank consider them as a customer?
>
> Look at the settings in your mobile device, under Accessibility, or locate general settings for language, color, font and size preferences, and dark mode. Web and mobile page layout considerations embrace visual design far more often than they account for people who can't see. Design for accessibility for the web and mobile apps is a specialized skill set worth investing in because it opens the doors to millions of potential new customers.

What Makes a Great Landing Page?

Designing for today's landing page is trickier because computer devices come in all shapes and sizes. A laptop web page has more room to display content than a mobile device. Sidebars on larger monitors are stacked below on mobile or excluded.

What is it? Why is it for me? Take me there. What is the value you are offering?

In its most simple state, a landing page meets needs for a well-structured value proposition. Figure 7.1 shows an example mockup landing page.

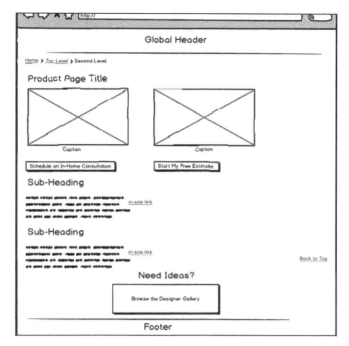

FIGURE 7.1 Example Mockup for a Landing Page

A few critical elements items should appear in the top third of your home page:

- **Company name or product brand.** Identify yourself right away. The number-one error in page design is forgetting to put the name of the brand or company on the home-page or landing page in text.

- **Why choose us.** State why your site visitor should choose your service or product. You have about 3 seconds to convince them to stay on the page.

- **Why you're better for them.** Clearly indicate that you understand who your visitor is and how you can meet their needs.

- **How to start.** Place your lead call to action task in this space. It can be a button ("download free trial") or a short form ("get started now"). Avoid forcing anyone to scroll to complete the top user task.

- **Here's how to buy.** Start a conversion funnel here. Some visitors will have been to your site earlier. They want to get past the formalities and start a task.

- **Emphasize the benefits, rather than the features.** How does the product or service make a positive impact? This is often directly related to feelings and an immediate reward.

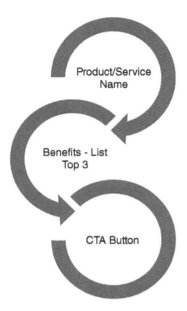

FIGURE 7.2 Structure the Order of Appearance to Aid in Understanding the Offer

Creating Calls to Action

Nothing is more unmotivating than reading a "Click Here" or "Learn More" link. Did you know that it is against website accessibility guidelines to indicate text links solely by color? Figure 7.2 shows the value proposition order.

Here are ways to improve the design of your buttons and text links.

- Always choose foreground and background colors that pass accessibility color contrast tests when designing buttons. The outer border can be darker. Padding between text and sides matters too.
- Tap targets for mobile devices must meet specific size requirements. If the finger misses the arrow, that's a risk.
- Always describe the landing page. "Learn More" and "Click Here" are not descriptive enough. Learn more about what?
- When you present a new product offering, show your visitor what it is with a product image or name. Figure 7.3 shows a simple example.

When providing a call to action, it must be placed at the moment when you inspired your readers to leave their train of thought.

FIGURE 7.3   What is on sale? Be sure to put in the details.

Note

Whenever a searcher lands on any page of your website, whether it is an advertised landing page, product page, or homepage, it is vitally important to quickly communicate what sets you apart from your competitors. Think of it as communicating what you do and are, as opposed to what you say or want. If you claim to be the "best," you need to provide proof.

Design Considerations

Computer technology changes at a fast pace, requiring us to update everything we traditionally tracked about user experiences.

Behavior from a generation that grew up with handheld devices is not like Boomers, who fondly recall reading the Sunday paper and watching TV shows delivered by the antenna on the house roof.

Small cellphone screens take getting used to, especially for people who are sight impaired. Not only is squeezing text, buttons, video, and images into a handheld device a challenge, but so is designing that content to connect with readers.

Conversion optimization teams stay on top of trends, especially when products and services are displayed for websites or within mobile apps. Let's take a look.

When someone lands on a web page, they need directions and reminders for what is referred to as "sense of place." They also need to be reminded where they are when comparison shopping or learning about a new company or brand.

Scarecrow Links

The following is taken from an article I wrote for Search Engine Journal *called* "Optimize Your CTA: Better Alternatives to 'Click Here'"

If you have watched the original film, "The Wizard of Oz," you will understand why I refer to these calls to action as scarecrow links.

These are calls to action that provide many choices, usually with vague labels and often to the same destination.

In the film, when Dorothy is traveling the Yellow Brick Road to find Oz, she comes upon the scarecrow and asks for directions.

> ***DOROTHY:*** Now which way do we go?
> ***SCARECROW:*** Pardon me. That way is a very nice way. . . *[pointing]*
> ***DOROTHY:*** Who said that?
>
> *[TOTO BARKS AT THE SCARECROW]*
>
> ***DOROTHY:*** Don't be silly, Toto. Scarecrows don't talk!
> ***SCARECROW:*** It's pleasant down that way too! *[pointing in another direction]*
> ***DOROTHY:*** That's funny. Wasn't he pointing the other way?
> ***SCARECROW:*** Of course, people do go both ways. *[pointing in both directions]*. That's the trouble. I can't make up my mind. I haven't got a brain. Only straw.

Humans are impulsive. That's why digital marketers agonize over where and when calls to action are placed within web page content.

What if we put a button in a spot before they're ready? Did we confuse them? What if they have too much time to think about it?

Okay. You HAVE seen the endless landing pages with the repeat buttons to take action that appear after every other paragraph, right? (In bright orange and green to make an impact!)

Website visitors just want to be directed to that cool thing you just showed them, now.

The number-one error in page design is forgetting to put the name of the brand or company on the homepage or landing page in text. Sounds crazy, right?

Eye-tracking studies show us that we read top to bottom, left to right, unless you live in a country that reads right to left. Most web pages are designed for "F" pattern.

To commit a brand name, product name, company name, or service description to memory, you should present it three times near the top of a web page, or what is sometimes referred to as "above the page fold."

My favorite way to test how often the brand name appears for search engines, screen readers, and reading cognition is to remove all images to see what's in the text. Hopefully the brand, company, or product name is!

However, many companies rely on their logo as the only place the brand name appears. If there is no ALT text for the logo, the company name is not available. Images don't stick in our memory if shown just one time.

To remedy this, the brand could be placed into a navigation menu as part of a category or page title such as "About Brand Name," but once that menu is reduced to a hamburger menu icon, the text display disappears.

This leaves you with headings, subheadings, paragraphs, bulleted lists, and picture captions.

Be sure the brand is in text three times at or near the top of the page because this is how long the normal attention span is. If you have not held the attention of your web page visitor long enough for them to remember your company, they will not remember they stopped by.

Remember that on mobile apps, there is no page fold, creating innovative design challenges for guiding our eyes down the page.

Design touches that increase conversions help more people by making content perceivable and understandable. Here are more ideas:

- Add ALT text to product images.
- Remember to create ALT text for images in Twitter too!
- Avoid inserting ads inside articles.
- Transcribe content for YouTube and include links to product landing pages within the text. Demonstrating a hobby with how-to instructions is a sales bonanza when adding affiliate links for your viewers.
- Many visual learners benefit from listening to instructions and blind customers who can't see the visuals benefit from the transcribed step-by-step details you provide in a video to help them understand what you are offering. This is another way to reach out to new customers.
- Images can be powerful motivators. We are more likely to trust credible information. Allow customer demos. Real-life pictures of products in action are helpful.

This summer I purchased a yurt-style tent for the backyard. I wanted to find something within my budget, which would help handle a larger group of people for a party in the event of rain. And I always wanted a yurt. This was my opportunity to get the experience.

The manufacturer I went with provided videos to help with decision-making. As you would expect, they were professionally produced and focused on a key benefit, which was how easy it is to set up the yurt. They invited customer videos too. By allowing prospective customers to see the product in action, they added another layer of authenticity. Add the written feedback and five-star ratings and bingo, they won the sale. They even beat Amazon!

Welcome new ideas. Customs may have changed. Brides on a budget are finding wedding dresses on Etsy rather than bridal boutiques. Wedding photographers and videographers familiar with new traditions add packages to include "First Look," and couples expecting a baby may invite a video of a "Mother's Blessing Ceremony."

Research into trends increases opportunities.

Copywriting for Conversions

Limited space and a growing sense for inclusion has created an even deeper need to find the right words to use.

ALT text character limits have been expanded to grant more room to describe scenes or images with diagrams. Because you are trying to convey information to people who may just be listening to your web pages, describing images takes on new relevancy for conversions.

It can be interesting to read content from the perspective of someone who can't do what you are recommending. One example is to write, "Tell your friends" about something. How might a blind person do this? Or "Show me how" takes on new meaning for demonstrations for deaf, blind, deaf/blind, or people with cognition impairments.

Writing for Screen Readers

Mobile apps and web pages are accessible with screen readers and other assistive technologies used to interpret content.

Android devices come with Talk Back, a free built-in screen reader with settings to meet many preferences from font sizes and colors to listening speed.

Apple's iOS provides VoiceOver for free, the same as it provides for Macs. VoiceOver is a robust screen reader that provides audio. The Rotor command is used to sort content by headings and links content, making the use of keywords important for understanding content.

NVDA for Chrome and Firefox PCs provide audio for free. JAWS is popular but requires a fee for a license after a free trial.

The crux of writing for screen readers is that conversions are less likely to occur if the audio version is not precisely described. A button must be announced as a button and must also describe where clicking it will go. This includes warnings if a link or button takes the listener off the website. They do not have visual aids and require the added assistance.

Ableisms

We make choices every day. What influences those choices falls into human behavior research. We pull a tremendous amount of data and work it like putty in our hands to form new ways of saying the same things.

What we don't consider is who the reader may be when writing marketing copy. Trained to write for SEO? Most of us are. We're not trained to consider the meanings for words.

One example is the use of "Call Now." This is not going to fly for people who require assistance to make a phone call.

Another example is "Tell Your Friends." There is an assumption that talking is as simple as opening up a mouth to speak, but for people who are deaf or hard of hearing, "telling" is not a natural response.

With accessibility and design for people with disabilities growing as its own discipline, it's important to understand how to not offend people.

Ableism assumes that the physical, cognitive, and sensory differences with which disabled people live are deficits that need to be "fixed." It's not hard to offend readers.

I've found that the best way for me to understand people who are different from myself is to listen to their stories and watch how they get through the day. I've taken these observations and researched more if I'm not sure how my own behavior should be.

Conversions are traced to empathy.

Lessons Learned

I've audited and tested thousands of web pages over 25 years. There is no end to what you can learn. Here are some of my favorite discoveries:

- The chances are likely that you are missing from your story. Your website design doesn't feel like you are there. Its marketing strategies are not you and don't seem to represent what you really want to say.
- Content is written for search engines rather than your targeted visitors. What may be "soda" to someone is "pop" to another.

- Ads inserted inside content interrupt reading. Why send someone away from the page?
- Clutter and distractions include providing too many links and too much reading, making decisions nearly impossible.
- Always test color contrasts.
- Forms require information. Providing options and choices is more welcoming and helps to create trust.
- Forms can have too many steps and are prone to functional errors.
- Poorly designed shopping carts make it difficult to continue shopping.
- Provide a visible customer service page or help during specific tasks such as entering data into forms.
- Always prevent user errors. If they make a mistake, show where it is and how to fix it. (And don't use the color red for error messages. It's a color-blind issue.)
- An oldie but goodie: Create a text tagline containing your site's unique selling proposition with one or two top keywords in it. This verifies in an instant that a search query has found a good match.
- Page content should clarify with more detail the meta description displayed in the search results. If your meta description is written in a way that creates an incentive to click, be sure to fulfill that desire.
- Maintain fresh content. Sometimes a conversion is lost because there's no sign that anyone's home.
- Concise is the new way to deliver content in the age of brief attention spans. An overwhelmed visitor becomes frustrated and is more likely to leave for the organized competitor.
- Related to shorter content is writing for people with disabilities or impairments who perceive information easier when delivered in brief bursts.
- Never mislead site visitors with false claims.
- Build global navigation that offers directions to groupings of pages (hubs). Base the dropdown order on what you know about your target user. Navigation should be designed to meet their top needs and interests.
- All navigation labels must describe a category in terms your customers use (machine parts and products fall into this rabbit hole).
- Avoid orphan landing pages. It's like sending the worker ants out to find food and then moving the ant hill so they can't get back.

Conducting UX Audits

When the options discussed in the previous section fail to uncover blocks, marketers turn to UX audits. These audits include functional testing and evaluating business and website requirements for missed opportunities.

Sometimes an audit requires journey mapping and a complete review of the information architecture of a website. Have you ever lost your keys? You can't start your car without them. The same is true for generating revenue from websites. There is always one lead CTA that is given the job of driving in the most revenue.

One day a client arrived with a mystery. They had built a website they loved and had followed everyone's advice. Of course, they invested thousands of dollars in marketing campaigns and were puzzled at the dismal results.

Finally, they consented to a usability audit, which meant looking under every nook and cranny of the website. And wouldn't you know it? The number-one revenue-generating lead CTA was hiding in a poorly labeled button in a dark corner of the homepage.

Nobody saw it there. So, they didn't click on it.

The Authentic Voice

One day a website owner was describing to me his business. When he was finished, I told him I was moved to tears and that everything he just told me was nowhere to be found on his website. My recommendation was to rewrite his content so that it sounds like him rather than forced marketing content. Adding a brief video would also help communicate the human side that I could detect over the phone. In his particular business, I sensed his conversions would shoot up if his website visitors heard his story from him and watched him tell it.

Conversion Opportunities and Considerations

Email conversions are a trendy way to discover how well campaigns are going. When used for announcements, adding a button or text link tagged for click tracking is one straightforward way to conduct A/B or multivariate testing.

For email, remember to add a privacy statement and provide directions to painlessly, unsubscribe. People's lives change. They may need to leave.

The questions some businesses ask during the unsubscribe process are not answered because there is a form field to tell a story. While the feedback may be helpful, the effort to describe why an email newsletter is no longer needed is time consuming. Try a list instead:

- Not enough time to read
- Outgrew the topic
- Career change
- Other

Social websites like Facebook, Twitter, Pinterest, LinkedIn, and others are like tribes. Each one has rules for their community, and those rules are always changing. Trust is a major concern for Facebook because ads appear based on algorithms. If you look at a Toyota sporty SUV, there's an excellent chance your Facebook feed will erupt with SUV vehicles from other automobile manufacturers.

There is a larger issue with social marketing, however. It has to do with consumer trust. Many clothing ads point to stores that do not exist. Over time, after chasing down payments to nonexistent companies, Facebook users stop buying at all.

To convince people on social sites to make a purchase or follow a link requires just as much user research and the same attention to content writing as you apply to any other campaign.

In many ways, when it all comes down to it, the best approach to conversions is to network with your tribe. In fact, "tribe" is a new label for online communities that gather online to share on specific topics of interest.

The experience is satisfying because for starters, everyone is there for a common cause or shared interest. Conversions between members create trust and that feeds into authenticity, which makes presenting something for sale lucrative.

Facebook Marketplace understood the value of trust and how to help local communities sell their old John Deeres to their neighbors. When you can see someone with many sales and an excellent reputation, it's easier to make decisions.

Online communities gather people together. Friendships and business relationships result from this common ground. It's an enormous positive contribution from the Web.

Twitter and LinkedIn are not used to persuade people to buy a product. However, they too contain the ability to segment into topical groups and communities. When people are comfortable with one another, word-of-mouth advertising increases.

Knowledge of local customs and use of language contribute to the conversions experience when the words are familiar. "Add to Cart" may mean something different to someone who is used to "Add to Bucket" because a cart and bucket may be different items in everyday use.

"Buy Now" is universally understood.

We all like that one.

CHAPTER 8

Mobile Marketing

By Cindy Krum

Mobile marketing is a newer and evolving specialty in the discipline of digital marketing. Most marketers know that consumers are spending more and more time accessing the Internet using mobile devices, but many also forget that mobile devices can have a substantial impact on the design, execution, and measurement of their digital marketing campaigns. In 2021, it is estimated that there were 4.32 billion active mobile Internet users in the world and that mobile Internet traffic represented 56.89 percent of all Internet traffic worldwide. This number continues to grow.

In this chapter, you'll learn about the following:

- Various technologies and concepts that fit under the mobile marketing umbrella
- Rules and regulations around mobile marketing
- Marketing strategies for mobile websites
- Marketing strategies for mobile apps
- Strategies for gathering and interpreting mobile and cross-device analytics data

Components of Mobile Marketing

Mobile marketing can be defined as any type of marketing or brand engagement that is consumed on a mobile device. This may seem simple, but it can actually be a bit wide-ranging because embedded in the concept is the idea that you as a marketer will "know" how or where your digital marketing message will be consumed and engaged with, which is not always the case. Sometimes you don't know. That is what makes it tricky! So in truth, mobile marketing can focus on marketing that is specifically designed for mobile devices but is often consumed across multiple digital devices and often involves adapting marketing messages that were designed to be consumed on much bigger devices, like computers, laptops, or TVs, to work well on mobile devices.

While the growth and evolution of mobile phone technology may now be slowing to some degree, there is still a lot of innovation happening as more and more nontraditional devices are connected to the Internet to become part of the Internet of Things (IoT). IoT refers to the increasing number of industrial and commercial items that can now be digitally controlled via the Internet, Bluetooth, or other wireless technologies. Controls for these devices generally come in the form of websites, mobile apps, or voice controls. Devices include connected security cameras, doorbells, thermostats, digital assistants, and speakers where consumers may receive digital communication. While these devices are often stationary and, thus, might not immediately be considered mobile, IoT devices are most frequently set up and controlled via mobile apps and websites and, thus, act as an extension of the smartphone. This will likely be where the mobile marketing innovation of the future happens, and it should not be ignored.

With the inclusion of IoT, you can see that the definition of mobile marketing can be wide-ranging, so it is useful to start by breaking down all the different kinds of devices and technologies that are included in mobile marketing. Most of these topics can be best understood in the context of each other, and since many of the terms are commonly used and understood, we will not dwell on the precise definitions but instead will focus on the larger concepts of how all of these technologies fit together. The following table provides a basic breakdown and the subsequent sections address each set of technologies as a group:

Mobile Devices	Mobile Operating Systems	Mobile Connectivity	Mobile Marketing Communication	Mobile Marketing Assets
Feature Phone	iOS/iPhone	CDMA	SMS	Mobile Website
Smartphone	Android	GSM	MMS	Native Application/App
Tablet	Windows	EDGE	NFC	Web Application/App
Connected Home Device	Other*	LTE	Push Notification	Progressive Web App
IoT Devices		2G/3G/4G/5G	Digital Assistant	Widget
Digital Assistants		WiFi	Chatbot	Mobile Ads
		Bluetooth		
		Casting		

Mobile Devices

Mobile devices generally include smartphones and tablets, but it can also include a wide range of connected home and IoT devices. You can think of feature phones as the first generation of mobile phones, including some that were connected to the Internet, but not in any kind of sophisticated way. Feature phones were often flip-phones and worked only with button-pushes, often on the traditional qwerty keyboard rather than a touchscreen, with nearly no ability to shop or add new apps from app stores. The main method of mobile marketing to these devices was with text messaging. Feature phones that could access information from the Internet did it with a very limited browser that often focused on text and static images and struggled with more sophisticated code and designs.

The next level up in sophistication of mobile devices is the smartphone. The main thing that makes a smartphone different from a feature phone is that it has a much higher level of capability, including the ability to access the Internet in a more capable browser and to download apps from app stores. Smartphones generally have high-resolution touchscreens that allow users to interact with websites and apps in a more user-friendly, intuitive way. Tablets are similar and are generally used like a larger version of a smartphone, but they don't have the ability to place traditional cell phone calls over a mobile network (they often can make calls over an Internet-enabled calling app).

The last group of mobile devices is connected home devices, IoT devices, and digital assistants. These are different from the other mobile devices because they are often less mobile; they are not meant to move around with the user, like a phone or a tablet, but instead, are meant to interact with the user through applications on the phone. Devices can include Google Home, Nest Thermostat, Ring doorbells and other WiFi-enabled security cameras, Amazon Echo and other Alexa devices, and a growing list of similar types of devices. In most cases, these devices are connected to a local WiFi network and are controlled either by voice commands, by a mobile app, or both. In some cases, these devices will include a visual touchscreen, but it is not required. In many ways, these devices act as extensions of the capability of the mobile devices that they are connected to.

Mobile Operating Systems

An operating system is simply the software that is loaded on a device that allows people to operate the device. All different types of technologies, including computers and modern cars, have operating systems, and so do mobile phones. In the world of mobile marketing, the main operating systems that we work with are called iOS for iPhone devices and Android for most other mobile phones, including phones that are not made by Google, the creator of Android. Apple has a closed system where only phones that they make can include their phone OS, but Google allows the Android OS to be used on mobile phones made by a variety of different manufacturers. There are other mobile phone operating systems, like Windows and the BlackBerry OS, but these are much less common, and the marketplace is now dominated by iOS and Android.

The most important thing to understand about operating systems is that they are generally not interoperable, meaning that software that is written for one OS will not work on a different OS. You might not think about phones using software, but mobile apps (mobile applications) are just a specific kind of software. This means that if you develop an app for Android devices, it will not work on iPhones. The two operating systems work differently with different code, and thus, the apps need to be developed separately, sometimes even by different development teams, because not all developers can code for iOS and Android. While there are some technical solutions that are striving to unify the code and the effort needed to make an app, they still require some separate effort, and the resulting software is often more buggy, limited, and problematic than code built specifically for each OS.

Not everyone knows this or understands it, including potential customers, so they may not understand when an app exists for one OS, but not the other. This is generally because most of the big, well-known apps always release very similar apps for iOS and Android. Similarly, many consumers don't have a clear understanding of the differences between app and web experiences, and since websites work natively on Android and iOS without extra effort, it can be difficult to clarify the distinction. As you can see in Figure 8.1, the populations in most countries are nearly evenly split between iOS and Android users, so these complexities make it best to build and launch iOS and Android versions of an app at the same time if possible, but to also have a web version of the app available so that potential customers don't have to download an app to interact with your brand. Mobile applications are often described as *native apps* to differentiate them from web apps, because they have to be built to work natively on the operating system.

Mobile Connectivity

Having a basic understanding of mobile connectivity is especially important for mobile marketers when they are evaluating what types of technology will be most useful for their audience. Connectivity is all about how the devices send and receive information. The first generations of mobile data transfer were CDMA (Code Division Multiple Access) and GSM (Global System for Mobiles). The various carriers offered mobile data services using one or the other of these two bands. Some devices were built for one communication band or the other, and then some devices were "dual-band" and could work

Symbol	Generation	Standard	Max Download Speed	Max Upload Speed
2G		GSM	14.4 Kbps	14.4 Kbps
G	2G	GPRS	53.6 Kbps	26.8 Kbps
E		EDGE	236.8 Kbps	59.2 Kbps
3G		UMTS	384 Kbps	384 Kbps
H	3G	HSPA	14.4 Mbps	5.76 Mbps
H+		HSPA+	168 Mbps	22 Mbps
4G	4G	LTE	100 Mbps	50 Mbps
4G		LTE-A	1 Gbps	500 Mbps 4

FIGURE 8.1 The Difference Between Internet Speeds (Andrea Saravia, **www.ufinet .com/whats-the-difference-between-internet-speeds**)

on either. Now most phones are dual band. CDMA is more commonly associated with the United States and the Verizon network, but Worldwide CDMA only represents 20 percent of connections; the rest of the data connections are GSM. Verizon has transitioned their network to also support GSM. The main benefit of GSM over CDMA is that GSM allows you to simultaneously transmit data and have a voice call.

Mobile connectivity is often described in terms of its generations (Figure 8.2). The first generation of mobile connectivity, or 1G, included analog calling only, with no data. 2G, 3G, 4G, and 5G are all better levels of connectivity that represent multipliers of the speed and capability of the mobile connection and its ability to pass data. For example, 5G is about 100 times faster than 4G. There are sometimes subsets within the different numeric groupings. For instance, LTE, which stands for Long-Term Evolution, is considered part of 4G but still relies on some analog radio transmission and some digital transmission of data, and it is slightly slower than regular 4G but faster than 3G. The chart in Figure 8.1 compares the different levels of connections.

In addition to mobile networks, smartphones can also use traditional WiFi signals to send and receive data, and in some cases, the WiFi is even used to make calls. 5G mobile data connections are sometimes referred to as *fiber* because they use fiber-optic cables to help speed up the transmission of data. 5G and WiFi signals are comparable in terms of speed, but in general, 5G connections tend to be faster for upload and download than a low-quality WiFi connection, like one that you might get in a public place, but 5G is not always better than a high-quality WiFi connection that you might get at home or work. 5G has a longer range and a higher capacity than WiFi, so in the future it is expected to be the backbone of IoT communication, connected cities, connected cars, and other types of future IoT technologies.

According to Erickson's research, it is expected that 5G mobile networks will carry 62 percent of the world's smartphone traffic by 2027. WiFi will still be critical for the growing number of stationary connected devices in the home, such as doorbells, security cameras, connected speakers, gaming

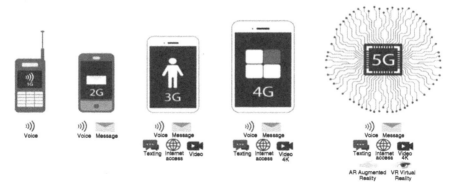

FIGURE 8.2 How to Think About the Evolution of Mobile Technology and Capabilities (**https://justaskthales.com/us/generations-mobile-networks-explained/**)

systems, app-enabled TVs, and computers, and the two technologies will work together.

Like mobile connectivity, WiFi is also going through advancement, as the standard advances from 2.4Ghz to 5Ghz, which are both still common, but the next generation of WiFi will be WiFi 6, which "will deliver 4× higher capacity and 75 percent lower latency, offering nearly triple the speed of its predecessor, Wi-Fi 5," according to Intel.

Casting is a concept that is related to WiFi because it is a technology that allows one device to stream a constant signal to a separate device over WiFi connection. Chromecast, Amazon FireTV, and AppleTV all rely on or can use casting to send audio, video, or both to different devices, while also maintaining the controls of the streaming on the primary device rather than just the "receiving" device using native controls. Bluetooth connections are similar to casting but rely on a different type of connection. All of these technologies should be kept in mind when evaluating methods and technology for mobile marketing.

Mobile Marketing Communication

A few different communication technologies are common in mobile marketing. The two most obvious types of communication that are mobile-specific are SMS and MMS communication and marketing. SMS (Short Messaging Service) is more commonly known as text messaging. MMS (Multimedia Messaging Services) is more commonly known as image messaging. Both can be used to communicate with potential customers in a similar but more abbreviated way than you might communicate in an email. This communication could be for announcing a sale or a special event or following up on a previous interaction, purchase, or behavior. These messages are generally short because of character limitations in SMS technology. Messages used to be limited to 140 characters, including spaces, but now most phones can accept more, through iMessage, the iOS messaging software, or Multimedia Messages, or MMS, which can include images, videos, and other attachments, much like email. Push notifications are similar in that they are short messages that are meant to drive engagement and re-engagement, but they are initiated by native applications and websites rather than working independently like SMS and MMS.

The next, more sophisticated types of mobile-oriented communication tools that can be used in mobile marketing are digital assistants and chatbots. These types of mobile methods of communication can include voice controls or text-based communication. They are more commonly used as part of an engagement campaign designed to help potential customers understand, appreciate, or use the brand or the product offering. Chatbots and digital assistants often use language understanding technology and machine learning to determine what is needed or being requested by the customer and program a specific response to these needs. It is expected that these types of opportunities to interact with customers will grow by leaps and bounds because they are more deeply incorporated into IoT devices, which are likely to become more important aspects of a mobile marketing program.

Mobile Marketing Assets

When we talk about mobile marketing, the marketing that you design or promote will generally attempt to direct customers to a mobile-friendly waypoint or destination that you build to work on the mobile device and use the communication methods that others build. You can choose to build a number of different types of mobile assets. Most often, that will be things like a native application (app) or a mobile-friendly website, but it can also be less-known variations of those assets, such as a web app, watch app, a progressive web app (PWA), a widget, a mobile banner, or text-based mobile ad copy. Some of these assets, like apps and websites, can be for discovery and long-term engagement, and others, like text-based mobile ads and mobile banners, are just focused on the discovery and generally pass users over to an app or a website for longer-term engagement. We get more into specific distinctions, along with the pros and cons of many of these assets, later in the chapter.

Rules and Regulations

Mobile marketing efforts must also follow the same rules and regulations as other types of digital marketing, including the U.S. Canned SPAM Act and

Canadian Anti-Spam Legislation (CASL), EU General Data Protection Regulation (GDPR), U.S. Children's Online Privacy Protection Act (COPPA), and others. In the United States, the Federal Communications Commission (FCC) and the Federal Trade Commission (FTC) regulate much of the marketing that happens on the Internet, including on mobile phones. The most important regulations for mobile marketing limit calling and text messaging, especially the Telephone Consumer Protection Act (TCPA).

The main limitations to keep in mind in mobile marketing tend to be common sense, which will also ensure that you are not being too aggressive and irritating potential customers. Basically, if you have a commercial interest, you need to have written consent to send people SMS marketing messages, and recipients need to clearly understand if they are consenting to a one-time communication or ongoing communication. Written consent from potential customers generally happens with a response to an initial text message that says it is okay for a company to message you. In most cases, there will be a call to action that is not in a text message, instructing people to "text XYZ to 12345 to begin receiving special text message communication, alerts or deals!" Once a customer does that, a message with a deal is sent, along with instructions to reply with YES if you would like to continue receiving deals via text message, and this is usually followed with instructions that the customer can also text STOP at any time to stop receiving text messages.

You are not permitted to simply buy lists of phone numbers and message them. There can be numerous variations in the regulations based on what you are sending and what you are marketing. For instance, if you are marketing items that are age-restricted, like alcohol or tobacco, you need to only send those messages to people who have had their age verified. You also can't send copyrighted or trademarked material without appropriate licenses, and you can't send confidential information or anything violent, including hate speech, threats, or descriptions of potential violence. The restrictions for nonprofits are slightly less stringent than those for consumer goods and services; specifically, you don't need to have consent in writing to send text messages, but you do still need to have some type of consent before sending the SMS messages.

Reaching Mobile Users

Now that you know the basics of mobile technology, you need to think about your potential customers and determine how and where you will have success getting their attention with your marketing message. Knowing who your users are and where they spend their digital time will be helpful for reaching the best possible mobile customers. Often, social media sites can be used to learn about your customers and their preferences and what types of marketing messages they respond to. If you don't know much about your customers, it can be useful to start with the more ubiquitous platforms like Facebook to test the success of your messaging and begin learning about your audience so that you can eventually segment users into different groups. On the other hand, if you feel like you already know a lot about your ideal customers, you might be able to start with more niche social media marketing, especially if you know that your users tend to spend more time engaging socially in online venues with similar people, or if they are tied to certain social networking sites like LinkedIn or Reddit.

The demographic and psychographic profile of your ideal customers may lean more toward mobile or more toward desktop, but at least in the United States and most developed countries, you can generally assume that potential customers will probably actively engage with your marketing with both and may bounce between the different marketing channels and devices. This means that the wisest marketers will not put all their budget on mobile or all on desktop, but they will split efforts between both and then reallocate funds to support the most successful efforts while deprioritizing or redesigning less successful aspects.

Mobile Marketing Strategy and Planning

The mobile marketing strategy that you choose can be very important, but mobile marketing can be leveraged many different ways so there isn't a single right or wrong way to plan and evaluate a strategy. In general, you need to look at your budget and goals and find the options that will be the most effective at reaching your target audience with the most compelling messaging and offers possible, taking the various types of technology on both sides of the equation into account.

One of the biggest questions that you have to answer is how much of your marketing budget will be used for digital marketing and, from there, how the budget will be divided between mobile, desktop, and other digital marketing options. To help you make this evaluation, it is often useful to think about the product or service that you are selling and what causes a potential customer to choose it over the competitors'. With that in mind, you can think about the various ways that current customers have gone about researching and finding your offering, or you can look at competitors' offerings and how the different mobile marketing options can fit, expedite, or support that customer's purchase process. If you are launching a new product or service, you can look at the existing competition and make your best guess about these aspects of the strategy.

Products and services that will skew more toward mobile will be ones where the core offering is a mobile app, a social network, news, information, gaming, entertainment, and offline or local businesses that people may be searching for when they are out and about. In general, the cheaper and the lower the level of consideration needed for the purchase, the more likely it is that a product or service can be marketed successfully on mobile. Examples include meals, transportation, movies, games, and general consumer goods. Products that will skew less toward mobile and more toward desktop digital marketing are more expensive and more consequential, like cars, homes, vacations, and expensive technology, although mobile marketing can still help support these products too. While this trend is shifting, it is still more common for people making bigger purchases to research these options and make the digital purchases on desktops rather than mobile devices.

Just because what you are selling may skew one way or the other doesn't mean that either should be ignored. It may simply mean that you need to plan calls to action based on the device where the potential customer will be most likely to take the action. For example, it might be tough to convince someone to purchase a car on their mobile phone, but if your mobile call to action encourages the viewer to book a test drive or call and talk to a sales representative, those requests will be more reasonable and more likely to eventually lead to a purchase. Similarly, it generally doesn't make sense to market an app or mobile game on desktop devices with a call to action that encourages the user to "download now," since the product is not meant to be consumed on the device they are on.

The other question that comes up a lot in mobile marketing is the question of which is better—app or web marketing. As discussed, the safest option is to always do both whenever possible. The reality though is that the budget limitations can make that option impossible or impractical, so you may actually have to make a choice. The best option will always be a judgment call that you will need to make for your individual company and its ultimate goals, but in general, if you have to choose, we recommend starting with the website rather than the app.

You can use a lot of different statistics to inform this decision, but some can be confusing and misleading, so we would like to address them quickly here. First, it is true that on average, users spend more time on mobile applications than they do on the mobile web. Unfortunately, this can be deceiving because there is a lot of long-form app behavior that can skew the statistics. If you think about apps like Netflix, Hulu, Facebook, Uber, GrubHub, YouTube, Instagram, WhatsApp, TikTok, Audible, Google Maps, and all the email apps—these are all very popular applications that people use and forget that they are actually interacting with apps. Similarly, gaming apps are very popular, especially with younger generations, and those can also skew the data dramatically.

The next statistic that comes up a lot is that when customers convert, they tend to convert at a higher rate and value in apps than web users. The problem with this statistic is that it is heavily skewed because of the behavior of highly loyal users in branded apps. For example, people who are already huge fans of brands like Target, Lululemon, The Gap, or Crate & Barrel are much more likely to download the branded apps, which they intend to use a lot, especially when compared to people who are only lukewarm or completely uninterested in the brand. What is important to understand here is that these brands already have strong brand loyalty and an ongoing relationship with their customers. The customers are likely searching the app stores for the apps by brand name. If you have this kind of brand awareness, the likelihood that you already have a website is very high.

Problems arise, however, when this statistic is provided to young startups that are eager to make money and please their investors. The reality is that apps and app stores are not great places for users to discover new brands, and in fact, many users go to the app stores with an app that they would like already in mind. They are not casually browsing for new apps to download. Companies who start with apps instead of websites will likely have to do much more promotion and marketing, working even in advance of the app launch, to create demand for their app because the chances of casual app discovery in the stores are not good. Conversely, search engines are eager to index and surface new websites—especially when they have unique and authoritative continent, and search engines are great at surfacing deep, detailed content on a website, reaching customers who are searching specifically for that information or product, which is just not the reality of the app store search capabilities.

To put it in simple terms, apps are great if you have existing brand awareness and strong, well-established brand loyalty already. They are not great for discovery of new products and services; websites that are crawled and indexed by search engines like Google are much better for that. You will need to do marketing and promotion for both, whichever you decide to start with, but the effort will likely be much more if you start with an app, unless you have a very clever social media or other campaign that you can fully expect to go very viral, and with that, it can still be more work. Also, mobile apps are meant for mobile phones, limiting any potential for desktop discovery, but the same is not true for websites. It is for these reasons that we recommend starting with a website whenever you can, even if it is only a few pages to describe the app that is being developed, and not a replica of the app functionality. If the desire to start with an app first can't be overcome, at least build a very small website to market the app and collect email addresses of interested consumers before the app launch, so that you can market to them and notify them when the app actually goes live or is updated.

With an understanding of the basics of mobile customer acquisition and strategy, it is time to think in detail about what types of mobile assets will be the most useful in your marketing mix. This section of the chapter includes details about the goals and strategies that apply to mobile websites, mobile apps, mobile incentive and loyalty programs, location-based mobile services, and mobile advertising.

Marketing on Mobile Websites

Mobile-friendly websites are one of the most basic options for mobile marketing and are almost a de facto requirement if you plan on engaging your customers on their mobile devices. Anymore, we don't talk about mobile websites and desktop websites because the best practice is to have one set of website URLs that works on both. There are a variety of ways to make website code work on mobile and desktop, but the most common and well-known way to do this is with a development process called *responsive design*.

Responsive design requires website developers to separate the content of each page from the design and layout. This way, you can have the same content on the page for mobile and desktop users, but you can use different technical cues to trigger different design and layout options, based on the size of the device that is requesting the page. This type of flexibility makes it much easier to build websites that can work on a variety of different devices, including small phones, large phones, tablets, laptops, desktop computers, and even smart TVs.

The technology that allows responsive design websites to adapt to different screen sizes is called Cascading Style Sheets (CSS). Developers include code, called media queries, to set up slightly different layouts or styles for the content, based on the screen width of the device. This can mean that a page will have three columns on a desktop or laptop display, but those three columns may be rearranged to fit into two columns on a tablet or just one on a mobile phone. This way, when a new size of mobile device is released, developers don't have to build a new page—they just have to make sure that the new device screen size is included in the ranges of screen widths that have instructions in the CSS.

Other than testing between the different operating systems and browsers, you should also try to test devices with a wide array of screen sizes. Focus mostly on width rather than height. Many phones now have extra-large size options, and some have small or compact options, and now, with mobile phone screens that can bend and fold coming into the marketplace, we can expect to see more and more variable phone screen sizes being released.

The basic tenets of responsive design should accommodate a variety of different phone sizes, and the resizing that happens is based on the pixel-width of the screen. Pixels are a tiny increment that has historically been used to describe the level of detail on digital displays. One pixel is 1/96th of an inch or 0.26 millimeters. When a device is above a certain pixel-width, it gets one mobile design and layout, and when it is below that width, it will get a design layout that is slightly, sometimes imperceivably different. The goal is to set up the website to display properly in whichever mobile "viewport" is displaying it. The viewport is basically the view settings for how something should display based on the height and width of a screen. Remember that while desktops and laptops have viewports that are set up for landscape viewing, most mobile devices consume content in a portrait orientation, so if you simply scale down some content that you want to display above the fold, it may still be below the fold on mobile screens.

One problem with responsive design was that developers who are just getting into it can inadvertently create new problems for mobile users while trying to adapt their content to be responsive. In an attempt to fix these issues, Google released an updated version of HTML, called Accelerated Mobile Pages (AMP) HTML, which is meant to be more streamlined. AMP was meant to speed up mobile page loads. There is also AMP JavaScript, AMP CSS, and specific guidelines for being "AMP compliant."

Developers could build separate versions of AMP pages to connect with their slower counterparts using a pair of meta tags. They also had the option to build a "canonical AMP" page, which meant that there was no slow version of the page and that the fast AMP page could be shown on mobile and desktop as the main version of the page. Since Google prefers to rank fast pages and users prefer to view fast pages, AMP was a great thing for some companies, though it did add a lot of extra work and complexity in some cases—especially in terms of measurement and maintenance.

There was a time that AMP-compliant pages were rewarded with a visible lightning bolt in Google search results, but this was only for certain kinds of content, and the types of pages that could get the reward expanded over time until the reward for being AMP compliant was dropped. AMP code libraries still exist and are still great for replacing slow code with a faster alternative, but it is unclear if there are any benefits associated with AMP compliance aside from a linear benefit of making pages faster. As you rely more on AMP code, the page gets faster and faster, and AMP-compliant pages are generally almost as fast as they can be.

Core Mobile Products and Services

In some cases, companies will focus their products and services on a mobile-only or primarily mobile. Usually these are app-based businesses like Uber, DoorDash, and Facetune; we describe these businesses as core mobile products and services. In some cases, companies like this will believe that they don't need a mobile-friendly website because they are so focused on the mobile app. This assumption is generally disadvantageous, and frankly wrong, especially in a marketing context, because of the pronounced differences in how people discover new businesses and how people engage with brands that they have an existing relationship with. The reality is that most brand discovery and product discovery now happen on the Internet and in search engines. While some search engines index apps and Google claims that they can index app content, it is rare that app-only content shows up well in search results. This is because search engines, and especially Google, have historically not been good at crawling, indexing, and ranking app content unless very specific and intentional measures are taken. This is because apps are built-in code that search engines are not designed to crawl and index.

The caveat is that Google can index apps, but only if they have corresponding websites, and only if the corresponding websites have pages and a URL structure that matches the screens and the structure of the app. When this is the case, Google can index native iOS or Android app content, but based on the requirements, it seems mostly like Google is indexing the web content, and noting that there is an app landing page alternative rather than actually crawling and indexing the apps.

This possibility only emphasizes the idea that app-focused brands still can benefit significantly from natively having a mobile-friendly web presence. With this process, called *app indexing*, people can discover your brand when its contents rank in search engines, then as they get more engaged with the brand, they become more likely to download the app. The converse, however, is rarely true. People are not likely to search for products or brands that they have never heard of in the app stores, and they are also somewhat unlikely to download and immediately engage financially with an app from a brand that they have never heard of.

Even for companies that are very app-focused, like Uber, it is important to have corresponding web content. App indexing is the process of communicating to search engines how pages in the website correspond to screens in the app. To connect the specific screens in the app to the specific corresponding pages on the website, you must set up something called *deep links,* which allow mobile browsers to detect when an app is installed that corresponds to a website deep link that is requested. When this happens, the browser can launch the app and open it directly to the corresponding screen in the app rather than simply linking to the website. This can be great for driving periodic re-engagement with an app directly from Google, but it can also be fantastic for creating a better potential for the initial discovery, engagement, and conversion within an app.

Setting up deep links and app indexing can be technical and tedious processes, especially when your app content or organization does not exactly match your web content. Even then, it is important to understand that you will have to do all of the deep linking and app indexing work twice—once for the iOS app and again for the Android app. Since the two systems use different code, they require different steps to set up the deep links for this kind of website-app transitioning and functionality. Apple and Android have documentation, but in many cases, it can be barely enough to get the job done, especially if the person doing the work has never done it before or is not somewhat familiar with how search engines work.

Incentives and Loyalty Programs

One type of mobile marketing that has exploded in the past couple of years is the use of SMS marketing and push marketing to help drive engagement and conversion with purchase incentive and loyalty programs. Since a mobile phone is almost always with our target customers, it is a great vehicle for reminding people about any exclusive program where they can get rewards in a physical store or online. To create an incentive or loyalty program, it is best to have a customer relationship management system (CRM) that can handle email and SMS communications to help manage customer communication. This is especially true because email and SMS require specific levels of opt-in or permission to be legal, and if you are marketing to customers in multiple countries, the requirements can vary. A CRM can help make sure that you have all the permissions that you need for the user's country of residence and lets you focus on one or the other if the customer has not opted into both.

One important point to remember is that no matter how much we follow any local marketing rules and regulations for opt-in, many companies ignore them, and thus, potential customers are likely already receiving a barrage of mobile marketing communications in email and text messages all the time. That can be a double-edged sword for decision-making because it is critical not to send too many messages and annoy your customers, but you also want to send enough that even if some are missed or ignored, your loyalty messages are registering and being seen by potential customers—especially the ones who are most likely to respond with additional purchases.

One of the best ways to achieve this balance is by using email and SMS campaigns together, to support each other in loyalty communication—especially when it comes to messages about loyalty deals and things that are time-sensitive. The time-sensitive nature of loyalty communication makes the combination of email and SMS especially useful because you can plan an email campaign that focuses on reminding people that a deadline for some loyalty benefit is approaching and you can alternate reminders between emails and SMS. For example, emails can count down at 10 days, 5 days, and 2 days before the redemption deadline, and those email reminders can be supplemented with SMS messages that count down at 7 days, 3 days, and 24 hours in the text messages. This kind of planning can be enough to prevent users from feeling overwhelmed with the communication. The two different channels, which are potentially received in different contexts or at different times of day, make it less likely that the recipient will feel overwhelmed or annoyed with the communication—especially if you assume that they will miss or ignore at least some of the messages in either channel.

Location-Based Services

Whether you are focused on driving customers to a mobile app or a website or to a physical store, location-based services can be an especially valuable type of mobile marketing. One of the best and most unique qualities that mobile devices have over other digital devices is that they are so portable. They generally have GPS capabilities and other location services, which can be used as part of a marketing campaign. When it comes to location-based services for mobile marketing, there are really only a few that are commonly used, and this type of mobile marketing is one where there is still potential for more innovation, evolution, and growth.

Location-based mobile marketing can be broken roughly into two categories: GPS and proximity-based location-based marketing. GPS-based marketing is all based on users and their phone's physical location, based on the GPS coordinates of the phone. Constant GPS location monitoring can feel invasive, or like a violation of privacy, and this has been a limiting factor in the growth of this type of marketing. Proximity-based mobile marketing, on the other hand, shows a bit more promise because the phone only reaches the marketing when it is physically within a certain range of wireless signals, like a WiFi signal or a Bluetooth beacon, and the interaction completely stops when the device is out of that range, making it feel slightly less invasive.

WiFi Geo-Targeted Marketing   One of the easiest ways to use a person's physical location to market to their mobile phones is by using a WiFi signal. Since WiFi has a limited range (up to about 150 feet indoors and 300 feet outdoors, per network router), it is naturally location-specific. By offering free WiFi in a physical location, you can reach people with a marketing message, or you can request that the customer participate with some minor engagement in exchange for access to the free WiFi. Companies like Starbucks, Target, and Walmart actively use this method of marketing in their physical locations and seem to achieve at least some good engagement with this strategy.

The basic model for using WiFi in location-specific marketing is generally somewhat standard, even when the implementation or goal differs. The main part of the customer engagement starts when you add physical signage in your locations to let visitors know that there is free WiFi available in the location. In locations where there are multiple companies that might be offering WiFi, it may be important to note the name of the WiFi network and to mention the name of the company offering the WiFi, which is sometimes listed with a "sponsored by" attribution.

Once users turn on the WiFi on their phone or try to connect to the network that is specified on the signage, the system automatically redirects them to a landing page that the visitor must interact with in order to get to the WiFi. These landing pages can have a variety of goals; in some cases, they just collect the visitors' email addresses in exchange for access to the WiFi, but the interaction can also be more involved. The landing page can request the visitor fill out a form or a survey, rate their service, watch a video, vote on a poll, or basically anything else. The landing page does not have to be limited to promoting one single interaction that will get visitors to the Internet—it can also focus on visitors in a branded experience, giving them information about the physical location that they are in, highlighting specials, deals, or important information, or linking people to other branded experiences like app downloads, coupons, or SMS signup. (Airlines are notorious for this with their in-flight WiFi.)

By engaging visitors on a WiFi network, you will benefit from whatever information or interactions that you get on the branded landing page that you have created. This can include seeing how willing visitors are to engage with the landing page, what information they are willing to share, what links they are willing to click, and what calls to action visitors are willing to engage with from your landing page beyond just accessing the free WiFi. This can all be great research for learning more about your customers.

When visitors do submit their information and click past the landing page, you will also get aggregated information about what types of content people are accessing on your network. It is obviously important to protect your visitors' privacy, and you shouldn't be able to see specific inputs on the Internet once visitors leave your landing page, but you will be able to see aggregations of how much time visitors spent on your site, using the Internet, or on other sites on the web. This might be useful to see when and how visitors comparison shop while in your store, what products they are most interested in, what competitive sites they visit when searching for more information, what social networks they visit, and so on.

Bluetooth Beacon Marketing Bluetooth beacons are another location-based marketing option. These were previously more popular, but interest has waned because of a variety of technical difficulties that have limited their performance and scared companies off from trying it in many cases. Apple and Google both have Bluetooth marketing technology on offer. Apple has the iBeacon, which was specifically targeted at iOS users, and Google has Eddystone, which is interoperable between iOS and Android devices and creates an encrypted connection, designed to be more secure than traditional Bluetooth beacons. Both options were popular because of their simple setup and low cost, but they have lost favor because of security concerns and limited consumer adoption and interest.

Bluetooth beacon marketing works in a similar way to WiFi marketing, but the messages travel over Bluetooth. This means that your visitors either have to have their Bluetooth on, or you need physical signage to suggest to them that they turn it on. After that, they need to know to opt into a specific Bluetooth connection permission request sent from the beacon. From there, the brand can send the visitor push notifications with advertising, relevant deals, or other similar types of information.

You can simply send text prompts over Bluetooth, but to have an interactive experience, it is best for the prompt from the Bluetooth beacon to send people to a mobile website, landing page, or in-app experience. The transition between using Bluetooth to initiate the communication, then using WiFi or a data connection to access content from the web or in an app, can cause problems, but the main problem is related more to users' perceptions about the security of Bluetooth as well as the low likelihood that they are walking around with Bluetooth on or that they are willing to receive Bluetooth marketing communication from potentially unknown brands. It turns out that for many users, allowing this type of connection is a big request—especially when the reward of the interaction is uncertain.

One of the benefits of Bluetooth beacons is that if you have more than one of them located in a particular area, you can use the signals to triangulate exactly where users are when they respond to a prompt. This information may be useful to understand the context that causes them to interact—for instance, are they lost or looking for help, have they picked an item to purchase, and are looking for a discount, or is there something else driving the interaction? Beacons have also been used to help attribute offline purchases after someone clicks on an ad. For instance, if someone is using their phone to search for a dress and clicks on an ad for a dress, then goes into a store to try the dress on, and eventually purchases it, that purchase can be attributed back to the digital ad even if it happened offline.

Geo-Fence Marketing   Geo-fencing is a method of marketing that relies on GPS to set up a digital perimeter that can be used to send specific marketing messages to potential customers within the perimeter of the designated area. Similar to Bluetooth beacons, geo-fencing received a lot of attention in the early days of mobile marketing but has lost steam due mostly to technical complexity as well as security concerns. To reach potential customers in a geo-fenced area, their mobile phones need to have location services turned on in their mobile phones, and this was more of a hurdle than marketers expected.

The technology requirements for working with geo-fencing generally require working with a third-party to help with the technical setup of the geo-fence. Given the right conditions, a marketing campaign that used geo-fencing could send push notifications or text messages to potential customers, but it is much more common for geo-fencing to be used in collaboration with a branded app that uses location data and already has the user opted into push notifications. This, however, limits the potential to use this type of mobile marketing for driving brand discovery; instead, it makes it better for engagement or re-engagement of existing customers—especially for people who have a branded app and go to a related event, store, or location.

Google Business Profile   Previously known as Google My Business, Google Business profiles are a mix of a location-based services and search engine optimization and marketing. Google Business profiles are something that any small or local business can set up by going to Google Profile Manager and entering the business details. From there, you can go through a verification process with Google, and the business listing can start to rank in local Google searches. When people search for terms related to the business, the business listing has the potential to rank in mobile search results, generally as part of what is called a *map pack,* which generally includes a few other related businesses in the area.

Since mobile phones that search Google send basic geo-coordinates of the mobile searcher, Google can change their search results when they believe that the searcher is trying to find a local business, and these types of results are slightly more likely to rank on mobile than they are on desktop searches. Google's local rankings generally only rank within a relevant radius of the location of the business, unless the search is for the exact brand name, in which case, the business is more likely to rank outside of the relevant local range.

Different strategies can help Google Business profiles rank in Google searches. The basic tenets of a good local search optimization strategy are to fill out the Google Business profile as much as possible, with a lot of good information about the business as well as pictures, product listings, and accurate contact information, focusing on always using the exact same name, address, and phone number, exactly as the location is listed in other websites on the Internet. After that, it is important to choose all of the most relevant categories, and if possible, link the Business Profile to the business website, which also includes the same address and phone number information. Having good reviews on the Google Business profile and getting links to the website from other local business can help improve the business's local rankings in Google, which means it will show up for more searches in a wider local radius.

Mobile Marketing Channel Management

With all of the mobile options in marketing, and all of the traditional marketing channels that they can support, channel management within mobile marketing can build up and get complex pretty quickly. Channel management in mobile marketing is most often determined based on the most dynamic and lucrative mobile channel that is in the marketing mix. This will be different for each company, and it may be heavily dependent on the unique skills and experience of the marketing and technical teams that are working on the project. Of course, it may also depend on the nature of the product or service that you are trying to market. For example, a company that is promoting a new app will likely have a vastly different strategy than a company that is just a local restaurant trying to drive foot traffic or a clothing brand that is trying to drive both on- and offline purchases.

When you are determining how mobile marketing fits into your marketing mix, it is often useful to think about what mobile technology offers are not available in the other marketing channels. Usually, the most relevant benefit of mobile marketing is the location-specific nature of the mobile devices, the ubiquity and constancy and personal nature of interaction that consumers have with their phones, and the potential for simple, multi-modal interactions on mobile devices. Thinking about these benefits, it is easy to understand why a local business would see value in ranking well in mobile search results in Google Maps, or why a new mobile game app might benefit from push notifications and SMS reminders to keep users engaged with the app during their downtime.

Conversely, a clothing brand with both on- and offline commerce could really benefit from multi-modal mobile interactions, leveraging email, mobile web, SMS, and possibly even an app to support loyalty, customer service, and conversion goals for their shoppers, in ways that allow them to shop online or in an app from wherever they are, but also driving them into the store for special events, to avoid waiting on shipping, or to pick up or return items in a quick, hassle-free way. This chapter goes into further detail about how you can effectively leverage elements of mobile marketing like mobile search, mobile video, mobile advertising, and other mobile channels to work together, and with traditional marketing channels to create the perfect marketing mix.

In large campaigns, mobile channel management can become more and more complex, especially as each additional channel is added and as different target markets, cohorts, and funnels are identified. As the level of complexity increases, it may become more useful to create a combined dashboard that brings all of the different channels together so that they can be understood as a group. In some cases, many of your marketing channels may be part of a larger entity, like Google, Apple, Chrome, Microsoft, or Amazon. If that is the case, it may be useful to see if a combined management platform exists within that larger company; it can be useful to leverage that for channel management.

As you read this chapter, you may notice that Google is mentioned a lot. This is primarily because Google has an incredibly dominant presence in the mobile marketing world—especially for advertising, marketing, browsers, handsets, and apps. Rather than fighting against this, it is generally best to allow the different Google products to work together as best as possible, using systems like Google Ad Manager 360 and Google Analytics to measure and combine whatever you can. Their products are often free and generally have easy integrations that help the different channels and lines of business work together more seamlessly than they otherwise might if they were all part of different platforms. This is why the preference for Google and Apple products will seem especially strong in the mobile marketing world.

Mobile and Other Marketing Channels

One of the best ways to think of mobile marketing is as the glue that can bring other marketing channels together. That means that it can be very useful to keep your mobile projects top-of-mind when you are working on the overall channel management or even when focusing campaigns in one specific channel. Mobile technology and advertising are generally a great way to learn more about your target audience and home in on your messaging, segmentation, and conversion funnel development mobile marketing. This tends to be perceived as somewhat more personal, as long as you get your messaging right and show the right level of respect for your customers.

Mobile Search

Mobile search marketing is generally described as *search engine optimization* (SEO, or in this case, mobile SEO). It is the process of building and improving websites to make them more appealing for computer programs like the ones that Google uses to rank them for relevant queries when customers search. In general, mobile search marketing is not that different from other search marketing; it is about making content that is simple and easy for Google and other search engines to understand and rank. More searches are submitted from mobile phones than computers now, and Google uses what they call *mobile-first indexing*, which prioritizes the mobile rendering of a website over the desktop when they are evaluating the pages that should rank in their search results.

Google uses the same basic website information to rank websites on mobile and desktop search but results can be different on mobile—especially when there is local intent, like to find a local business, or app intent, when it appears that the searcher is looking for an app. Most companies that consider mobile marketing important should already have a website that is mobile-friendly. This is the first requirement for showing up well in mobile search results. This means building your website in responsive design so that the same content can be presented clearly and in a usable way on mobile and desktop devices.

If this is not possible, then other more technical solutions, like adaptive design, cloud-based selective, or adaptive serving options, can be used to switch to different variations of the content for mobile and desktop users. What is important for search engines is that the URL and the actual content of the page—that is, the text and images—are basically the same between desktop and mobile, even if they are in different locations or if the images are smaller or of lower quality when they are on mobile.

Once this is done, the next most important thing to do is make sure that your website is easily crawlable by Google and other search engines and that the keywords that you want to rank for appear on the pages. There are a couple of things that make a website easy to crawl, but they can basically be summed up as minimizing the impact of JavaScript and maximizing page speed and load time. In both of these, what you have to remember is that Google's main limitation is its crawler, so the longer time and the more computational effort that a website takes to load, the more of Google's resources it takes to crawl, and the less incentive they will have to crawl it completely or regularly.

The JavaScript Conundrum

Google takes active measures to prevent individual websites from hogging too much time with the crawler because the websites are slow, take a high amount of computational power to render, or rely heavily on more complicated code like JavaScript. This is a bit of an over simplification, but Google computationally tries to balance the value of ranking content from the site with the effort it takes to crawl it.

As the web advances, more and more websites use JavaScript to make their websites more interactive and to make them look and feel more like native apps. What you need to know about JavaScript is that for many years, Google totally ignored it because it slowed down their crawlers and created security risks for the crawler. Now, especially since most of the web has transitioned from HTTP to HTTPS, JavaScript is less of a security threat for a search engine, but other risks are still present.

JavaScript can contain a lot of information and be slow to load it into a page. In some cases, certain types of website coding practices, technically called WebApps and Single Page Apps (SPAs), allow developers to build entire websites on one URL, using JavaScript interactions with the server to refresh the contents of the web page rather than requesting a new page on a new URL. Since search engines use URLs to organize their index of information, these JavaScript solutions can be very limiting for SEO success. Similarly, even pages that require a lot of JavaScript to load their content can be problematic for search engines to rank.

The best option, if you have a site that uses a lot of JavaScript, is to maintain separate URLs for separate pages on the site whenever you can. The other thing that you should do is to server-side render (SSR) or prerender your pages so that the JavaScript is already executed and processed when it is sent to the browser and also to the search engine crawlers. This is a technical service or setting that can usually be controlled by your hosting company or your content delivery network (CDN), if you have one. SSR basically executes the page code before it is sent to the browser. It saves a copy of that executed code and sends that to the browser, so that it does not have to take time for the code to be processed by the browser. It is great for users because it makes the page load much faster, and it also decreases the computational power needed for a search engine to render the page.

If SSR is not possible, the next best option is to make sure that all of the links on each page of your site are written in HTML instead of JavaScript. This means that each link should include the "<ahref=" code for an HTML link rather than linking with "ID=" or other JavaScript code. Google and other search engines look specifically for HTML links when they are crawling, so this will ensure that they can at least find the internal pages that are linked to, even if some of the page code might still be in JavaScript. These steps will make it much easier to crawl, despite the inclusion of JavaScript.

Even if your site does not rely heavily on JavaScript, you need to make sure that the pages on your websites load quickly so that the search engine doesn't stop before the page is fully loaded and so that they don't leave the site early because the pages are loading too slowly. Google has a variety of tools that are designed to help website owners figure out if their pages are loading slowly and to give them feedback about what can be fixed to make the pages load more quickly. The most well-known one is called Google Pagespeed Insights.

There is also a related set of standards called *core web vitals*, which is about both the load time and the user experience that is associated with the load time and about how much things move or change, during the time when the page is loading. Basically, you want your pages to load as quickly and stably as possible, without movement or a refresh once an asset is in place. This makes it easier and faster for Google to load and render the page when it crawls it.

Mobile Advertising

Mobile advertising is another potentially powerful marketing channel that can be used alone or combined with other mobile marketing initiatives, and it is capable of a wide range of impacts, from simply supporting and generating brand awareness, all the way to driving very targeted and adaptive marketing campaigns that are designed to create very specific types of engagement and conversion.

According to eMarketer statistics, in 2021 all segments of U.S. industries spent more than 50 percent of their ad budget on mobile advertising, with retail and consumer packaged goods as the two industries with the highest focus on mobile (based on total spending and on the percentage of the ad budget focused on mobile).

Oberlo, a digital business and entrepreneurship portal, explains the growth in mobile advertising spend like this: "According to the latest data, mobile advertising spend in the United States in 2022 is expected to reach $137.13 billion, after surpassing $100 billion for the first time in 2021. This refers to expenditure on everything from classified ads and display ads to email, lead generation, and search on mobile devices such as smartphones and tablets. This will represent a whopping 16.86 percent year-over-year increase in mobile ad spend, a slowdown from 2021's 22.15 percent growth rate. . .. If it does continue to grow as experts forecast, this will mean that mobile ad spend will have doubled in the few years from 2019 to 2024." With this perspective in mind, it is important to understand the many options that are available in mobile marketing.

One digital advertising tactic that has become common on mobile and desktop experiences is called *remarketing*. Remarketing can be controversial because it is when websites and apps use third-party tracking code called *cookies* to track users' behavior across different websites and apps, and sometimes even across different devices, including mobile phones. As a consumer, you know it is happening when ads for certain brands or products seem to follow you around the Internet. Customers who recognize when it is happening claim to dislike it, but conversely, it is actually one of the best digital advertising tactics for driving brand awareness and eventual conversion. The personal nature of mobile phones makes remarketing even more effective, but they also can make it seem even more invasive and sometimes like a violation of privacy. It is this type of digital marketing especially that has pushed the industry to create more stringent privacy protections for digital customers, which are discussed more at the end of this chapter.

Understanding Your Mobile Advertising Options

Mobile advertising is one of the most straight forward mobile marketing channels for people who are new to mobile because the basic concept does not change much between mobile and traditional variations of the channel. In mobile advertising, you purchase different types of ads like banners, text ads, or sponsorships, and you pay for either the number of views or impressions that the ads get, or the number of interactions that the ad gets, which could be based on clicks, form completions, or conversions or purchases.

There are a variety of mobile advertising options that you can choose from, depending on your goals and the assets that you have to work with. The key thing to remember when you are designing mobile advertising campaigns is that the users' context when they are consuming advertising is less predictable on mobile than it might be on desktop. They could be at home, at work, in transit, traveling, or basically anything else. They are living their lives and interacting with their phones while doing that, so the more information that you can glean, know, or control about the context in which they see the ad, the better, because it can be used to inform and modify your ad campaign to make it more targeted. The following sections outline the major mobile advertising models and platforms where the ads can be purchased and the basic ways you can optimize them for conversion and budget efficiency.

Google AdWords Pay-per-Click

Google AdWords is one of the most popular ad platforms for digital advertising. It has great reach because ads have the opportunity to show up on Google search results pages. The model that they use is called pay-per-click (PPC). As a reminder, in this ad model, advertisers pick the keywords that they want to bid on and write the ads that they would like to show, then Google shows their ads along with regular search results when people search. This works basically the same on mobile as it does on desktop, except that there are a few more options on mobile that are not available or useful on desktop. You can request that ads be shown on mobile by setting a percent that you want the ads to be shown on desktop and mobile.

There are other ad options in AdWords. They focus on nontext ads, but instead on more contextually relevant ads. The most relevant option here is within the Ad Exchange platform called Native Ads, which strives to let apps and websites that host ads adapt the ads to some degree, to make them feel more natural in the experience, while still conveying the advertising message. The concept involves the advertiser providing either app or web content promotion assets that can be manipulated in terms of layout, font sizes, and font colors to match the layout of other non-ad content that it will be displayed with. The ads are still labeled as ads, but they are used to maintain a fluid look and feel in a native app. The advertiser provides things like headlines, body copy, landing pages, and images or videos, and the app hosting the ad makes the minor modifications necessary to make the ad feel like a naturally occurring part of the app.

Website Banners and Google AdSense

Another option for mobile advertising that is also common in desktop digital advertising strategies is web banners. Banners are visual ads that can be purchased on other websites and apps to drive awareness and conversion by linking visitors from the site or app that they are on to your content. Unlike PPC ads, banners are sold based on the number of impressions, or times the ad has been shown to a user. This model means that you will get a much lower cost per impression but that you will pay even if there is no click. This makes it an especially good way to create and support brand awareness. Like on desktop, one of the most prolific options is from Google, called Google AdSense, but it is not the only option. Companies like AdRoll, Taboola, and Mobile Banners can be placed on mobile-friendly websites or apps. Many of the same struggles that are common with desktop banners, such as relevant placement and banner-blindness, are also a reality on mobile, but there can also be additional complications that are more mobile-specific, which should be taken into consideration.

For many years, Google's mobile ad network was DoubleClick, a company that Google acquired in the early days of mobile advertising and that they evolved and grew over time. Now the company has been rebranded and incorporated with other Google advertising options as part of Google Display, Video, and Search 360. This platform combines a variety of digital advertising options that are prominent on mobile devices. The standard mobile banner sizes are listed in Figure 8.3.

To make banners mobile-friendly but also mobile-performant, it is important to adapt desktop banner designs. In your design process, be careful not to overwhelm the ad unit with too much information or imagery, which can hurt more on small mobile screens than it does on desktop. In terms of colors, high-contrast designs tend to perform best, but the more a banner looks like it belongs on the website or app, the more likely it is to get the user's attention, so there is a delicate balance to be had. Limit the number of fonts, colors, and text used in the ads, and make sure that calls to action are meaningful

The table below lists the standard banner sizes.

Size in dp (WxH)	Description	Availability	AdSize constant
320x50	Banner	Phones and Tablets	BANNER
320x100	Large Banner	Phones and Tablets	LARGE_BANNER
300x250	IAB Medium Rectangle	Phones and Tablets	MEDIUM_RECTANGLE
468x60	IAB Full-Size Banner	Tablets	FULL_BANNER
728x90	IAB Leaderboard	Tablets	LEADERBOARD
Provided width x Adaptive height	Adaptive banner	Phones and Tablets	N/A
Screen width x 32|50|90	Smart banner	Phones and Tablets	SMART_BANNER

FIGURE 8.3 Standard Mobile Banner Sizes (**www.publift.com/blog/mobile-banner-ads**)

and actionable for mobile users. Make sure that the buttons that users are expected to click are large enough, even if the ad is resized for smaller mobile phone screens. Also, make sure the landing pages that the banners link to are mobile-friendly and optimized specifically for mobile conversion.

Many ad platforms allow advertisers to use HTML 5 to make their banners interactive with rich media. The interactivity can include things like geolocation, videos, and interactive animations or games. Adding HTML 5 to a banner ad means including HTML code or sometimes a bit of JavaScript that controls the interaction. This can be intimidating for some designers, but the change in success rates that these types of improvements can drive in your ad campaign will often easily justify the extra effort, and it may be worth contracting the work out or potentially even learning this as a new skill to create a more long-term benefit. Also, some tools can help designers add these types of elements to a banner design. Whenever possible, dynamic personalization in ads can also be included with HTML 5, sometimes called dynamic creative optimization (DCO) or real-time banner optimization, and this also can make a big difference in the response rate of the campaign. Companies like Celtra, Bynder, and Automation can help with this kind of ad creative optimization.

In some cases, usually in apps, banner ads can be shown as an interstitial. Interstitial ads are simply ads in which the banner opens over the app view that the user is on and must be interacted with or closed before the user gets back to the app engagement. Some apps use interactions like this to make their app or game profitable, but in many cases, users find these kinds of ads invasive, so be sure that if you choose to launch this type of ad, it is deployed in apps where the messaging and product offering is highly targeted to the audience and somewhat expected so that the interaction will feel less discordant and intrusive and more useful and actionable.

Video and YouTube Ads

As mobile phones and their digital connections get faster and more capable, more and more mobile time is spent watching videos or, in some cases, casting videos from phones to other devices, so you can consider the potential of mobile video marketing a lot like making regular TV commercials that are super-targeted and potentially even interactive. This type of advertising becomes even more important when you consider the number of "cord cutters" who have stopped paying for cable TV services and replaced them with subscription streaming services like Hulu, Netflix, Amazon Prime Video, and YouTube TV. All of these streaming services are heavily focused on mobile use cases and can incorporate various types of video ads.

The assumption that the mobile video trend is focused only on younger generations is not quite accurate. Younger generations are more likely to stream video over the Internet, on their phones, and through social networks,

Generation Z may not be "video first"
Respondents across generations ranked their favorite entertainment activity

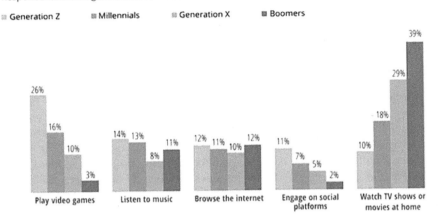

Source: Digital media trends, 15th edition.

Deloitte Insights | deloitte.com/insights

FIGURE 8.4 Comparison of Generations and Entertainment Preferences (**www .mediapost.com/publications/article/363472/gen-z-may-be-challenge-for-video-streaming-service.html**

but all age groups like watching videos, as you can see in Figure 8.4. As the number of cable-cutters continues to grow, more people are consuming on-demand streaming videos, and fewer people are watching live network programming. Video ads will soon become more available to the masses of digital advertisers, tending more toward a self-service, digitally mediated, and targeted advertising model. These ads will more easily be available to a higher number of digital advertisers, further blurring the line between traditional TV advertising and digital video advertising.

YouTube is the world's largest searchable video platform. In fact, YouTube now represents more than 25 percent of mobile traffic worldwide, and more than 70 percent of YouTube traffic is from mobile devices. Therefore, this section focuses on its ad offerings and specifications. In video platforms, video ads are generally sold as pre-roll, post-roll, or mid-roll, depending on when the ad is shown. When you are working with Google, they offer skippable and non-skippable in-stream video ads, in-feed video ads, outstream video ads, video bumper ads, and masthead ads, for display on the YouTube website home page. Skippable and non-skippable in-stream ads are ads that show up before, during, or after a video on YouTube and on any of Google's video ad partners. For skippable, in-stream ads, the videos can be as long as you want, but Google recommends a maximum of 3 minutes for any video ad. YouTube video ad views are only charged for when a viewer watches 30 seconds or more of the ad or interacts with the video.

Alternatively, non-skippable video ads are limited to 15 seconds and are charged based on a CPM bidding model, so advertisers pay based on impressions. The ads often occur in the middle of another video, interrupting the flow of the experience, so the more targeted and useful they are to the viewer, the less likely the viewer is to be irritated by the interruption and consequently, the more likely they are to not keep a negative view of the brand on the ad because of the interruption. Bumper ads are similar, but only last 6 seconds on YouTube.

Outstream ads are another video ad option that is a bit different; they are mobile only and will begin playing on Google partner sites with the sound off, somewhat like a banner ad. According to Google, "Outstream ads can run across a variety of different mobile placements. For mobile web placements, outstream ads appear in traditional banner placement locations. In mobile apps, however, outstream ads appear in banners, interstitials, in-feed, native, as well as in both portrait and full-screen modes." These ads are charged when anyone views the ad for two seconds or more so budgets run out more quickly and you have minimal time to get a viewer's attention with a memorable marketing message.

Masthead ads are another unique option for video ads that will be seen, which can be shown on the YouTube home page, where they auto-play without sound for up to 30 seconds. On mobile, Masthead videos include a customizable headline and an external call to action, outside of the video itself, and it also shows the advertiser's channel name and icon. These ads can be shown on mobile, desktop, and TV, and this is becoming more and more common for video ads, as the lines between mobile, desktop, and TV use cases blur— especially for video consumption. These ads can be very valuable for driving massive brand awareness for a company because of the huge level of traffic and exposure from the YouTube homepages, but these must be reserved and booked directly with a Google sales representative, and they require specific editorial approval, so they can be quite costly.

In general, all video ads should be recorded and saved as MP4 files, with a minimum frame rate of 30 frames per second. The shape of the video is normally 16:9 for landscape videos, but some video platforms also allow 1:1 square video ads, and 9:16 portrait video ads. If it makes sense, you may also want to save a copy of video ads as an audio-only MPG4 file type; this can be especially useful if the audio is particularly entertaining or informative even without the support of the video because this audio-only version of the ad can be used to advertise in specific podcasts that are relevant to your audience or even in podcasting platforms, which also focus on a mobile listening audience.

Social Media Ads

One of the simplest ways to get into mobile advertising is to start with social media ads. As with many other ad options, social media ads are not exclusively

How does Gen Z and Millennials' social media usage compare to a year ago?

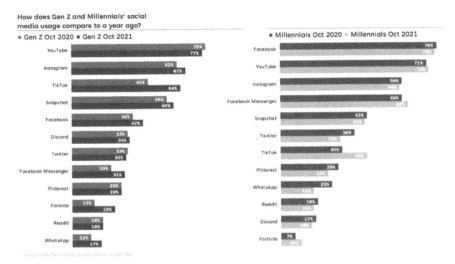

FIGURE 8.5   Social Network Users Often Self-Select and Are Organized Based Roughly on Age-Groups and Interests (YPulse Survey Data, **www.ypulse.com/ article/2021/12/21/this-is-how-gen-z-millennials-social-media-use-has-changed-in-2021/**)

mobile. A majority of social media is accessed on mobile devices, so it is heavily weighted toward mobile, and often the social network ads are more capable of segmenting mobile users from desktop users because most mobile users are accessing the network from apps. One of the best things about social networks is that the social networks have access to and report on a lot of good demographic information about themselves and their audiences. As you can see in Figure 8.5, users of social networks often self-select and are organized based roughly on age-groups and interests. Doing your research before deciding where to focus advertising dollars can be crucial.

YouTube is the top social network for Gen Z, and it is growing for that age group, and while it is shrinking a bit for Millennials, it is still the second largest social network where Millennials congregate. Facebook is the largest social network for Millennials, and it is still showing growth, whereas for Gen Z, the Facebook audience is much smaller and shrinking with time.

Social media ads are a good way to achieve targeted reach effectively because the social network ad platforms allow you to target your ads based on what the networks already know about their users. This means that you can do a pretty good job of targeting ad campaigns for your mobile app or website and landing them accurately at the intended destination for top conversions from social media sites. Often, social networks like Facebook and LinkedIn will also allow you to start with a seed list of "known users" who fit certain criteria and then expand it to build out specific cohorts and lookalike groups of users that you don't know directly but who have demographic characteristics of your happiest existing customers, for example. With the right messages, this can be a very powerful way to quickly expand your brand reach and exposure to the target markets and demographics that are most likely to convert.

One important thing to look out for in social media marketing on mobile is the behavior of the ad or post when it is clicked from the social media app rather than the website. Some social networks will open any link in the phone's default mobile browser, like Chrome or Safari. Others will keep users in their app in a window that looks more like the browser but is actually still part of the social media app. These social media hosted, in-app browsers are sometimes not as capable as regular mobile browsers and, thus, can struggle more with complex code like stylesheets that are used for layout and JavaScript. In the worst cases, entire ad campaigns can be built to take visitors to a landing page that has been extensively tested on a traditional mobile browser, but not tested in the in-app browser of the social network where the ad is placed, potentially hurting the engagement or limiting conversion all together. That means the money spent to get traffic from that app was almost entirely wasted.

To add more complexity, some social media apps use their own in-app browser for one OS but the default mobile browser outside of the app for the other. That means that if you are placing ads in any social media site, it is important to test the landing page not only in all the popular mobile browsers, but also in the in-app browsers for both iOS and Android versions of the social network app. The effort might be a bit more extensive than expected, but this is important to ensure that your ad budget is not wasted.

In-App Ads

Companies like InMobi and Tapjoy allow you to place ads for your app (or sometimes website) in other apps. This can be a great way to target app ads by operating system because you can easily segment specific ads to only show up in iOS apps, to promote your iOS app for iPhone, and only show up in Android apps to drive downloads for the Android version of the app. App ad networks can work in a variety of ways, sometimes allowing you to pay for impressions in certain types of apps or for impressions with certain types of audiences.

Google says, "Each time your ad appears on Google or the Google Network, it's counted as one impression. In some cases, only a section of your ad may be shown. For example, in Google Maps, we may show only your business name and location or only your business name and the first line of your ad text." With other models, ads only cost money when a click leads to a conversion, or the ads can be priced based on a variety of similar pricing models that vary based on volume, app targets, demographic targets, or cohorts. Google defines a cohort as "a group of users who share a common characteristic that is identified in this report by an analytics dimension. For example, all users with the same Acquisition Date belong to the same cohort."

If you like working with Google, they have an app ad network called Ad Exchange (discussed previously), which allows for a variety of different types of in-app advertising, including full-screen app interstitial ads that happen at natural transition points in other apps, video interstitials, native ads, banners, and animated banners. These ads generally include fallback options in case something unexpected limits the availability of your ad to be shown—a nice perk. One benefit of Google is that they allow a few different ad destinations, including of course driving viewers to an app download, using a deep link to move viewers from the app that they are in, to your app, to a call, or to a website URL.

On-Site App Ads

When you have an app and a website, it is always a good idea to use your website to help drive downloads for your apps. This may seem obvious, but it is often overlooked. You can promote a branded app from a website in a variety of ways. You should obviously have a landing page that describes your apps and links people to their pages in each of the app stores where they can download it, but you can also use on-site app promotion to drive downloads throughout the site. Even though you may be giving it away for free, it is best to think about apps like another product or service that you sell and promote it accordingly.

You can use a system called *smart app banners* to promote your app directly from your website. Code is added to the website, and if the system determines that a visitor does not have the app installed, the banner will link them to the app download page. If they do have the app installed, it can detect the operating system of the visitors' phone and use a deep link to get them directly to the corresponding screen in the correct version of the app, so that they can continue their engagement or take advantage of a promotion directly in the app rather than on the website. There are different methods for setting this up for iOS and Android, but the good news is that these "ads" are actually free, and they can be very useful if you know that your app converts better than your website.

From a user perspective, smart app banners are nice because the ads take up only a fraction of the mobile screen, unlike other types of app interstitials that are common on websites. The small footprint of the smart app banners makes it easier for the users to continue interacting with the website as they wish and then engage with the smart app banner when they are ready or dismiss it entirely. Smart app banners load at the top or the bottom of the mobile page and stay present even as the users scroll. These are also considered the

SEO-friendly option for actively promoting an app from a website, especially when compared to full-screen app interstitials on a website, which can create a frustrating mobile experience and can prevent Google from crawling and indexing your content.

Choosing Your Mobile Ad Strategy

Like desktop ad strategies, mobile ad strategies can run the gamut from very simple to very intricate. Also, it is important to acknowledge that not all ad strategies need to be mobile or desktop-specific—in fact, they often shouldn't be. If you have a responsive design website, for example, you may not need to create separate campaigns for the separate devices. The best way to decide what mobile advertising option will be the most effective for you is to start with the goals and the mobile assets that you have to support the ad campaign and then work backward from there. Often simply altering the ad copy, creative, or landing pages, and adjusting the percent to target for mobile can do the trick. This is easier than completely segmenting campaigns, which sometimes is not even possible. For instance, you can consider the following based on your key mobile assets.

Website Only

If you have a mobile-friendly, responsive design website where your top conversion or engagement activity can take place, then nearly every type of traditional ad network could be used to drive mobile traffic to the website. Website banners, retargeting campaigns, PPC ads, video and YouTube ads, and social media ads can all generally be targeted at mobile users to some degree. If you want, you should also be able to place ads in apps, and clicks from the apps will launch a browser to open the landing page on your website, meaning you can generate traffic from apps even if you don't have an app.

When mobile ads are designed to take a user to a mobile-friendly or responsive design website, the potential goals to be as wide-ranging as they are on desktop; anything from awareness campaigns to micro-targeted conversion campaigns should work, as long as all of the necessary assets on the path to conversion are mobile-friendly. This includes the ad imagery or ad copy as well as the ad landing page and all of the utilities and forms through the end of conversion, including follow-up emails and other subsequent communication. It is especially critical that any forms or pages related to the sign-up, registration, or purchase process be tested extensively on mobile. If the conversion is a download, a calendar invite, or something similar, it will also be important to send the link to the asset in an email in case the user initiates the conversion on a mobile device but intends for the final consumption of the asset to take place on a different device, like a computer or tablet.

When you are testing your ads and landing pages for mobile friendliness, it is important to test on multiple devices and in multiple mobile browsers. You can do this on free digital emulators like the ones offered by MobileMoxie, but you should also test on real devices to ensure that there are no problems or conversion limitations in the process. This means testing on Android and iOS devices, but you should also text in the mobile versions of Safari, Chrome, and Opera. You may also want to test on the mobile versions of Firefox, Edge, and the Samsung Internet mobile browsers. Note that a browser that is built for iOS may have slight differences from the same browser that is built for Android. If your target market is young or likely to be interested in gaming, or if you are promoting a mobile game, it may also be relevant to test your mobile advertising assets on handheld Nintendo Switch and PlayStation devices.

The points that determine which styling is used in a responsive design are called *breakpoints*, and one page template can have many breakpoints to accommodate many different ranges of screen widths. This is what allows a page that works well on a desktop rendering of a website to also work well on a mobile device, without having to be built multiple times. If things in your ads or landing pages are not lining up properly on certain screen sizes, it is usually because a new screen width specification (called a breakpoint) needs to be built into the page. You can read more about this in the mobile website section of this chapter.

App Only

If you have a mobile app, then many of the same options will be available, with one additional complication. You need a way to know if the potential customer is using an Android or iOS device when viewing the ad, and ideally you also want to know if that user already has the app installed. There are mechanisms for this, and they are sometimes built into the ad networks, but they are not always reliable. This can get somewhat technical, so if you don't have strong support from a tech team, nuanced advertising options could be a frustrating option.

If your technical options are limited, but you have an app that you want to advertise, the best path forward is to focus your ads in the realm of apps rather than relying on web-to-app advertising options. This works well because, when you place an ad in an iOS app or the Apple AppStore, you can safely assume that the potential customer is on an iOS device, and the same can be true for Android. With knowledge of the operating system in hand, you can then more easily segment your marketing for customers with and without the app already installed. For instance, you could target people without the app with a message about downloading the app and target people with the app installed about specific conversions or engagement opportunities within the app. The same is true on Android and the Google Play app store.

If all you are trying to do is drive app downloads, the first thing to think about is using the in-store PPC options. The App Store and Google Play both allow you to purchase ads directly in the store. In these advertising models, you identify keyword searches that are related to your app and set a price that you are willing to pay for clicks when the platform shows your ad to people who search for that keyword. It is important to understand that different rules apply between the two app platforms, and those rules are also different from the rules that apply in Google AdWords. In some cases, those differences can be used to your advantage. Specifically, it is important to understand that Google AdWords does not let you bid on your competitors' trademarked terms, but both of the app stores do. This is why, for example, you can search for the Amazon app and see that the top paid result is from their competitor, eBay, or you can search for Facebook, and the top ad will be from their competitor, LinkedIn. This means that a very simple strategy for increasing downloads is to bid on all of the names of your competitive apps.

If your goal is to target existing app users with your ad campaign, then there is only value in the app store ads if the action that you are targeting is the download of a subsequent, companion app, such as a premium version of the app or an add-on, or if you are trying to achieve downloads of the same companion app on a different device, such as a watch or tablet version of the app. If none of these scenarios apply and you want to target existing app users with more specific ads that drive the app users toward in-app purchases or deeper in-app engagement, then a different type of ad is needed.

This is true for iOS and Android, though iPhone users can actually browse in-app purchases directly on the app store and start a purchase even before downloading your app. While it is possible, it is not common, so if your goal is to drive in-app purchases, the best way to proceed is usually to work with an app ad network like Tapjoy or InMobi, described earlier in this chapter.

Website and App

If you have an app and a website, then you have a lot of options, and the trick is just making sure that you are segmenting your ads and messaging correctly and testing all of your scenarios to ensure that the ads are working as expected for all of the users and potential use cases. One of the best options for making this possible is to use deep linking to join the screens in your app to the corresponding pages on your website. Obviously, this is easiest if the two assets were developed together, with the intent that at least some content and interactivity in one asset will be replicated in the other. If this is not the case, and the interactivity and use cases between the app and the website are different, this will complicate the implementation of the ad campaigns and will make accurate targeting more critical for success.

The nice thing about deep links is that they can allow devices with and without the app to interact seamlessly, even if, for example, a link is shared from someone with the app on iPhone to other people with and without the app on Android devices. When the deep link is requested by either operating system (assuming that deep links have been set up for both), then the operating system will automatically check to see if the app is installed. If it is, the app will open directly to the specific screen in the app that is being requested. If the app is not installed, the system will simply open the corresponding version of that page on the website. All of the information is contained in the deep link.

If the deep links are taken a step further and they are used to initiate app indexing, then the deep links can be indexed by Apple and Google search engines. When a link is clicked from one of the search engines, the same process of checking for the installed app and opening to a specific screen or failing over to the corresponding web experience can take place. Deep links can even be included in emails and other marketing links, especially if you have a heavily engaged app audience, or if the app is likely their primary interaction with your brand, such as with companies like Facebook, Uber, and Twitter. While they can sometimes be frustrating to set up, if deep links are well integrated for iOS and Android, they can make it easy for users to share mobile content across different mobile devices, without needing to know what operating system users are on or if the app is installed.

Mobile Marketing Measurement and Control

When it comes to mobile management and control, things are in flux, and there is a lot to know. In general, mobile marketing can be a great way to learn about your potential customers and drive conversion in online and offline scenarios. Most types of digital marketing have their own unique types of measurement and control mechanisms, but then also, many companies will choose to do what they can to bring all the different channels of data together into a central dashboard. This can give you a great understanding of what is working and what is not.

Like other forms of digital marketing, it is common to use strategies like A/B and multivariate testing to determine what parts of your mobile apps or websites are resonating well with customers and driving conversions and what tweaks can be made to improve the performance. Some tools like Optimizely and Taplytics can be used for ongoing A/B testing of web content, and also again, Google offers a competitive option called Google Optimize 360 that is quick and easy to integrate.

The difficulty associated with mobile measurement and control is caused by the data limitations that are associated with privacy. This is the other side of the proverbial privacy coin. Mobile devices are inextricably tied to specific people and all the parts of their life, so the privacy protections must be more significant. Since most of the mobile landscape is covered by devices from Google and Apple, it is important to understand how they protect the privacy of their users and how that can filter down to impact the measurement of your mobile campaigns.

Apple is better known for protecting its users' privacy than Google is. Starting with their iOS 14.5 operating system, Apple began to require app developers to state clearly what information they collect in their apps and how it is used, and Apple also requires apps to ask for permission before tracking users' activities in third-party apps and websites. In more recent updates, Apple has taken this further, by also showing when apps share your information with third parties, and sometimes even exactly where the data are being shared. This is part of a project that Apple calls App Tracking Transparency (ATT). It turns out that when given the choice explicitly, only 6 percent of iOS users choose to allow apps to collect and share their data, so in terms of users' privacy protection, the effort has been successful, but for advertisers and marketers, it has been a new change.

Apple has its own trackers that it calls IDFA, which stands for ID for Advertisers. This is a long string of letters and numbers that is unique to each phone, a bit like a person's Social Security number. If an iOS user gives an app permission to track him or her, it is this ID that is shared with websites and apps, to associate the user's behaviors on apps and websites with the ID. It is what allows apps to do things like advertising themselves on a social network like Facebook and then track and attribute the download to a specific user, showing that the ad actually resulted in a download of the app.

Google is less known for its privacy protections, but it has also recently announced multiple avenues of protection for Android phone users. Google also has its own unique identifiers that are used for tracking in Android; these are simply called an Advertising ID. Google has said that it will limit the use of Advertising IDs for sharing user data or data associated with a specific device to other apps and websites. It has announced similar limitations in its Chrome desktop and mobile browser, limiting the use of third-party cookies for tracking, but most of the changes have yet to be deployed. This move by Google has been mostly just announced, and it will be slower to fully launch. It is expected to finally roll out in 2023 or later.

Google calls its multiyear privacy initiative and the associated APIs the *privacy sandbox*. Google's goal in moving more slowly is to preserve the mobile data that have historically been the backbone of mobile-first business marketing programs—especially for mobile apps and games, which rely on the targeted mobile ads to drive downloads and engagement. It has mechanisms that allow different web and app properties that are owned by the same company to set up sharing across different domains and apps; it also creates a way to anonymize some data so that they can still be reportable in aggregate. It also creates topic groupings that can be associated with user groups in a more general, less invasive way, and it is trying to design a system where ad remarketing, which has historically been driven by third-party cookies, might still work with more privacy protections and no third-party cookies that identify specific users or devices. This all has yet to be seen though, so marketers will have to watch and wait.

Additionally, Google has launched a developer initiative called *Checks*, to help Android and iOS app developers make their apps more secure and privacy-conscious. Google's ultimate solution appears to focus more on conversion modeling and potentially AI-data-driven attribution with aggregation and sampling, focusing more on first-party data and information rather than third-party affiliations and cookies.

Mobile Marketing Analytics

All of these advancements in privacy laws are definitely going to impact the ability of marketers to track and segment user data to hone their marketing messages and tactics. Some new methods and options may come out of this change, but until we see how these things all shake out, we are basically left to rely on the first-party data that we have now, and whatever third-party data that are available and, hopefully, learn as much as we can from it before it is possibly more limited. This means that using traditional and mobile methods of analytics to evaluate the success and opportunity in marketing campaigns may be more crucial now than ever, while there is still some third-party data available. Mobile analytics software is designed to do exactly this, combining first- and third-party data wherever it can, recording as much information as is available about interactions with your ads, marketing campaigns, and put it all into a platform that allows you to visualize and manipulate the data to answer questions and learn about the results of your marketing efforts.

In general, most of the traditional analytics software available now includes the ability to segment out or geo-target information about mobile interactions. Segmenting mobile and desktop campaigns is one of the simplest but most impactful ways you can view your data, especially if you can compare mobile and desktop campaigns side-by-side, simultaneously, without the hassle of using two different platforms. In mobile marketing there are a nearly infinite number of possible combinations of analytics software because it is difficult or almost impossible to accurately track every marketing channel with one solution. Different software is often required for tracking detailed success metrics in the different channels, and you will generally benefit from using software that is tailored to the needs of the channel. Most companies benefit from setting up a variety of channel-specific analytics software to capture data from the different channels, and then in some cases adding a layer of software for combining and visualizing the various data streams together in one place. Here, we focus on the measurement options for the different marketing channels first, then go into the more holistic marketing views for combining data sources and channels.

SMS, Push Messaging, and Geolocation Marketing Analytics

In most cases, the company that sends out your text messaging campaigns, MMS campaigns, or geolocal campaigns will be able to provide basic statistics about how and when the SMS messages are being sent out, how many people are opting in versus opting out, and in some cases, how many people are clicking on any links included in the messages. In many cases, this can be enough, especially if you are using tracking code on the links or unique landing pages to help you measure which SMS campaigns drive traffic to which pages. This is a channel where the data are clear, simple, and straightforward.

Mobile Website Analytics   In general, when measuring mobile website traffic, you want to start with the end in mind. The location of the most valuable conversion or engagement events should be the nexus of your analytics setup. Often, the website will be the nexus of a campaign, so these are the most important places to have tracking. Other marketing channels, like SMS, generally send traffic to the website for conversion. Some of the long standing web analytics software that includes reporting on mobile traffic are Google Analytics, Adobe Analytics, Clicky, and Coremetrics. All of these can segment mobile and desktop web traffic so that you can understand how your website is working on mobile. Google Search Console is great for tracking the success of your website rankings in Google, but it only shows organic search traffic and not ads or sponsored campaigns, so it is not enough.

If mobile ads, email, SMS, Bluetooth, or other mobile channels are sending traffic to the website, then tracking code should be appended to all of the links included in these campaigns, so that the traffic can be correctly attributed in the analytics software or in a separate layer of data analysis. This is more accurate and can often be more informative than just looking at the website referrers (i.e., sources that sent traffic to the website). This is true unless unique landing pages are being used for each channel that are only accessible from one specific campaign, in which case tracking codes are less necessary, unless you are A/B testing any messages or calls to action in acquisition campaigns. Different tools are available for this and should be used whenever possible.

App Analytics While you can see some basic information about app downloads in the native app management platforms—Apple's App Analytics and Google's Play Console—it is generally not enough to help marketers perform advance analysis about the source of the download. Most mobile and app ad networks will offer some reporting on their own performance, but the level of sophistication and accuracy can sometimes be limited and may not have all the advanced tagging and modeling capabilities for more sophisticated measurement and analysis.

App analytics can be a bit more complicated to measure because there are always more steps that a user must take. To complete a conversion in the app, the user must first download, install, and open the app, which can be a significant hurdle. To get more information about the specific path and in-app behavior of the users, and if they were brought in through paid ads, organic searches, emails, or something else, you will want to set up additional analytics. More sophisticated app analytics options can also help you group different users by their demographic and psychographic similarities.

These platforms for deeper app analysis are often referred to as mobile measurement platforms (MPPs). According to Incipia, "MMPs such as Apps-Flyer or Adjust are attribution tools which record the source/date of each new app user and tag each event that user completes in the app back to the user's origination source/date. This gives marketers a 'source of truth' for calculating the cohorted ROI of marketing campaigns."

The nice thing about using Google Analytics to track your website is that it can also track app interactions, but this is not its historic specialty. Similarly, Google Search Console can also be used to track Android app rankings for deep links, but this is not what it was designed for, and more sophisticated Google platforms like Firebase and Google Analytics can give you more and better information about how the iOS and Android apps are performing. Analytics software that focuses more exclusively on apps includes Flurry, which is one of the most long standing options. There is also Firebase from Google, App Analytics by Apple, AppsFlyer, AppRadar, and Singular. Kochava is great if you are measuring deep links, and Game-Analytics is ideal if you are marketing a game app. In some cases, these app analytics solutions can be free, especially for simple integrations or small apps, but they may also have costs associated with them based on traffic volume.

You can choose from a variety of MMP options, and their goals are all primarily to help you understand what is driving different positive and negative behaviors within the app and tie those back to aspects of the marketing and app development that you can control. Some MPP options can also help report on web interactions and interactions with deep links between the app and the website; others include features like email integrations, to help connect the app with email messaging about the app to drive more long-term

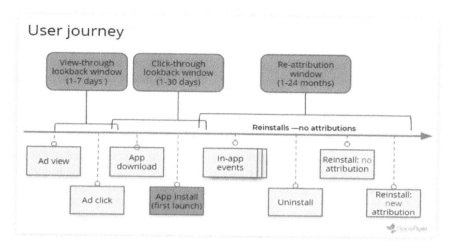

FIGURE 8.6   AppsFlyer Attribution Model (**https://support.appsflyer.com/hc/en-us/articles/207447053-AppsFlyer-s-Attribution-Model**)

engagement and re-engagement with the app. MPPs are great for modeling campaign attribution and to help understand which mobile marketing channels, ad networks, and campaigns are driving the best conversions. Each MMP will use a slightly different attribution model. The models are designed to help the marketing team understand and ascribe the app user activity in a meaningful way. A sample attribution model from one of the leaders in the space, AppsFlyer, is shown in Figure 8.6.

Combined Data Layers and Visualization   In some cases, separate channel analytics will be enough for your mobile marketing efforts, but when many campaigns and channels are involved, you may need an additional data layer to pull everything together. When you get into the combination and visualization of your data, there are a number of good options, but the best option for you will be the one that you can easily set up and maintain to aggregate and present the data in a way that is most useful for your marketing team. Some of the most popular options that also include a free, entry-level option are Google Data Studio, Power BI by Microsoft, and Tableau. There are also some less-known options, like SAS and KNIME, which can also be quite useful. The learning curve on these types of data visualization software can be a bit steep. Consider contracting with an expert or at least someone who is familiar with the chosen platform to ensure that the setup is stable and the calculations and visualizations are accurate. If this is your single source of truth for evaluating your mobile marketing efforts, you need to get it right.

Interpreting Your Analytics

As you are looking at your analytics, either in a combined visualization or in channel-specific platforms, you should approach the interpretation of the data carefully. The first thing to know is that your numbers will rarely match exactly across different platforms. This can be related to a number of factors caused by the analytics measurement technology, time zones, methodology, setup, and sometimes a normal margin of error or chance. You might not be able to consider the numbers in your analytics software to be an absolute truth, but you should expect them to be proportionally and directionally accurate. It is often good to have at least two types of analytics solutions in play at once because they can be used as a backup for each other. If ever the two systems show major differences, especially in relation to direction or proportion, it is a good indicator of a larger problem.

If you are working with large-scale data, it can be important to segment mobile data by country and device. Different countries have different types of mobile behavior that is common or effective as a means of marketing or communication, and the same can be true of different mobile devices, operating systems, or even mobile carrier networks. These differences are generally caused by the local infrastructure, the cost, and availability of fast mobile data connections, and of course, by the cost and availability of high-end mobile devices. To illustrate this point, the following sidebar looks at an example.

How Mobile Internet Traffic Affects Analytics

Even though the mobile Internet penetration rate in the United States is about 83 percent, it's not the country with the highest share of mobile Internet traffic worldwide. Nigeria is! Facts like this mean that a mobile campaign in Nigeria could look very different than a campaign in the United States because almost all of the Internet traffic in Nigeria will be from mobile devices, whereas in the United States, it is more likely to be somewhat split between mobile and desktop.

The apparent discrepancy between the United States and Nigerian mobile traffic comes from the historical lack of digital infrastructure in Nigeria. The United States had a well-established high-speed Internet infrastructure with high user-penetration on the desktop before mobile devices were as widespread. Conversely, in Nigeria, infrastructure for wired Internet was not well-established, and thus, penetration for desktop computers was not high. This made it possible for mobile phones to achieve dominance very quickly. Mobile data networks are a faster and easier infrastructure to build, and mobile phones have a lower cost and, thus, a lower barrier to entry for users.

In 2021, only 47.28 percent of all U.S. Internet traffic was from mobile devices. Even though mobile penetration in Nigeria is only at 42.12 percent, a full 82.73 percent of all web traffic in that country is being generated by mobile devices. When you are working on large-scale, international mobile marketing campaigns, information like this can be vital to understanding your own analytics. (FYI: India is just behind Nigeria, at 76.65 percent of all Internet activity coming from mobile devices. This data juxtaposition illustrates a theme that is especially common in mobile marketing statistics, and that is the importance of context for understanding and interpreting the implications of data, statistics, and your own analytics.)

CHAPTER 9

Email Marketing

By Michael Stebbins

mail is one of the most enduring digital marketing channels, and it remains one of the most effective. It's easy to find reports that claim it places in the top three channels for customer acquisition, sale conversion, and content promotion. Email is also one of the highest rated channels for customer retention and follow-up sales.

When email campaigns are properly coordinated with other channels, this amplifies the effectiveness of your overall campaign results. On a budget or under pressure to show results? Email marketing is among the most affordable and measurable channels in digital marketing.

With all these benefits, this is a vital channel to understand for your campaigns, for your OMCP and OMCA exams, and for your career in digital marketing.

This chapter covers what a marketer needs to know to manage basic email marketing campaigns (or teams that implement them), and the concepts of integrating email marketing with adjacent channels.

By the end of this chapter, you will know the following:

- Principles that will guide you, even when email marketing practices and rules evolve
- Enough history of email marketing to understand some of the present challenges
- Key regulations and how to stay up to date to protect your company from complaints or fines
- Some basic email strategy, planning, and implementation practices
- How your choices can affect deliverability and how many messages make it to the inbox
- How email marketing can integrate with other channels
- Basic email marketing measurement and control systems

Guiding Principles

For those who have practiced digital marketing for more than a decade or two, certain practices tend to remain evergreen while some details change. For example, for SEO, we teach that the relevance and accessibility of our content tends to win over the latest tips and tricks to influence search engines. There are similar guidelines for email marketing.

So the first guiding principles may not be on your OMCP exam, although they can certainly help candidates guess at some questions. These will likely remain applicable—even as our technology changes over the next decade.

Do modify and make them your own, memorize them, and put them on the wall. Your campaigns will be better for it.

Every Email Is a Wanted Email

- Our recipients must be delighted to receive every message we send.
- Our messages must help recipients or build trust whether they chose to do business with us or not.
- Every email represents a chance to earn an unsubscribe, so we will deliver what our subscribers hope for, consistently.

We Are Lawful and Responsible

- Our email marketing practices will comply with all relevant regulations and laws.
- We will always require consent before adding an address to our list and make it easy to leave our lists.

We Earn Our High Deliverability

- We are committed to great content, reputation, and proper implementation of technology to maintain deliverability.
- We will keep only engaged recipients on our list.
- We will only use highly reputable transaction email services.

The first principle (every email is a wanted email) can be very difficult. But all too often we marketers get so excited about conveying our product features, or we are under pressure to send something—*anything*—to get the newsletter out, that we fill it with self-beneficial, minimally personalized messages that don't delight the recipient. Like most things, it takes time and investment to create and manage good email campaigns.

One of my favorite emails to receive in 2003–2004 was from Cathay Pacific Airlines. I could count on it to share surprisingly low airfares for travel to and within Asia. I'd browse every email, imagining the travel I could experience for a fraction of typical airfare. It was my chance to dream and to consider. I made sure I received their emails and read each one for several years. Every email was delightful and they never mis-stepped.

Staying up with the laws and regulations related to email marketing is essential to protecting your organization, but also to treating your recipients with respect and earning their trust. This chapter gets you started with ensuring compliance. All of these things contribute to deliverability—the ability to ensure your campaigns get delivered and read.

You may not achieve customer delight in every message, but to the degree that you do, your recipients will anticipate and mark your emails as welcomed or high priority and remain open to do more business with your company. And this is good marketing, no matter what changes behind the scenes.

Establishing Campaign Goals

What gets measured gets done, and your email marketing strategy must have a measurable goal, established early in the planning phase to guide your tactics. The professional email marketer will interview internal stakeholders and management to establish campaign goals and measurement systems. Even better to include interviews with some prospects and customers to derive what's important to them, your recipients. Ensure that your campaign goals align with overall marketing strategies within the organization.

Email applies well across the entire buyer journey from demand generation (interest) through conversion (decision) to retention for lifetime value. Even customer support emails are important touchpoints for building a long-term relationship with your customers and your market.

Knowing some of the more common campaign goals will help you establish your own. Here are a few campaign goals with a brief description of each.

- **Content delivery:** The primary measurement of the email campaign is engagement with published content. For example, gain 10,000 views of our recent whitepaper.

- **Revenue or sales:** The primary measurement of the email campaign is attributable revenue. For example, earn $10,000 in sales. Each message can move the prospect closer to a purchase, upsale, cross-sale, or a larger purchase. While this may be the ultimate goal of all marketing campaigns, more success is found when we focus on delighting the recipient. That we want to sell something is implied. The customer will order when ready.

- **Acquiring customers:** Each message can move the prospect closer to a first purchase engagement. For example, acquire 1,000 new customers or 400 new leads for our new service. Common tactics include sales or "subscriber-only" offers that create a sense of exclusivity or urgency, loss-leaders (selling for less than your cost just to get the customer invested), and low-cost, high-value samples (first course or first month for $1). Email can also be effective at remedying shopping cart abandonment.

- **Reader behavior:** Many campaigns are measured by a series of actions made by the customer. For example, earn one public review for every four customers. Goal examples include earning written reviews, social media engagement (interact with us), amplification or sharing of social media content, or setting an appointment.

- **Customer satisfaction (or similar sentiment):** These campaigns are designed to enhance the reader's satisfaction as measured by the absence of complaints, a survey result, net promoter score, or other review system. Examples might include open feedback channels: "Is there anything we can do better?"

Other goals can include branding and perception, growing a social media following, fundraising, appointment confirmations, lead nurturing, demand generation, and survey and data collection.

Email Metrics and Reporting

It's important to set goals that *can* be measured. So you, as a digital marketer, must understand what is measurable and enable reports that use measurable metrics to show whether a campaign is reaching its goals or falling short.

The most popular email metrics tend to be engagement metrics. Engagement metrics include *email opens, clicks,* and other intentional interactions such as an *email forward.* Decades ago we measured email opens by placing a small image in each email, annotated with information that could identify the recipient. Upon opening the email, the email client (mailbox providers such as Outlook, and so on) requested the image from our server, creating a trackable event each time the email was opened (presumed read). But as recipients demand privacy, more and more email clients obfuscate the image request and reduce the reliability of this classic measurement. While there are some new technologies to track opens, a surer sign of engagement is a click from within an email. This makes it pretty likely that the recipient opened the email and (hooray!) clicked on a trackable link.

Here is a partial list of email metrics that are commonly captured:

- Opt-ins (subscriptions)
- Opt-outs
- Subscriber activity
- Email sent
- Email delivered
- Email hard bounce
- Email soft bounce
- Email open
- Email link click
- Time of open
- Time of link click
- Email forwarded
- Email client (mailbox type, platform)
- IP address of reader
- GEO IP location of reader
- Spam complaints
- List segment name
- Message type (newsletter, promotion, and so on)

Here are some examples of metrics based on extended activity that can be tracked in web analytics tools or in other integrations (e.g., CRM or ecommerce):

- Revenue
- Conversions
- Goals reached
- Bounce rate
- Pages viewed
- Purchase completed
- Lifetime revenue captured
- Webinar attended
- Meetings completed

We combine these to gain insights and progress toward goals:

- Revenue per subscriber trailing 30 days
- Conversion rate by segment
- Content view rate by campaign
- Unsubscribe rate by message type
- Mobile click rate
- Campaign ROI

Where Email Marketing Fits

Email is rarely used as a sole marketing channel. Often categorized as "owned media," it integrates well with other channels, including social media, content marketing, and digital advertising. It is a pillar of marketing automation implementation, CRM, and customer support systems.

There isn't enough room in this chapter to teach the details and implementation of email integrations. But a marketer should be *aware* of some of the possibilities of channel integrations with email marketing. The OMCA teaching standard requires education programs to teach at least four examples of integrations, and some exam questions cover this area. So here are just a few examples of email channel integrations to pique your curiosity and creativity:

- **Content marketing and email:** Email can be a great way to distribute free or gated content. Campaigns can be purposed to invite recipients to promote content.
- **Social media marketing and email:** Many marketers use emails as a channel for broadcasting what happened in their social media channels. Your emails are also opportunities to invite readers to connect or engage on your social media channels. Social channels can be used to announce upcoming emails and create anticipation. It is also a generally accepted practice to use interactions on relevant social media channels as inspiration for email content topics that are important to your audiences. I have seen very effective email campaigns that ask a loaded question in email but direct readers to answer it on the social media channel. By uploading your email subscriber list to social networks like Twitter, Facebook, or LinkedIn, you can often connect a name and face to the email address in your list. Many get good results by following their email subscribers to get a clear idea of their preferences and requirements. Plus, if your social media content is engaging enough, you increase the chances of return follows and content consumption and promotion from your audience.
- **Mobile marketing and email:** Mobile responses can be used for list building. For example, "Text us your email for a special deal." Consider

texting subscribers to let them know an email message is coming and the value within. For recipients who welcome such text messages, this warms them up and increases open and engagement rates. Communication improves when a customer can interact with either an SMS or an email for the same goal, such as tracking a shipment or updates on an event. Note that, like email marketing, SMS marketing requires specific consent and is regulated by region.

- **Email and digital advertising:** Many top tier advertising platforms can create and target custom audiences based on uploaded email addresses from your list. We have had success creating custom audiences in, say, Google Analytics, based on actions taken in emails, with follow up targeting using custom messages in Google Ads.

Email Marketing Work Within Organizations

The email marketer within a large organization, say with 20-plus marketers, will coordinate how email marketing interacts with all of these channels and more. This marketer will usually rely on others for content but will establish the formats, measurement systems, data governance, list management, service providers, and integrations. In larger organizations, the in-house email marketer will work with other technical teams to agree on email marketing implementation, technology choices, data management, and sending practices.

Mid-size entities, from 3 to 20 marketers, may use an email marketing contractor service to handle the technical side of list management and newsletter campaigns, but the in-house team must understand and set policies for compliance and data governance. Email service contractors can bill by an hourly rate, a monthly retainer, or by the number of campaigns each month.

And at the smallest businesses, email marketing is one of many tasks that the owner or marketing manager performs. Some choose to outsource to independent contractors or marketing agencies that include email and newsletter services.

Tools for Email Marketing

Gone are the days of sending mass emails using a blind carbon copy (Bcc:) from your personal account. While sending campaigns from your own accounts is certainly possible, the effectiveness will be rightly curtailed by many checkpoints that attempt to filter out unwanted emails from recipients' inboxes. Enter the era of the email service providers and tools. Many are free for smaller campaigns. You will need to know at least these two basic tool classifications:

- *An email service provider (ESP)* is a company that provides bulk sending, email formatting, and/or list management. Examples include MailChimp and Constant Contact. Higher email volume may require a transaction email service, also called a *deliverability service.* Examples include Twilio Sendgrid and SparkPost. The alternative of using your own mail account—your company's Gmail account or your own hosting service—to send volumes of email is a bad idea, as this can reduce deliverability (how many messages actually reach the inbox and get read) and incur a lot of manual work to handle unsubscribes and remain in compliance with regulations. An ESP can help marketers stay in lawful compliance, handle bounced emails and unsubscribes, and report on campaign effectiveness. List management and segmentation can happen using these tools, in other dedicated list management tools, or in a marketing automation tool. We cover these concepts later in this chapter, but the net-net is that email marketing tools have become essential to even the smallest campaign.

- *Marketing automation tools* help track, trigger, and coordinate messaging based on your recipient's actions, including website behavior, clicks in email, or updates in your sales team's CRM system. Examples include Hubspot, Salesforce Pardot, and Adobe Marketo. Marketing automation can start and stop timed sequences of messages (auto-responders and drip campaigns) to a subscriber based on behavior. Your automation tools can coordinate messaging and timing with social media campaigns and sales interactions (via CRM), as well as SMS and mobile campaigns.

- *Analytics and reporting capabilities* are usually baked into your email service provider toolset, but it is worth mentioning that web analytics tools like Google Analytics or Adobe Analytics can be used to measure the effectiveness of your email campaigns as it relates to reader behavior on your web pages.

There are many other tools that can enhance your campaign integration, measurement, deliverability, analysis of your servers (I like MxToolBox) and list management that are beyond the scope of this chapter.

Stay Up to Date on What's Possible

The capabilities and requirements of email marketing tools are constantly evolving. If you are just starting out in email marketing, a nice shortcut into what is possible is to research and compare the current capabilities of email service providers and transaction/deliverability services. Another technique is to follow the social streams of email marketing specialists. One trick to choose whom to follow: see who had been invited back to the same reputable digital marketing conference to present on email marketing techniques—at least twice. This implies that the speaker has survived peer review and consistently stays up on the latest in the practice. It also helps if they are OMCP certified. Lastly, join some active email marketing groups online to see what the more seasoned email marketers are discussing. This is a great way to stay up to date on what is possible.

Growing Your Email List

Your email address list is your precious crucible, to be kept in a velvet-lined case, locked in a secure vault, behind the best security with lasers and private armies to defend it. Too far? Okay, then know this: the best email address lists are grown organically, from infancy to maturity, and are maintained with love and compassion. They are full of data that enable the email marketer to personalize each message and segment each send. And they are indeed protected from bad addresses that can infect your reputation.

If this sounds like a lot of work, it is—much like raising a child. And it's rewarding.

Building a New Email Marketing List

The new marketing entity must build a list from scratch, one opt-in at a time. Generally accepted practices to invite prospects to get on your email list include the following:

- Offer valuable content: whitepapers, newsletters, guides, ebooks, and so on.
- Offer discounts and deals.
- Offer loyalty programs.
- Offer exclusive notifications.
- Use social media to promote your content.
- Include an invitation in your email signature.
- Include an invitation on your contact page.

Some brands use scroll popups or exit popups to put email subscription offers in front of visitors. Be careful with these because they can degrade your users' experience and affect their perception of your brand.

When it comes to enticing new subscribers, it isn't hard to get into the mindset of the visitors. Most are evaluating your reputation and your offer, trying to decide as quickly as possible, "Why should I give you access to my inbox?"

Attracting or Repelling Subscribers

It helps to imagine that everyone has a price for access to their inbox. Your job as an email marketer is to earn that access by making offers so attractive that your prospects can't help but sign up, eagerly anticipating your next message. This is hard to do for most marketers and competition is everywhere. Do you want newsletter signups? Then share exactly what subscribers can expect in terms of content and frequency. Which message is more likely to earn signups?

"Sign up for our newsletter about investing,"

or

"Get exclusive stock tips from Wall Street giants who average 30 percent year after year."

Testing is the surest way to know, but the emphasis on believable benefits is a good starting point. The barrier grows as reader's inboxes fill up to capacity, so your offer has to be irresistible *and* easy to accept.

The Data You Collect

Each additional field adds value to your list and future messages by enabling personalization and segmentation. That's a good thing, right? Well, yes it is, but not at the cost of conversions.

The more data you request on your forms, the higher the barrier to subscribers and the more likely it is your visitor will leave without completing the subscription form.

The less data you request on your forms, the higher the likely conversion rate. The highest converting forms simply ask for one thing—the email address. I like to also ask for the first name, which is a great start to personalizing the messages.

Where's the balance? Well, the more attractive the offer, the more your audience will tolerate additional fields and questions. Offer a $1,200 analyst report as a free download, and you might be able to ask for more than a company name.

Ascertaining the balance takes a lot of work and testing.

Here's a workaround solution: collect more data on subsequent interactions. For example, when your subscriber uses the same email address to purchase, you can add the collected data to the subscriber record. When the customer returns to download a whitepaper, you could offer to text updates or additional chapters via SMS to a valid phone number. Modern marketing automation tools can supplement your email list with implicit and explicit data collection.

Which brings us to two data categories that you'll need to understand: Implicit and explicit data.

- *Implicit data* are data derived from visitor behavior and available data streams, but not explicitly offered by a visitor. Examples include geo-location as associated with IP address, pages visited, referring source, and time of each interaction. For example, if your subscriber has visited your water filtration product page multiple times, this can indicate interest in water filters. If your subscriber clicked on a link in your email content related to water filtration, this suggests or further confirms this interest. Some email and marketing automation systems track and correlate this data, adding it to records in your email list.

- *Explicit data* are information that is knowingly provided by your visitor/subscriber, usually via form fields on subsequent interactions. This can also include notes and data entered by representatives of your company who interact live with the customer. For example, customer support, customer service, or sales reps can enter data in a CRM system in a structured format (e.g., "The customer is interested in water filtration systems," or "The customer has received a quote."). You may choose to mail water filtration content to the former and suppress emails to the latter, at least until a record in CRM indicates that the transaction is closed. Some email and marketing automation systems collect or correlate this data, adding it to records in your email list.

Knowing what types of data are available will help you plan your campaigns for success. Start with what data you can collect without repelling your prospects, and as you build value and trust, use that data responsibly to enhance the experience and conversation.

Personalization

When sorting through the waves of incoming emails, your recipient's eyes naturally scan for something that qualifies an email for attention. One signal is that "the sender knows me." The more signals we can put in that are specific and unique to the recipient, the stronger the "personalization" of the email is.

Email personalization is the process of using the data that you have to tailor message content to be unique and personal for each recipient. Personalization, when done well, builds trust and can improve the relationship with the recipient. At minimum it can show that you care enough to provide individualized experiences in your email campaign. The benefits of personalized campaigns include higher response rates, open rates, click rates, and retention (lower unsubscribe rates). Personalization can help create a more conversational tone as well.

Here's an example message that some of you might have seen already; it uses personalization in the subject and on every line.

Subject: OMCA Certification dates for Nikola

Hi Nikola, About two months ago, you chose May 13 as your goal date for your OMCA.

That's coming up soon, but it seems you haven't registered for your OMCA exam yet—an important step.

Given that, I thought you'd like this stat:

Your LinkedIn OMCA course has a 92 percent pass rate when candidates sit for the exam within 30 days of course completion.

So. . . the sooner you take the exam after finishing the course, the higher the likelihood of your passing score.

This is the perfect time to register, get it on the calendar, and create some urgency to completing your OMCA goal.

And when you finish the registration, let me know and I'll provide a free practice assessment voucher so you can move toward your certification with even more confidence.

—Rachel and the OMCP Team

This message content, which continues to be tested over the years, generates a 62 percent response rate at the time of this writing. The prior nonpersonalized messages generated less than a 5 percent response rate. Now, the data in the system behind this email are comprehensive. Each line is dynamically changed based on the recipient's prior behavior and our records of what has already been sent to the recipient. For example, this message won't be sent if the candidate has registered for an exam or received any other email from us in the past 24 hours. That's a 1,200 percent (12 times) increase in response rate. Personalization pays off.

Personalization can include what you know about the recipient. Here are just a few of hundreds of possibilities:

- First name
- Time of signup
- Last visit to the website
- Pages visited on the website
- Geographical region via GEO-IP or provided address
- Interests derived from past interactions (product, service, delivery preferences, and so on)
- When your company last sent the recipient an email
- When the recipient last opened or responded to an email

- Whether the recipient has purchased a product/service
- Plans as captured in CRM by sales representatives
- Data from customer service interactions
- Conditional phrases or words based on logic (e.g., liquid)
- Many more

If you are just starting your email campaigns and data management, you can start small. The recipient's first name is a good start. Knowing what's possible for personalization helps you plan your data collection for the future.

Too Much Personalization

Avoid personalization that does not align with the voice of your company or that adds no value to the message. While writing this, I received a soliciting email selling website development services; it asked about the weather here in Santa Cruz, California, stating that it was cloudy and (52° F). That's clever, but could be considered disingenuous since it is unrelated to the message. So it is a better practice to ensure that the personalization that you do use is relevant to the message and the user.

Segmentation

Email segmentation achieves a similar goal through a different process. Email segmentation controls delivery or inclusion of content in email messages based on data that you have collected. The purpose of segmentation is to ensure that only *relevant* messages are sent to each recipient on our list. The benefits of segmentation in campaigns include higher response rates, open rates, and click rates as well as higher retention (lower unsubscribe rates).

Here are just a few of many ways to segment your email list.

- Past purchase history, e.g., toys for a 3-year-old
- Activity on your website, e.g. content interest or site search history
- Responses to past emails, e.g., opens or clicks
- Stage of the sales funnel, e.g., Aware, Interested, In Evaluation, at Decision, as set in CRM
- Time zones or geolocation, e.g., likely to be home from work
- Inactivity, e.g., three months of no activity
- Device and email client, e.g., Gmail on a Mac

Can you think of how each message would be so much more relevant and effective when only the most qualified people are receiving them?

Your list management system, be it CRM, an ESP, or even a spreadsheet for those starting out, can have data fields associated with each email address. These data fields are also used for personalization. The word "segment" can bring up images of cutting up a list. But the actual application of segmentation is usually *additive*. When you send a message about winter clothing, for example, you would add those addresses you know are from colder regions *and* have shown interest in jackets and hats. Some might exclude addresses that are from warmer regions. But instead of excluding addresses in warmer regions, some email tools can customize the email content specifically for those recipients who meet specific criteria. For example, recipients known to be interested in jackets and hats, but are from a warmer region, might get a paragraph about traveling to the ski slopes based on this data.

These types of personalization and segmentation conditions can become overwhelming very quickly. So if you're feeling lucky to craft just one newsletter a day before the deadline, these techniques may have to get designed into future campaigns. At minimum, being aware of them can alert you to the possibilities and can define your list architecture and data collection systems earlier in your process.

List Hygiene

Keeping your company's email list accurate and up to date is a continual commitment. It takes some work. The following sections discuss the main steps in getting the most out of your curated email list.

Avoid Auto-Subscribe

Every subscriber on your list should remember *asking* to be on your list. When you capture an email address in conversation, from a business card, or even from a transaction, it is not an implicit subscription to your newsletter or promotional emails. Some marketers cave in to temptation and automatically add these to the campaign list. A better practice is to send an invitation to these people, asking them to expressly sign up for your campaigns or newsletter. If they don't respond, then don't add them to the list.

Scale Down Inactive Subscribers

Make it your goal to keep only engaged subscribers on your list: those who interact with your messages or content. How long until a subscriber is considered inactive? It'll be different for each entity, but a good starting point is twice your normal sales cycle time.

Responsible email marketers regularly clean lists, removing inactive subscribers in order to maintain high deliverability. Some more experienced marketers simply delete inactive users based on a time-without-interaction. Some put inactive subscribers on a less frequent schedule.

Another effective practice is to send farewell messages to inactive subscribers prompting for a resubscribe confirmation. Then remove those who do not confirm a desire to remain subscribed. This may seem counterintuitive to marketers who want to maintain a large list. It's a painful process for some of us! We think, "What if they don't see my reconfirmation message?" But know that the reputation of your domain or sending server is at risk if your emails are being sent to recipients who ignore them or fail to interact. Conversely, it stands to reason that, if a high majority of your recipients are observed to open, click, or "favorite" your messages, mailbox providers like Gmail or Outlook are much more likely to ensure that your messages are delivered to a recipient's inbox.

Clean Out Poison Addresses

Most of the email addresses in your list will be acquired through an online form. And with most online forms there is inevitable bot traffic or "form spammers," where the email addresses entered are not associated with a person who is interested in your content or products. The reasons behind these illicit form completions are varied, from email relay hack attempts to security breaches to link spam and more, but the savvy email marketer will ensure these are removed from all lists.

Why? The primary guideline is that every email you send should be a wanted email. Addresses used by bots do not correlate to a "real" email or to a recipient who wants your content. Beyond this, there are security and email reputation issues with sending messages to unverified addresses.

But there is more. Did you inherit a list, rent one, or add someone else's list into your own? A responsible marketer would never buy a list to target via email. But in case you know someone who is tempted, it's important to understand some history.

In ancient times, some marketers engaged in the questionable activity of email harvesting. Email harvesting was a method of building email lists by deploying crawlers or bots that scan public or private content to extract email addresses. To combat this, some mailbox providers or filtering service providers placed "honeypot" addresses as traps, and blacklisted servers/domains that sent to those addresses. An email blacklist is a list of IP addresses or domains that are suspected of sending spam or sending to harvested (or poisoned) lists. Some blacklists are publicly searchable, and some are kept private by mail service providers. You now know the danger in buying and using a list that might include these email addresses.

An attendee of one of my sessions stood up and challenged me to come up with any scenario where procuring an email address list could be of *some* advantage. I could think of only one use, and that would be specific to digital advertising—to upload a high-reputation email address list to test custom audiences on platforms that support it (many do). But adding any of those addresses to your own subscriber list directly would be like adding poison to your company's marketing mix. Earn each subscriber address and confirm it is from a person who genuinely wants your email messages and campaigns.

Deliverability

One important principle to remember is that *wanted* emails get opened and *delightful* emails earn interaction. Interactions (opened, clicked, forwarded, or "favorited") improve your deliverability. Email deliverability measures how many of your sent emails are delivered to recipients' inboxes. As our incoming mail load increases, mailbox providers continue to develop ways to detect unwanted messages, and they categorize mail in a way that helps the recipient focus on what's important or urgent as needed.

Filtering Spam   You might wonder how filters attempt to block messages that look like spam and how this affects your deliverability to the inbox.

Imagine that you run the Gmail team at Google or the Outlook team at Microsoft or an ISP who provides email mailbox services. One of your primary objectives is to ensure your users only see legitimate, wanted emails in the inbox, to route promotional emails accordingly, and block unwanted and dangerous emails.

How do you do it? You might try the following:

1. Filter emails that have spammy words, phrases, or punctuation, like FREE!!!! Or the latest scam phrases, like "Passive Income."

2. Detect messages from sending servers or domains that have sent a high volume of messages with largely the same content in a short period of time and block them or categorize them as "promotional."

3. Block sending servers or domains that have a high rate of unsubscribes or deletion.

4. Block sending servers or domains that have a bad reputation already, such as those that are blacklisted or are associated with open relays.

5. Block sending servers or domains that have a no established reputation and are also triggering numbers 2, 3, or 4.

6. Block messages that contain only a single image.

7. Detect messages that have excessive CSS or HTML, tables, or indicators common to newsletters and categorize them as "newsletters" or "updates" instead of inbox.

8. Categorize messages with the word "unsubscribe" as mass emails.

9. Block messages that contain attachments that could be dangerous or offensive.

10. Detect messages with complex tags on links or tracking pixels and categorize them as "promotions."

Now let's look at the positive side. What signals would you look for to indicate a "wanted" email?

- A "starred," favorited, or whitelisted email domain
- Emails with a high "read" or interactivity rate, e.g., replied to, forwarded, favorited, or images loaded
- Emails from a domain to which the recipient has already sent an email
- Emails with words or phrases that are used in conversational or transactional interchanges, e.g., "from your report" or "sales order receipt"
- Emails that differ significantly from others sent from the same domain in a short period of time
- Emails from sending servers or domains with established reputations and accountability systems

There are plenty of arguments about whether all of these checkpoints are in place, but most agree that they do reflect reasonable measures that could be used by mailbox providers. Here's the key: when we craft our email campaigns and methods to avoid triggering these possible filters, we increase the chances that our emails will make it to the inbox. Now this isn't about fooling the filters. Schemes like avoiding the word "unsubscribe" or trying to make a newsletter seem like a sales receipt will be a losing battle over time. Instead, the following sections discuss some methods that attempt to address these possible filters *and* may delight the recipient as well.

Email Frequency, Timing, and Limits One technique that can increase open rates is to set email message timing to correlate with the times of day that a recipient has most often interacted with your business. Bulk sends can be batched by these time blocks over a day or even a week. So if Raul subscribed at midnight in his time zone, messages from my servers will be sent to him within two hours on either side of midnight. If Ayat clicked at 2 p.m. in her time zone, then you could update her sending time to be a few hours on either side of 2 p.m. in her time zone.

It is a common practice for email marketers to put limits on total outbound emails per minute, per hour, and per day. This is called "throttling." Email throttling is the process of limiting how many emails are sent from your servers in a given time frame. For example, we might limit our sending server to 1,000 emails per hour. Controlling the volume can help reduce the indicators that suggest your messages are spam. Remember, if you ran an email service and detected, say, 900 emails per second from the same sender to your clients, it would be pretty easy to label that as a bulk or promotional email.

For larger entities, it is a healthy practice to put limits on total number of emails sent to any one recipient in a set period, excepting transactional or customer support emails. A sudden high volume of emails to one recipient increases the chances of earning a spam label or an unsubscribe from the recipient.

Other Techniques to Increase Deliverability Besides the preceding practices, email marketers should be aware of a few vestigial indicators.

- **Spammy words:** In the early 2000s, Microsoft Outlook was prone to mark a message as spam if it included specific words—even certain names generated a spam score. While mailbox providers are using more advanced methods now, it still helps to avoid using words and punctuation that correlate with spam emails. Words like "FREE!" in the subject line or "make more money" in the body are obvious examples. You can browse the content in your spam folder to get ideas for the most recent phrases to avoid.

- **Complex code:** Emails with complex CSS or extraneous HTML are reported to trigger spam filters. It's unlikely that a person-to-person email has 200 lines of HTML for each paragraph. So here again, it can help to simplify. Favor technology that keeps HTML, CSS, and formatting directives simple.

- **One last practice that could seem counterintuitive to sum up the deliverability section: Be genuine.** If your email is a newsletter, then don't attempt to portray it as something else. I often call out [Newsletter] in the subject text so subscribers know exactly what is being sent. Wanted emails are opened and read, and opened emails help your reputation directly or indirectly. Yes, your newsletter may be categorized as a "Promotion" or "Update" but this is better than eroding trust or earning an unsubscribe.

The overall rule for deliverability, aside from some vestigial technical faux pas to avoid, is to generate content that is wanted and eagerly anticipated.

Creating Email Content Designed to Persuade and Get to the Inbox

Emails that are *wanted* get opened and read, and emails that are *opened* and read tend to get delivered to inboxes. So, it makes sense to invest in the most persuasive, delightful content to entice your recipients to anticipate your messages.

Whether your messages are long or concise, persuasive or passive, plain text or graphic art pieces is up to you and your brand. A generally accepted practice is to know your recipients and what messages will delight and persuade them. OMCP's OMCA exam does not test for copywriting or persuasion skills, but it does cover some essentials for delivering effective messages. So here they are:

- It is generally accepted that your email content must agree with what is promised in the subject line. In the same way, landing pages must deliver what is promised in the email call to action. The concept of "scent" or common design and wording from email to landing page can also assure recipients that they are in the right place, on the intended path. If your email offers 50 percent discounts on red hearts, then the landing page should feature 50 percent discounts on red hearts as the first thing your reader sees.

- For email campaigns where the goal is to persuade the reader to action, it is a good practice to have one *primary* goal for the email and include a clear and prominent call to action for that goal. The call to action might be a button, a highlighted link, or an invitation to reply. There is some dispute on how many calls to action are effective, so to know what's best for your campaign, run an AB test.

- AB testing can reveal which components (e.g., subject line, call to action, style) of your email will perform most effectively. Many experienced campaign managers start each campaign by testing two variants to 10 percent of the target list to see which one should go to the remaining 90 percent of the target list.

Format for Email Clients

Each mailbox technology (email client or email reader) has its own method for rendering emails. So it follows that, to get the most engagement, your campaigns need to render well in the majority of mailboxes. Imagine if your call to action button does not show up for Outlook users or your message text doesn't wrap for mobile clients. Some email service providers have tools to predict rendering, and some have attempted to create common markup frameworks that render consistently in the most popular email clients. Avoiding complex HTML and CSS in your messages can help here, but testing is a must. At minimum, ensure that your emails render well in the majority of your recipients' mailboxes ahead of any significant campaign.

Many email clients reveal a portion of the email content in the inbox list before the recipient opens the email. This is called preview text, as shown in Figure 9.1.

Preview text can scale differently in each email client, but it usually follows the subject line in inbox message lists.

			Hootsuite's Global .	Everything you need to know about creators · Join this webinar for the inside scoop from the experts. To view this ...	5:11 AM
			Lauren @ Search Mar.	Unlock expert-led training in your search marketing specialty · Actionable tactics, in-depth training, and Q&A – $1...	Jan 24
			MarTech Webinars	"It's Now or Never: Prioritize Your Customer's Digital Experiences in 2022" · Dear Michael, The world's leading bra...	Jan 24

FIGURE 9.1   Preview Text

The preview text often includes the first words of the email body: Hi Pat, Your car didn't quite make it to. . ..." There are several techniques for controlling what shows up in the preview text including pre-header text and use of multipart email components, or even hidden text. Some ESPs provide a specific markup for this. Accepted practices include using preview text as a continuation or enhancement of the subject line. When used properly, the preview text can significantly boost your chances for engagement.

Domain and Server Reputation

Your sending domain and the servers used to deliver your email can earn a reputation, good or bad, that helps mailbox providers, like Google's Gmail or Microsoft's Outlook, to decide which emails go to the spam folder and which ones go to the inbox.

One way mailbox providers do this is by authenticating that each email message is truly from the claimed sender, domain, server, and/or IP address and that there is some accountability from the sender when things go wrong. The industry has tried several ways to do this, and the ones that are most prevalent now, SPF, DKIM, and DMARC, are essential for email deliverability. While you may not implement these yourself, an OMCA must know the importance of each and ensure that they are implemented properly.

Sender Policy Framework (SPF)   SPF, or Sender Policy Framework, is an email-authentication technique that helps email senders specify which email servers (often specific IP addresses or domains) are permitted to send email on behalf of their domain. So, for example, if a domain like omcp.org, uses Sendgrid as a mail server, the SPF record would list Sendgrid's server name, sendgrid.net (or IP address), as a legitimate source for emails. Most email clients and mailbox providers will mark a message as suspect or spam if there is not an SPF record set. SPF is typically configured in the DNS (Domain Name Service) settings for your domain. If you don't have SPF configured for your email systems, your deliverability is likely to suffer.

DomainKeys Identified Mail (DKIM)   DKIM, DomainKeys Identified Mail, is an email authentication technology that uses an encryption key and digital signature to verify that an email message and sender address was not forged or altered. DKIM is typically configured by generating a public/private key pair and entering this information in the DNS settings for your domain.

Domain-Based Message Authentication (DMARK)   If only there was a way to set procedures and be notified when emails from our domain fail authentication and show the world that we care about our email reputation. Well, that would be DMARK. DMARK, Domain-based Message Authentication uses SPF and DKIM mechanisms to enable email senders to declare how they would like to handle emails that fail an authorization test. It also sends reports when those events occur. These data can help ensure that your recipients will only see emails that you have sent yourself. Proper use of DMARC improves email delivery and can prevent others from hurting your domain and brand reputation.

While the technical implementation may be done by someone else, a responsible email marketer will ensure these minimum three technologies are properly set up and tested before sending any email campaigns.

Warm Up New Servers

It is a generally accepted practice to warm up a new sending domain or server IP by gradually increasing the message volume. This can differentiate your campaigns from a fly-by-night spammer who burns through servers as fast as possible. Want to be sure you don't share a server address with such a spammer? Use an established, reputable ESP who doesn't tolerate such behaviors. When your ESP is strict on compliance, it's a good sign that they are reputable.

One way, of many, to warm up your servers is by sending some interactive, highly personalized emails to your most loyal group, preferably signed by you. Leave out the tracking pixel and the link tags for these initial emails because these are common signals of high-volume campaigns. The goal is to get replies or some interaction for the first batches. Ease into your volume by slowly increasing the list size. There are other ways to warm up the reputation of your domain and sending server. Talk to your email service provider for recommendations on what rates of volume increases are appropriate for your campaigns.

Compliance with Regulations

This section covers issues involving regulations. Even though they aren't always fun to follow and keep track of, they are important to the success of your email marketing campaigns.

How the History of Email and Spam Affects Your Campaigns Today

Some will roll their eyes in contempt of studying the history of email marketing. Do so at the peril of your campaigns and your company's bank balance. If that seems dramatic, you might look at some of the regulations that are now in place to curtail historical practices. When your outbound emails get caught in filters or end up in spam folders, knowing your history will help you to understand why. Knowing why will help you stay in the spirit of new laws and regulations. Also, knowing the bad practices will help you to avoid the appearance of evil in your email marketing processes.

The term *spam* in its earliest days referred to unwanted posts in news-groups but later grew to be almost entirely associated with unsolicited emails. When you are aware of how spammers work, you can avoid the appearance of evil in your own campaigns.

How Spammers and Bad Actors Work and How to Avoid Looking Like Them

Let's start with just a few examples of how spammers have shaped the practice, whether we like it or not.

- **Email harvesting:** This is a method of building email lists by deploying crawlers or bots that scan public or private content to extract email addresses.

- **Spoofing through open relays:** Essentially sending email under a sender domain or address that is unauthorized, falsified, or doesn't belong to the sender.

- **Subject content disagreement:** Sending an email with a misleading subject line to lure recipients into opening/reading the email.

- **Burning a domain to test a list:** A spammer will buy or use a temporary sending domain to send an email to a large list just to see which ones bounce, or who clicks, thus verifying the list without damage to the primary domain.

- **Using a single image for content:** A spammer will send a message with the content in a single image to circumvent filters for certain text words. Filters are now catching these, but you need to know that it was a spam technique.

A reputable marketer doesn't want to be associated with any of these, but some bad actors can spoil the reputation of the entire industry, and when the masses complain, elected officials listen and do their best to appease their constituents. Committee-built regulations often come with misapplied rules, but once established as law, we must protect our practice, company, clients, and reputation by staying in compliance with all parts of the regulations that apply.

Government Rules and Regulations

As a result of complaints from the masses, elected officials and industry associations have made efforts to enact regulations to control the abuse of email as a marketing channel. The resulting rules range from reasonable to ridiculous, from vague to concise, and they sometimes conflict with each other and even themselves. Nonetheless, marketers must know the rules and regulations for each region where their emails may be received and comply with those regulations to protect their company, campaigns, and brand reputation.

The teeth are sharp when a government chooses to enforce these regulations. Marketers outside the United States should note that for large offenses, U.S. courts have shown a willingness to bring foreign defendants within their jurisdiction.

In the 2008 case of *Facebook, Inc. v. Guerbuez,* U.S.-based Facebook successfully sued Montreal-based spammer Adam Guerbuez in a California court for contravening the provisions of CAN-SPAM and then successfully sought to enforce the $873 million judgment it was awarded in the United States in a Canadian court (in the province of Quebec). In her September 28, 2010, ruling, Quebec Judge Lucie Fournier ordered Guerbuez to pay $100 U.S. in damages and $100 U.S. in punitive damages for each of the 4,366,386 spam messages he sent to Facebook users in 2008. That's $873 million in fines at $200 per message, but violators of U.S. CAN-SPAM regulations can face up to $16,000 per message that is in violation. So for reputable marketers, the chances are currently low that a simple mistake in your campaign would result in a court order of that magnitude. Currently, the resources are in place to prosecute only the most egregious offenses. But why put your company or clients at risk at all? Know the regulations and comply with them. It's responsible marketing at minimum. Here are some overviews of the more prominent regulations.

United States The United States has the CAN-SPAM Act. This is called the Controlling the Assault of Non-Solicited Pornography and Marketing Act of 2003. The CAN-SPAM act covers commercial email messages where the primary purpose is advertising or promotion of a commercial product or service. It's not going to cover an email between you and your relatives or private emails. If you're trying to influence someone to engage for future business, your email falls into the category of commercial email.

Senders who violate the CAN-SPAM Act can face fines up to $16,000 per message that is in violation, and there have been prosecutions of guilty verdicts since the act went into place. So, marketers need to know the key areas for CAN-SPAM compliance.

Opt-In, Opt-Out Oddly enough, at the time of this writing, the CAN-SPAM Act doesn't require an opt-in. And it doesn't prohibit the sending of direct marketing email messages without permission *until* the recipient explicitly requests that they stop, usually via an opt-out. While it may not be a good practice to send unsolicited email, it is not specifically prohibited by the CAN-SPAM Act until somebody says "Stop," and the opt-out needs to be a service or an easy event for the recipient to opt-out of commercial email in the United States.

Unsubscribe or Opt-Out More explicitly, each email message must include opt-out instructions, and subscribers can't be required to pay to unsubscribe or to provide information other than their email address and opt-out preferences. Also, they can't be required to take any steps other than sending a reply email message or a visit to a single web page to opt out of receiving future email from a sender. In short, marketers must make it *easy*. You will only anger your recipients if you require a password to unsubscribe (that's one of my pet peeves). The sender must honor the opt-out request within 10 days.

Identity The CAN-SPAM Act covers identity rules as well. It prohibits falsifying information in the email header: your from, to, reply-to, and routing information, including the originating domain, the email address, have to be accurate and identify the person or business who initiated the message.

More Bad Practices Also prohibited are open relay abuses using multiple sending email addresses, address harvesting, dictionary attacks, and a number of other ways of sending spam where fraud is involved. I can't imagine any OMCP or OMCA using any of those, but what you do need to know is that the email subject line cannot mislead the recipient about the content or the subject matter of the message.

Subject Line Must Correlate Now this was largely enacted to stop porn purveyors from misleading recipients into looking at an innocent email that contained offensive images. But it applies to marketers across the board. So let's make an example. You could not use an email subject line that says, "Your child's insurance policy," and then try to sell vacation timeshares in the body of the message. Those two are clearly unrelated and should not be combined because it misleads a recipient into opening an email under false pretenses.

Identification Including a valid physical postal address in a commercial email is required in the United States under the CAN-SPAM regulations. It is acceptable to use a post office box address. Typically the physical addresses appear in the footer or at the end of the email so they don't distract from the primary message. If the address is in there and is readable, you're likely in compliance as far as including a physical postal address.

The United States also requires identification that the message is an advertisement or solicitation. Now, even the U.S. government admits that there are no set guidelines for this. So, for now, OMCP is monitoring this. It's not part of the exam or the standard until a generally accepted practice evolves.

Liability Also note that the *business* behind the email is liable for a lack of compliance by U.S. standards. So, even if there's an agency or a third-party sending out on behalf of the business behind the message, it does not absolve responsibility. In fact, both the company whose product or services are promoted in the email *as well as the company that actually sent the message* can be held legally responsible for violations under CAN-SPAM. That *is* important for you to know in order to protect your company and clients, and it is on the OMCP and OMCA exams.

Canada, the European Union, and Other Regional Regulations Now, let's look at Canada, the European Union, and other countries' regulations.

Canada has the CASL, the Canadian Anti-Spam Legislation. And some of Europe has the EU opt-in directive. The two differ from each other as to coverage on nonprofit, political, and charity messages, but both are largely inclusive of the U.S. regulations and then, and this is important, are *much, much stricter* than the U.S. regulations in obtaining explicit prior consent before sending commercial email to recipients.

The CASL and the EU opt-in directives prohibit sending any commercial email messages unless the recipients have given express prior consent. So where the U.S. CAN-SPAM is lax and you *can* send unsolicited email, when you're targeting areas covered by the EU opt-in directive, or addresses in Canada, you cannot.

Now, transactional email content must stick to the product or services that are part of the transaction, and the recipient must, again, give explicit permission to receive other types of email. So, for example, if a recipient bought your company's pretzel making machine, you can continue to send transactional emails about the pretzel making machine. But if you really want to send them something that sells a system to make spun cotton candy, well, then you would have to receive explicit permission to start sending them promotional emails about a different product.

When sending to addresses in Europe, senders need to state their company details on every electronic business communication sent from the organization, and it should include the full name of the company in its legal form, the place of registration of the company, the registration number, the address of the registered office, the VAT number, and a valid return address. So, again, the regulations are a little bit more strict when sending to those regions, and something marketers should know. Now, the commonalities and the safest route is to get explicit agreement from your audience to receive promotional or informational email. One of the safest routes to do this is what is called the double opt-in.

Double Opt-In: The Safest Route   A double opt-in typically consists of a second action on the part of email recipients confirming that they want to continue receiving the emails that promote your products or services.

So the sequence looks like this: Jeff fills out a form on your website to get a whitepaper. Jeff gets the whitepaper, but also gets an email that requests his confirmation that he wants to receive a monthly newsletter from your company. So to confirm, Jeff clicks a link in the confirmation email and his consent is recorded in your email systems. Jeff has supplied explicit confirmation.

Double opt-in, as we've just described here, aligns with the current email regulations that we are seeing in the United States, Canada, and the EU opt-in directives. The rules can change any time. The EU directive does not cover all European countries so, again, responsible marketers need to watch for changes in the regulations in countries where they are going to send email.

Other Regulations That Overlap with and Affect Email Marketing

Other regulations will certainly affect how you may collect, store, protect, delete, and use data in your marketing efforts. Consider and track India's Personal Data Protection (PDP), China's Consumer Rights Protection Law (CRPL), and the Measures for the Administration of Internet Email Services that govern email marketing in China. Individual states in the United States are enforcing regulations, such as the California Consumer Privacy Act (CCPA) as well as Virginia's HB 2307 Consumer Data Protection Act. These are representative of the laws being adopted around the country. If your emails could land in an inbox in these regions, you must know and comply with each of these regulations. At the time of writing, some countries don't yet have comprehensive regulations in place, but most are headed in that direction. The tough truth is that *it is your responsibility to stay up-to-date on the regulations and consumer privacy laws for the areas where you're sending your emails*. A marketing email professional will stay up to date by scanning for current laws and regulations for each target region. Your ESP can be a great place to start.

Common Denominator Practices

So let's bring it all together to look at the common denominator and practices that cover some of these regulations *and* are best practices for marketing.

- First, ensure prior explicit and verifiable permission from the recipient to receive your emails. This is an opt-in. Double opt-in is the minimum.
- Ensure a clear and accurate sender identity and use an accurate subject line.
- Provide clear and easy opt-out instructions and a physical postal address and required company details.
- Use a valid return and reply-to address.
- Test and ensure systems are in place to handle unsubscribes, replies, or any subscriber requests promptly.
- But most importantly, provide wanted, expected, relevant, and delightful messages to each recipient.

And that last one is a good guideline for marketing overall.

CHAPTER 10

Careers and Hiring

By Michael Stebbins

This chapter will answer the most common questions related to role requirements, getting hired in digital marketing, and how to leverage your OMCP or OMCA certification. By the end of this chapter, you will know the answers to these questions:

- Can my OMCP certification get me a job?
- Why don't I get a response from hiring companies when I'm clearly qualified?
- Why are job postings unrealistic?
- Should I apply if I don't meet all the qualifications?

This chapter also includes a section for hiring managers, which can be illuminating for candidates as well.

Can the OMCP Certification Get You a Job?

At a New York digital marketing conference, one of this book's other authors, Matt Bailey, was signing books in our booth. After waiting in the long line, a lady held up her book and asked Matt, "Will this make my website rank better?" Matt politely replied, "The book won't do anything on its own, but when you *apply what's in it*, your digital marketing is likely to improve."

A certification—like OMCA, OMCP, or PMP—quantifies hard skills, experience, education, and training. But in the end, "*You* get you the job." A reputable certification certainly helps you stand out from the crowd.

Note
Those who are willing to test and measure their skills are most often those who maintain and improve those skills.

When a hiring manager is aware of the requirements and reputation behind these certifications, candidates who have earned them can become preferred candidates over those who have not. So it benefits you to claim your industry certification, whether OMCA or OMCP, with a link back to your certification profile. There a hiring manager can confirm that you have earned an industry certification with verified skills, experience, education, and training.

Those who haven't yet heard of OMCP (a shrinking crowd) are usually impressed with the quality and requirements behind it as an industry standard. More than 1,000 colleges and training institutes teach to OMCP standards to enable careers worldwide. That's an impressive number in itself. And what matters even more to you is that a growing number of companies and managers prefer, or recently *require,* OMCP or OMCA certification within the company. Here are some quotes from just a few hiring managers related to OMCP:

"I see the resumes upfront and note if anyone has OMCP, then I ask for phone screens. . .in case someone doesn't have it on their resume."

—Senior Manager, Digital Marketing, Dell

"We found that OMCA and the organization at OMCP had the industry-leading guidance on how we should be certified in this space."

—Global Marketing Technologist Leader, P&G

"I look for OMCP certification to know that candidates are qualified to perform the level of online marketing necessary for our initiatives. . . .The certification, and the fact that they can take that away for a year in their resumes, is good for Home Depot and good for the industry. "

—Senior Manager SEO, Home Depot

"As a hiring manager who sees many resumes come across my desk, the OMCP certification is a great indicator of which ones to put at the top of the stack. Having been through the OMCP process myself, I can attest to the thorough and careful vetting process—earning the OMCP designation is the real deal."

—Director, Customer Experience Group, Yamaha

So you are wanted and in demand. But there is even better news. Our surveys repeatedly show that OMCP certified earn 16 percent to 20 percent more than noncertified. And 80 percent of those who initiate team certification programs within their organization are promoted to a higher position within one year.

That last one might be causation or correlation, but either way, we see that those who invest in their own knowledge and are willing to measure it tend to get the better results.

One recently certified OMCP author, expert, and agency owner, Tarek Riman, left advice for those following in his OMCP footsteps: "Yes, the certificate is important, but in digital marketing, there are no experts, there are learners. Digital marketing is about continuous learning and acquiring a patient learner mindset."

This is wise advice for those practicing digital marketing or aspiring to improve and quantify their skills

So yes, an OMCP certification increases your chances of placement, your salary prospects, and correlates well with the practice of continuous learning—which is essential to the practice of digital marketing. You are wanted. You are in demand. Now, let's ensure you increase your chances of the best role possible.

Approaching the Digital Marketing Job Market

A role in digital marketing is fun, creative, and rewarding; it pays well. But for some the prospect of landing a first job in digital marketing can be overwhelming. Some approach with inflated confidence, and others underestimate their own skills. Your OMCA or OMCP certification has quantified your hard skills, experience, education, and training, so it's time to look at the process and approach to connecting with hiring managers.

The purpose of this chapter is not to help you choose which digital marketing specialty you plan to pursue as a career. For that, enjoy each practice area chapter in this book, and you'll get a sense of the components of the practice. However, you should know that hiring managers overwhelmingly prefer those with strong hands-on skills in *at least two digital marketing disciplines and conceptual knowledge across five to eight practice areas.*

The demand for digital marketers is high. A scan of open jobs related to digital marketing consistently shows well over 250,000 open roles in any month. In the United States, the Department of Labor reports the median salary for promotions and marketing managers is $141,490 per year. Entry-level will be less; senior roles can be much more.

Which should you apply for? Well the quick answer is, "Apply for those where you can contribute the most, thrive, and be compensated fairly." But when addressing the overwhelming demand for your digital marketing skills, it can be difficult to decipher job descriptions. Many are not accurate, requirements can be overstated, and our resumes end up in the black hole of "no response." So what's going on and how can you optimize your chances of a good match? Read on.

Do You Really Need SQL?

From my experience, OMCPs are hired quickly. Very quickly. But one exception caught my attention last year. This OMCP was articulate, well educated, and had enough experience in one field to make a diagonal jump into digital analytics. In fact, this OMCP took initiative and volunteered to perform analytics reporting for a charity to further boost his analytics experience claims. I thought it was perfect.

But it wasn't.

The candidate called OMCP to let us know that SQL programming wasn't covered in the OMCP standard, yet it was on almost every job description for analytics roles. We took that very seriously. More than 4,000 managers tell us what they need candidates to know and show the priority of each practice. SQL wasn't on the analytics list. Yet, sure enough, we confirmed it was on many analytics job postings. When we polled our community and managers and asked, "Do you really require SQL?" the answer was stunning. "Not really. We just put it on the job description as a filter."

A filter?

So I asked, "Do you realize how many candidates you may be missing who *know* digital analytics but haven't learned SQL?" The responses were all over the map. Some removed from the job posting; some kept it. The point is that candidates cannot know for certain which job posting requirements are must-haves and which are filters (you'll learn more about why filters are there later in this chapter).

The same can apply to filtering on specific tools. On a recent online meetup with digital marketing agency owners, the conversation quickly went, as it often does, to the lack of hirable candidates. I asked, "How do you filter?" and most agreed that they post or filter for specific tool knowledge, e.g., SEMrush or Adobe Analytics, as these suggest that the candidate has experience in the practice.

The problem is that some candidates will back away from applying if they lack experience in those specific tools. Once again, employers miss out on good candidates by using an inaccurate filter. While this may sound dismal, it is intended to be enlightening to the candidate. When you have a picture of what's going on behind the job description, this can help you tune your message for each hiring manager.

Finding the Right Match

Reading job descriptions can be discouraging when the requirements seem unreasonable or even impossible. How do we decipher what the real requirements are? Here are two recommendations to increase your chances of finding a match.

- When you match roughly 80 percent of the hard skills listed on a job description, you are probably okay to apply. This can be disputed for as long as people have opinions, but it's a guideline to start with.
- Next, and even more important, it's time to get into the heads of the hiring managers.

If you're reading this, you are a marketer, or on your way to becoming one. So it's time to treat your career like a marketing campaign. To do that, we must understand our target market, which in this case includes hiring managers or potential clients. One way to understand our target market is to uncover the scenes, wants, and knowledge needed to persuade our prospects.

Answer these: What is the scene where a manager must hire for digital marketing talent? What do they really want? And what knowledge do they need to make a decision?

First let's immerse ourselves into a *scene* of a hiring manager. Here is a pretty common, albeit slightly dramatized example:

The hiring team is short on staff and full on deadlines, wading through internal hiring requirements and with little time to interview, let alone write a clear job description in one pass. Sometimes an "everything and the kitchen sink" job description goes out. Sometimes a template is all the human resources team will allow. The posting goes out on the job boards.

The hiring team is flooded with the initial wave of "spray and pray" resumes ranging from interior designers to senior managers in retail to those who studied some marketing in school.

The managers wanted to know, early in the process, if candidates are exaggerating a skill or underselling themselves. It's too hard to know with so many resumes coming in, so a meeting is held with the recruiting team.

Now the recruiters and/or the applicant tracking system (ATS) are instructed to reject any candidates who don't claim 5 years of experience or a prior title with specific keywords. Nonetheless, the team is still flooded with resumes, most unqualified. Another meeting is held and now the ATS is set to filter resumes by skill keywords. But this has problems as well. The recruiting team, or ATS, have been looking for "web analytics" experience and overlooked "digital analytics" experience. They also filtered for CRO but missed resumes that mentioned conversion rate optimization.

Nonetheless, some resumes get through the filters, and some interviews are set. After the first few interviews, the hiring team starts to get a picture of what talent is out there and what might work for the role that differs from the initial needs. So requirements change, but the posted job description doesn't get updated. Applicants are still seeing the old job description.

There is no time to interview everyone. A hiring decision is made on a hunch. It doesn't work out, and even more time is lost, as well as costs, and company reputation when the new hire is dismissed weeks into the role. Then managers must start all over again, with an even stronger bias against what caused the prior hire to fail.

Sometimes the hiring process isn't the well-oiled machine that the world imagines! How can the hiring team know, early in the process, if candidates are exaggerating a skill or underselling themselves? Some hiring managers resort to filtering on "years of experience," which they believe correlates with skills in the practice. Others filter based on tool names or phrases that suggest expertise in the practice. This isn't ideal or fair in all cases. In fact, I chuckle when I see required experience years exceeding the years the practice has been known to the industry! But the resumes that come through the "higher-experience" filter *do* tend to *correlate* with established skills. Knowing this can give you, the candidate, some edge in addressing the pain of the hiring team. For example, you may format your resume to indicate total years of marketing experience instead of role by role.

And yes, more and more managers are turning toward skills tests or proof of industry certifications to establish levels of hard skills *early* in the interview process. So if you've already earned your OMCA or OMCP, you're ahead of the game.

Now that we have a scene, let's establish the "wants."

To a marketer, complaints are more informative than compliments. To solve a problem, we look for pain or complaints and use the words of the customer to shape our product and message as well as the "knowledge" they need to make a decision. It's no different in marketing yourself for a job in digital marketing.

So how do we get those complaints? We could *survey* hiring managers, but managers aren't often accessible to candidates. And I can help here. It turns out that OMCP must survey and/or interview hiring managers in the digital marketing industry. Hundreds of them. And in my role at OMCP, I get to participate in this, interviewing hiring managers year round. Honestly, their answers are so consistent, I have to stop myself from silently mouthing the words as they say them. (My wife told me doing this is rude.)

And here they are. The top complaints of hiring managers, specifically in digital marketing are, roughly in order:

- Can't find qualified digital marketing candidates
- Candidates exaggerate skills
- Not a fit for the team
- Work habits lacking
- Invested in them and they left (Mayson 2019)

So with those complaints, let's list the most likely "wants" or "wants to avoid" of a hiring manager as it relates to deciding on whom to interview.

- Wants to avoid: Loss of time interviewing unqualified candidates
- Wants to avoid: Loss of reputation and time/resources when making a hiring mistake
- Wants to: Verify soft skills, work habits, or fit for team *after* hard skills are established

Can you think of others?

Now, let's establish what "knowledge" we as candidates need to provide to resolve the hiring team's "wants."

The hiring manager and recruiting team must know and, ideally, verify the qualifications of the candidate, as much as possible *ahead of time*. Why? Because person-to-person interview time is precious, and the limited amount available can only go to the top handful of qualified applicants. With that, we can predict that the hiring manager will value the following:

- Resumes or online profiles containing keywords for skills, tools, or certifications
- Resumes or online profiles containing position titles or minimum years of experience
- Personas who share domain knowledge under some amount of peer review

Are you starting to see a path here?

Now, let's shape our product and messaging to address these wants and, as much as we are able, provide the knowledge the hiring teams are most likely to need through the vehicles most likely to get you that interview.

Choosing Apt Words and Phrases in Your Resume, CV, or Profile

Like it or not, your resume (or CV) or online profile is often the front runner in establishing a likely match for busy employers. If you don't clear that hurdle, then it's unlikely that you'll win a person-to-person conversation.

Your goal is to portray your product (you, your online profile, and your resume!) accurately and in an easily accessible way. I don't condone keyword stuffing to game the system, but it is a good practice to select phrases that will most likely match what the hiring managers will be looking for and work these fluidly into your resume and cover letter.

Hints for this can come from the job postings and from the hiring manager's social streams. Scan past and recent job postings for phrases and words used to describe skills. If it is too difficult to pinpoint the hiring manager's name through online searches, pick the most likely three and search their posts on social streams like LinkedIn or Twitter to look for keyword usage in the context of the work they do. These are the most likely keywords to be used as filters. While you may specialize in digital analytics, the hiring team may use a tool name, "Adobe analytics," as an indicator of this skill. The hiring team may also use the phrase "web analytics" instead of "digital analytics." These are your hints.

If you see consistent trends, then it's time to work these keywords and phrases into your profile. The key here is to do it *fluidly* and not in eye-straining tiny fonts and long bulleted lists. Using the previous example, if the job posting lists "web analytics" as a required skill, then change at least one of your experience or skill statements to use "web analytics" instead of "digital analytics." So, for example, "At Mondelēz, I lead two initiatives to implement web analytics data collection that brought us into compliance with GDPR requirements."

Getting the Most from Your Work and Platform Experience

As mentioned, some hiring managers filter for qualified candidates using tool or platform names as a substitute for the related experience. So the presence of a phrase like "Google Ads" might signal experience in digital advertising while the keyword "HubSpot" might signify marketing automation.

To avoid long keyword lists, one method to improve your presentation is to roll popular platform names in with your narrative, "...increasing conversion by 23 percent deploying marketing automation through HubSpot." Or if the likely filter is Google Analytics, then you could list your Simplilearn course experience as "...completed 26 hours of accredited digital analytics training that covered Google Analytics and Data Studio reporting tools." See how that works? We're being accurate *and* are more likely to get our resume through the system.

If you are missing that experience, you may be able to volunteer for non-profits who use such platforms. Six months of managing email marketing to a charity can put the right words and platforms in your profile. And you're helping a charity.

Another technique to handle the experience filter is to format your resume to indicate total years of marketing experience instead of role by role. So instead of listing employment for each company, you could list, "Web analytics practitioner, three years, 2019–2022" to summarize your experience in web analytics across multiple projects or roles. Don't stretch the truth. Be sure that you can back up all claims.

Your goal is to be noticed for that search whether it's your resume or your online profile.

Does this suggest creating custom resumes for each role? Yes! Absolutely. Does this suggest changing your online profiles to match your top job application? Yes again. Some successful job seekers modify their LinkedIn profiles each week to match the most important application of the week. Your social platforms have other ways to support your search, and that's by sharing your knowledge no matter where you are in your learning experience.

Standing Out by Giving Back

Managers are learning that digital marketers who consistently share expertise under the bright lights of peer review are more likely to have the required skills. And I heartily agree.

This one piece of advice brings the most benefit, but also gets the most pushback from candidates. And understandably so. Fear of revealing ignorance, stage fright, struggling with writing, and other hesitations are common. But a career in digital marketing could be challenging without overcoming these very hesitations. You'll see in the soft skills section ahead that hiring managers are looking for persuasion skills, the ability to present, and the ability to write. What better way to showcase these essential skills than by sharing your expertise with others?

Sharing your expertise online, or in person, has several additional benefits:

- Sharing, in most forms, forces you to structure your processes and thoughts.
- Sharing invites constructive criticism from your colleagues and community.

- Sharing showcases your knowledge and helps hiring managers and clients find you and get an idea of your capabilities.
- Sharing can also create some "celebrity" effect, making you a preferred catch for a hiring team or client.

The venerable Bruce Clay sat opposite me at a memorable speaker's dinner after a digital marketing conference. We were taking a moment to look back at meaningful decisions in our careers. Bruce pointed out that very early in his career, he decided to share everything he learned—all his SEO expertise—no matter how "special" or "secret" the method was at the time. Bruce's practice grew into one of the most prominent digital marketing agencies in the industry and if you asked him, he'd tell you that sharing his expertise openly was a cornerstone of that growth. People hire who they learn from, who they understand.

"But I can't share anything authoritative yet," says the newly graduated. It may be true that you won't come out of the gate as the next Bill Slawski, but you can find a way to convey the basics that you have learned in a new and interesting way. Matt Bailey once taught basic web analytics concepts by mapping the process to patterns in *Star Trek* episodes. It was a hit. You can curate information and present it in a channel that others will value. Why not interview some of your fellow OMCP and OMCA certified and collate their wisdom? Ask questions in those interviews (live or in online forums) that tease out new insights valuable to others. Your role as a marketer will require this type of thinking, so for the astute hiring manager, these signs make you stand out from the crowd.

In the soft skills section ahead, you'll learn what else hiring managers are looking for, and hopefully start to see the connection between sharing your expertise and persuading others.

About Soft Skills and Work Habits

Here are the top requests for soft skills from hiring managers looking for digital marketing talent:

1. Ability to persuade
2. Ability to turn data into decisions
3. Writing skills
4. Traditional marketing skills
5. People skills
6. Ability to turn strategy into tactics

While digital marketing has transformed over the last decades, these requirements have remained consistent. Let's look at each one and make a plan for how to address each need.

Ability to Persuade, Ability to Write

We combine these two as they are close cousins.

There are several interpretations of what these requirements mean that depend on the role and the size of the organization. The smaller the organization, the greater the hours spent on persuading the target market. The larger the organization, the greater the ratio of hours spent persuading internal stakeholders.

One hiring manager at a leading consumer products company told me, "I look for candidates who dance, play music, or perform in their off hours. They are more likely to be able to present. I can trust that when I put them in front of an executive, they will be able to present well."

So managers and clients are looking for signs of your ability to persuade a target market, whether it's via advertising, media, press, affiliates, community management, written content, or the talent to recruit and manage those who do these jobs.

There are really only three channels commonly used to confirm these: an in-person interview, testimony to your prior work in these areas, or a cursory scan of your online presence.

To stand out here, there are four to-dos:

- **Clean up your online presence, profiles, and posts to showcase your persuasion abilities and your ability to write.** No need to change your profile to Shakespearian prose. If you write informally, then be consistent. It's up to you if you choose to keep or eliminate content that could offend the hiring manager or be at odds with the values of the organization. If they'd criticize or avoid you because of who you are, then you may not be comfortable in a role on that team. Conversely, there is a time and a place for everything. Even though in the United States it isn't proper for a hiring manager to scan what you intended for private use, most admit to looking anyway. If those videos of your drunken pool party are less important than attaining your new role, it could be time to mark those as private and keep public what enhances your personal brand.

- **For managers who haven't heard of you through your history of sharing and don't look at your online presence, your primary showcase of your ability to persuade will be your resume and cover letter.** Some managers prefer long-form passionate cover letters, and some value brevity. Either way, most guides will encourage you to use the cover letter to show your passion for the company and the role (which you researched, of course) and quantify relevant work habits and soft skills that are not already covered in the resume. Perhaps the hiring manager will look at your cover letter in the context of an internal briefing. Would it stand up to scrutiny as error free and fact rich? Would it persuade the executive team? If yes, then you can check this box.

- **Impeccable grammar will impress many managers.** Use a reputable tool and have someone check your writing.
- **When you do get an interview, prepare, prepare, prepare.** The hiring team will rightly want to verify that you have a history of persuading others as well as additional soft skills and work habits. Anticipate the types of questions covered in the next section. Though they may not ever come up, you'll be ready to steer the conversation toward highlighting your skills and habits.

Ability to Turn Data into Decisions, Strategy into Tactics

We combine these as they are both action related. When have you turned strategic initiatives into actionable steps? When have you taken a table of data and made decisions from it? It turns out that hiring managers want to verify that you have done this and are likely to do it well in your digital marketing role. Be prepared to steer the conversation to examples where you exhibited these habits or if the hiring manager asks, you'll have some stories to tell. Here are some example questions in each category.

Questions that can test your ability to turn data into decisions:

- Tell me about a time when you turned data into decisions.
- The AB test data is inconclusive, roughly 50/50. What do we do next?
- The majority of site visitors exit after searching for shipping options. What is the next action?
- Our survey data indicate that our prospects want a free demo, which is too expensive. What is the next step?

Questions that can test your ability to break strategies down into tactical actions:

- Tell us about a time when you created tactics from a strategy.
- Our strategy is to dominate the luxury market first and then move our name into the mass market. What content marketing models will achieve this?

- We will empower the community to spread the word about our products. What are the first three steps to curate and build that community?
- Our email campaigns will be the core of our conversations with our market. They should be inspiring, educational, and entertaining whether our prospects buy or not. What are the steps to build a list?

The chances you'll be asked these *exact* questions are very low. But a trial run through these will help bring to front-of-mind the answers and stories that are likely to align with the needs and wants of the hiring manager.

Traditional Marketing Skills

There is an iconic scene in the movie *Raiders of the Lost Ark*. Our hero, Indiana Jones, is stopped in a Cairo marketplace during a chase and confronted by what appears to be an expert swordsman. The swordsman laughs and brandishes his weapon to intimidate Indy who, so far, has been using hand-to-hand techniques. The crowd backs away, prepared for an epic sword fight. But Indy doesn't have time for this. He thinks for a moment and surprises everyone by simply using a gun to end the fight.

As digital marketers, we are not exempt from knowing basic marketing principles and concepts such as market definition, unique selling points, clear definitions of benefits to our audience, and when needed, magazine, catalog, print, outdoor, radio, direct mail, or event marketing. Much of what underpinned marketing in the 20th century still works today, and hiring managers will avoid those who don't know it.

Your takeaway? Know your Ogilvy and Godin. Study the marketing strategies of Steve Jobs, Walt Disney, Henry Ford, and John Brinkley. Does the hiring manager "like" or "follow" a well-known marketing author? How much can it hurt to study up on those marketing methods?

People Skills

If it isn't obvious so far, a digital marketer can rarely work in a vacuum. Technical SEOs must convey concepts and value to managers and colleagues. PPC managers must present results and earn support for new initiatives. Analytics specialists must extract business goals from busy managers and then convey meaningful reports that drive action.

It's not enough to be good at implementing your channel expertise. Your digital channels affect many stakeholders and service providers, and you must influence and persuade them all. Executives may not understand the channel or requirements or even the potential. To convey these effectively without hyperbole or drama can earn you a reputation and the relationships needed to make your digital channels effective.

Being right isn't enough. I once joined a marketing team at an EMC/ Dell division only to be aghast at the site load times, deletion of pages (with no redirect) that had thousands of valuable inbound links, landing pages without conversion tracking, and key content in PDF or uncrawlable forms. In my second week, the execs were asking why we weren't ranking number 1 already. When laying out these inhibitors along with paths to rectification, my strident tone caused some upheaval, and I unintentionally insulted a lot of people. I was right (of course!), but I wasn't getting the changes implemented. A wise middle manager took the challenge and coached me on how to come alongside the stakeholders better and help them move toward solutions. After experiencing this, it's even more impressive to see how other in-house digital marketers build relationships, friendships, and trust by knowing their audience and dispensing just enough information to help the team succeed as a whole.

If you have intrinsic "people skills," you'll know it if others naturally want to join you in projects, if your colleagues repeatedly include you in their decision-making process. Was this the case in your last job or school experience? If you don't know if you have people skills, then it's likely you'll need to do some practice runs, perhaps starting in your community or by volunteering to help a nonprofit organization or charity with their marketing. Some candidates will benefit from courses on "soft skills" or a reputable book covering these principles.

Preparing for Interview Questions About Soft Skills

Hiring managers have a tough time identifying and verifying soft skills and work habits. Unfortunately, some trust their gut, a hunch, or a feeling. Others will try to derive this from specific questions in the interview. The most common interview questions for verifying soft skills start with "Tell me about a time when you...." The interviewer is looking for stories that portray your situation, tactics, actions, and results related to the particular soft skill requirement. "Tell me about a time when you influenced others." The prepared candidate will have stories at hand. The best answers to these questions start with "There was this one time at _____ company...." The prepared candidate will not resort to generalist statements, such as the cringe worthy, "Influencing others is an important skill and I'm very good at it. Really I am."

If you, the candidate, after multiple tries, cannot come up with one story related to a required soft skill or habit, then it is much less likely that the interviewer will perceive that you have that skill. There are exceptions, and a well-trained interviewer will detect distress or simple memory lapses and come back to the question later in the interview.

In preparation for a live interview, scan the job description for hints on the soft skills the hiring team is looking for. The requirement to "multitask" can be translated into "the ability to prioritize." "Team player" can be translated into the need for persuasion skills. Make a list of up to five of the most prominent and jot down stories where you showed these skills. It may not come up at all, but you'll be ready to speak to the required skills whether asked or not.

About the Interview

The goal of an interview isn't always to get hired. Sometimes it's to dodge a bullet. I once interviewed at Genentech, and it was an incredible success. We decided not to work together.

There was a ton of love, affinity, and confirmation bias in the interview. We loved each other and didn't want the interview to end. The skills matched, but in an open and honest conversation, it became clear that in the long term, working together would not be a good match. We were both sad and thrilled that we discovered this. The perfect interview! Can you imagine discovering this 8 months later? Much better to move on and find a better match.

I once interviewed for a full day for a senior director role at a large company in Salt Lake City. I was in my mid-20s at the time. Once it was pretty clear that we had a match and all other candidates had gone home, I asked, "How many non-Mormons have been promoted to VP?" After a very long, thoughtful, and uncomfortable silence, the honest answer was, "None." We both knew it wasn't a match, sadly shook hands, and I flew home that night. Dodged a bullet.

That experience shaped my own processes as a hiring manager. I learned to ask candidates to share three things that would make them walk out of a role with an hour's notice. Why three? The first two are usually the same, related to abusive or unethical behavior. Those are a given. But the third is usually off the cuff, honest, and the most telling. "If the company keeps changing processes," or as one lady said, "The smell of food in the office." It so happened that my teams did both of these often, sometimes a few times a day. While not a show-stopper, these mismatches could support a case where the candidate may not be happy in the role in the long term.

By the way, I do follow up and ask, "What are three things that would make you want to stay forever, no matter what?" At this point, most marketers understand the intent, but the answers are more genuine. Of course we hear the expected ones related to pay, advancement, and work-life balance. But then the third and subsequent ones are again telling: "I'd like to know I am making a difference in people's lives," or "If I know the company is giving back to the community," or "If the team likes to hang out after work." All of these help predict whether we'll be happy working together. Or not.

Do not view the interviewer as an enemy or opponent. This will go a long way to ease anxiety and interview jitters. Your time together is to uncover skills and habits that predict that you'll both be happy. It's also to uncover what might make it miserable for you or the team. It's bi-directional. If the interviewer is condescending or creates a confrontational environment, it could be a sign that you won't enjoy working together. Bullet dodged! If you are lacking the skills or habits to be successful, then it is much better to figure it out quickly. Not all interviewers are skilled at this, but you can be. Go into your interview with questions that will uncover what the work environment will be like, that reveal what might make you unhappy.

Strident questions for stronger managers might include the following:

- Tell me about a time when you discovered that a staff member was lacking a needed skill. What did you do?
- By what criteria do you determine allocation of stock options to new employees?
- In this department, what are the most measured performance indicators and how do you celebrate achieving them?

Your questions for teammates or recruiters might be a bit different:

- What are three things you love about working for _____?
- Three things that are most challenging?
- Knowing what you know of my skills and habits, what causes the most concern?
- Knowing what you know of my skills and habits, can I count on your recommendation to hire?

Smart interviewers look for curiosity and welcome questions from candidates as a sign of intelligence. So, make your own list ahead of time. Your goal is to uncover the probability that you'll be happy in this role in the long term. What are the chances you'll end up where you want to be, doing what you enjoy, in an environment that you thrive in?

I'll acknowledge there is some idealism here to make the point. There may not be dozens of jobs beyond the one you are interviewing for. And sometimes a partial match is better than none at all for either or both parties. Not all interviews are ideal enough to extract the facts. You may not have an opportunity to ask your questions. Both candidates and interviewing managers make mistakes. But you are now prepared, and this exercise underscores the bi-directional nature of the interview. This isn't a trial where you are sentenced to the outcome. You can approach your interview as a bi-directional discovery process where a no-hire or a hire decision are considered a success.

Maintaining Your Skills

Few professionals involved in digital marketing training or talent development will dispute this: those who constantly invest in improving their skills consistently get the better jobs, better clients, and experience more success in the industry. It's a mindset and it can be practiced and learned. We see bestselling authors, agency owners, keynote speakers, marketing professors, and marketing leaders taking digital marketing courses and many test with OMCP every year. I used to call them to ask why. Now I don't bother because the answer is the same: digital marketing is a moving target, so we don't become complacent and we keep on learning. Stay fresh, review, teach, and grow.

So to maintain your skills and career, here are some essentials:

- Sign up for accredited courses.
- Attend the most reputable conferences.
- Fill out applications to speak at conferences, and if approved, attend all the other sessions that you can possibly fit in.
- Create relationships with fellow marketers and share your expertise generously.

Do this as many times a year as you can fit in to see your career thrive. Ask your employers for a budget and help them create a list of approved courses and conferences. You can also borrow the list of approved courses and conferences from OMCP at `omcp.org`. The most successful teams allocate $2,000 U.S. to skills development every year per employee. It becomes an employment perk, and it benefits you and the team.

At this point the following section is specifically for hiring managers. Candidates may benefit from reading it too. This could be how your next interview is conducted.

For Hiring Managers

Hardly a week goes by where I don't hear the same complaints over and over from hiring managers. Earlier I shared these complaints to help candidates shape their own presentation and improve the interview process. But this section is specifically to help hiring managers in finding and scaling talent for your digital marketing team.

Just as this chapter is being written, an email came from an experienced manager with the following, *"Our dominant problem is getting qualified applicants into the pipeline. The general consensus in agency recruiting right now is that everyone is hiring and not many candidates are looking. Those that do apply exaggerate their skills or just don't respond after the interviews."*

Common. And not ideal.

So to be sure we are addressing the complaints across the industry, let's review the top five complaints from surveying more than 4,000 hiring managers in digital marketing.

Top Five Complaints from Hiring Managers

1. Can't find qualified digital marketing candidates
2. Candidates exaggerate skills
3. Not a fit for the team
4. Work habits lacking
5. Invested in them and they left (Mayson 2019)

A perfect summary is the phrase, "The talent pool is too shallow." And when we look at the interview process, the job description, and the recruiting efforts, it sheds some light on that perfect description, "shallow."

Over the last decade I've had the privilege of working with dozens of the world's leading marketing teams, large and small, agency or in-house, to set competencies and requirements to increase talent. It's a unique perspective, and like that famous insurance commercial, "I've seen a thing or two." So in this section, I'll share ways to develop the most qualified talent when you can hire, ways to scale your team's performance when you can't hire, and what worked (and didn't work) for teams working to deepen the talent pool.

Developing Deeper Talent Pools

A deeper talent pool means that you have digital marketing talent available when you need it. Some less experienced managers assume this is only on the hiring side. But it turns out that there are three core elements that consistently underpin the scaling of a talented digital marketing team. We will call them:

Team Performance Candidate Qualification Finding Talent

You might ask, "Aren't those backward?" Well, yes, they appear to be at first, and we *will* get to the hiring side in upcoming pages. But for now, it turns out that one piece of information, one *answer*, is key to support all three elements: finding talent, qualification, and scaling performance. All three are substantively dependent on your answer to a simple question:

How well can you define and measure what your team DOES?

Quick. You're on an elevator, and someone asks you: What is it that your digital marketing team does and how do you know if it is successful? What's your answer? Can you say it out loud right now in a few sentences?

If we know what our outcomes are, we know what to measure. If we know what to measure, we all know that what gets measured, gets done. And this applies to marketing campaigns as well as scaling the talent of our team. Let's start with what to measure.

Knowing What to Measure: Using a Job Description

More than half the managers I work with turn to a job description when quantifying what a particular role must do. Is this you? When you first started thinking about scaling the team, you probably centered your attention on a job description. So that's a baseline. I've seen some great job descriptions. I've also seen some that repel qualified candidates.

But a job description is *not* an ideal way to define and measure what a role needs to do. The primary purpose of a job description is to open the funnel on the incoming end, and address the number-1 complaint from hiring managers—not enough applicants. Indeed, just because we are flooded with applicants doesn't mean we have the time to interview them all. So just ahead, I'll show you one way to filter by hard skills automatically and then validate the soft skills of the few qualified candidates in the interview process.

So now that the primary purpose of our job description is to open the funnel on the incoming end and to make the position and company as attractive as possible, I suggest you leave out the requirements for soft skills as well as company-specific requirements. Get rid of generic fillers like "the ability to multitask." Do you really care if someone can multitask as long as they get the job done? Can you imagine a candidate being more attracted to your role and company if your job description requires the ability to communicate, multitask, or be a team player? Yet how many applicants will balk at some of these statements, either out of insecurity or by interpreting them as subtle ways to say, "expect to work long hours with constantly changing priorities." There is little to gain and much to lose. So keep your job descriptions simple, remove the fillers, and list only the minimum hard-skill requirements.

It's a revealing exercise to pull up your go-to job description and circle each *measurable* requirement. Is this the whole picture? What is "fluff" or filler? What needs to be added, or removed? And a very telling test: What are you doing to develop and measure these skills in your *existing* people?

Knowing What to Measure: Use a Role Competency Document

One step above using an old job description is a *competency document* that can be used to know what to measure, whether in hiring, interviewing, training, testing, employee reviews, promotions, or in writing a job description that reflects what your ideal candidate really needs to know and do. A competency document is a hierarchical outline that codifies what skills are required to do the work your team needs to produce.

Need to filter those masses of incoming candidates? Your competency document is the basis for doing this efficiently and without bias. Whether through up-front testing or as a guide for your recruiters, you save the in-person interviews for the candidates who have *proven* themselves to have the hard skills you need.

Let that sink in for a moment. Managers are learning to use one template guide that is the basis for hiring, interviewing, training, testing, employee reviews, promotions, or in writing a job description that reflects what your ideal candidate really needs to know and do. Do it once, and all of those become much easier.

It's worth it. It pays back in spades.

I've helped countless teams do this, and I'll show you a few shortcuts to doing it yourself and how this can improve your scaling and hiring in all three phases.

So what goes in a competency doc?

A competency document starts with a list of practice areas where your marketing team performs. I recommend bulleting out between 6 and 16 practice areas. A practice area can be a short answer to "In this role, you must perform or manage _____." So what level of practice areas go on the document? Well, OMCP must create these as part of the digital marketing standard. So from OMCP, here's an example for digital advertising:

- Advertising Strategy, Communication of Practice
- Advertising Keyword Research
- PPC Account Structure
- PPC Bid Management
- PPC Keyword Match Types
- Text Ads for Paid Search
- Video Ads
- Display (Graphic & Banner) Channel Ads

- Programmatic and Media Channel Ads
- Shopping and Product Listing Ads
- Landing Page Definition
- Ad Serving and Scheduling
- Quality Score for PPC
- Targeting and Audience Definition
- Digital Advertising Testing and Reporting

Your list will likely be different. If you end up with more than 16, trim it down a bit.

Here's how to validate and trim your practice area list: start with a larger list (like the previous one) and then have your team distribute a set number of hours in a typical work cycle across your areas of practice. A work cycle is the time it takes until all practices are performed at least once. Most use a workweek. Some use a month or a quarter. This doesn't have to be complex or precise. We often host a shared spreadsheet and ask each team member to distribute a set number of hours across the practice areas. You'll notice a long tail fairly quickly for practice areas that aren't taking that much time. Remove those. Keep the top 10 or 12 practice areas with the highest amount of applied hours. We will use these distributions of hours later to prioritize testing and interview time for candidates.

Focusing on Common Practice Areas and Competencies
Many teams I work with believe that they have a secret recipe for helping clients or generating demand. This is good! But some portion of the practice of digital marketing is common. We don't want to test incoming candidates for knowledge of your special recipe! So focus your competencies on generally accepted practices. What is a generally accepted practice? Here's a test: if three out of five outside specialists, author experts, or repeat conference speakers would agree on these practices, you probably have a generally accepted practice (OMCP requires 7 of 10!). If you suspect a practice area won't pass that test, it's better to leave it out of the competency doc. You can always teach your secret recipes to your hired staff *after* they join the team.

Completing Your Competency Document
For each practice area, define the *actions* that a person in that role must take to achieve success. These are "primary competencies," and it's a good practice to start each one with an action (identify, describe, perform, structure, build), or even better, to use Bloom's Taxonomy verbs that match the level of the role, as shown in Figure 10.1.

The next indent, the "First Detail" is a list of possibilities. Usually only a subset of the list of first details, e.g., 4 of 10 listed, is actually used in training,

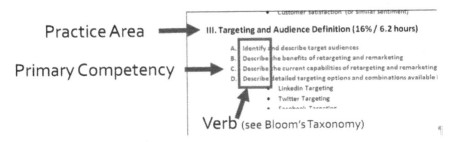

FIGURE 10.1 Using Bloom's Taxonomy Verbs to Match Roles

performance reviews, interviewing, or testing. Lastly, we set ratios to know where to put priority. Ratios can be established by polling existing staff to allocate hours to each practice in a given work cycle.

Note

Your final competency document will be a hierarchical outline listing competencies and details under each practice.

Primary competencies are perfect to establish training and reviews. The first detail level is great for writing skills tests.

In the excerpt in Figure 10.2, we expand two of the digital advertising practice areas to include primary competencies with a first detail list.

Now we have a document that can guide the requirements for each phase of the team and talent scaling process.

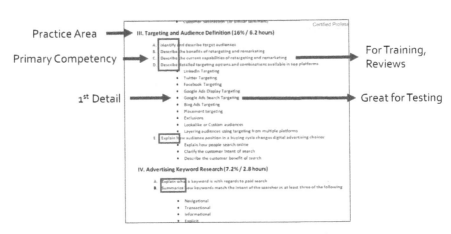

FIGURE 10.2 Two Digital Advertising Practice Areas Expanded

Now we know what to measure. Let's apply it to scaling the teams with this process:

- *Test* for what's missing.
- *Train* to weaknesses.
  - Use the competency guide to make in-house training or vet accredited programs.
- *Annual* readiness testing (e.g., Facebook Blueprint, OMCA, Google Ads).
- *Celebrate* certifications and completions.

Leveling Up the Existing Team

Would you like to retain a highly skilled team? One way to do that *and* be a hero to your digital marketing staff is to grant each one a budget for training or certification every year. Budgets vary, but in the early 2020s, I see $2,000 per employee per year as a midpoint that correlates with high-performance teams. Make sure you create a list of accredited training, conference workshops, and industry certifications. If you want a shortcut, you can borrow the accredited training provider list from OMCP and also look at OMCP's Professional Development Unit list for conferences that have been evaluated by your peers. Or make your own from scratch. Either way, it proves that you care about your employee development and the return comes back multifold from the performance of your team.

I'm biased about this since I serve on the OMCP standards body and a number of you do as well. Employees might value a certificate of completion from your internal "XYZ Agency" course. But covering the cost of an industry certification that will be valued in their next role shows that you care about their career and life success, not just your team's success.

Using Your Competency Document to Guide Training

It is a crime against your team to require everyone to slog through the same training. Treat your staff like adults and let the experts test out. The key is to level up, not to lose hours of your best people to train for what they already know. So create your test from your competency guide, or use an industry exam that shows areas of strength. Train to weaknesses. If a team member can't pass an industry standard test, then any related training is bound to be more appreciated and applied. Celebrate certifications. You'll find your team leveled up faster than others who just assign training.

Now your competency document can be used to make your own in-house training *or* to vet training programs. Rather than burning time evaluating 20 training vendors, here's a secret: send the training vendors your competency doc and hire only the ones who prove that they teach to your competencies.

It's like magic. It becomes obvious very quickly who will fall short and who is not teaching to your standards. They do all the work because you know exactly what you want. If you do your own in-house training, your competency document can be the starter for your slide deck.

Testing for Skills   Of course you can use OMCP and OMCA exams to test for skills, but if you do it on your own, here are some of the criteria that OMCP uses to build exam items from the master OMCP competency guides.

- Present items in ratio of your practice areas, e.g., 7 percent keyword research.
- Use only generally accepted practices/competencies.
- Never use platform-specific details (it's okay to say "such as" for leading platforms).
- Larger teams compare individual results to team's average (or industry averages like those from OMCP).
- Each item maps to published works.

Lastly, make testing a regular event. The most successful teams celebrate annual readiness testing companywide. I've also seen it work on a per-employee cycle, but the group annual testing gets more internal publicity for larger organizations when the C-level execs celebrate milestones and achievements.

Cross-Training for High-Demand Periods   Special teams can help fill in gaps when demand increases faster than you can hire. For example, cross-training your Google ad specialists in programmatic is a great investment. Train your Facebook ad specialists in landing page and conversion AB testing. Sure, some can leave with the new talent, but most stick around because you are investing in *their* careers and talent.

Bias Can Cost You 15 Percent to 35 Percent in Performance   If you had interviewed with me 10 years ago at one of my companies, there's a much higher chance you'd be hired if you showed interest in vintage motorcycles. This can be called an "affinity" bias or a "halo" bias. Now that I'm *aware* of the bias, this won't work quite as well (so don't tweet that), but do tweet that your interview biases (and you do have them) can correlate with 35 percent lower performance than teams that reduce bias and build highly diverse teams. This is data from the McKinsey 2015 report entitled "Diversity Matters: 15–35 percent performance (EBIT, revenue and ROE) correlations with team gender diversity and ethnic diversity."

Don't think your interview process has bias? Freeform interviews and "gut" decisions trend toward bias. Profiling by name, location, school, or even speech patterns can contribute to bias.

Blind	Chat	Audio	Visual
Hard Skill Testing		Soft Skills & Work Behaviors	
Cert confirmations		Assign Qs to interviewers	

FIGURE 10.3   Structuring Interviews for Performance and Lack of Bias

Note

Structured interviews reduce bias, and by proxy, increase performance.

The antidote is structured interviews. To create a structured interview process and save considerable time for your managers and staff, managers can verify hard skills in advance, and gradually increase live time based on those who progress through the steps. See Figure 10.3.

The best practice: verify hard skills through blind testing or by proof of industry certification. Instead of resume Bingo, you will only invest interview time with candidates who have proven hard skills. It is very hard to "exaggerate skills" when taking a proctored industry exam!

> True story: For research, I've been known to go through some interview processes myself. I once applied to a company who wisely did testing up front. The exam rules stated, "No calculator, no assistance." Well of course I used both. The next morning, the recruiter gave a cheery welcome and announced that I'd be taking the same test, proctored by her right then and there. I was caught; and not only did the hiring company see my true hard skills, they could also derive how likely it was that I cheated on the first exam.

I don't recommend this exact process for testing your candidates! But it illustrates the point that high-stakes exams can filter candidates *before* a hiring manager invests the time to interview. Also, online proctored exams are becoming easier and less expensive every year. Do be careful to respect the time of the candidates. There is a fine balance between demanding too much up-front time from candidates and filtering for those essential skills. A well-written exam, vetted with item P-values and item discrimination analysis, can do this much more quickly than an exam that lacks these verifications.

Note

High-stakes exams can filter candidates *before* a hiring manager invests the time to interview.

You now know how to write your own exam. If you'd rather not do that, you can purchase OMCP and OMCA exams to test candidates and staff. In all cases, be up front about the time investment for candidates. "This interview will require a 20-minute exam to verify digital marketing hard skills *or* proof of existing OMCA or OMCP certification."

Using Live Interview Time on Soft Skills and Behaviors   Live
interview time is expensive. It also introduces many opportunities for bias, whether intended or not. Some teams are experimenting with initial anonymous "chat" interviews to reduce the chance for gender bias, age bias, or cultural bias based on speech patterns.

The final step is to determine soft skills, work habits, and behaviors through live interviews. I recommend distributing a list of required attributes among many interviewers—e.g., the ability to make decisions from data or the ability to persuade others. Here we can determine fit for the team without any one interviewer skewing the process with a "hunch" or unintended bias.

Until we see reliable technology for verifying soft skills, work habits, and behaviors, most managers still default to, "Tell me about a time when. . ." questions. The interviewer notes that if the candidate cannot recite a specific story where the hopeful attributes were in place, then it is less likely that the candidate possesses these attributes. Managers can research further by looking up "behavior-based interviewing" or by learning systems that supersede it.

Overlooked Sources of Talent   Managers often complain that there
is too much competition for hiring digital marketing talent. Here are seven nontraditional sources to scaling your team that less-experienced hiring managers might miss:

- **Level up your existing team.** Cross train. Your internal talent pool can be developed and verified by using the methods set out in this chapter. Invest in who you have, and your reputation as a great place to work is more likely to spread.

- **Recruit from known educators.** Some of the most successful hiring managers I have interviewed have built a close relationship with professors and program directors at local colleges and reputable training institutes. Share your competency document with them. They'll appreciate the perspective of teaching what you need to hire. The symbiotic relationship casts your company in the best light, while the school benefits from good placements in the industry. Win-win and it can start by treating your local professors to lunch.

- **Incentivize your employees to repost your job postings.** Reports suggest that when employees promote open jobs, it can generate between 3 times to 8 times more engagement (Edelman 2014) and extend your reach beyond standard postings. Beyond a referral program, reward visibility earlier in the funnel. Offer gift cards or other rewards to employees for post view thresholds. For example, $500 to the first two job post shares that get either 100 reported views, 10 likes, or 5 reposts.

- **Mine association member lists, certification directories.** Oftentimes industry associations will allow members to create online profiles or will publish lists of participants. Lists that suggest that members are investing in their own skills or are helping others to learn are pre-filtered lists for recruiting. For example, steal from OMCP by doing a site search from Google to scan **Linkedin.com** for all profiles with OMCP in them.

- **Recruit from new conference speakers at reputable digital marketing conferences.** Conferences that have thrived have done so because of the management's ability to vet speakers. You can borrow this filtering by having someone on your team harvest the newest speaker names from each conference. Chances are that if a first-time speaker took the time to pitch a talk and made it through the gauntlet, this could be the hard-skill and soft-skill match that you've been looking for.

- **Recruit from unlikely majors.** When John Marshall and I were building ClickTracks, our local university did not have a strong marketing program. Yet, we had interest from students to come join our web analytics team. We learned to recruit reliably from the economics department for marketing talent and from the genetics department for digital analytics. We also learned that sales reps tended to make great PPC and digital advertising specialists (with some minimal training).

- **Pay a well-known speaker/author/influencer to teach an evening session on one of the primary practices you need to hire for.** This last one is my favorite. Recruit from the attendees. For example, host Cindy Krum to speak on mobile marketing when you need to recruit mobile marketing talent. See if you can get Kim Krause Berg to teach conversion optimization in your Boston location. The attendee list is your richest source of talent who are investing in improving their own knowledge.

Scaling and Staying Together

Retaining and developing internal talent is less expensive than hiring new talent, with very few exceptions. One manager commented last week that salaries are skyrocketing so fast that he must increase incumbent salaries when hiring new talent for just short of *double* last year's salaries.

Note

Dollar for hour, your investments in your *existing* teams will bring the most reward for all involved.

Yes, you can pay to develop skills and then see some employees leave, but the benefits are proven to outweigh the costs. Only short-sighted managers teach internal processes and are perceived to fear employee defection. Strategic managers empower the employee to develop transferable career strength.

Which do you think an employee will value more: an internal certificate of completion of XYZ methods course signed by you, or an internationally recognized industry certification valued by many employers?

Here are just a few best practices I've seen after helping hundreds of teams improve digital marketing talent:

- *Pick approved courses and certifications in advance and send out the list.* Those who teach to your competency document are a great start. In fact, it saves you hours of evaluation time when you simply send your competency document to a training firm and let them do the work to prove to you that they teach to your standards. Either award a training budget for expense reimbursement program to each employee for approved courses, purchase access for the team, or even better, use gated entitlement (see next).

- *Create a group goal that is celebrated at the highest levels.* For example, the CEO will publicly congratulate the first 10 who attain OMCP certification by name. This broadcasts to the company and the outside world that you invest in your employees. It sets a goal for internal staff to achieve the same level.

- *Treat your staff like adults.* Instead of forcing everyone through the same hours of courses, use a passing score on an exam as the goal. For example, those who can pass an industry standard OMCA exam get celebrated and get back to work, with the option to attempt an OMCP-level exam. Those who cannot pass the initial readiness testing will value the company-funded training even more as they work to earn an industry certification.

- *Use gated entitlement to save hours and costs.* With OMCP, the following processes consistently yield the best results. You might use these four steps for other standards, training, and certifications:
  - Evangelize the program 1 month in advance or more, with C-level support.
  - Everyone starts with the same readiness assessment (in this example, the OMCA practice assessment), due in 2 weeks, celebrating completion.
  - Training access is available to those who score 69 percent or less, and certification exam vouchers are awarded to those who score 70 percent or higher.
  - Celebrate those who earn certification (OMCA in this case) and offer them support for advanced training or higher level certification, e.g., OMCP.

- *Friendly competition* among teams for progress through training, tests or final certification yields great results. "Lunch and learns" where staff discuss the training or techniques for passing the exams build unity. We've seen bonuses to staff who create short how-to videos to help others follow.

These are examples, but the overall spirit of investment in your team's skills goes beyond performance and retention. It helps you scale for far less than it costs to recruit and hire new talent.

Need to scale momentarily? Your cross-trained employees can stand in if needed. Some managers tap former employees to fill temporary workloads. How can they do that? By investing in people and relationships.

At Market Motive, I regularly invited our interns into my conference rooms when I spoke with my attorneys about patents or with my co-founders about budgets. Where else will they get this type of education? It cost me little but helped them with their career paths. When we could not pay our developers what the Silicon Valley giants were paying, we'd help them navigate to the best new job possible.

Do the same. Invest in your employees' lives by funding personal development that empowers them to move beyond their current role, whether it's with you or not. It's personally rewarding and business wise; it pays back multifold. Your reputation as an employer will improve. Your relationship with local educators will be stellar and attract better talent. Former employees will remember you well, and send business, talent, and help when you need it. Your own talent pool will grow because your loyal staff will perform better, bringing in new methods and skills that increase your overall performance.

Digital Marketing Glossary

The following terminology is frequently used within digital marketing. To create a successful digital marketing presence and ongoing strategy, knowledge of these common terms is imperative. Terms are listed within their marketing discipline and then alphabetically within those sections.

Digital Marketing Strategy

Brand Equity: The importance of a brand in the customer's eyes.

Brand Value: The financial significance the brand carries.

Business to Business (B2B): Describes businesses working with other businesses for profit. A commercial transaction takes place between them.

Business to Consumer (B2C): Describes businesses working with consumers for profit. A commercial transaction takes place between them.

Buyer, Customer, or User Personas: Semi-fictional representations of your different types of audiences. They are created based on data and research, which helps you to create content that is more meaningful to your target audience.

Buying Cycle and Journey: An experience your target audience goes through to purchase a product or service. This is the point of view of your audience.

Cascading Style Sheets (CSS): A computer programming language for adding style to web documents. CSS can include fonts, colors, structure, spacing, and page behavior.

Channel: A marketing medium of distribution, such as pay-per-click and email marketing.

Customer Experience: The totality of cognitive, affective, sensory, and behavioral consumer responses during all stages of the consumption process, including the pre-purchase, consumption, and post-purchase stages.

Customer Insight: An interpretation of trends in human behaviors that aims to increase the effectiveness of a product or service for the consumer as well as increase sales for the financial benefit of those provisioning the product or service.

Customer Relationship Management (CRM): The ability to manage and analyze the interactions with past, current, and potential customers by using software or online platforms.

Data and Measurement: Can show how people experience a brand across platforms and can help marketers gain a better understanding of the performance of each channel in their marketing mix.

Distribution: The process of making a product or service available for the consumer or business user who needs it. This can be done directly by the producer or service provider or using indirect channels with distributors or intermediaries.

Friction: Anything that impedes your target audience from moving throughout the sales funnel and ultimately keeping them from making a purchase.

Funnel: Think of the funnel as an organizational process. It is based on the target audience's journey, illustrating the steps to take toward making a purchase. This is the point of view of the company and aligns to operations.

Hypertext Markup Language (HTML):   A markup computer language and one of the most basic forms of languages. It is assisted by other computer languages, such as Cascading Style Sheets (CSS) and JavaScript (one type of scripting language).

Integrated Marketing Communications: A planning process designed to assure that all brand contacts received by a customer or prospect for a product, service, or organization are relevant to that person and consistent over time.

JavaScript: A computer programming language used to make web pages interactive. It gives web pages interactive elements that engage a user.

Landing Page: A page used to capture leads or sales for specific promotional initiatives. The standalone web page is designed specifically for a campaign in mind.

Lead: When a user shows interest by conducting a defined action, such as filling out a form to receive a content offer, that user then becomes a lead.

Lead Nurturing: A way of developing a relationship with acquired leads through marketing initiatives. This can be done through a scoring system within a CRM.

Market or Customer Orientation: A marketing approach that puts the needs of the market or customer over the needs of the business.

Marketing Strategy: A plan of action designed to promote and sell a product or service.

Platform: A tool used to engage with your target audience to achieve specific marketing goals.

Positioning: The process of promoting a brand so that it occupies a unique place in the minds of customers. This also distinguishes the brand from the products of competitors. Positioning is different from the concept of brand awareness.

Segmentation: The process of dividing your target audience into homogeneous subgroups based on certain criteria, such as purchase history and demographics.

Small to Medium Business (SMB): A business with fewer than 100 employees is considered small, and a business with more than 100 but fewer than 1,000 is considered medium.

Targeting: The process choosing the segments of customers to pursue with digital marketing and advertising campaigns.

Digital Analytics

A/B Testing: Also known as split testing, this is a process of comparing two versions of either web pages, emails, ads, and so on. The testing measures the difference in performance between the two versions.

Behavioral: Reveals the actions users take within a digital product by organizing events taken and analyzing the user's journey.

Bounce Rate: The percentage of website users who leave rather than continuing to view other pages of the website.

Call to Action (CTA): A term for any type of desired action on a marketing deliverable, such as "Learn More" or "Add to Cart." It most often refers to words or phrases to get a target audience to act.

Click-Through Rate: Measured by the number of clicks received compared to the number of people who saw the content.

Conversion: A sale or desired action you want a user to take.

Conversion Rate: Calculated by totaling the number of conversions and dividing them by the number of visitors.

Cost per Conversion: Also called cost per action, shows how much it costs to acquire a conversion.

Dashboard: A reporting tool that displays different types of metrics and possibly key performance indicators, depending on the software used.

Data Collection: The process of gathering and then measuring data about a specific variable in an established computer system. It enables you to answer questions and evaluate outcomes.

Data Sampling: A technique used to manipulate and analyze subsets of data points while identifying patterns in larger data sets.

Demographic: A particular group within the population.

Dimensions: Typically, an attribute of the user of your website or mobile app. In most modern practice, they appear in rows in your web analytics tools or spreadsheets. Commonly used dimensions are user attributes, like source (referring websites, campaigns, countries, and so on) and technical elements (browser, mobile phone, screen resolution, and so on). Dimensions also include attributes of a user's behavior, such as landing pages, internal site searches, and product purchases; they are key building blocks of digital analytics segments.

Engagement: Refers to the way users interact with your content. This can look like shares and comments on social media posts.

Events: User interactions within Google Analytics to measure data around your content, which can be independently measured.

Exit Page: The last page the user is on before leaving the website, ending the sessions.

Frequency: Part of a marketing analysis tool used to identify the best customers. It is based on how "frequent" a customer makes a purchase.

Goals: In Google Analytics, you can measure specific actions by creating goals, such as clicks to call or email, order confirmations, and more.

Hit: Common interactions within Google Analytics, such as page tracking, event tracking, and ecommerce tracking.

Key Performance Indicator (KPI):   A metric that helps you understand how you are doing against your objectives. These indicators are directly aligned to business goals, telling you how successfully your tactics are performing based on what is ultimately necessary for the organization.

Metrics: The numbers and cold, hard data that measure a marketing initiative. In most modern practice, it appears in columns in your web analytics tools or spreadsheets. A metric can be a Count (a total), or a Ratio (a division of one number by another). Examples of Count metrics include Visits, Time on Site, and Page views. Examples of Ratio metrics include Bounce Rate, Conversion Rate, and Task Completion Rate.

Monetary Value: Part of a marketing analysis tool used to identify the best customers. It is based on how much "money" a customer spends.

Open Rate: The percentage of subscribers who open a specific email out of your total number of subscribers.

Page View: When a user visits a web page on your website.

Profit: The amount of income that remains after expenses, debts, and operational costs have been accounted for within the organization.

Psychographic: Tracks consumer shopping and online habits, showing advertisers where to allocate more resources.

Recency: Part of a marketing analysis tool used to identify the best customers. It is based on how "recent" a customer made a purchase.

Relevance: A score that serves as a barometer around your messaging, deciding if it appeals to your target audience. The measurement consists of a combination of variables, including the way a user moves from search to a website.

Return on Investment (ROI):   The ratio between net profit and cost of investment. It is often used to evaluate the performance of a marketing investment.

Revenue: The amount of income generated by a business or activity.

Segments: Subsets of your analytics data, such as users from a particular demographic. A segment contains a group of rows from one or more dimensions. Examples of segments include, but are not limited to, users from New York, users who visit more than three times, visits to the support content on the site, orders with more than five items, and so on.

Sessions: The amount of interactions by one user on your website, which happens at a particular time.

Unique Visitors: This metric generally refers to an approximation of the number of people visiting the website, measured using a persistent first-party cookie. In some modern digital analytics tools, the term *users* is used to refer to unique visitors. Users are best reported as trends.

Digital Advertising

Ad Extensions: To expand your ad, you can create extensions to provide more information about your business.

Ad Groups: Several ads within a group that are triggered by keywords.

Bids: The maximum amount of money you are willing to pay for a click on an ad.

Campaigns: It is where you can organize categories of products or services within a campaign. This is also where you determine your budget and bidding strategy.

Click Fraud: Fraud within pay-per-click in which owners of websites are paid money every time a visitor clicks on the ad.

Description: Your text ad consists of description fields where you can enter a limited number of characters, each to highlight details about your product or service. The description lines allow for deeper explanations than headlines, so you can go into detail as to why someone should choose your website over your competitors.

Destination URL: The final website address. This should be the landing page for your ads.

Display Network: A way to reach users on websites or YouTube with advertisements.

Display URL: The web page address that appears with your ad. Display URLs give people an idea of where they'll arrive after they click an ad. The landing page that you define with a final URL tends to be more specific.

Google Ads: An online advertising platform developed by Google where advertisers bid to display brief advertisements, service offerings, product listings, or videos to web users. It can place ads in the results of search engines like Google Search as well as on non-search websites, mobile apps, and videos.

Headline: A group of words or sentences that promote a product or service, typically emphasizing a product's primary purpose or benefit to a consumer. An effective ad headline draws in attention, summarizes the most prominent benefit of your product or service, and uses engaging words that appeal to the intended reader. Most digital advertising platforms limit the characters used in an ad headline. For example, Google Ads limits headline text to three lines of 30 characters each, so advertisers must be concise, craft headlines carefully, and test for the most effective headlines. Generally accepted practices for digital advertising headlines include use of search keywords your prospects are likely to use, and/or the addition of a "call to action"—the action you want your prospects to take.

Landing Page: The first page someone sees on your website after clicking on your ad. The landing page should contain information about your keywords and any specials or offers included in the ads.

Pay per Click (PPC): An Internet advertising model used to drive traffic to websites, in which an advertiser pays a publisher when the ad is clicked.

Programmatic: The process of automating the buying and selling of ad inventory in real-time through an automated bidding system.

Quality Score: A variable used by PPC advertising platforms that influences the position and cost of PPC ads. Click-through rate and keyword alignment are generally accepted to be most influential in the Quality Score calculation for major PPC platforms, such as Google Ads and Microsoft Ads.

Search Network: A group of search-related websites and apps where your ads can appear. For example, when you advertise on the Google Search Network, your ad can show near search results on Google Play, the Shopping tab, Google Images, Google Maps, and the Maps app when someone searches with terms related to one of your keywords.

Search Engine Optimization

Algorithm: A set of rules the search engine follows to understand the content. It then ranks the content according to value and relevance.

Anchor Text: The visible words that links display on a web page.

Canonical URL: The URL of the best representative page from a group of duplicate pages, according to Google. For example, if you have two URLs for the same page (such as `example.com?dress=1234` and `example.com/dresses/1234`), Google chooses one as canonical. Similarly, if you have multiple pages that are nearly identical, Google can group them (for example, pages that differ only by the sorting or filtering of the contents, such as by price or item color) and choose one as canonical. Google can only index the canonical URL from a set of duplicate pages.

Crawl: Search engines send automated programs called crawlers to determine what pages exist on the web.

Inbound Links: Links from other websites that point to your website.

Index: A large database where information is stored on a page after it is crawled and a search engine analyzes the text, images, and video files.

Keyword: Ideas or topics that define your content in the search.

Link: Referencing another web address on a web page.

Long-Tail Keyword: Keywords that are more specific and less common. They tend to focus more on a niche area.

Off-Page Optimization: The process of obtaining links. Refers to the activities done away from your website.

On-Page Optimization: The process of adding content, keywords, tags, and so on, to the individual pages of your website.

Outbound Links: Links on your website that point to another website.

Penalty: A deliberate action taken by a search engine to demote a previously higher ranking page or groups of pages on a website based on violating terms of service or published best practice. These deliberate actions can be algorithmic or manual in nature.

Permalink: A permanent, static hyperlink to a particular web page or entry in a blog.

Ranking: The position where your web page appears in the search engine's results.

Responsive Design: When the content of your website fits into several screen sizes and is made for mobile, tablet, and desktop.

Robots.txt: A text file that tells search engine robots which pages on your website to crawl.

Search Engine Optimization (SEO): The process of affecting the visibility of online content, a website, or web page in a search engine's natural or unpaid search results. It is essential to send optimized signals to search engines, enabling them to match relevant content with search queries, thus attracting qualified visitors to the best content. Practices include keyword research, web design and architecture, on-page optimization, link building, local search strategies, tracking and analysis, planning and project management, and staying current with search engine updates.

Search Engine Results Page (SERP): The pages that search engines show in response to a user's search query.

Short-Tail Keyword: Search phrases with only one or two words. They tend to be more general.

Sitemap: A blueprint of your website. It helps search engines and users understand the available content.

Snippet: A single search result in a set of search results consisting of a title, URL, description, and so on.

Structured Data: It is also called *schema markup*. This is the code that makes it easier to explain what content to crawl, organize, and display.

XML Sitemap: While acting as a blueprint for search engines, this is a list of your website's URLs, explaining what to crawl and index. These sitemaps are written specifically for search engines.

Content Marketing

Authority: The establishment of thought leadership within a specific field or industry by using content.

Content: More than just copy on a marketing deliverable, it is information provided to your target audience through a specific medium, such as images and video.

Content Curation: The process of gathering information relevant to a specific area and then adding value or analyzing what has been collected.

Content Frequency: How often new content is published on a blog or in social media. Understanding when and how often your audience will likely be active is key in determining the optimal frequency for posting content.

Content Management System (CMS): A computer system used to manage the creation and modification of content. Basically, it is computer software that allows multiple contributors to create, edit, and publish.

Content Marketing: This is a strategic marketing approach focused on creating and distributing valuable, relevant, and consistent content to attract and retain a clearly defined audience—and, ultimately, to drive profitable customer action.

Content Relevancy: This is all about your audience's perception of your content's pertinence to topics, issues, needs, or interests.

Content Usefulness: This refers to your content's ability to help users make decisions or make progress toward goals.

Content Value: Content can add value to viewers, listeners, or readers by enabling them to do something (tactical value) or to think something (strategic value).

Editorial Calendar: It can also be called an editorial calendar. It is a schedule for when you plan to publish upcoming content, such as promotional activity, existing content, and so on.

Evergreen Content: Content that never goes out of date and will always be valuable to the user.

Inbound Marketing: A technique that attracts current and potential customers through the use of content.

Multi-Channel Attribution: A set of rules that allow marketers to allocate appropriate values to each marketing channel based on its contribution to conversions or sales.

Whitepaper: A report or guide that informs readers concisely about a complex issue and presents the issuing body's philosophy on the matter. It is meant to help readers understand an issue, solve a problem, or make a decision.

Social Media Marketing

Affinity Segments: An ad targeting method for reaching people who already have a strong interest in relevant topics (e.g., "sports fans" on YouTube).

Amplification Rate: Indicates how many times on average each of your posts was shared/retweeted (Amplification rate = # of shares/ # of posts).

Applause Rate: Indicates how many likes each of your posts has received on average (Applause rate = # of likes/ # of posts).

Blogging: The process of creating and adding optimized and informative long-form content to your website.

Brand Lift: A measurement of the direct impact your social video ads are having on consumer perceptions and behaviors. A brand lift study can show marketers how their ads impact lifts in brand awareness, ad recall, consideration, favorability, and purchase intent.

Chatbot: A software application used to conduct an online chat conversation via text or text-to-speech, in lieu of providing direct contact with a live human agent.

Check-In Services: The process of checking into your physical location on social media.

Conversation Rate: Indicates how many Comments/Replies on average each of your posts has received (Conversation rate = # of comments/ # of posts).

Custom Audiences: An ad targeting option for finding your existing audiences among people across Meta's platforms.

Economic Value: Shows how much economic value each visit from a social network brings to your site by completing your site's goals. (Economic value = Per session goal value, which is calculated by Google Analytics when you assign a monetary amount to each completed activity, called a *conversion*, that contributes to the success of your business.)

Hashtag: A way of tagging in social media. Some users include hashtags for fun, and others include them as part of a campaign. It is a short, memorable way to get a message across.

Influencer: A person who has the ability to influence the decisions of their followers in a distinct niche or on a specific topic because of their authority, knowledge, position, or relationship with their audience.

In-Market Segments: An ad targeting option for reaching customers who are researching products and actively considering buying a service or product like those you offer.

Macro-Influencer: A person who has 40,000 to 1 million followers on a social platform.

Mega-Influencer: A person with more than 1 million followers on at least one social platform.

Microblogging: Typically short-form content and can be done through posting.

Micro-Influencer: A person who has 1,000 to 40,000 followers on a single social platform.

Monitoring: Involves tracking social media company mentions and responding to them.

Nano-Influencer: A person who has fewer than 1,000 followers.

Photo Sharing: The process of adding a photo to a social media post.

Publishing: Posting relevant and engaging content on social media.

Reach: The total number of people who see your post content.

Reputation Management: Influencing users to think a certain way or have a certain view on your company through the use of social media.

Reviews: The process in which you obtain reviews on particular social media channels.

Sentiment: The attitude and feelings users have about your company on social media.

Social Media: These are interactive digital channels that facilitate the creation and sharing of information, ideas, interests, and other forms of expression through virtual communities and networks.

Social Media Marketing: This is the use of social media platforms to market a business's products or services, connect with existing customers, reach new audiences, and build their brand.

Social Networking: Interacting with users through other websites or applications.

Video Sharing: The process of adding a video to a social media post.

Conversion Optimization

A/B Testing: Comparing two versions of the same web page to find which one performs better.

Multivariate Testing: Test that measures the conversion performance of variations of multiple elements of web pages. Multivariate tests provide a greater number of variable combinations than A/B tests and can test the impact of different fonts, colors, content, calls to action, buttons, and so on. This type of test reveals which elements have an impact on user engagement and can help optimize individual elements of a web page.

Persuasion Principles: Evolving from Robert Cialdini's six principles of persuasion, these heuristics enable marketers to harness the cognitive biases that shape consumer shopping behavior and influence why customers choose one product over another.

Usability Testing: Determining if users can complete the tasks that your website is meant to accomplish.

Mobile Marketing

Android: A mobile operating system based on open-source software, designed primarily for touchscreen mobile devices such as smartphones and tablets. Apps for Android are promoted by Google and Microsoft to run on a wide range of devices and platforms.

App Store: An online platform where users can purchase or download applications (apps). Examples include the Apple App Store and the Google Play Store.

Geofencing: A way to engage consumers based on a well-defined or "hyper-local" location as detected by a global positioning system or radio frequency identification. For example, a business can text a coupon or discount offer when an opted-in customer enters a defined geographical area.

Geotargeting: Also called hyper-local targeting on mobile devices, this is a type of targeting that uses a global positioning system, WiFi networks, and other location data to serve ads to prospective customers within a defined geolocation. Marketers can specifically target audiences who are in a certain city, district, postal code, or even a specific street.

In-App Messaging: A way to engage customers in the moment, while they are using your mobile application. For example, users can receive relevant offers, support messages, or invitations based on behavior in your application.

In-App Purchasing: The buying of goods and services from inside an application on a mobile device, such as a smartphone or tablet. Some application providers provide free applications in hopes to get paid afterward through in-app purchases.

iOS: A mobile operating system created and developed by Apple exclusively for its hardware, particularly iPhones and iPads.

Mobile App: A type of application, software, or service designed to run on a mobile device, which can be a smartphone or tablet.

Mobile Marketing: According to the MMA, mobile marketing is described as "a set of practices that enables organizations to communicate and engage with their audience in an interactive and relevant manner through any mobile device or network."

Progressive Web Apps (PWAs): These appear to users as mobile apps, but are really enhanced websites that can do many things a native mobile app can do, such as operate offline, send push notifications, access a mobile device's microphone or camera, and use GPS location. Using a PWA can circumvent some of the expenses and time investment required to develop and register an app with an app store.

Software Development Kit (SDK): A set of tools that can help build compliant, portable, and reliable mobile applications. For example, Apple offers an SDK for taking advantage of features built into iPhones.

Email Marketing

Auto-Responder: A program that sends emails based on a trigger or in response to a recipient's action. For example, an auto-responder can be configured to send a welcome email when a recipient subscribes to a newsletter.

Bounced Emails: An email message that gets rejected by a mail server and has not reached the intended recipient. Bounces can be either "hard" or "soft." Hard bounces typically correlate with an invalid or unavailable address. Soft bounces can be related to temporary conditions such as full mailboxes or servers offline.

Call to Action (CTA): A message or component in marketing that prompts the recipient to take an action. Examples include buttons and links (Click Here for a Free Package, Add to Cart, and Next Page, for example), audible instructions, or other visual prompts.

Double Opt-In: A second action on the part of the email recipient confirming the desire to continue receiving the emails that promote your products or services.

Drip Campaign: A campaign that uses an established time or trigger-based event to send emails as well as the rules that govern the sending of those messages. For example, a drip campaign might be configured to send three messages describing product benefits while the fourth message is a call to purchase.

Email Blacklist: A list of IP addresses or domains that are suspected of sending spam or sending to harvested (or poisoned) lists. Some blacklists are publicly searchable and some are kept private by mail service providers.

Email Click Rate: The ratio of sent emails that are reported to have received a "click" from the recipient, typically on a link, button, or a call to action.

Email Deliverability: A measurement of how many sent messages are delivered into the recipient's inbox. Often, it is a ratio or percentage of emails delivered versus those that bounce or are labeled as spam for a particular campaign.

Email Footer: A component at the lowest part of a message that typically contains the sender's identifying information, other options for contact or interaction (e.g., phone, address, and social links), and an unsubscribe option.

Email Harvesting: A method of building email lists by deploying crawlers or bots that scan public or private content to extract email addresses.

Email Open Rate: The percentage of sent emails that are reported to have been opened (and assumed read) by intended recipients.

Email Service Provider (ESP): A company that provides bulk sending, email formatting, or list management. Examples include MailChimp and Constant Contact.

Email Throttling: The process of limiting how many emails are sent in a given time frame.

Marketing Automation: This includes tools and processes that help track, trigger, and coordinate messaging based on your recipient's actions, including website behavior, clicks in email, or updates in your sales team's CRM system. Examples include Hubspot, Salesforce Pardot, and Adobe Marketo.

Opt-In: A purposeful action on the part of the potential recipient that confirms the desire to receive emails that promote your products or services.

Opt-Out (or Unsubscribe): A request to remove an email address from a list or campaign. The term *unsubscribe* can also refer to the option or link in an email content that offers that option to the recipient.

Spam: An unsolicited and unwanted email, usually sent out in bulk. Typically, spam is sent for commercial purposes. It can be sent by unscrupulous marketers, botnets, or by networks of infected computers.

U.S. CAN-SPAM Act: A law passed in 2003 in the United States that regulates certain practices in email marketing to control the levels of unwanted emails sent by marketers. The acronym stands for Controlling the Assault of Non-Solicited Pornography And Marketing Act.

Whitelisting: The process that a recipient (or their mailbox provider) takes to ensure that messages from a specific sender appear in the inbox (or as priority).

References

Chapter 1

Content Marketing Institute and Marketing. (2021). *B2B Content marketing benchmarks, budgets, and trends for 2022* [online]. Available from: **https://contentmarketinginstitute.com/wp-content/uploads/2021/10/B2B_2022_Research.pdf**.

Content Marketing Institute and Marketing. (2022). B2C content marketing: benchmarks, budgets, and trends—insights for 2022 [online]. Available from: **https://contentmarketinginstitute.com/wp-content/uploads/2022/01/b2c-2022-research-r3-1.pdf**.

Friedlein, F. (2017). *Introducing the Modern Marketing Model (M3)* [online]. Econsultancy. Available from: **https://econsultancy.com/introducing-the-modern-marketing-model-m3/**.

Jarboe, G. (2019). *Kraft Heinz: Isn't anyone going to help that poor brand?* [online]. Search Engine Journal. Available from: **https://www.searchenginejournal.com/kraft-heinz-trouble/315513/**.

Jarboe, G. (2021a). *Customer personas can transform SEO, PPC and content marketing* [online]. Search Engine Journal. Available from: **https://www.searchenginejournal.com/customer-personas-seo-ppc-content-marketing/397592/**.

Jarboe, G. (2021b). *Nostalgia marketing & what we can learn from John Lewis ads* [online]. Search Engine Journal. Available from: **https://www.searchenginejournal.com/nostalgia-marketing-examples/429066/**.

Kaushik, A. (2013). *Digital marketing and analytics: Two ladders for magnificent success* [online]. Occam's Razor. Available from: **https://www.kaushik.net/avinash/digital-marketing-analytics-ladder-step-by-step-success/**.

Ogilvy, D. (1985). *Ogilvy on advertising*. New York: Vintage Books.

OMCP. (2019). *OMCP digital marketing role delineation study* [online]. Available from: **https://omcp.org/2019-omcp-digital-marketing-role-delineation-survey-is-live/** [accessed 26 August 2022].

Chapter 2

Stephens-Davidowitz, S. (2017). *Everybody lies*. New York: Dey Street.

Chapter 4

Stephens-Davidowitz, S. (2017). Everybody Lies. New York: Dey Street.

Chapter 5

BuzzSumo. (n.d.). *400,000 article analyzed: Here's what we learned about content engagement* [online]. Available from: **https://buzzsumo.com/resources/creating-engaging-content/view/#section-method**. [Accessed 26 Aug. 2022].

Content Marketing Institute, MarketingProfs, and On24. (2022). *B2B content marketing* [PDF]. Available from: **https://contentmarketinginstitute.com/wp-content/uploads/2021/10/B2B_2022_Research.pdf**.

Gartner. (n.d.). *The B2B buying journey* [online]. Available from: **https://www.gartner.com/en/sales/insights/b2b-buying-journey**. [Accessed 26 Aug. 2022].

Hensler, V. (2020). *Consumer intent is better than demographic data for video ads* [online]. Think with Google. Available from: **https://www.thinkwithgoogle.com/consumer-insights/consumer-trends/consumer-intent-video-data/**.

Jarboe, G. (2020). *Is a Super Bowl ad the equivalent of lighting money on fire?* [online] Search Engine Journal. Available from: **https://www.searchenginejournal.com/is-a-super-bowl-ad-the-equivalent-of-lighting-money-on-fire/348076/**.

Jefferson, M. (2021). *Inside the Grand Prix winning Direct Line campaign that delivered against all measures* [online]. Marketing Week. Available from: **https://www.marketingweek.com/inside-direct-line-campaign/**.

Johnson, A. and Jones, C. (2019). *Content relevance and usefulness: Why you need it and 4 ways to achieve it* [online]. Content Science Review. Available from: **https://review.content-science.com/content-relevance-and-usefulness-why-you-need-it-and-4-ways-to-achieve-it/**.

Lieb, R. (2011). *Content marketing: Think like a publisher—how to use content to market online and in social media*. Indianapolis, IN: Que Publishing.

Kaushik, A. (2015). *The three greatest survey questions ever* [online]. Occam's Razor. Available from: **https://www.kaushik.net/avinash/the-three-greatest-survey-questions-ever/**.

Kaushik, A. (2014). *Digital dashboards: Strategic & tactical: Best practices, tips, examples* [online]. Occam's Razor. Available from: **https://www.kaushik.net/avinash/digital-dashboards-strategic-tactical-best-practices-tips-examples/**.

Kawasaki, G. (2012). *Enchantment: The Art of changing hearts, minds, and actions*. New York: Portfolio Publishing.

LinkedIn. (n.d.). *The B2B effectiveness code* [online]. Available from: **https://business.linkedin.com/marketing-solutions/b2b-institute/the-b2b-effectiveness-code#:~:text=The%20B2B%20Institute%20at%20LinkedIn,best%20lead%20to%20those%20effects**. [Accessed 26 Aug. 2022].

McKinsey Quarterly. (2020). *The quickening* [online]. Available from: **https://www.mckinsey.com/business-functions/strategy-and-corporate-finance/our-insights/five-fifty-the-quickening**.

Nelson-Field, K. (2013). *Viral marketing: The science of sharing*. United Kingdom: Oxford Press.

Raymond, K. (2022). 7 steps to a more strategic editorial calendar. *CMI*, January 6. Available from: **https://contentmarketinginstitute.com/2022/01/strategic-editorial-calendar/**.

Sullivan, D. (2019). *What site owners should know about Google's core updates* [online]. Available from: **https://developers.google.com/search/blog/2019/08/core-updates**.

Think with Google. (n.d.). *What the world watched in a day* [online]. Available from: **https://www.thinkwithgoogle.com/feature/youtube-video-data-watching-habits/**. [Accessed 26 Aug. 2022].

Chapter 6

Duggan, B. (2021). *Media KPIs that matter* [online]. ANA. Available at: **https://www.ana.net/blogs/show/id/mm-blog-2021-05-media-kpis-that-matter**.

Fishkin, R. (2022). *SparkToro & Followerwonk joint Twitter analysis: 19.42% of active accounts are fake or spam* [online]. SparkToro. Available at: **https://sparktoro.com/blog/sparktoro-followerwonk-joint-twitter-analysis-19-42-of-active-accounts-are-fake-or-spam/** [Accessed 26 Aug. 2022].

Geyser, W. (2021). Social Media Marketing Benchmark Report 2022 [online]. Influencer Marketing Hub. Available at: **https://influencermarketinghub.com/social-media-marketing-benchmark-report/**.

Geyser, W. (2022). *The state of influencer marketing 2022: Benchmark report* [online]. Influencer Marketing Hub. Available at: **https://influencermarketinghub.com/influencer-marketing-benchmark-report/**.

Heath, A. (2022). *How Facebook plans to become more like TikTok* [online]. The Verge. Available at: **https://www.theverge.com/2022/6/15/23168887/facebook-discovery-engine-redesign-tiktok**.

Institute for Public Relations. (2022). *2022 IPR Disinformation in Society Report* [online]. Available at: **https://instituteforpr.org/2022-disinformation-report/** [Accessed 26 Aug. 2022].

Jarboe, G. (2021). *How to calculate the ROI of influencer marketing campaigns* [online]. Search Engine Journal. Available at: **https://www.searchenginejournal.com/influencer-marketing-roi/416945/** [Accessed 26 Aug. 2022].

Jarboe, G. (2022). *A guide to social media algorithms & how they work* [online]. Search Engine Journal. Available at: **https://www.searchenginejournal.com/social-media-algorithms/453220/** [Accessed 26 Aug. 2022].

Kaushik, A. (2011). Best social media metrics: Conversation, amplification, applause, economic value [online]. Occam's Razor. Available at: **https://www.kaushik.net/avinash/best-social-media-metrics-conversation-amplification-applause-economic-value/**.

Kaushik, A. (2017). Stop all social media activity (organic): Solve for a profitable reality [online]. Occam's Razor. Available at: **https://www.kaushik.net/avinash/stop-organic-social-media-marketing-solve-for-profit/** [Accessed 26 Aug. 2022].

LinkedIn News. (n.d.). *What's in your LinkedIn feed: People You know, talking about things you care about* [online]. Available at: **https://news.linkedin.com/2019/January/what-s-in-your-linkedin-feed--people-you-know--talking-about-thi**.

Mizener, J. (2022). *[Podcast] Defining social media, part 1. channels, platforms, & changing rules* [online]. SiteLogic Marketing. Available at: **https://www.sitelogicmarketing.com/podcast-defining-social-media/** [Accessed 26 Aug. 2022].

Mosseri, A. (2021). *Shedding more light on how Instagram works* [online]. about.instagram.com. Available at: **https://about.instagram.com/blog/announcements/shedding-more-light-on-how-instagram-works**.

Puzzanghera J. (2022). *The world economic outlook turns grim as 'once in a lifetime' shocks take their toll* [online]. BostonGlobe.com. Available at: **https://www.bostonglobe.com/2022/06/18/nation/world-economic-outlook-turns-grim-once-lifetime-shocks-take-their-toll/** [Accessed 26 Aug. 2022].

Think with Google. (n.d.). *The car-buying process: One consumer's 900+ digital interactions* [online]. Available at: **https://www.thinkwithgoogle.com/consumer-insights/consumer-trends/consumer-car-buying-process-reveals-auto-marketing-opportunities/**.

Scott, D.M. (2009). *US Air Force web posting response assessment* [online]. **www.davidmeermanscott.com**. Available at: **https://www.davidmeermanscott.com/blog/2009/01/us-air-force-web-posting-response-assessment.html** [Accessed 26 Aug. 2022].

Stelzner, M. (2022). *2022 Social Media Marketing Industry Report* [online]. Social Media Examiner. Available at: **https://www.socialmediaexaminer.com/social-media-marketing-industry-report-2022/**.

Southern, M.G. (2022). *Facebook to restructure main feed around video content* [online]. Search Engine Journal. Available at: **https://www.searchenginejournal.com/facebook-to-restructure-main-feed-around-video-content/454480/** [Accessed 26 Aug. 2022].

TikTok. (2019). *How TikTok recommends videos #ForYou* [online]. Available at: **https://newsroom.tiktok.com/en-us/how-tiktok-recommends-videos-for-you**.

We Are Social Singapore. (2022). *Digital 2022: Another year of bumper growth* [online]. Available at: **https://wearesocial.com/sg/blog/2022/01/digital-2022-another-year-of-bumper-growth/**.

Chapter 7

Ash, T., Gindy M. and Page R. (2012). *Landing page optimization*, 2nd ed. Indianapolis, IN: John Wiley & Sons.

Berg, K.K. (2022). *Optimize your CTA: Better alternatives to "click here"* [online]. Search Engine Journal. Available from: **https://www.searchenginejournal.com/optimize-cta-click-here-better-alternatives/298591/**.

Renyard, A. (2021). *3 reasons why your marketing needs Unbounce's new smart builder* [online]. Available from: **https://unbounce.com/marketing-ai/smart-builder-launch/**.

Chapter 8

Agility Ads. (n.d.). *Start with where* [online]. Available at: **https://agilityads.com/agility-geo/** [Accessed 26 Aug. 2022].

Blancaflor, S. (n.d.). This is how Gen Z & Millennials' Social media use has changed in 2021 [online]. YPulse. Available at: **http://www.ypulse.com/article/2021/12/21/this-is-how-gen-z-millennials-social-media-use-has-changed-in-2021/** [Accessed 26 Aug. 2022].

Ericsson. (2020). *Mobile data traffic forecast—Mobility report* [online]. Available at: **https://www.ericsson.com/en/reports-and-papers/mobility-report/data-forecasts/mobile-traffic-forecast**.

Firebase. (n.d.). *Firebase app indexing* [online]. Available at: **https://firebase.google.com/docs/app-indexing** [Accessed 26 Aug. 2022].

Flynn, J. (n.d.). *Gen Z may be challenge for video streaming services* [online]. The Marketing Insider. Available at: **http://www.mediapost.com/publications/article/363472/gen-z-may-be-challenge-for-video-streaming-service.html** [Accessed 26 Aug. 2022].

Google. (2022a). Introducing Checks: simplifying privacy for app developers [online]. Available at: **https://blog.google/technology/area-120/checks/** [Accessed 26 Aug. 2022].

Google. (2022b). Introducing the privacy sandbox on Android [online]. Available at: **https://blog.google/products/android/introducing-privacy-sandbox-android/**.

Google Support. (n.d.a). *About video ad formats* [online]. Available at: **https://support.google.com/google-ads/answer/2375464?hl=en**.

Google Support. (n.d.b). About cohorts [online]. Available at: **https://support.google.com/analytics/answer/6158745?hl=en** [Accessed 26 Aug. 2022].

Google Support. (2020). Impressions: Definition [online]. Available at: **https://support.google.com/google-ads/answer/6320?hl=en**.

Insider Intelligence. (n.d.). *Mobile advertising is still king, but more industries are looking at nonmobile* [online]. Available at: **https://www.emarketer.com/content/mobile-advertising-still-king-more-industries-looking-nonmobile-thanks-ctv** [Accessed 26 Aug. 2022].

Intel. (n.d.). *Comparing 5G vs. Wi-Fi 6* [online]. Available at: **https://www.intel.com/content/www/us/en/wireless-network/5g-technology/5g-vs-wifi.html**.

Just Ask Thales US. (2018). *Generations of mobile networks: Explained* [online]. Available at: **https://justaskthales.com/us/generations-mobile-networks-explained/**.

Kwakyi, G. (2019). What is a mobile measurement partner (MMP)? Incipia Miniseries [online]. Incipia. Available at: **https://incipia.co/post/app-marketing/what-is-a-mobile-measurement-partner-mmp** [Accessed 26 Aug. 2022].

Levy, A. (2016). *Should you create device-specific PPC campaigns?* [online] Search Engine Land. Available at: **https://searchengineland.com/create-device-specific-ppc-campaigns-264902** [Accessed 26 Aug. 2022].

Oberlo. (2022). *US Mobile Advertising Growth (2019–2024)* [online]. Available at: **https://www.oberlo.com/statistics/mobile-advertising-growth** [Accessed 26 Aug. 2022].

O'Dea, S. (2019). *Mobile OS market share 2019* [online]. Statista. Available at: **https://www.statista.com/statistics/272698/global-market-share-held-by-mobile-operating-systems-since-2009/**.

Official GMI Blog. (2022). *YouTube statistics 2022 [Users by country + demographics]* [online]. Available at: **http://www.globalmediainsight.com/blog/youtube-users-statistics/#mobile** [Accessed 26 Aug. 2022].

PCSteps. (2017). *What is the difference between E, 3G, H+, and the 4G Mobile Network?* [online]. Available at: **https://www.pcsteps.com/10751-mobile-internet-e-3g-h-plus-4g-mobile-network/** [Accessed 26 Aug. 2022].

Saravia, A. (2020). *What's the difference between internet speeds? GPRS, EDGE, 2G, 3G, 4G & 5G [online]*. Ufinet. Available at: **https://www.ufinet.com/whats-the-difference-between-internet-speeds** [Accessed 26 Aug. 2022].

SimpleTexting. (n.d.). *Text Message Laws—Rules and Regulations for SMS* [online]. Available at: **https://simpletexting.com/in-depth-guide/sms-compliance-guide/text-message-laws-the-groups-who-make-them/**.

Statista. (n.d.). *Topic: Mobile internet usage worldwide* [online]. Available at: **https://www.statista.com/topics/779/mobile-internet/#dossierKeyfigures**.

Telecompetito. (n.d.). *Wi-Fi vs. 5G Speed Report: Not All Wi-Fi (or 5G) Is Created Equal* [online]. Available at: **https://www.telecompetitor.com/wi-fi-vs-5g-speed-report-not-all-wi-fi-or-5g-is-created-equal/**.

Specktor, Z.B. (2022). *AppsFlyer attribution model.* AppsFlyer. **https://support.apps-flyer.com/hc/en-us/articles/207447053-AppsFlyer-s-Attribution-Model**.

Statista. (n.d.a). *Nigeria mobile internet user penetration 2027* [online]. Available at: **http://www.statista.com/statistics/972900/internet-user-reach-nigeria/** [Accessed 26 Aug. 2022].

Statista. (n.d.b). *U.S. mobile internet users 2027* [online]. Available at: **http://www.statista.com/statistics/275591/number-of-mobile-internet-user-in-usa/** [Accessed 26 Aug. 2022].

Statista. (n.d.c). *U.S. percentage of mobile traffic 2022* [online]. Available at: **http://www.statista.com/statistics/683082/share-of-website-traffic-coming-from-mobile-devices-usa** [Accessed 26 Aug. 2022].

web.dev. (2022). *Digging into the privacy sandbox* [online]. Available at: **https://web.dev/digging-into-the-privacy-sandbox/**.

Chapter 9

Dhavate, N. and Mohapatra, R. (2022). *A look at proposed changes to India's (Personal) Data Protection bill* [online]. Available from: **https://iapp.org/news/a/a-look-at-proposed-changes-to-indias-personal-data-protection-bill/**.

Facebook wins judgment against alleged spammer. *New York Times,* October 24, 2008.

Federal Communication Commission. (2021). *CAN-SPAM Act: Unwanted commercial electronic mail* [online]. Available from: **www.fcc.gov/general/can-spam**.

Government of Canada. (n.d.). *Canada's anti-spam legislation* [online]. Available from: **https://fightspam.gc.ca/eic/site/030.nsf/eng/home**. [Accessed 26 Aug. 2022].

People's Republic of China. (2007). *China's consumer rights protection law (CRPL)* [online]. Available from: **http://www.npc.gov.cn/zgrdw/englishnpc/Law/2007-12/12/content_1383812.htm**.

State of California Department of Justice. (n.d.). *California Consumer Privacy Act (CCPA)* [online]. Available from: **https://oag.ca.gov/privacy/ccpa**. [Accessed 26 Aug. 2022].

Virginia's Legislative Information System. (2021). *HB 2307 Consumer Data Protection Act* [online]. Available from: **https://lis.virginia.gov/cgi-bin/legp604.exe?211+sum+HB2307**.

Chapter 10

Edelman. (2014). *2014 Edelman trust barometer* [online]. Available at: **https://www.edelman.com/trust/2014-trust-barometer**.

Mayson, A. (2019). *OMCP Digital marketing role delineation study* [online]. OMCP. Available at: **https://omcp.org/omcp-digital-marketing-role-study/** [Accessed 8 Sep. 2022].

McKinsey. (2015). *Diversity Matters. 15–35% performance (EBIT, revenue and ROE) correlations with team gender diversity and ethnic diversity* [online]. Available from: **https://www.mckinsey.com/~/media/mckinsey/business%20functions/organization/our%20insights/why%20diversity%20matters/diversity%20matters.pdf**.

About the Authors

Greg Jarboe is president of SEO-PR, which he co-founded with Jamie O'Donnell in 2003. Their digital marketing agency has generated award-winning results for a variety of clients, including Southwest Airlines, the SES Conference & Expo series, as well as Rutgers University. He has been the faculty chair of Video and Content Marketing at Market Motive, as well as an instructor at Simplilearn, Rutgers Business School Executive Education, and the New Media Academy. He's a member of the standards committee for OMCP.

Greg is the author of *YouTube and Video Marketing: An Hour a Day* (2009, 2011). He's also a contributor to *Complete B2B Online Marketing* by William Leake, Lauren Vaccarello, and Maura Ginty; *Enchantment* by Guy Kawasaki; *Strategic Digital Marketing* by Eric Greenberg and Alexander Kates; and *The Art of SEO* by Eric Enge, Stephan Spencer, and Jessie Stricchiola. Greg is also profiled in *Online Marketing Heroes* by Michael Miller.

Since 2003, Greg has written more than 1,600 posts for several online publications, including *Search Engine Journal, Search Engine Watch,* and *Tubular Insights*. He has also spoken at more than 80 industry conferences. He's also been a keynote speaker at the Be-Wizard conference in Rimini, Italy; the International Search Summit in London; and the ÜberTube Brand Summit in New York City.

Matt Bailey teaches digital marketing to the world's biggest brands and at the most recognized universities.

He has taught Google employees how to use Google Analytics.

He has taught Experian how to present data.

He has custom-developed digital marketing workshops for Microsoft, Disney, Nationwide, Orange, Hewlett Packard, Procter & Gamble, and IBM.

Matt's training curriculum is used at Duke University, Rutgers University, Purdue University, University of South Florida, George Washington University, Full Sail University, and many others.

According to Microsoft, "Matt has an uncanny ability to simplify the complexity of digital marketing into concepts that are understandable, relatable, and ultimately do-able."

From developing real-estate websites in 1996 to starting his own digital marketing agency, Matt has been at the forefront of entrepreneurship and digital marketing. In 2015, he pivoted from his agency business to focus full-time on training. In 2020, he earned his master of education in instructional design and technology and now offers coached digital marketing courses at Learn.Sitelogic.com.

Matt is the digital marketing instructor for the ANA (Association of National Advertisers), an instructor for LinkedIn Learning, and standards contributor for OMCP, the international standards certification and licensing program for digital marketing education.

He's also the author of *Internet Marketing: An Hour a Day* (2011), *Wired to Be Wowed* (2015), and *Teach New Dogs Old Tricks!* (2017).

Michael Stebbins is a director and co-founder of OMCP, curating best practices and certification standards in digital marketing in cooperation with industry leaders. Today, OMCP standards are taught by more than 1,000 colleges, universities, and training institutions worldwide.

Michael has led multiple companies from bootstrap to high-multiple acquisitions spanning ecommerce, digital marketing tools, and digital marketing curriculum for agencies and universities. As CEO and co-founder of Market Motive (acquired by Simplilearn), Michael and his team changed the way the world learns digital marketing. As vice president of marketing at ClickTracks (Acquired by Lyris), Michael was part of the team that disrupted the digital analytics market, showing the world a new way to look at analytics. In marketing technology, Michael was awarded the first patent for marketing automation lead scoring (US 7698420) in 2010 and continues to write poorly structured code for marketing automation systems.

After Market Motive was acquired, Michael returned to his passion to guide digital marketing, SEO, and advertising initiatives at Dell, RSA, and other companies. Through his boutique consultancy GrowingTwice https:// GrowingTwice.com, Michael advises business leaders and agencies on growth, digital marketing, and talent development.

Brad Geddes is a co-founder of AdAlysis, a PPC recommendation engine that has won multiple awards for the Best PPC Management Suite in multiple countries. He is the author of *Advanced Google AdWords,* the most advanced book ever written about Google's advertising program. He sits on the board of the Paid Search Association and is the PPC chair for Simplilearn and Market Motive.

Brad has spoken or keynoted at more than 125 conferences across the world. In addition, he has led more than 120 Google Ads workshops, which have been attended by over 10,000 digital marketers.

He started his PPC career in 1998. Over those years, he has started or expanded multiple agencies as well as started multiple software companies. Several of his projects have been acquired by other companies. Over those years, Brad has worked with many of the world's leading companies in managing and perfecting their PPC management and workflows. Companies that Brad has worked with or trained include Salesforce, Amazon, Oracle, Mailchimp, LL Bean, Capital One, GroupM, and Procter & Gamble.

One of his trademarks has been demystifying the complicated aspects of SEM. Not one to hold secrets, Brad prefers to educate marketers on the various aspects of crafting successful marketing campaigns to ensure the success for all parties involved.

Cindy Krum is the founder and CEO of MobileMoxie (previously Rank-Mobile). She has been bringing fresh and creative ideas about SEO and ASO to consulting clients and digital marketing stages around the world since 2005. She regularly speaks at national and international trade events and launched MobileMoxie in 2008 to address mobile-specific marketing needs within the traditional digital marketing industry. Cindy's leadership helped MobileMoxie launch the first mobile-focused SEO toolset, to help SEOs see what actual mobile search results and pages look like from anywhere and to provide insights about the impact of mobile-first indexing on search results. Free versions of these great tools are now available to all digital marketers as two easy-to-use Chrome extensions.

Outside of work, Cindy is an animal lover, spending as much time as possible with her dog, Barkley. She loves to travel and is also an avid audio-book listener, sometimes listening to two or three books per week or more. She lives in Denver, Colorado, and whenever the weather is nice, she strives to be outside, spending time at festivals and cafes, working in her yard, or just walking in nature. Otherwise, her hobbies are mostly creative and include painting, cooking, sewing, and crafts.

Kim Krause Berg, CPACC, accessibility specialist and QA analyst, human experience design, BM Technologies, Inc. (BMTX) f/k/a BankMobile, owns Creative Vision Web Consulting, LLC, where she has provided website consulting services for more than 25 years. Her work experience includes UX, accessibility, information architecture, software QA testing, and SEO.

An early pioneer in search engine optimization techniques in the late 1990s, her passion for user experience became known as Holistic UX and SEO. Today she specializes in website accessibility and works full time for BMTX as a QA analyst specializing in web accessibility. She earned the highly distinguished IAAP CPACC Certification and is a featured speaker and writer with an esteemed reputation.

An early adopter of blending SEO and UX methodologies, she launched Cre8pc.com (decommissioned) in 1996 as a search engine optimization teaching site. Trained in human factors in 2000, Kim created and taught what she called, "holistic UX and SEO," which included accessibility with persuasive user focused design practices. In 1998, she founded Cre8asiteforums, the first forums to discuss usability and accessibility topics. It was closed May 25, 2018.

Kim is a writer and speaker and taught basic website usability at the now closed Search Engine College for 12 years.

Index